THE RELIGIOUS RIGHT

A Reference Handbook
Second Edition

Other Titles in ABC-CLIO's
CONTEMPORARY
WORLD ISSUES
Series

Abortion, Second Edition, Marie Costa
Adoption, Barbara Moe
Affirmative Action, Lynne Eisaguirre
AIDS Crisis in America, Second Edition, Eric K. Lerner
    and Mary Ellen Hombs
American Homelessness, Third Edition, Mary Ellen Hombs
Campaign and Election Reform, Glenn H. Utter and
    Ruth Ann Strickland
Censorship in America, Mary E. Hull
Cults in America, James R. Lewis
Hate Crimes, Donald Altschiller
Pornography in America, Joseph Slade
Religion in the Schools, James John Jurinski
School Violence, Deborah L. Kopka
Single Parents, Karen L. Kinnear
Violence and the Media, David E. Newton
Work and Family in America, Leslie Stebbins

Books in the Contemporary World Issues series address vital issues in today's society such as terrorism, sexual harassment, homelessness, AIDS, gambling, animal rights, and air pollution. Written by professional writers, scholars, and nonacademic experts, these books are authoritative, clearly written, up-to-date, and objective. They provide a good starting point for research by high school and college students, scholars, and general readers, as well as by legislators, businesspeople, activists, and others.

Each book, carefully organized and easy to use, contains an overview of the subject; a detailed chronology; biographical sketches; facts and data and/or documents and other primary-source material; a directory of organizations and agencies; annotated lists of print and nonprint resources; a glossary; and an index.

Readers of books in the Contemporary World Issues series will find the information they need in order to better understand the social, political, environmental, and economic issues facing the world today.

THE RELIGIOUS RIGHT

A Reference Handbook
Second Edition

Glenn H. Utter and John W. Storey

A B C ❧ C L I O

Santa Barbara, California   Denver, Colorado   Oxford, England

Library of Congress Cataloging-in-Publication Data

Utter, Glenn H.
  The religious right: a reference handbook /Glenn H. Utter and John W. Storey.—2nd ed.
      p. cm.—(ABC-CLIO's contemporary world issues series)
Includes bibliographical references and index.
   ISBN: 1-57607-212-6 (alk. paper)
1. Conservatism—Religious aspects—Christianity. 2. Christianity and politics—United States. 3. Conservatism—Religious aspects—Christianity—Bibliography. 4. Christianity and politics—United States—Bibliography. I. Storey, John W. (John Woodrow), 1939— II. Title. III. Contemporary world issues.
   BR526.U88 2001
   277.3'0825—dc21

                                         2001003625

06 05 04 03 02 01   10 9 8 7 6 5 4 3 2 1

This book is also available on the World Wide Web as an e-book. Visit www.abc-clio.com for details.

ABC-CLIO, Inc.
130 Cremona Drive, P.O. Box 1911
Santa Barbara, California 93116-1911

This book is printed on acid-free paper ♾
Manufactured in the United States of America

Contents

Preface, ix

1 **Introduction,** 1

2 **Chronology,** 35

3 **Biographical Sketches,** 73

4 **Survey Data and Quotations,** 125
   A Survey of Conservative Christian Attitudes, 125
   Quotations, 138
   Responses to the Religious Right: Scholarly
      and Polemical, 152

5 **Directory of Organizations,** 157
   Organizations on the Religious Right, 157
   Organizations Critical of the Religious Right, 187

6 **Selected Print Resources,** 193
   Works about the Religious Right, 193
   Works from the Religious Right, 232
   Periodicals, 280

7 **Selected Nonprint Resources,** 291
   Audiotapes and Videotapes Presenting Religious Right
      Positions, 291
   Audiotapes and Videotapes about the Religious Right, 326
   Radio and Television Programs, 334
   CD-ROMs, 337
   Internet Resources, 338

Glossary, 347
Index, 357
About the Authors, 383

Preface

In 1930 Ludwig Wittgenstein, an eminent philosopher, remarked in a foreword that he would like to say "This book is written to the glory of God." But he thought better of it, fearing that readers of the time would misunderstand his intent, that he had written not out of pride and vanity but goodwill. A reference to the glory of God at one time would have been appropriate, perhaps even expected. That Wittgenstein thought the purpose of his expression would be lost on a large portion of the population of the 1930s attested to the trend toward secularization, a trend that haunts many Americans today, large majorities of whom have consistently expressed a belief in God. In weighing the potential for success of the contemporary religious right, the ongoing effects of secularization must be kept in mind.

Terms such as *religious right* and *Christian right* are difficult to pin down largely because they encompass groups of considerable diversity, ranging from mainline and evangelical Protestants to conservative Jews and Catholics. "Religious right" has generally been the expression of choice for the authors, as it is somewhat more inclusive than "Christian right." This latter phrase makes it awkward to include Jews, for instance, some of whom have identified with Christian conservatives on various issues. Another problem arises with regard to the term *evangelical*. Specifically, who are the evangelicals, and are they all on the political right? To answer the second half of the question first—no. Evangelicals are to be found on both sides of the political spectrum. The Sojourners offer a case in point. Theological conservatism notwithstanding, this group is on the left with regard to matters such as poverty and nuclear disarmament. It looks at issues from the vantage point of those at the bottom of society. African American evangelicals likewise often join the left in debates over civil rights and other concerns.

Evangelical is almost as elusive a term as *religious right.* Theologically, an evangelical is one who claims a personal relationship with Jesus based upon a "born-again" experience, accepts the authority of the Bible in matters of faith and practice, and spreads the gospel through evangelism. Since the early 1800s most American Protestants, save Episcopalians, have been evangelicals. Historically, the term is derived from the Greek *evangelion,* meaning "good news," and it was applied in the sixteenth century to Lutherans in Germany; in the eighteenth century to those Anglicans who introduced hymn singing, Sunday schools, and missionary societies; in the late nineteenth and early twentieth centuries to those American Protestants who were dubbed fundamentalists; in the early twentieth century to Pentecostals in America; and since the 1940s to conservative American Protestants who wish to be differentiated from fundamentalists. In this last sense, the difference is more a matter of temperament than theology. Jerry Falwell is a fundamentalist; Billy Graham is an evangelical. Although in this book we frequently use *evangelical* as a catchall for all conservative Protestants, we just as frequently distinguish between mainline bodies, such as Presbyterians, Methodists, Episcopalians, and Disciples of Christ, and evangelical groups, such as Southern Baptists, Assemblies of God, Missouri Synod Lutherans, and Churches of Christ.

Individuals such as J. Gresham Machen and Cyrus Scofield have been included in this study because they provide continuity, showing that various facets of the contemporary religious right have roots in the nineteenth century. The premillennialism of Jerry Falwell can be seen in John Nelson Darby, for instance, and Francis Schaeffer's repudiation of secular humanism bears similarities to Machen's earlier condemnation of liberalism. Otherwise, this study deals only with individuals and organizations on the religious right that have endeavored since World War II to influence public policy through the political process. Thus, we treat the religious right as an essentially political movement that courts voters for "moral" candidates, lobbying Congress on everything from public school prayer to abortion, and joins religious conservatives in judicial proceedings involving home schooling, sex education, and textbooks. Accordingly, the focus is upon people such as Billy James Hargis, who fashioned the Christian Crusade, and Pat Robertson, founder of the Christian Coalition. In this second edition we have added religious right figures such as D. James Kennedy, R. C. Sproul, and Marvin Olasky.

Alexis de Tocqueville, that observant Frenchman who traveled America during the presidency of Andrew Jackson, was impressed by this country's separation of church and state. Indeed, he noted that the American clergy prided itself on aloofness from politics. This stance was wise, he thought, for in nations such as his own, where the flag and the cross were allies, there was no way to criticize the state without rebuking the church. Americans, by contrast, could indulge in bitter political debates without trampling religious institutions. Of course, de Tocqueville was not altogether correct. The great political controversies in this country, from slavery to abortion, have always involved fundamental moral considerations. And the churches have readily joined the fray, fighting and dividing over these concerns. Still, de Tocqueville's observation seems basically sound. When religion identifies itself intimately with a political cause, and then wraps that cause in the flag and anoints it with God, the opposition has little recourse but to attack both its political and religious adversaries. Over time, both the religious left and right have invoked God's blessing in behalf of political objectives and in so doing have at times shown a certain self-righteous arrogance; but the contemporary religious right has carried the identification of God and Caesar to a new level through its "moral" report cards, which on the basis of voting records designate politicians as basically godly or ungodly. Most significantly, perhaps, these report cards disclose the intimacy between the current religious right and conservative Republicans. Among other things, this study helps to elucidate this development.

We have introduced extensive revisions in this second edition. In addition to several new biographical sketches, we have brought the chronology up-to-date, including events from 1995 to the election of George W. Bush as president and the political struggle in the U.S. Senate over his nomination of John Ashcroft as attorney general. Both the print and nonprint resources chapters include many new entries, the survey data and quotations chapter has updated information from the 1998 General Social Survey, and the organizations chapter includes several new organizations on the religious right, as well as groups opposed to the Christian right agenda.

Acknowledgments

The authors are indebted to numerous individuals, and it is a pleasure to acknowledge them. Professor James True, the Jack

Brooks Chair of Government and Public Service at Lamar University, and his research assistant, Mariam Stepanyan, provided valuable assistance in analyzing the General Social Survey data. Patty Cargill and Karen Wright, members of Bethlehem Lutheran Church in Beaumont, Texas, volunteered useful insights for this second edition, as they did for the first. Carol Stokesbury-Atmar, a graduate student in the Lamar University History Department, proofed much of the manuscript and offered suggestions regarding both style and content. Patty Renfro, the History Department secretary, assisted in typing the manuscript, and Mark Asteris, Media Services Coordinator at the Lamar University Gray Library, furnished information on video materials. The authors, of course, accept full responsibility for any errors of judgment or fact.

Glenn H. Utter
and John W. Storey

1

Introduction

Thomas Jefferson's famous metaphor to the contrary notwithstanding, there has never been an absolute wall between church and state in American society. Ever since the Puritans came ashore in the early 1600s, religious leaders have often sought to influence public policy on a variety of social issues, and political leaders of all persuasions have just as readily appealed to the divine. A generation before the Civil War, for instance, the churches had already clashed and divided over slavery. In the late nineteenth and early twentieth centuries the social gospel inspired many churchgoers to pursue legislative remedies to urban, industrial ills. The adoption of the Eighteenth Amendment on prohibition in 1919 was a crowning achievement for the religious establishment. And today many religious bodies maintain lobbyists in the nation's capital to sway politicians on everything from prayer in public schools to racial justice.

To many religious leaders, political activism in no way violates the separation of church and state, for in their view religion has a responsibility to address vital issues. Likewise, public officials have often invoked the authority of religion, hinting that a divine force directs American history. Both Abraham Lincoln in his second inaugural and John F. Kennedy in his 1961 address, for instance, used a religious framework to explain national purpose. In 1949 Harry Truman described the Cold War as a contest between the powers of light and darkness; in 1953 "God's Float" led Dwight D. Eisenhower's inaugural parade; and in 2000 religion figured prominently in the hotly contested race between Vice President Al Gore, the Democratic nominee, and Governor George W. Bush, the Republican standard-bearer. Indeed, the governor, in a declaration that appealed to many Christians but aroused the ire of many Americans of other persuasions, proclaimed June 10,

2000, "Jesus Day" in Texas. Further blurring the line between church and state has been the tendency of many Americans to shroud their history in religious symbolism, with George Washington likened to Moses and July 4 and December 25 both serving as occasions for nationalistic and religious exaltation.

Despite the religious shallowness of many Americans, there is no denying the religiosity of the American public. This impressed Alexis de Tocqueville, that discerning Frenchman who crisscrossed the nation from New York to New Orleans in 1831. There was "no country in the world," he observed, "where the Christian religion retains a greater influence over the souls of men than in America."[1] De Tocqueville's observation has a contemporary ring, for surveys from 1947 to 2000 suggest that America is the most religious of the modern Western nations. And "nothing in the last half-century," wrote George Gallup, Jr. in June 2000, has "dislodged the conviction of Americans that there is a power in the universe . . . greater than ourselves—not wars; not the problem of evil and the obvious sufferings of innocent people; not the 'death of God' movement; not social upheavals nor the lures of the modern world."[2] Indeed, current surveys show that 96 percent of all adult Americans believe in God, 84 percent maintain that God is actively involved in their lives, 85 percent insist that God performs miracles today, 70 percent belong to a church or synagogue, 40 percent actually attend church weekly, 59 percent believe religion is an important aspect of daily life, and 65 percent consider religion the answer to many of the nation's present ills.[3] This augurs well for calls to political action rooted in religious principles, as shown only a generation or so ago by the "religious left." In pursuit of racial justice, for instance, the National Council of Churches pricked the nation's conscience in the 1950s and 1960s. This coalition of religious groups, along with Presidents Kennedy and Lyndon B. Johnson, challenged Americans to live up to the egalitarian ideals of their faith. Accordingly, the Council brought the power of religion to bear on the civil rights legislation of the 1960s.

So in light of this country's long-standing interaction between religion and politics, why has the religious right attracted such attention since World War II? Why have Jerry Falwell and the Moral Majority and Pat Robertson and the Christian Coalition aroused such alarm in some quarters? What is so different about the religious right? In terms of fundamental theological concerns, nothing is particularly new. Contemporary Christians on the right are no less disturbed by higher criticism of the Bible and Darwinian evolution than their conservative forebears of the late nineteenth and early twentieth centuries, as attested to by persistent efforts over the last decade or so to have "creation science" accorded equal time with Darwinism in public school classrooms. Two recent developments in this ongoing tug-of-war have had an unsettling effect on much of the scientific community. In August 1999 the Kansas Board of Education, dominated by religious fundamentalists, made the teaching of evolution in the state's public schools optional and announced that questions dealing with evolution would no longer be included in state assessment tests. "Disgraceful" was the American Association for the Advancement of Science's description of the new Kansas standards, but Linda Holloway, the former chairperson of the Kansas Board who had pushed for adoption of the guidelines, blithely dismissed the national scientific organization. "Clearly," said she, the scientists "have an ax to grind about evolution."[4]

On another front, in October 1999, Baylor University, a reputable Baptist institution in Waco, Texas, established the Michael Polanyi Center to study "intelligent design," the idea that some life-forms are too complex to have evolved by chance through a process of Darwinian natural selection. Proponents of this view, which has gained strength since the 1980s, believe that mathematical models can prove that some intelligent agent outside the universe has been responsible for directing creation. To opponents, this kind of academic activity amounts to just another cloak for creationism, and the ultimate purpose of Baylor's new center, they insist, is to promote the teaching of intelligent design in the public schools.[5] Disclosing the ambivalence of the American public on such issues, a poll released in March 2000 showed that overwhelming majorities supported the teaching of both evolution and creationism in the public schools.[6] Even Vice President Al Gore, with an eye perhaps on evangelical votes, professed to see no harm in this. But to Nobel Laureate Steven Weinberg, a world-renowned physicist, the current vogue for equal time, sounding so fair and innocent, did not bode well for science.

But it is not theology and concern about evolution so much as active involvement in the political process that separates the contemporary religious right from conservative religious forces of the pre–World War II era. Believing Armageddon to be nigh, conservative Christians, especially those of a fundamentalist and evangelical variety, have traditionally concentrated more on redeeming sinners and preparing themselves for the imminent return of Jesus than on active political involvement. The Joneses of

South Carolina—Bob Sr., Bob Jr., and Bob III, leaders of the fundamentalist Bob Jones University in Greenville, South Carolina—still reflect this viewpoint, and so did Jerry Falwell until the 1970s. Agitated by the political activism of the religious left in behalf of civil rights reforms, the future leader of the Moral Majority informed his Lynchburg, Virginia, congregation in 1965 that God had given no command to engage "in marches, demonstrations, or any other [political] actions."[7] Preachers, he added, were "not called to be politicians but soul winners."[8] But Falwell underwent a dramatic metamorphosis. At a special bicentennial service on July 4, 1976, the Virginian fused a nationalistic love of country with an intense religious zeal. "The idea that religion and politics don't mix was invented by the Devil to keep Christians from running their own country," asserted Falwell. "If [there is] any place in the world we need Christianity," he continued, "it's in Washington. And that's why preachers long since need to get over that intimidation forced upon us by liberals, that if we mention anything about politics, we are degrading our ministry."[9]

Falwell's political awakening, as well as that of multitudes of other Americans on the religious right, can be understood only in terms of foreign and domestic developments since World War II. To people on the religious, as well as political, right, the years since 1945 have been fraught with peril. Abroad, the communists appeared to be winning the Cold War, as exemplified by the triumph of Mao Tse-tung in China, the failure to achieve victory in Korea, the costly quagmire in Vietnam, the continuing presence of Fidel Castro in Cuba, the "giveaway" of the Panama Canal, and leftist successes in Central America. And at home, "socialist" governmental programs (the religious right tends to equate liberalism with socialism and socialism with communism), the teaching of evolution in the public schools, a soaring divorce rate, Supreme Court decisions banning organized prayer in the public schools, growing numbers of abortions, urban violence and crime, the Equal Rights Amendment (ERA), the assertiveness of the gay and lesbian communities, "smutty" television programs, the AIDS epidemic, and President Bill Clinton's misbehavior in the White House with Monica Lewinsky confirmed the religious right's belief that cherished moral values were in decline.

Uniting the voices of the religious right in the late 1940s was an intense fear of communism. Indeed, a symbiotic tie swiftly emerged between the religious and political right. Politicians such as Senator Joseph McCarthy of Wisconsin drew support from the religious right, for instance, while otherwise obscure preachers such as Carl McIntire gained national prominence through close association with the political right. Thus, in defense of God and country, preachers and politicians of the right embraced in a righteous crusade to save America. McIntire was typical. Now in his early nineties, this autocratic and self-righteous Presbyterian has become an elder statesman of sorts for a certain segment of the religious right. Fiercely independent, he forged his own denomination in 1937, the Bible Presbyterian Church, and through the weekly columns of the *Christian Beacon* kept his followers advised on matters of God and Caesar. By the 1950s he had established a network of educational institutions, such as the Faith Theological Seminary in Philadelphia, and had begun to broadcast his messages for religious and political redemption on a regular program entitled *The Twentieth-Century Reformation Hour*. Basically, McIntire told Americans that national well-being hinged upon a return to the "old-time" Christian values upon which the nation presumably had been founded. Accomplishing this would not be easy, however, because of the communist conspiracy. To McIntire, the major Protestant bodies all harbored communists, the National Council of Churches was nothing but a communist front, and the Revised Standard Version of the Bible was communist inspired. At the height of his influence in the early 1960s, McIntire's call for national salvation, as heard daily on *The Twentieth-Century Reformation Hour*, was carried by at least 200 stations.[10]

By 1960 the religious right had become more cluttered, as additional crusaders joined the cause, notably the trio of Edgar C. Bundy, Frederick Schwarz, and Billy James Hargis. Bundy, an ordained Southern Baptist minister without a congregation, took charge of the Church League of America in 1956. This ultraconservative agency, which Bundy moved from Chicago to Wheaton, Illinois, labored to awaken Protestant ministers to the reality of the communist conspiracy. Schwarz, an Australian physician and lay preacher who had come to the United States initially at the request of McIntire, launched the Christian Anti-Communism Crusade in 1952. His prominence was enhanced considerably by Billy Graham, who in 1957 arranged for him to address a group of congressmen on communism. Schwarz repeatedly told American audiences that the communist method of conquest was infiltration, a process he believed already far advanced in the halls of academe, the press corps, and the State Department. More zealous perhaps than the other two, Hargis, a Disciples of Christ minister, began in 1951 the Christian Echoes

National Ministry, better known as the Christian Crusade. Although closely associated in the mid-1950s with McIntire's organizations, Hargis increasingly went his own way. From radio in the 1960s he moved to television in the early 1970s with smoothly packaged programs. At one stage, 146 stations telecast his messages. In 1973 he founded American Christian College.

These ministers often enjoyed cordial ties to secular counterparts, thereby obscuring the line in the public's mind between the religious and secular right. Such was the case of Robert Welch, who founded the John Birch Society in 1958. Welch was a well-educated, widely traveled, and successful businessman who had become disillusioned with politics after running unsuccessfully for lieutenant governor of Massachusetts and supporting the failed presidential candidacy of Senator Robert A. Taft, an Ohio Republican, in 1952. In 1956 he retired from business and became an anticommunist warrior. Welch was not a minister, but he named the John Birch Society for "a young fundamentalist Baptist preacher from Macon, Georgia," who allegedly had been murdered by Chinese communists after World War II. And ministers on the right certainly saw an ally in Welch and his organization. McIntire called the society "a good patriotic American organization," and Hargis referred to Welch as "a great American patriot." Such admiration was not surprising, for Welch and the preachers had much in common.

The early ministers of the religious right, as well as Welch, were as one not only in their intense anticommunism, but also in their conspiratorial view of history. The "paranoid style in American politics" was historian Richard Hofstadter's description of the tendency to see conspiracy as the causal force in American history, a tendency prompted by morbid suspicion.[11] And men such as McIntire, Hargis, and Welch were nothing if not suspicious of those with whom they disagreed. They took for granted that their adversaries were pawns of Satan, and thus parties to a sinister conspiracy in which outward acts concealed darker intentions. Within this context, for instance, Supreme Court decisions regarding prayer in the public schools were just one aspect of a broader communist conspiracy to destroy the Christian moorings upon which the Founding Fathers supposedly had anchored the nation. More an article of faith than a product of empirical observation, such a view of history remained unaltered by evidence. Consequently, the recent collapse of communism in Central and Eastern Europe fooled everyone but Hargis. He asserted in August 1994 that while the American news media "looks the other way," communism "is making a dramatic, secret comeback." Continued Hargis: "There is a Red threat and it is alive and thriving."[12] Time has changed nothing for Hargis. The conspiracy is ongoing, protected by the reticence of the liberal media.

Preachers such as McIntire and Hargis have remained active, but they have been forced into the background by the easing of the anticommunist hysteria that spawned them in the 1950s. For all but the most devout true believers, it is difficult to sustain a belief in a communist conspiracy in light of the removal of the Berlin Wall, the unification of Germany, and the collapse of the Soviet Union. Consequently, the resurgence of the new religious right in the 1970s was led by a group of broadcast media preachers: Pat Robertson, president of the Christian Broadcasting Network (CBN) and host of *The 700 Club*; James Robison, a Texas Southern Baptist; and Jerry Falwell, leader of the Moral Majority. Preachers such as these still employed apocalyptic imagery in discussing the global struggle—liberty against atheistic communism, light against darkness—but the constant emphasis upon conspiracy was absent. Instead of communism, "secular humanism" unified these newer leaders of the religious right. Many religious conservatives sensed that secular humanists, who supposedly were entrenched in the courts, media, and schools, systematically undermined the supernaturalism of Judeo-Christianity. Robertson was typical. In 1986 he rebuked the "small elite of lawyers, judges, and educators" who had "taken the Holy Bible from our young and replaced it with the thoughts of Charles Darwin, Karl Marx, Sigmund Freud, and John Dewey."[13] Like "modernism" of an earlier era, secular humanism quickly became an evangelical catchall for every imaginable "sin," from violence in the streets to the lack of discipline in the public schools. And to combat these ills the more recent religious right has been much readier to join the political fray than its counterpart of the 1950s. Whereas McIntire and Hargis often spoke to political issues and frequently endorsed specific bills, such as those seeking to "restore" prayer in the public schools, Falwell and Robertson have been far more inclined to instruct their followers on issues, conduct voter registration drives, engage in legislative lobbying, and target specific politicians for defeat.

The religious right of the 1970s differed in yet another significant respect from that of the 1950s. The former has been more ecumenical. A mutual concern over such family-related issues as abortion, sex education in the schools, and the ERA enabled many Protestant fundamentalists and some conservative Jews,

Mormons, and Catholics to rise above theological differences and join hands in the quest for "family values." Particularly illustrative here was Phyllis Schlafly. Stung by the ERA, which was approved by Congress in 1972 but never ratified by the required three-fourths of the state legislatures, and the Supreme Court's decision on abortion in 1973, Schlafly, a Roman Catholic, started the Eagle Forum in 1975. This organization spearheaded the drive to kill the ERA, and in so doing drew support from Falwell. If the Catholic conservative Schlafly and the Baptist fundamentalist Falwell could set aside theological differences in behalf of common social values, so could other religious conservatives.

The ecumenism of the religious right, to be sure, has been more across denominational and religious than racial lines. Although African American Christians, for instance, especially those in the South, were as theologically conservative as Falwell, they never moved in sizable numbers to the religious right. A possible explanation is that many religiously conservative whites have all too frequently opposed political and social initiatives beneficial to minorities. The close association between the religious right and Senator Jesse Helms, a North Carolina Republican, illustrates the problem. It would be difficult for many African Americans to feel comfortable in a movement that welcomes a politician who has always objected to civil rights legislation and now criticizes federal programs to assist the poor. Making matters worse was a voter guide distributed across the South by the Christian Coalition in the 1996 presidential race. It used the image of a black man to represent issues the organization opposed and a white man for measures it favored. Claiming a printer error, Ralph Reed, executive director of the Christian Coalition, apologized, but Julian Bond, a board member of the National Association for the Advancement of Colored People and a former Georgia congressman, was unimpressed. He all but accused Reed and the Christian Coalition of hypocrisy, suggesting that the director's lofty preachments "about racial equality and Christian morality" were easily "tossed aside in favor of racial wedges and voter manipulation at election time."[14] Given such suspicion on the part of African Americans, the ecumenism of the religious right does not extend much beyond white Americans and their social concerns.

By the mid-1970s the social issues that brought diverse but predominantly white groups together on the religious right generally fell into one of three categories—educational, family, or moral. As evidenced by the Supreme Court's 1962–1963 school prayer decisions, the growing trend toward secularization in the public schools not only alarmed many conservative Christians, but also prompted some of them to seek private schooling for their children. Just as many Catholics had insulated themselves within a system of parochial schools in the nineteenth century, some Protestant evangelicals sought to do the same in the twentieth century. Robertson voiced the mood when he wrote in 1980: "Christians must educate their youth in new schools which teach biblical principles and a biblical life-style in which the Lordship of Jesus Christ is acknowledged in every facet of their lives."[15] A logical consequence of the private school movement was support for tuition tax credits and vouchers, and therein lay the possibility of cooperation between Protestant evangelicals and Catholics.

Another area of likely agreement among people of differing faiths was the family. Of special concern were the ERA and the Supreme Court's 1973 decision on abortion. Paradoxically, many conservatives affirmed their support of women while simultaneously denouncing the ERA. Their opposition supposedly was not to equality of treatment for women, but rather to any fundamental restructuring of the family allegedly at odds with the Bible. Consequently, religious conservatives opposed the ERA, convinced it would alter scripturally rooted male-female roles and even legitimize homosexuality. Robertson spoke for many others when he asserted that the proposed amendment would protect "homosexuals, lesbians, sadomasochists, and . . . anyone else who engaged in any other sexual practice whether or not that practice was prohibited by the Bible, religious dogma, existing federal or state law."[16] Just as disparate elements of the religious right of the 1950s had been as one in opposing communism, so now, as Robertson's remark suggests, divergent strands were unified against homosexuality. Or, to borrow Cal Thomas's words, "softness on gays" had "replaced Communists as the Religious Right's No. 1 enemy."[17]

As for abortion, the position of many evangelical Protestants and the Catholic hierarchy was essentially the same: except when the mother's life was endangered, the rights of the unborn fetus were paramount to the mother's choice. The intensity of this debate was undiminished by the Food and Drug Administration's approval in fall 2000 of the French abortion pill, RU-486. Stubbornly resisted for years by the religious right, RU-486 was no more likely to ensure privacy for women and physicians than that promised by *Roe v. Wade* in 1973. From different sides of the religious spectrum came immediate expressions of outrage over the FDA's decision. Although Richard Land, head of the Southern Baptist Convention's Ethics and Religious Liberty Commission, labeled the pill "a dangerous drug that is fatal for unborn babies and hazardous to their mothers."[18] Fran Maier, chancellor of the Catholic Archdiocese of Denver, served notice that "RU-486 only streamlines the process of destroying a human life."[19] More ominously, the director of Operation Save America, Flip Benham, threatened to discover physicians who prescribed the pill and expose them "doctor by doctor."[20] Those who administered RU-486, Benham warned, would "put their practice in jeopardy."[21] With polls showing that 47 percent of Americans disapproved of the pill, RU-486 reenergized antiabortion forces and strengthened the sense of unity among people of diverse faiths on the religious right.[22]

The moral concerns of the religious right revolve around drug abuse, pornography, television programs, and movies. With its constant barrage of nudity, profanity, and violence, television has been a frequent target. Donald E. Wildmon, a Methodist minister from Tupelo, Mississippi, believed the industry undermined family values, and in the mid-1970s he launched a movement to purify the airwaves. Adding weight to the claims of the religious right was a recent report by ten major health organizations, including the American Medical Association, which attributed much youthful violence to television, movies, videogames, music, and the Internet. Of the twenty-six wealthiest nations, the United States, according to the American Academy of Family Physicians, had the highest homicide and suicide rates among young people. The report concluded with a call to Hollywood to be more responsible.[23] This indicates that at least some of the moral concerns of the religious right are also the concerns of multitudes of other Americans. And politicians, ever mindful of the next election, have paid some attention. Witness the V-chip, which allows parents to filter out unwanted television programs, and the posturing about "filth in Hollywood" by all sides in the 2000 presidential campaign.

The outcome of the 1976 presidential race brought hope to many religious conservatives, for Jimmy Carter was an acknowledged "born-again" Southern Baptist from the Deep South, a Georgian with whom many on the religious right could easily identify. Moreover, by focusing national attention on and enhancing the stature of conservative evangelicals, Carter's victory emboldened many on the religious right to increasingly measure public issues against biblical standards of morality. As a result, matters of moral concern to Christian conservatives became politicized, and in turn Christian conservatives increasingly entered the political fray, not only to protect their way of life but also to "restore" the nation to its moral roots. Ironically, it was not long before President Carter himself incurred the wrath of his religious kinfolks. They were dismayed by his endorsement of the ERA, his failure to prevent federally subsidized abortions, his refusal to support voluntary prayer in the public schools, and the suggestion in 1978 of his commissioner to the Internal Revenue Service (IRS) that Christian schools should be taxed. Tim LaHaye's judgment was common. "Between 1976 and 1980," he wrote in 1981, "I watched a professing Christian become president of the United States and then surround himself with a host of humanistic cabinet ministers" who "nearly destroyed our nation."[24]

LaHaye's frustration was matched by Falwell's. The articulate Virginia pastor had become by the late 1970s an institution of sorts. His Thomas Road Church, an independent Baptist congregation, numbered approximately 15,000; his Sunday services, broadcast on *The Old-Time Gospel Hour*, entered millions of homes via radio and television; and his capacity for fund raising was already well established. Coincident with the disenchantment of people such as LaHaye and Falwell with the Carter administration was the appearance of several conservative lobbyists, men who saw in disaffected religious conservatives a reservoir of potential voters for conservative political causes. The key figures were Howard Phillips, leader of the right-wing lobbying group Conservative Caucus; Edward A. McAteer, a marketing specialist from the Colgate-Palmolive Company and a Southern Baptist layman; Robert Billings, head of the National Christian Action Coalition; Richard Viguerie, a direct-mail expert who began the *Conservative Digest*; and Paul Weyrich, a Catholic who in 1974 had organized the Committee for the Survival of a Free Congress. Credit goes primarily to Billings and McAteer for bringing Falwell and Weyrich together, thereby wedding secular and religious conservatives.

Whether secular conservatives such as Weyrich subsequently dominated and used religious conservatives such as Falwell is debatable. John Buchanan, the director of People for the American Way, a liberal lobby, insists that the political right actually created the religious right.[25] This is clearly inaccurate. The religious right had been around for a long time, and the relationship that evolved between it and the political right in the late 1970s was symbiotic. The politically savvy Weyrich coined the term "moral majority" and brought organizational talent to the movement, while Falwell added righteous indignation and promised voters for the cause. Together, Weyrich, Falwell, and others forged Moral Majority, Inc., in 1979 and set out to rescue America from secular humanism. And, popular perception to the contrary notwithstanding, the Moral Majority was more than a Christian fundamentalist organization. From the outset it appealed to, and drew at least some support from, conservative Catholics, Jews, and Mormons. Indeed, Falwell's willingness to broaden the religious base of the Moral Majority sometimes offended his fundamentalist allies.

The Moral Majority was only one of three conservative religious agencies created in 1979. The other two were the Christian Voice and the Religious Roundtable. A California-based organization that by 1980 claimed the support of 37,000 pastors from forty-five denominations and a membership of 187,000, the Christian Voice assumed the task of evaluating the morality of public officials.[26] To do this, it developed a morality scale based on fourteen key issues, and a politician whose position coincided with that of the Christian Voice was deemed "moral." Disturbed and angered by societal changes involving the family, women, sex, divorce, homosexuality, and television programming, the Christian Voice was against abortion, racial quotas, forced busing, the Department of Education, gay rights, the Strategic Arms Limitation Treaty (SALT) II, pornography, drugs, higher taxes, and sex education without parental consent. It was for the "restoration" of prayer in the public schools, free enterprise, the defense of Taiwan, and a balanced federal budget. Republicans usually came closer to meeting the Christian Voice's standard of Christian morality than Democrats. However, when convicted defendants of Abscam (an FBI sting operation in the late 1970s that ensnared one senator and five U.S. representatives) scored higher on the Christian Voice's morality scale than congressional proponents of alleviating world hunger and poverty, it became glaringly obvious that the moral report cards had more to do with "correct" political behavior than morality.

The Religious Roundtable, McAteer's principal organizational contribution to the religious right, attempted to connect prominent figures from the political and religious right. In August 1980 it sponsored the National Affairs Briefing in Dallas, Texas. Nonpartisan billing to the contrary, this was a Protestant fundamentalist and conservative Republican affair. The Southern Baptist patriarch W. A. Criswell, the longtime pastor of the First Baptist Church, Dallas, attended, as did Ronald Reagan, the only presidential candidate present. This meeting attracted national attention, not all of which was positive. The stridency of some of the speakers, along with hints of anti-Semitism, bothered many Americans.

Although the Moral Majority shared the field with other organizations on the religious right in 1979–1980, it soon became the primary focus of national attention. With the presidential race of 1980 looming, the Moral Majority hastily established local chapters in forty-seven states, conducted voter registration drives and educational seminars for religious conservatives, and targeted several prominent politicians for defeat. Although it claimed to be nonpartisan, in 1980 the Moral Majority invariably opposed liberal Democrats, such as senators George McGovern of South Dakota, Frank Church of Idaho, Alan Cranston of California, John Culver of Iowa, and Birch Bayh of Indiana. And Falwell's eagerness to discredit President Carter prompted him, just weeks before the election, to fabricate an unflattering story about homosexuals on the president's staff. Although unapologetic, the minister later confessed his lie.[27] The Moral Majority, tending to equate morality with a narrow set of political options, was clearly more comfortable with conservative Republicans.

The results of the 1980 elections thrilled the religious right, although analysts disagreed sharply over the causes for the defeat of incumbents Carter, McGovern, Church, and Bayh. To be sure, Falwell, as well as Weyrich, Phillips, McAteer, and Viguerie, claimed considerable responsibility. As Viguerie put it, "the white followers of the TV evangelical preachers gave Ronald Reagan two-thirds of his 10 point margin in the election."[28] But other postelection observers were far more skeptical, suggesting that Falwell and his followers merely rode, but did not create, the antiadministration sentiment so evident in the election. Bayh agreed, explaining his loss more in terms of high interest and unemployment rates than opposition from the religious right. By this analysis, President Reagan was not especially beholden to religious conservatives. Accordingly, he did not appoint a representative of the Moral Majority to a major administration post and disregarded Falwell's objections to the appointment of Sandra Day O'Connor to the Supreme Court. On the other hand, Reagan, with an eye toward the midterm congressional elections, soothed the religious right by choosing Billings for an important post in the Department of Education, appointing C. Everett Koop, an evangelical opponent of abortion as surgeon general, taking a stronger stand against abortion, and endorsing a constitutional amendment allowing organized prayer in the public schools.

Although probably never as influential as either its followers or detractors supposed, the Moral Majority, assailed from within and without, definitely ebbed as the 1980s progressed. Falwell and Weyrich had faced a dilemma from the beginning. How could the Moral Majority broaden its base by appealing to moderate religious conservatives without alienating its staunchly fundamentalist core? The difficulty of this situation was apparent by the early 1980s. As Falwell eased toward the evangelical center, territory long occupied by Billy Graham, he quickly aroused suspicion. By softening somewhat his opposition to abortion, allowing that it was permissible if the mother's life was endangered; endorsing equal rights for women, once the ERA had become "a dead issue"; and distancing himself from the virulently anti-Catholic Bob Jones, Jr., Falwell gained few converts from the evangelical mainstream and angered many on the fundamentalist right. Jones, for instance, called the Moral Majority the instrument of Satan and named Falwell "the most dangerous man in America today as far as Biblical Christianity is concerned."[29] Such outbursts supported the assessment of Graham, who doubted Falwell could move with his constituency into the evangelical mainstream.

Many critics outside the religious fold were just as biting as Jones. To arouse Americans to the allegedly intolerant and dangerous views of the Moral Majority, several former senators who had been defeated in 1980 took to the stump in 1981–1982. McGovern organized Americans for Common Sense to counter Falwell's group. And Senator Barry Goldwater of Arizona, the elder statesman of Republican conservatism, castigated the Virginian for his ideological rigidity. Goldwater's rebuke had been sparked by Falwell's opposition to the Supreme Court nomination of O'Connor. Meanwhile, John Buchanan and People for the American Way loudly observed that the Christian Voice's "morality report cards" consistently gave low marks to African American, Jewish, and female lawmakers. Coincidentally, Buchanan had been one of the lawmakers the Moral Majority opposed in 1980. Although an ordained Southern Baptist minister and a Republican congressman from Alabama, his vote to extend the time allowed for passage of the ERA had angered Falwell. Buchanan lost in the GOP primary.

One of the more discerning critiques of Falwell and the religious right came from the distinguished historian Henry Steele Commager. Addressing a Conference on Church and State at Baylor University in 1982, he charged that the likes of "Oral

Roberts and Jerry Falwell and their camp followers" concerned "themselves not with public sin but with private vice, or what they conclude is vice—especially the sins of the flesh and of infidelity, which they interpret by their own standards."[30] Although wringing their hands over "personal sin," in other words, they had little if anything to say of "social sins." Listen again to Commager: "They have much to say about the wickedness of limiting posterity, whether by birth control or abortion, but very little if anything to say about the kind of world children will be born into or about the systematic destruction of a rightful inheritance of natural resources."[31]

As Falwell discovered, political activism by one side invariably generated counterattacks by the other side. After all, the religious right itself had been to some extent a response to the activism of the religious left in the 1950s and 1960s. The result for Falwell and the Moral Majority was a negative public perception. A Gallup Poll in late 1981 disclosed that over half the people who were aware of the Moral Majority viewed it unfavorably, and the response to Falwell personally was equally critical.[32] The consequence of Falwell's growing unpopularity was that many conservative politicians refused to be identified with the Moral Majority in the elections of 1982, 1984, and 1986. With his influence apparently waning, Falwell changed the name of the Moral Majority to the Liberty Federation in January 1986 and thereafter lowered his political profile. "I've redirected my priorities," he later explained, "and have no intention of working as hard in the political arena as I have in the past."[33]

If Falwell had expected calm to accompany his political retreat, he was sorely disappointed. With glaring evidence of material excess and sexual misbehavior, the Praise The Lord (PTL) ministry and Jimmy Swaggart scandals unfolded in 1987–1988. Stunned, the faithful retaliated against all the major televangelists by withholding contributions and voicing disapproval. A Gallup Poll in 1987 showed that 62 percent of the American public now viewed Falwell unfavorably, a negative rating surpassed only by Oral Roberts, 72 percent, and Jim Bakker, 77 percent. Even 24 percent found fault with Graham.[34] By mid-1988 the PTL was ruined, Swaggart was disgraced, Robertson's presidential foray was a shambles, and Falwell faced financial disaster. In 1989 the Moral Majority was dissolved.

Although the Moral Majority collapsed, the religious right survived. Indeed, it became more aggressive, particularly at the local and state levels, under the leadership of Robertson and his

Christian Coalition. Never close, the relationship between Falwell and Robertson sheds some light on the religious right itself. Contrary to popular assumption, the religious right has never been very cohesive. Although they usually shared the same social concerns, people on the religious right often followed different drummers. Robertson, for instance, after initially agreeing in 1979 to serve as a director of McAteer's Religious Roundtable, soon recoiled from active involvement in any of the new organizations of the religious right. His explanation was vintage evangelical conservatism. Christians were to concentrate on saving souls, not winning votes. Later, in fall 1980, he remarked that critics had found "an easy target" in the religious right "because the conservative Evangelicals involved in politics—Christian Voice, Moral Majority, and Religious Roundtable—have been, at times, unsophisticated, simplistic and inept."[35] As for Falwell, his professed friendship for Robertson did not translate into support of the latter's bid for the presidency. "I personally wish," Falwell said in 1987, "that no minister would ever run for . . . political office."[36] George Bush, not Robertson, was Falwell's choice to succeed President Reagan in 1988. As exemplified by Falwell and Robertson, the religious right was a union of kindred spirits in which there were many fissures.

Robertson's withdrawal from religious right organizations in 1980 in no way diminished his support of conservative social causes. On the contrary, he maintained close ties to prominent figures on the religious and secular right, such as Weyrich and Senator Jesse Helms of North Carolina, and gave conservative commentators easy access to *The 700 Club*. He also began building a political apparatus of his own. In 1981 Robertson founded the Freedom Council, an organization designed to educate Christians on political issues, followed in 1982 by the National Legal Foundation, which offered legal assistance to religious causes. And in 1985–1986 he presided over the Council on National Policy, a conservative group that was periodically briefed on issues by figures such as Senator Helms and Secretary of Education William Bennett. By 1987 the successful televangelist clearly had his sights set on the presidency, apparently convinced he could overcome an unfavorable Gallup Poll rating of 50 percent. But amid the lingering PTL and Swaggart scandals of 1987–1988, as well as serious reservations among many Americans about electing a charismatic preacher to the presidency, the effort foundered. Robertson's political ambition had exceeded his grasp. Columnist William F. Buckley's assessment probably was correct. He wrote in 1987 that while Robertson said all the things conservatives wanted to hear, Americans nonetheless were overwhelmingly unprepared "to believe that any minister is, ultimately, a serious candidate."[37]

Following the presidential debacle, Robertson regrouped, forming in 1989 the Christian Coalition. This organization differed in at least one significant way from the Moral Majority. Whereas Falwell's group operated largely from the top down, seeking to achieve its ends by swaying politicians in the nation's capital, Robertson's Coalition was a grassroots effort to influence policies at the local and state levels. By 1994 the movement claimed almost 1,500,000 members, and its effect on local school board and state races was apparent from coast to coast. Indeed, Christian conservatives had gained control of the Republican Party leadership in Texas, Virginia, Oregon, Washington, Iowa, South Carolina, and Minnesota, and comprised substantial voting blocs in New York, California, and practically all the southern states. One of the more closely watched races of 1994 was in Virginia, where Republican Oliver North, the darling of the religious right, eventually lost a bitterly fought contest to the Democratic incumbent, Senator Charles Robb. Among other things, this race disclosed the willingness of the religious right to overlook the "sins" of the candidate who supported its political agenda, while assailing the other for his "weakness of the flesh."

As for school board elections, these traditionally attract only a small percentage of the electorate, thereby enhancing the chance of any well-organized and determined group to obtain control. And Christian conservatives, sharing with multitudes of other Americans the current frustration with the public schools over everything from low scores on achievement tests to controversial textbooks to violence in the hallways, were quick to seize the opportunity. In 1993 it was estimated that of the nation's 95,000 school board members 7,153 were conservative Christians.[38] Texas was one of the major battlefields in the 1994 fall elections. With 60,000 members and 136 chapters in the Lone Star State, the Christian Coalition had its eyes on the state's fifteen-member Board of Education. To avoid jeopardizing its nonprofit status, the Christian Coalition endorsed no candidate by name, but rather encouraged its membership to support "conservatives." This left no doubt as to the anointed candidate in six of the districts. Republicans subsequently won in three of those races, giving candidates beholden to the religious right an eight-to-seven majority on the Texas board.[39]

The political activism of first Falwell and then Robertson raises anew the issue of religion and politics. Preachers certainly have the right to run for office, and organized religion is entitled to bring pressure to bear on matters of public concern. That is exactly what the religious left did in the 1950s and 1960s, and so also the religious right since the late 1970s. The dispute arises over the arrogation of God by one side to support a specific set of political objectives, thereby implying that the other side is ungodly and irreligious. And of this practice the religious right has been guilty. Admittedly a biased observer, John Buchanan nevertheless put it aptly. "The fatal flaw of the Religious Right," he said, "is to baptize the mentality of the John Birch Society."[40] This assurance of God's support perhaps accounts for the religious right's propensity for harsh, judgmental rhetoric. How else could one explain Robertson's outburst in Iowa in 1992? "The feminist agenda is not about equal rights for women," he asserted. "It is about a socialist, anti-family political movement that encourages women to leave their husbands, kill their children, practice witchcraft, destroy capitalism and become lesbians."[41] The religious right has all too often indulged in this kind of inflammatory speech, apparently convinced that its opponents on everything from the ERA and abortion to guns and homosexuality are Satan's minions.

The religious right was especially active in the 1994 elections. The Christian Coalition alone distributed about thirty-three million voter guides and manned a vast network of telephone banks shortly before the November balloting. And the effort paid off. Overall, the Republicans elected seventy-three freshmen to the House and gained control of both houses of Congress for the first time since 1954. An exhilarated Louis Sheldon, leader of the Traditional Values Coalition, bespoke the mood of many fellow religionists. "The election of 1980 with Ronald Reagan was great," said he, but the 1994 outcome was "like we've died and gone to heaven."[42] Whether the Republican landslide was due more to the failure of Democratic leadership, pervasive frustration within the general populace, or the political activism of the religious right is debatable. Nevertheless, the Christian Coalition's Ralph Reed promptly claimed considerable credit for the religious right in the high-profile Republican victories of Steven Stockman over House veteran Jack Brooks of Texas, Rick Santorum over incumbent Senator Harris Wofford of Pennsylvania, and George W. Bush over Governor Ann Richards of Texas. There were, of course, some setbacks for religious conservatives, most notably North's loss in Virginia.

With so many of the first-year Republicans, such as Stock-man, Randy Tate of Washington, Lindsey Graham of South Car-olina, Helen Chenoweth of Idaho, Steve Largent of Oklahoma, Mark Souder of Indiana, and Van Hilleary of Tennessee beholden to it, the religious right had cause for optimism in 1995. To the ex-tent that the 1994 elections had aligned Congress more closely with the country's conservative mood, they seemed to portend good things for many of the religious right's objectives. For in-stance, a constitutional amendment on prayer appeared close to reality. "We need a moral guidepost for our children," pro-claimed Jay Sekulow, chief counsel for Robertson's American Center for Law and Justice, who saw momentum for prayer "coming from the soul of America."[43] Sekulow's perception ap-peared well founded. Laws in Alabama, Georgia, Maryland, Mis-sissippi, Tennessee, and Virginia already permitted a moment of silence, and similar legislation was pending in Florida, Okla-homa, Pennsylvania, and South Carolina. And television, long the bête noire of the religious right, had begun to treat religious subjects more sympathetically, as seen in such programs as *Picket Fences, L.A. Law, Northern Exposure,* and *Christy.* A special com-mentator on religion even joined anchorman Peter Jennings on ABC's evening news. The chairman of the conservative Media Research Center, L. Brent Bozell, who noticed these changes in programming, exclaimed "something's happening out there."[44]

Ironically, what subsequently happened out there was far from satisfactory to many religious conservatives. The first-year Republicans in whom they had such high hopes soon alienated much of the American public, created doubt about the judgment of Republican leadership in the House, and reenergized the Clin-ton presidency. Youthful, brash, and outspoken, these novice Re-publicans stormed into town in 1995 like some gunslinging posse of frontier marshals bent on routing evil and restoring virtue. They were going to trim the size of government by bal-ancing the budget and cutting taxes, and they were going to dis-lodge career politicians by setting term limits. And all the while they would curb government interference in religion, put prayer and the Ten Commandments back in public schools, make fed-eral money available to sectarian groups performing worthy so-cial tasks, and allow certain students to attend private schools at public expense.

Apparently it never occurred to many of the freshmen that there would be opposition to some of these objectives, that other points of view existed. They were confident to the point of arrogance, perhaps hubris. Knowing that they were "right," they gave no heed to anyone else's point of view. Compromise was a "four-letter word" to them. As one astute observer remarked, "they didn't know what they didn't know."[45] Although the so-called Contract With America, the platform on which the freshmen had run, sailed through the House in early 1995, it stalled in the Senate. For all the fanfare, not much had been accomplished by late 1995, at which time House Republicans shut down the government in a contest of wills with President Clinton over the budget. This was a public relations disaster, one the House Republicans unwisely repeated in 1996. Instead of principled newcomers, as they had been seen in 1994, the first-year Republicans were now increasingly perceived as stubborn children who flew into a tantrum if they failed to have their way. Senator Bob Kerrey (D-NE) said it best: "What we are trying to do is compromise with a minority in the House of Representatives which is basically saying, 'We will hold our breath until we get our way. We do not care if our face turns blue. We do not care if the government shuts down!'"[46] The Nebraska Democrat obviously was not alone in this sentiment, for some public weariness with the religious right and the "Revolution of '94" was soon evident. Although the Christian Coalition raised and spent over $26 million in the 1996 midterm elections, twelve of the freshmen, along with six senior House Republicans, were defeated for reelection.[47] The House Republicans had overreached themselves, and in so doing demonstrated qualities many Americans had come to associate with the religious right: intellectual rigidity, intolerance of differing views, inability to compromise, and a determination to impose itself on an unwilling public.

The failure of the 104th Congress to deliver on the social objectives of religious conservatives, along with the outcome of the 1996 elections, was not the only sign of trouble on the religious right. The Christian Coalition, the nation's largest organization of religious conservatives, soon encountered hard times. Announcing his pending resignation as executive director in April 1997, Ralph Reed, who had guided the Christian Coalition since its inception, prepared to forge his own political consulting firm, Century Strategies, and offered his talents to aspiring conservative politicians. Randy Tate took the helm of the Christian Coalition in August. Like Reed, this Washington native was something of a whiz kid. Only twenty-two years old and not yet out of college, he was elected to the state legislature in 1988, the same year in which he endorsed the presidential candidacy of Pat Robertson.

Six years later, in 1994, he was one of the first-year Republicans elected to the U.S. House of Representatives. A Christian conservative, Tate's congressional votes against abortion and for repealing the assault weapons ban and defunding the National Endowment for the Arts and Humanities earned him a 100 percent rating by the Christian Coalition and the National Rifle Association, but failed to gain him reelection by Washington's voters in 1996. Even so, Tate was Pat Robertson's kind of conservative, and so he was a suitable successor to Reed.

Whereas Reed had presided over a steadily expanding and influential organization, one that exercised considerable power within Republican ranks, Tate inherited a Christian Coalition soon beleaguered by dwindling membership, sagging contributions, internal dissent, external competition, and trouble with the IRS. Some skepticism has always existed about the size of the Christian Coalition, detractors arguing that the organization inflated its membership rolls. Nevertheless, the organization's size apparently peaked in late 1996, claiming some two million members and reporting contributions of $26.4 million. Following the 1996 elections contributions fell off sharply, slipping to $17 million in 1997, a drop of 36 percent in one year. This forced the Coalition to cut its staff from 110 to 90 and to cease publication of its flagship magazine, *Christian America,* which was replaced with a bimonthly newsletter. By 1999, after additional bad news for Republicans at the polls in 1998, the Coalition had lost at least 700,000 members, several key aides had resigned, and the organization had an outstanding debt estimated at $2.5 million. Symptomatic of the internal turmoil, in January 1998 Jeanne Delli-Carpini, a top financial officer, was given a suspended six-year prison sentence for embezzling $40,346 in 1996 and 1997. Compounding these problems, by 1999 other voices, such as the Family Research Council, had begun to challenge the Christian Coalition for the hearts of religious conservatives.[48] It appeared to many observers by 2000 that the Christian Coalition was headed the way of the Moral Majority. In April 2000 the organization's last lobbyist in Washington, D.C., resigned, and a former field director for the northeast pronounced the Coalition "a defunct organization."[49]

As if it did not have troubles enough, the Christian Coalition also ran awry of IRS rules for tax-exempt nonprofit organizations. Robertson's avowal of nonpartisanship had always been suspect, particularly given the Coalition's obvious preference for Republican candidates. With the approach of the 1998 midterm elections, for instance, the Christian Coalition released its congressional scorecard, ranking all members of Congress on the basis of votes on twelve specific issues. Republicans in the House and Senate received average scores of 89.8 and 80.3, respectively, whereas Democrats in the two chambers earned average marks of 13.1 and 6.1, respectively.[50] To critics, such statistics mocked the Coalition's assertion of evenhandedness, a conclusion already reached by the Federal Election Commission (FEC). At stake was the Coalition's tax-exempt status as a nonprofit religious organization.

In 1996 the FEC sued the Christian Coalition on grounds that it was little more than an arm of the Republican Party. As early as 1992, according to the Commission, the Coalition had been working "hand in hand" with President George Bush's reelection campaign. Robertson fought back, claiming First Amendment rights to free speech, but in 1998 the IRS sided with the FEC and denied the Coalition tax-exempt status. Among other things, the IRS pointed to the Coalition's distribution of about seventy-two million sample voter guides in 1998 that invariably supported Republicans. This decision was upheld in 1999, leaving the Christian Coalition owing the IRS between $300,000 and $400,000 in back taxes.[51] Barry Lynn, executive director of Americans United for the Separation of Church and State and a longtime foe of Robertson, applauded the outcome, asserting that the Coalition was "a hardball political machine . . . masquerading as a religious group." According to Lynn, "overwhelming" evidence proved that Robertson's organization had "been operating as virtually an arm of the Republican Party."[52]

The outcome of the IRS suit prompted a restructuring of the Coalition. In mid-1999 the organization split, creating the Christian Coalition of America and the Christian Coalition International. Because the Texas chapter, the Christian Coalition of Texas, retained its tax exemption, it was rechristened the Christian Coalition of America and charged with continuing the nonprofit practice of "voter education." Observed Robertson: "Christian Coalition of America will continue to be a force in American politics and will remain a prominent fixture on the political landscape as the nation's number one pro-family, pro-life organization."[53] The Christian Coalition International would be a for-profit political action committee. As such, it would endorse candidates, contribute financially to political causes, and continue the distribution of voter guides before elections. Robertson hailed the reorganization as a way of keeping the Coalition active in American politics, but the ever-vigilant Barry Lynn called it a shabby ploy to evade the recent IRS ruling. "This is the kind of disgraceful shell-game you find in a second-rate carnival in the middle of nowhere," declared he.[54] Americans United for the Separation of Church and State planned to file suit against the Coalition's restructured tax-exempt status.

Although her decision had no effect on the IRS ruling, Federal District Judge Joyce Green handed Robertson a partial victory in August 1999. She dismissed FEC charges that the Christian Coalition, through its literature, telephone banks, and other means, had improperly assisted candidates, including Senator Jesse Helms of North Carolina and former President George Bush, but nevertheless imposed a civil penalty against the organization for supporting Newt Gingrich's bid to become House Speaker in 1994. Green also ruled that the Coalition had inappropriately shared its mailing list with senatorial candidate Oliver North in 1994. Nevertheless, Robertson was clearly pleased, declaring "this is a decisive victory for First Amendment Freedom for all groups that want to involve themselves in federal issues."[55]

In many ways, the problems of the Christian Coalition reflected an emerging disillusionment within the religious right at large. An overview of the past twenty years left many religious conservatives feeling frustrated, perhaps even betrayed by their secular allies in the Republican Party. Long-sought objectives appeared no closer to reality in 2000 than in 1980, from obtaining a constitutional amendment on school prayer to repealing *Roe v. Wade*, improving the quality of television programming and Hollywood films, blunting the gay rights movement, winning the war on drugs, and providing vouchers and tuition tax credits to children to attend private, even religious, schools. The matter of school prayer was especially galling, for polls since the early 1960s showed that most Americans joined hands with religious conservatives on this issue. A Gallup Poll in June 2000 was typical. Some 70 percent favored daily spoken prayers in the nation's classrooms, and 74 percent wanted the Ten Commandments displayed.[56] Yet, the Supreme Court, dominated by Republican appointees, consistently thwarted such efforts. Thus, unable to make America once again a shining city upon a hill, a moral beacon to the rest of the world, many religious conservatives asked themselves whether the time had come to forsake the political arena and to concentrate anew on spiritual concerns.

That question echoed through the religious right in the late 1990s. Perhaps no group had worked harder to raise money, compile mailing lists, recruit foot soldiers, and make telephone calls for Republican causes than religious conservatives. And Republicans had dominated the White House for twelve years under Ronald Reagan and George Bush, and that party had controlled both houses of Congress since 1995. But what did the religious right have to show for it all? Not very much, at least in the opinion of James Dobson, the popular psychologist whose radio and television programs reached approximately twenty-eight million Americans every week. Originating from Colorado Springs, Colorado, his radio program, *Focus on the Family,* was heard by about five million listeners every day. By mid-1998 Dobson was in open rebellion against the Republican Party leadership. He warned that if the social agenda of religious conservatives continued to be ignored, there would be a price to pay in upcoming elections. Specifically, Dobson wanted Congress to eliminate the National Endowment for the Arts, defund Planned Parenthood, and require parental consent for abortions. And if the Republicans failed to deliver, the radio host vowed he would "try to beat them this fall."[57] Dobson's irritation disclosed a growing rift between grassroots religious conservatism and political conservatism in the capital, a conflict between idealism and pragmatism.

Despite the scandals swirling around President Clinton, the Democrats gained ground in the 1998 midterm elections, gains that forced Republican Newt Gingrich to relinquish the Speakership and resign from the U.S. House. And of the original seventy-three freshmen from 1994, only fifty-one remained. If the Republican "Revolution of '94" was not dead, it had certainly lost steam, and so had the religious right. Two prominent voices spoke the mood of many in 1999. The time had come to leave the political arena. "Politics has failed," announced Paul Weyrich on February 16. Coming from a man who perhaps had done more than anyone else to wed religious and secular conservatives, one present at the creation of the Moral Majority and the Christian Coalition, Weyrich's words reverberated widely. The way to improve American culture, he elaborated, was through nonpolitical means, and he offered as an example the home-schooling movement. Had those "parents stayed in the [political] battle to reform the public schools, they would have lost," he argued.[58] But by simply separating "themselves from the public schools," over "a million young people are growing up with decent values."[59] Similar paths supposedly were open to other religious conservatives. To be sure, the separatism Weyrich proposed was not a complete withdrawal from society. "I'm not suggesting that we all become Amish or move to Idaho," he explained.[60] He argued that religious conservatives should remain engaged as voters, if for no other reason than to protect themselves from greater government hostility.

While Cal Thomas and Edward Dobson in their book, *Blinded by Might: Can the Religious Right Save America?* (1999), shared Weyrich's assessment of politics, they offered a slightly different remedy. Instead of cultural separatism, they suggested that Christian conservatives resume the spiritual task of redeeming individual sinners. Both formerly associated with Jerry Falwell and the Moral Majority, Thomas was now a nationally prominent columnist with the Los Angeles Times Syndicate; Dobson was now pastor of a fundamentalist congregation, Calvary Church, in Grand Rapids, Michigan. According to the authors, religious conservatives had been right on the issues but wrong on strategy. They would have been better served by preaching the gospel than organizing for political battle, for "real change must come from the bottom up or, better yet, from the inside out."[61] Aggressive political activism by the religious right, the authors believed, had contaminated the message of Jesus rather than uplifted the moral fiber of society. Just as "too-close [an] association" with the Democratic Party in the 1950s and 1960s had diminished the moral authority of the National Council of Churches, so too had the contemporary religious right because of its association with the Republican Party. This was unavoidable, the authors observed, because politics was "about a kingdom of compromise" and the advancement of an "agenda incrementally," whereas "the kingdom of God" was "about truth and no compromise." Moral revival, they concluded, was "not the job of politics or politicians," but rather "the unique work of the church."[62] Even Pat Robertson seemed somewhat in agreement with Thomas and Dobson. Although showing no signs of leaving the political playing field himself, he nevertheless acknowledged that evangelicals had "been thoroughly disabused of the notion that the kingdom of God will come through political influence." Thus, "getting people into the kingdom of God," Robertson insisted, was now "the main thrust" of his life.[63]

Weyrich, Thomas, and others not only raised significant issues, but also revealed some uncertainty of purpose among religious conservatives by 2000. To be sure, neither Weyrich nor Thomas spoke for all their religious kinfolks. Jerry Falwell was unhappy with his old colleagues, as was Jay Sekulow, head of the American Center for Law and Justice. Sekulow accused Thomas and Dobson of encouraging religious conservatives to "unilaterally disarm and withdraw from politics." That would be a mistake, for "a lot of good has come out of political activism by religious people."[64] Yet others faulted Thomas and Dobson for failing to give convincing alternatives to religious conservatives. In part because of such internal turmoil, the religious right did not play as prominent, certainly not as visible, a role in 2000 as it had in previous presidential campaigns.

Evidence that something was changing in the religious-political landscape was apparent as George W. Bush edged toward the Republican presidential nomination in 1999–2000. Although the favorite of such religious conservatives as Robertson and Falwell, the Texas governor, with an eye toward the political center, kept a respectful distance from the religious right. Indeed, since 1995 Bush had clashed with the religious and social conservatives, all Republicans, on Texas's fifteen-member State Board of Education. At issue was everything from vouchers and textbook selection to investment of educational funds and federal ties to local schools. To the governor, the religious conservatives were intractable unless they got their way; to the religious conservatives, the governor had failed to keep his 1994 campaign pledges. It was not until 1997, when the state legislature enacted a religious freedom statute and a parental notification law on abortion, that the Bush administration delivered on matters dear to the state's religious right. But this did not mean that Bush, while admittedly wanting to retain their support, had surrendered to religious conservatives. In 1999, for instance, Bush ignored the hard right wing of the California Republican Party; in June 2000 he skipped the Texas Republican Party convention, an affair permeated by religious sentiments; the National Republican Convention in summer 2000 kept the Christian Coalition at bay; and Bush did not make the usual courtesy call on Pat Robertson at the Christian Coalition's annual gathering in September 2000. Neither Bush nor his vice presidential running mate, Richard Cheney, for instance, attended the Coalition's Washington, D.C., rally, although Bush did address the gathering via television from Texas.

Instead of being angered by Bush's aloofness, many powerful figures on the religious right were curiously silent as the 2000 race gained momentum. It was as if both sides had come to an unspoken understanding. Bush subscribed to most of the values and objectives of the religious right, but made no binding, public profession of such as he courted moderates with talk of "compassionate conservatism," a term borrowed from conservative

Republican guru Marvin Olasky. Meanwhile, on the religious right, people like Robertson, Falwell, and Ralph Reed, apparently satisfied that the governor's heart was in the right place, remained in the background and made few demands so as not to jeopardize Bush's prospects. For instance, regarding Bush's failure to appear in person at the Coalition's September rally, Robertson remarked: "I'm sophisticated enough to understand the strategy here, and it's a very deliberate and delicate strategy."[65] In other words, the Virginia preacher understood the Texas politician's need to attract moderates. Likewise, on abortion, a bedrock principle of evangelical conservatives, Robertson reflected a similar comprehension. When the Food and Drug Administration in fall 2000 finally approved RU-486, the televangelist refused to make it an issue. "It's a distraction," Robertson asserted, one cleverly designed to trap Bush just weeks before the November election. As the televangelist explained, if Bush "says he strongly opposes the pill ruling, the women will go against him. And if he says he's for the ruling, then the pro-life people will go against him."[66] In Robertson's opinion, the governor had avoided the pitfall by playing it "very well so far."[67]

Such an attitude demonstrated that the religious right, at least many of its leaders, had matured politically. The movement had become more pragmatic, recognizing the need to give a little, to compromise a bit, to win at the polls. Some concessions for victory felt better than moral purity in defeat. And what did religious conservatives expect in return for giving Bush an easy ride in the 2000 campaign? Robertson again is illustrative. The next president would likely nominate two or more justices to the Supreme Court, and Robertson wanted to be sure Bush made those recommendations. Even though the Texas governor had made no promises, he was definitely more likely than Al Gore to consider only pro-life candidates.[68]

The Texas governor's stunning loss to Senator John McCain of Arizona in the New Hampshire Republican primary in early 2000 almost wrecked this delicate balancing act between the Bush campaign and the religious right. Now desperately needing a victory in the upcoming South Carolina Republican primary, the heretofore presumed front-runner made a hard right turn politically in February 2000 and threw himself into the waiting arms of religious conservatives. All of a sudden the Republican presidential race turned nasty, as Ralph Reed, operating largely behind the scene, and Robertson helped orchestrate a ferociously negative attack on McCain. By telephone, e-mail, and other means South

Carolinians were "informed" of the senator's first wife, alleged marital infidelities, usage of profane language, and "softness" on the gay issue. In a telephone message sent to thousands, Robertson even accused McCain of being allied with "vicious" anti-Christian bigots.[69] Bush handily won, but some observers wondered at what cost. To Cal Thomas, the South Carolina contest proved that "people who are supposed to serve a higher kingdom . . . can get down and dirty with the best of the pagans."[70] Likewise, to *Washington Post* columnist E. J. Dionne Jr., it gave the lie to Bush's professed "compassionate conservatism," to the idea that "being Christian meant just not delivering votes to the ballot box but meals to the poor, mentoring to the young, comfort to the afflicted."[71] And to William Kristol, a staunchly partisan Republican and publisher of *The Weekly Standard*, it signaled the "crackup" of the religious right. Reasoned Kristol: "The Christian Right . . . is finished because of what Ralph Reed and Pat Robertson have done in South Carolina, because of the meanness of the assault."[72] Kristol was correct about the sordid nature of the South Carolina campaign, but mistaken about the anticipated demise of the religious right. People committed to a "higher calling" have often proved remarkably adept at rationalizing whatever means necessary to accomplish a desired end.

Once the South Carolina primary was over, Bush, though damaged in the eyes of some moderates, moved back toward the political center, and religious conservatives resumed a lower profile. To be sure, Jerry Falwell soon announced "People of Faith 2000," a plan to register at least ten million voters, and in May and September, respectively, Robertson warned against McCain's selection for the vice presidency and cautioned that the Christian Coalition should not be taken for granted. That the religious right was far from dead in 2000, however, came from the politicians themselves. The public square was anything but naked of religious sentiments during the presidential campaign, as candidates seemingly vied with one another for claims to the divine. Bush confided that Jesus was his favorite philosopher, while Gore countered that he always consulted Jesus before making any decision. And Joseph Lieberman, Gore's running mate and an Orthodox Jew, the first to be nominated by a major party in a presidential race, intoned that America was "the most religious country in the world," that all Americans were the "children of the same awesome God,"[73] and that "there must be a place for faith in America's public life."[74] Displaying some partisan jealousy, Cal Thomas called Lieberman an "itinerant Jewish evangelist" who used "God as a campaign surrogate to bless his and Al Gore's policies."[75] *New York Times* columnist Maureen Dowd, with her usual wit, put it all in perspective. "The main battleground state is the state of grace," she observed. "Democrats and Republicans are seeking a geographical advantage, but it is celestial. Both sides seem weirdly obsessed with snagging a divine endorsement."[76]

If Bush snagged a divine endorsement, he snared no heavenly mandate. Indeed, the election's outcome offered a lesson in biblical humility. Bush lost the popular count by over 500,000 votes, and he gained the necessary electoral margin only after a heated legal battle for Florida's twenty-five electors. At first glance it would seem that President-elect Bush owed more to Ralph Nader for taking votes away from Gore than to the religious right. Yet, the future president did have a debt to evangelicals for rescuing his faltering campaign in the South Carolina primary, and there was an early indication that the religious right would be rewarded. By naming several women, two Hispanics, and two African Americans, Bush drew praise for the diversity of his cabinet nominees. But the recommendation of John Ashcroft to be attorney general set off an alarm among many moderates and liberals. Defeated in his bid for reelection to the U.S. Senate from Missouri by a dead man, Mel Carnahan, who was killed in a plane crash just three weeks before the November 2000 election, Ashcroft was resurrected as Bush's attorney general designate. A devoutly religious member of the Assemblies of God Church, Ashcroft does not drink, smoke, or dance; he opposes most abortions and affirmative action; and he favors charitable choice and the carrying of concealed handguns. Notably, the Missouri senator was Robertson's first choice for the presidency. "I'm interested in picking a winner, not a loser," commented the televangelist in 1998, "and among Christian conservatives John Ashcroft's certainly number one right now."[77] In December 2000 another prominent minister on the religious right, Louis P. Sheldon, head of the Traditional Values Coalition, praised the nomination of Ashcroft, calling him "a committed Christian" who understood "that true justice" came "not from the laws of men, but from the ultimate lawgiver: God."[78]

Attorney General Ashcroft may be the religious right's Trojan horse in the Bush administration. He almost certainly will give a favorable nod to many objectives dear to religious conservatives. He will most likely oppose abortion, perhaps seeking to overturn *Roe v. Wade*; he will object to affirmative action, incurring the wrath of the National Association for the Advancement of Colored People and other civil rights groups; he will promote a greater presence of religion in the public arena, probably including school prayer; he will support voucher programs, permitting public funds to be used to finance private sectarian schooling for some children; and he will sanction charitable choice, directing federal tax dollars to religious institutions for conducting certain social service programs. In short, the nomination of Ashcroft suggests that the religious right, while probably never as strong as once believed nor as weak now as its detractors would like to think, is still very much alive, splintered somewhat by the defection of key voices, but also more mature and wiser in the ways of politics.

Notes

1. Alexis de Tocqueville, *Democracy in America,* vol. 1, 12th ed. (Reprint, New York: Vintage, 1945), 314.

2. Princeton Religious Research Center, *Emerging Trends* (June 2000), 1–2.

3. Ibid. (December 1992), 1; (April 1993), 3–4; (January 1994), 1–3; (March 1994), 1–2; and (June 2000), 1–2.

4. *Houston Chronicle* (September 27, 2000): 14A.

5. *Houston Chronicle* (October 20, 2000): 31A.

6. *Houston Chronicle* (March 11, 2000): 23A.

7. Richard V. Pierard, "Religion and the New Right in Contemporary American Politics," in *Religion and Politics* (Waco, TX: Baylor University Press, 1983), 64.

8. Ibid. 64.

9. Ibid. 64.

10. John W. Storey, "Religious Fundamentalism and Politics of the Far Right," in *Conflict and Change, America 1939 to Present.* St. Louis, MO: River City, 1983), 67–68.

11. Richard Hofstadter, *The Paranoid Style in American Politics and Other Essays* (New York: Vintage, 1967), 3–40.

12. Billy James Hargis, *Christian Crusade* vol. 42, no. 8 (1994): 1.

13. David Edwin Harrell, Jr., and Pat Robertson, *A Personal, Religious and Political Portrait* (New York: Harper & Row, 1987), 212.

14. The Interfaith Alliance, "Religious and Civil Rights Leaders

Urge Christian Coalition to Repudiate Use of Race as a Wedge Issue by Candidates and Organizations." Accessed October 21, 1996.

15. Harrell, 207.

16. Ibid.

17. *Beaumont Enterprise* (February 23, 2000): 11A.

18. "Pro-Life Forces Outraged by RU-486 Approval," *Maranatha Christian Journal* online at http://www.mcjonline.com/news/oob/20000929a.html. Accessed November 21, 2000.

19. Ibid.

20. *Newsweek* (October 9, 2000): 28.

21. Ibid.

22. Ibid.

23. *Houston Chronicle* (December 13, 2000): 4A.

24. Harrell, 184–195.

25. Harrell, 185.

26. *Houston Chronicle* (July 8, 1980): 4:28.

27. *Newsweek* (September 15, 1980): 32.

28. Richard Viguerie, *The New Right: We're Ready to Head* (Falls Church, VA: Caroline House, 1981), 128.

29. Walter H. Capps, *The New Religious Right: Piety, Patriotism, and Politics* (Columbia: University of South Carolina Press, 1990), 99.

30. Henry Steele Commager, "Religion and Politics in American History," in *Religion and Politics* (Waco, TX: Baylor University Press, 1983), 53–54.

31. Ibid.

32. *U.S. News & World Report* (June 21, 1982): 43–44.

33. *Houston Chronicle* (April 5, 1987): 1:7.

34. *Newsweek* (July 13, 1987): 52.

35. Harrell, 187–188.

36. *Houston Chronicle* (April 5, 1987): 1:7.

37. Harrell, 226.

38. *Houston Chronicle* (September 4, 1994): 20–21A.

39. *Houston Chronicle* (November 10, 1994): 25A, 27A, 30A.

40. Harrell, 218.

41. *Houston Chronicle* (September 4, 1991): 21A.

42. *Houston Chronicle* (November 10, 1994): 26A.

43. *Newsweek* (October 3, 1994): 48.

44. *Houston Chronicle* (June 4, 1994): E1.

45. Linda Killian, *The Freshmen: What Happened to the Republican Revolution?* (Boulder, CO: Westview Press, 1998), 14–22.

46. Ibid. 185.

47. *Houston Chronicle* (June 11, 1999): 4A.

48. "Politics: Christian Coalition Retrenches," *Christianity Today* (March 2, 1998): 74.

49. "End of the Road," Freedom Writer online at http://apoca-lypse. berkshire.net/~fas/fn0006/coalition.html. (Summer 2000).

50. Steve Benen, "Christian Coalition Congressional Scorecard Flunks Democrats." Americans United for Separation of Church and State online at http://www.au.org. Accessed June 1998.

51. *Beaumont Enterprise* (June 11, 1999): 8A.

52. Ibid.

53. *Houston Chronicle* (June 11, 1999): 4A.

54. Ibid.

55. *Houston Chronicle* (August 3, 1999): 3A.

56. Princeton Religious Research Center, *Emerging Trends* (September 2000): 5.

57. *U.S. News & World Report* (May 4, 1998): 20–21.

58. *Washington Post Weekly Edition* (March 8, 1999): 10.

59. Ibid.

60. Ibid.

61. Keith J. Pavlischek, "Blinded by Might: Can the Religious Right Change America? (Review)," *The Christian Century* online at http://www.findarticles.com/cf_1/m1058/16–116/54898666/p1/article.html. (Accessed May 19, 1999.)

62. *Beaumont Enterprise* (March 28, 1999): 3B.

63. *Newsweek* (August 24, 2000): 41–42.

64. "What Role for Religious Conservatives?" American Enterprise online at http://www.findarticles.com/cf_1m2185/3_11/61402621/p1/article.htm1. Accessed April 2000.

65. *Beaumont Enterprise* (September 30, 2000): 9A.

66. *Newsweek* (October 9, 2000): 30.

67. "For Now, Robertson Sees RU-486 as Issue to Avoid," *The Inquirer* online at http://inq.philly.com/content/inquirer/2000/109/30/front_page/right30.html. Accessed September 30, 2000.

68. *Newsweek* (April 24, 2000): 43.

69. *Houston Chronicle* (February 29, 2000): 1, 4, 5A.

70. *Beaumont Enterprise* (February 23, 2000): 11A.

71. *Beaumont Enterprise* (February 19, 2000): 40A.

72. *The Washington Post National Weekly Edition* (October 9, 2000): 21.

73. *Houston Chronicle* (August 30, 2000): 16A.

74. *Houston Chronicle* (September 4, 2000): 26A.

75. *Beaumont Enterprise* (October 29, 2000): 2B.

76. *Beaumont Enterprise* (August 14, 2000): 10A.

77. Benen, June 1998.

78. *Houston Chronicle* (December 29, 2000): 45A.

2

Chronology

1835– *Life of Jesus* by the German theologian David Friedrick
1836   Strauss creates a sensation in Europe and comes to
       symbolize the kind of biblical scholarship that will ap-
       pall American religious conservatives in the latter nine-
       teenth century. Relying upon the "myth theory,"
       Strauss argues that Jesus represented not a divine inter-
       vention in history, but rather a psychological projection
       of the beliefs of people at a particular moment. This
       kind of "higher criticism" offends many religious con-
       servatives.

1843   William Miller, a New York farmer and Baptist
       preacher, predicts that Jesus will return to earth on
       March 21. The failure of Jesus to appear forces Miller to
       adjust his calculations, which are based primarily on
       the prophecies of Daniel. He announces that the return
       will occur on October 22, 1844.

1859   Charles Darwin's *The Origin of Species* sets forth a the-
       ory of evolution based upon natural selection. To the re-
       ligious community, Darwin's implications are
       astonishing. In one fell swoop the British naturalist re-
       places purpose, direction, and spirit with a random,
       nondirected, and thoroughly materialistic explanation
       of existence. Although many Christians seek to recon-
       cile their faith with the new science, just as many recoil
       and prepare for battle against the new ideas.

1871   James Freeman Clarke's widely read *Ten Great Religions*
       disturbs many Christian conservatives, for it suggests
       that Christianity is just one of many important religions

1871
cont.
and that many things thought to be unique to Judeo-Christianity, such as floods, crucifixions, resurrections, and virgin births, are actually common to other religions.

1874
Francis L. Patton of McCormick Theological Seminary, a Presbyterian institution in Chicago, charges the pastor of the Fourth Presbyterian Church in Chicago, David Swing, with heresy for his liberal ideas allegedly ignoring the denomination's traditional position on original sin and atonement. Although acquitted by the local presbytery, Swing nonetheless resigns and establishes an independent congregation.

In *Outline of Cosmic Philosophy*, John Fiske, a popular philosopher and historian associated for a while with Harvard University, seeks to resolve the conflict between religion and Darwin by simply asserting that evolution is God's way of doing things.

1876
Religious conservatives led primarily by Presbyterians launch the Niagara Bible Conferences. Influenced greatly by John Nelson Darby (1800–1882), an Anglican minister who helped establish the Plymouth Brethren movement in Great Britain, these conferences, which will occur annually for about a quarter century, concentrate on biblical prophecy. Darby's sway is readily apparent in the widespread acceptance by many religionists who attend these meetings of dispensational premillennialism, the twofold belief that history is divided into seven distinct dispensations and that Christ's return will inaugurate a thousand-year reign of earthly righteousness.

1878
Professor Alexander Winchell of Vanderbilt University is censured by the General Conference of the Southern Methodist Church for taking a more allegorical rather than literal approach to the Genesis account of creation. When the professor refuses to resign, the Methodist school eliminates his position.

1879
Southern Baptist Theological Seminary in Louisville, Kentucky, forces one of its professors, Crawford H. Toy,

to resign for questioning the absolute authority of the Bible.

1882   Professor Ezra P. Gould is fired from Newton Theological Seminary, a Baptist school in Massachusetts, for his views on biblical criticism, which conservatives believe undermine the Bible's authority.

1886   The uncle of Woodrow Wilson, Professor James Woodrow of Columbia Theological Seminary, a Presbyterian school in South Carolina, is fired as a result of an address in which he argued that Darwinian evolution and religion were reconcilable.

To educate students in an institution untainted by modernist sentiments, the world-renowned evangelist Dwight L. Moody establishes the Moody Bible Institute in Chicago. Its curriculum is steeped in missions, evangelism, and Bible prophecy. The school becomes the prototype for countless other "Bible institutes" across the nation.

1891   Professor Charles A. Briggs of Union Theological Seminary (New York) faces heresy charges because of his rejection of the idea of biblical inerrancy, the notion that the Bible is without error in all matters. Although Union Seminary, a Presbyterian school, stands behind him, Briggs resolves the problem for the Presbyterians by becoming an Episcopalian.

1892   Professor Henry Preserved Smith of Lane Theological Seminary, a Presbyterian school in Cincinnati, Ohio, is convicted of heresy by the Presbytery of Cincinnati for denying the inerrancy of the Bible even in its original manuscripts. Smith subsequently obtains a librarian's position at Union Seminary and becomes a Congregationalist.

1895   The Niagara Bible Conference enunciates the five "essentials" of Christianity that will guide fundamentalists from this point forward: the inerrancy of the Bible, the deity and virgin birth of Jesus, the substitutionary atonement, the bodily resurrection of Jesus, and the second coming.

1896   The founding president of Cornell University, Andrew Dickinson White, writes *A History of the Warfare of Science with Theology*. At sharp variance with the fundamentalists, who fear the pernicious effect of science on religious belief, White argues that religion has retarded scientific thought.

1909   An annotated edition of the scriptures, *The Scofield Reference Bible*, perhaps the most influential source of dispensational premillennial ideas in the twentieth century, is prepared by Cyrus I. Scofield (1843–1912), a lawyer turned preacher who pastored the First Congregational Church, Dallas, Texas, from 1882 to 1895 and again from 1902 to 1907. Scofield's commentaries subsequently become "the Bible" for many fundamentalists.

1910–   *The Fundamentals: A Testimony to the Truth,* a set of twelve
1915   pamphlets each about 125 pages long, is published over a five-year period at the expense of two wealthy Presbyterian laymen from California. Distributed free to ministers, seminary professors, theology students, Sunday school directors, and YMCA leaders throughout the country, these booklets, each written by a prominent religious conservative, not only reaffirm the "essentials" of the Niagara Bible Conference of 1895, but also denounce evolution, higher criticism, Catholicism, Mormonism, Jehovah's Witnesses, Christian Scientists, Spiritualism, and much more.

1919   In an effort to give direction to their crusade against modernism, some 6,000 like-minded believers, spurred on by William Bell Riley, pastor of the First Baptist Church, Minneapolis, from 1897 to 1942, gather in Philadelphia and create the World's Christian Fundamentals Association. This organization, which includes the country's most prominent fundamentalists, leads the charge in favor of antievolution laws and later against John T. Scopes for teaching evolution in Tennessee.

Ratification of the Eighteenth Amendment, which ushers in national Prohibition, is viewed with justifiable pride by many church people, for they, working closely with the Anti-Saloon League and other agencies, contributed measurably to the amendment's success.

1920   Curtis Lee Laws, editor of *The Watchman-Examiner*, a Northern Baptist paper, coins the term "fundamentalist," asserting that such a Christian is one willing to battle for the fundamentals of the faith.

1922   President Frank L. McVey of the University of Kentucky urges the people of his state to oppose the antievolution bill being debated by the state legislature. McVey's courageous stand contributes to the bill's subsequent defeat in Kentucky.

1923   The Oklahoma legislature passes the nation's first antievolution law, followed a short time later by Florida, the adopted home of William Jennings Bryan, who crusades tirelessly in behalf of antievolution laws.

1924   Reflecting liberal sentiment within Presbyterianism, the Auburn Affirmation, a document signed by some 1,274 church members primarily in the northern United States, rejects such basic fundamentals as inerrancy of the Bible, the virgin birth, substitutionary atonement, bodily resurrection of Jesus, and the reality of biblical miracles. Appalled by this statement, J. Gresham Machen rallies the denomination's conservative forces.

1925   The Tennessee legislature enacts a measure making it illegal to teach evolution in the public schools. A few months later John Thomas Scopes, a young teacher in Dayton, is brought to trial for violating the new statute. The resulting "monkey affair" attracts national attention, for it pits two prominent figures against one another. The American Civil Liberties Union retains the famous Chicago criminal attorney Clarence Darrow for the defense, while the World's Christian Fundamentals Association brings in the former secretary of state and frequent presidential contender William Jennings Bryan for the prosecution. Inasmuch as Scopes is convicted and the antievolution law upheld, the fundamentalists prevail at Dayton. On the other hand, many Americans are appalled by the whole spectacle and

1925
cont.   wonder about the wisdom of state-mandated "solu-
         tions" to moral and religious questions. The World's
         Christian Fundamentals Association declines rather
         abruptly after the trial.

         Upon Bryan's death, which occurs just days after the
         conclusion of the Scopes trial, Paul W. Rood, a Califor-
         nia evangelist, organizes the Bryan Bible League in Tur-
         lock, California. Fiercely opposed to the theory of
         biological evolution, Rood and the Bryan Bible League
         spearhead the failed attempt to enact an antievolution
         law on the West Coast.

1926   The Mississippi legislature passes an antievolution law.

         Bob Jones, Sr., founds his college in College Point,
         Florida. This fundamentalist school is unaffiliated with
         any religious denomination.

1928   Arkansas, which is the only state to do so by popular
         referendum, outlaws the teaching of evolution by a
         vote of almost two to one. Although this is the last of
         five southern states to pass such legislation, the same
         objective is achieved throughout the country, north and
         south, by applying pressure at the local level, notably
         on school boards.

1929   J. Gresham Machen abandons Princeton Theological
         Seminary because of its liberal teachings, exemplified
         by the Auburn Affirmation, and founds his own West-
         minster Theological Seminary in Philadelphia.

1933   Thirty-four American humanists, including educator
         John Dewey, sign "The Humanist Manifesto," which
         fundamentalists will later point to as the "bible" of sec-
         ular humanism.

1936   The liberal wing of the Presbyterian Church defrocks J.
         Gresham Machen, who promptly establishes the Pres-
         byterian Church of America.

1941   To counter the Federal (later National) Council of
         Churches, Carl McIntire founds the American Council of

Christian Churches. Made in the image of its creator, this fundamentalist organization is rigidly separatist, admitting to membership only those who share its narrow theology and who eschew association with nonbelievers.

Under the auspices of the Moody Bible Institute, five evangelical scientists journey to Chicago to discuss formation of a creationist society. The result is the American Scientific Affiliation, whose growing membership is dominated by Mennonites, Baptists, and Presbyterians in the middle Atlantic and midwestern states. Tension soon emerges within the Affiliation between strict biblical literalists and evangelical scientists inclined toward a more metaphorical view of Genesis.

1942   The National Association of Evangelicals, which welcomes both individuals and denominations into its membership, is established as a fundamentalist alternative to the Federal Council of Churches. It soon becomes an alternative for many conservative Christians who are uncomfortable with the rigid dogmatism of fundamentalists such as Carl McIntire and Bob Jones.

1947   Radio evangelist Charles Fuller establishes Fuller Theological Seminary in Pasadena, California. This institution becomes identified with a more moderate, less separatist variety of fundamentalism. In the tradition of John Nelson Darby and C. I. Scofield, Fuller is a dispensationalist.

Bob Jones University moves to its present site in Greenville, South Carolina.

1951   With headquarters in Cincinnati, Ohio, Circuit Riders, Inc., is organized to combat socialism, communism, and all other forms of alleged anti-American teachings in the Methodist Church. Actually, Myers Lowman, founder of this group, scrutinizes virtually all the major religious bodies in America and identifies sizable numbers in each as either communist or procommunist. He considers approximately one-third of the scholars who collaborated on the Revised Standard Version of the Bible to be procommunist.

1951
cont.
Another crusading anticommunist, Billy James Hargis, incorporates the Christian Echoes National Ministry, better known as the Christian Crusade.

1953
At the behest of Carl McIntire, Billy James Hargis takes charge of a Bible Balloons project to use gas-filled balloons to float portions of the Bible into Eastern European communist countries. On May 7 some 10,000 balloons are set aloft from West Germany.

1954
The phrase "under God" is added to the Pledge of Allegiance to the flag.

Bernard Ramm, a Baptist theologian and philosopher of science, publishes *The Christian View of Science and Scripture*, which provides theological support for a more progressive approach to creationism, an approach more in harmony with conventional geology regarding the age of the earth and humankind.

1956
"In God We Trust," which was inscribed on American currency the previous year, becomes the national motto. Coming at the height of Cold War tensions, this and other gestures of government support for religion appeal to many Americans.

1958
Named for "a young fundamentalist Baptist preacher from Macon, Georgia," who allegedly was murdered by Chinese communists after World War II, the John Birch Society is launched by Robert Welch. This organization and its leader enjoy cordial relations with such figures on the religious right as Carl McIntire and Billy James Hargis.

1960
Pat Robertson launches the Christian Broadcasting Network (CBN).

1962
In *Engel v. Vitale*, popularly known as the School Prayer decision, the Supreme Court declares it unconstitutional to recite a brief, nondenominational prayer in the public schools that was composed by the New York State Board of Regents. The prayer seems inoffensive enough, declaring simply: "Almighty God, we ac-

knowledge our dependence upon Thee, and we beg Thy blessing upon us, our parents, our teachers and our Country." But to the Supreme Court, this public encouragement of religion violates the establishment clause of the First Amendment. The decision ignites a furor.

Disturbed by the content of many public school textbooks, Mrs. Norma Gabler of Longview, Texas, makes her first trip to the state capital to protest to the Texas Education Agency. The teaching of evolution, as well as anything else contrary to Mrs. Gabler's religious and patriotic views, offends the Texas housewife.

1963   The Supreme Court's decision in *Abington Township School District v. Schempp* involves two cases of required Bible reading in the public schools of Pennsylvania and Maryland. Mindful of the public outcry against its decision of the previous year, the Court takes pains in this case to explain the government's position of neutrality in matters of religion. Taking into account both the establishment and free exercise clauses of the First Amendment, the justices declare that statutes that either advance or inhibit religious expression violate the Constitution. On this basis, the Court rules against the states of Pennsylvania and Maryland. The Maryland case is all the more appalling to many religious conservatives because it has been brought by atheist Madalyn Murray.

Although the public reaction in 1963 is somewhat more restrained than it was to the decision of the previous year, many Americans are nonetheless angered. Hence, almost immediately several congresspersons and senators, notably Representative Frank J. Becker of New York and Senator Everett Dirksen of Illinois, seek to amend the Constitution to allow school prayer. These efforts are unsuccessful.

Henry M. Morris, a Southern Baptist engineer known primarily for efforts to reconcile science and biblical literalism, joins several like-minded creationists in founding the Creation Research Society in Midland, Michigan.

1963   Although the Society initially is dominated by Missouri
cont.   Synod Lutherans and Baptists, it also draws some sup-
        port from Seventh-Day Adventists, Reformed Presbyte-
        rians, Reformed Christians, and Brethren. Morris and
        his group object vigorously to the "creeping evolution-
        ism" of the older and more "liberal" creationist society,
        the American Scientific Affiliation.

1965   Rousas John Rushdoony, a California evangelist,
        founds the Chalcedon Ministries and initiates an effort
        to "reconstruct" society in accordance with God's laws,
        a society comparable to that of the seventeenth-century
        Puritans. Although these reconstructionists discard
        premillennial and dispensational eschatology, they
        stand with religious fundamentalists against "secular
        humanism," abortion, higher taxes, and bigger govern-
        ment. Evangelist Pat Robertson often speaks highly of
        Rushdoony. Although opposed to abortion, the recon-
        structionists do not support the militant tactics of Op-
        eration Rescue.

1969   Conservatives and fundamentalists among the Mis-
        souri Synod Lutherans elect J. A. O. Preus as president
        and embark upon a campaign to purify both the Synod
        and Concordia Seminary in St. Louis. Committed to
        biblical inerrancy, conservative Lutherans rail against
        the "evils" of Darwin, Marx, and Freud.

1970   Tim LaHaye and Henry Morris establish the Christian
        Heritage College in San Diego, California. Their objec-
        tive is to offer a liberal arts education in full accord with
        the Bible. The advancement of scientific creationism is
        a special concern, and so Morris launches the Institute
        for Creation Research, which in turn spearheads several
        efforts to find the remains of Noah's ark.

        With funds from the National Science Foundation,
        Jerome Bruner of Harvard University develops a new
        social science curriculum for the nation's fifth and
        sixth graders. Titled *Man: A Course of Study*, the new
        textbooks arouse the ire of many religious conserva-
        tives because of their emphasis upon cultural relativity
        and de-emphasis of religion. The resulting controversy

not only shelves the books and threatens the National Science Foundation itself, but also shows the ability of the religious right to mobilize its forces for a national campaign.

1971   In *Lemon v. Kurtzman* the Supreme Court sets forth a three-pronged test for determining whether a statute runs afoul of either the free exercise or establishment clauses of the First Amendment. According to the Court, a statute must have a secular legislative purpose; its principal effect must neither promote nor inhibit religion; and it must avoid excessive government entanglements with religion. Laws transgressing any one of the three criteria are unconstitutional.

1973   By a margin of seven to two, the Supreme Court in *Roe v. Wade* holds that laws restricting abortion during the first three months of pregnancy are unconstitutional. No decision of the Supreme Court since the prayer cases of the early 1960s so angers the religious right. Along with "restoring" prayer in the public schools, organizations on the religious right are as one in their resolve to restrict abortions. Indeed, opposition to abortion enables many religious and political, Protestant and Catholic conservatives to overlook their differences and to cooperate in behalf of a common objective.

Mel Gabler takes early retirement from Exxon Pipeline and joins his wife Norma in a full-time crusade in Texas to purge public school textbooks of unsatisfactory material. To accomplish this objective, they found Educational Research Analysts. The Gablers believe too many textbooks undermine both Judeo-Christian values and pride in America.

1976   Jimmy Carter, a "born-again" Southern Baptist layman, is elected president. Because of Carter's religious persuasion, the media suddenly show considerable interest in evangelicals and fundamentalists. Ironically, many on the religious right, initially hopeful because of Carter's victory, are soon disappointed.

1977   The National Federation for Decency, better known as
        the Coalition for Better Television, is organized by Don-
        ald Wildmon of Tupelo, Mississippi. Working closely
        with other religious right groups, particularly the
        Moral Majority, the Coalition endeavors to make the
        airwaves "safe" for family viewing.

1978   Jerome Kurtz, President Jimmy Carter's Internal Rev-
        enue Commissioner, announces plans to withdraw tax
        exemptions from private, including church, schools that
        were established presumably to avoid court-ordered
        public school desegregation. This decision infuriates
        many figures on the religious right who see it as another
        example of government hostility toward religion.

1979   With the help of Paul Weyrich, a conservative political
        strategist who coins the term, Howard Phillips, leader
        of the Conservative Caucus, and Edward McAteer, a
        marketing specialist for the Colgate-Palmolive Com-
        pany, Jerry Falwell establishes the Moral Majority, Inc.
        The purpose is to give political expression to Ameri-
        cans on the religious right, Americans who feel their
        sentiments have been ignored too long. With the 1980
        presidential race on the horizon, the Moral Majority
        embarks upon a crusade to destroy "secular human-
        ism" and to restore the nation's religious heritage.

        The Religious Roundtable is organized under the lead-
        ership of Edward McAteer. This organization labors to
        bring the religious and political right together.

        Headquartered in Pasadena, California, the Christian
        Voice identifies fourteen specific issues by which the
        Christian morality of politicians supposedly can be as-
        sessed. Like many other organizations on the religious
        right, the Christian Voice is more "anti" than "pro." It
        opposes higher taxes, sex education without parental
        consent, forced busing, abortion, racial quotas, homo-
        sexual rights, the Department of Education, the Strate-
        gic Arms Limitation Treaty (SALT) II arms agreement
        with the Soviet Union, drugs, and pornography. It fa-
        vors free enterprise, prayer in the public schools, and a
        balanced federal budget.

Led by Texans Paul Pressler of Houston and Paige Patterson of Dallas, Southern Baptist fundamentalists elect one of their own president of the Southern Baptist Convention and set out to purge the denomination's schools and agencies of "liberals." By controlling the presidency and the vast appointive power that goes with that office, the fundamentalists hope to gain control of the denomination's numerous committees and boards.

1980   Sponsored by Edward McAteer's Religious Roundtable, the National Affairs Briefing at the Reunion Arena in Dallas brings together prominent figures from the religious and political right. Presidential candidate Ronald Reagan attends.

In *Stone v. Graham* the Supreme Court declares unconstitutional a Kentucky law requiring the posting of the Ten Commandments in each public elementary and secondary classroom. In the eyes of the Court, the purpose of the statute is clearly religious, for the first five Commandments prescribe religious, not secular, duties.

Jerry Falwell's pamphlet, *Armageddon and the Coming War with Russia,* voices the belief, so typical of many figures on the religious right, that a Russian invasion of Israel will precipitate a nuclear war, the battle of Armageddon, in which the world will be destroyed. Echoing the same sentiment, Pat Robertson, in his *700 Club Newsletter,* goes so far as to suggest that the titanic battle will occur by fall 1982.

Ronald Reagan is elected president with the strong support of religious right organizations, such as Jerry Falwell's Moral Majority.

1981   Jerry Falwell advises "every good Christian" to oppose President Reagan's nomination of Sandra Day O'Conner to the Supreme Court because of the abortion issue. This prompts the Republican Party's elder statesman, Barry Goldwater of Arizona, to retort that "every good Christian" should give the Virginia pastor a kick in the pants.

1982   President Ronald Reagan, in obvious deference to the religious right, becomes the first incumbent president to endorse a school prayer amendment. President Reagan informs Congress that the time has come to "allow prayer back in our schools."

Louis Sheldon founds the Traditional Values Coalition, a California-based organization, and aggressively seeks to defeat politicians at odds with his definition of "traditional values."

After serious consideration by Congress, an antiabortion amendment fails to receive approval.

1983   In *Bob Jones University v. United States* the Supreme Court strips the fundamentalist school of its tax-exempt status because of its racial practices. Convinced that the Bible prohibits interracial dating and marriage, Bob Jones University had excluded African Americans until 1971, at which time blacks who were married within their race were admitted. Applications from unmarried blacks were not accepted until 1975, at which time the university prohibited interracial dating and marriage among its students.

1984   On March 5 Senate Majority Leader Howard H. Baker Jr. opens the debate on President Reagan's proposed school prayer amendment. For two weeks the Senate grapples with the proposal. Senator Jesse Helms, a Republican from North Carolina, favors the proposal, while Senators Lowell Weicker and John Danforth, also Republicans, lead the opposition. When the vote is taken on March 20, a majority, fifty-six to forty-four, supports the amendment. However, failing to receive the required two-thirds majority, the president's amendment fails. A defiant Senator Helms vows the fight has only begun.

During the course of debate several senators on each side of the issue indicate support for "equal access" legislation, a measure guaranteeing equal access to public school facilities for voluntary religious activities. In August Congress passes the Equal Access Act.

The Evangelical Voter, an analysis by Stuart Rothenberg and Frank Newport, challenges the assumption that evangelicals constitute a monolithic bloc of Christian voters. According to this study, income, race, education, and occupation seem to influence voting patterns more than religious beliefs. Moreover, evangelicals are more likely to be Democrats than Republicans, and they embrace diverse viewpoints. This report raises questions about the efficacy of mobilizing Christian conservatives for political purposes.

1985   In *Wallace v. Jaffree* the Supreme Court strikes down a 1981 Alabama law that allows schoolchildren a moment of silence "for meditation or voluntary prayer." The justices rule that Alabama lawmakers have violated the establishment clause of the First Amendment.

1987   In *Edwards v. Aguillard* the Supreme Court rules against Louisiana's Balanced Treatment for Creation-Science and Evolution-Science in Public School Instruction Act. This act had made it illegal to teach Darwinian evolution in Louisiana's public schools without making allowance as well for the teaching of "creation science." According to the Court, the Louisiana law promoted neither academic freedom nor scientific knowledge.

On March 4 Judge W. Brevard Hand of the United States District Court for the Southern District of Alabama in Mobile bans thirty-one textbooks from the public schools of Alabama, ruling that they illegally teach the "religion of secular humanism" and thus violate the establishment clause of the First Amendment. Agreeing that secular humanism is a religion, many conservative Christians hail Judge Hand's ruling, which will be reversed by the Eleventh U.S. Circuit Court of Appeals in August.

Televangelist Jim Bakker, founder of the Praise The Lord or People That Love (PTL) Club, is accused of adultery and financial wrongdoing. Jerry Falwell, momentarily given control of Bakker's empire, soon becomes embroiled in a nasty struggle to retain PTL.

1987   The Southern Baptist Convention faces another battle
cont.   between fundamentalists and moderates. Despite efforts by a Peace Committee to resolve the conflict, the
fundamentalists score another victory, electing inerran-
tist Adrian Rogers to the presidency of the convention.
However, later in the year the fundamentalists lose the
fight for control of Mercer University and several state
governing boards.

Reflecting growing conservative control, the Southern
Baptist Convention's Public Affairs Committee votes
by a narrow seven-to-five margin to support the U.S.
Supreme Court nomination of Judge Robert Bork,
whose positions on pornography, homosexuality, and
the role of religion in American history strike a respon-
sive chord within the convention.

The National Conference of Catholic Bishops voices
concern over the influence of Protestant fundamentalism on certain Catholics, notably Hispanics. Protestant
theologian Carl F. H. Henry quickly retorts that the
bishops are still waging war against the Reformation.
This mild exchange highlights the problem facing conservative Catholics and Protestants who attempt to rise
above theological differences in behalf of common social and political objectives.

In the case of *Mozert v. Hawkins County Board of Education* in Tennessee, a three-judge appeals court panel
unanimously overturns an earlier ruling of U.S. District
Court Judge Thomas G. Hull, who had allowed the
children of Christian fundamentalists to take reading
classes at home rather than reading public school textbooks offensive to their beliefs. The books in question
supposedly contain passages on witchcraft, astrology,
pacifism, and feminism. To many conservative Christians, this decision is just another example of discrimination against fundamentalists.

1988   Although ultimately unsuccessful, Pat Robertson
mounts a campaign for the presidency and early in the
year outpolls Vice President George Bush in the Iowa
caucuses. Fissures on the religious right soon surface,

as many of the other right-wing evangelists support alternative candidates.

Jimmy Swaggart, the enormously successful Baton Rouge, Louisiana, Pentecostal, is engulfed in a sex scandal that undermines his ministry. This scandal, along with the PTL disgrace, has a damaging impact on televangelism in general. Donations fall sharply, forcing severe cutbacks in numerous ministries. For instance, Swaggart's college collapses and Falwell's faces bankruptcy.

Operation Rescue, one of the more aggressive antiabortion groups, emerges into national prominence by the use of civil disobedience against abortion clinics. This group not only pickets, but also attempts to block women from entering clinics. As a result of protests at the Democratic National Convention, demonstrators from Operation Rescue clog Atlanta's jails. Although religious fundamentalists applaud the objective, not all support the group's militant tactics.

The release of Martin Scorsese's film, *The Last Temptation of Christ,* angers the religious right. Pat Robertson denounces the movie, for instance, while Donald Wildmon runs counter-advertisements on 700 Christian radio stations and mails out over two million letters. Conservative columnist Pat Buchanan gives encouragement to the attack.

1989   The Christian Coalition, with headquarters in Chesapeake, Virginia, is organized in the wake of Pat Robertson's failed presidential bid in 1988. Describing itself as profamily, this organization opposes abortion, pornography, condom distribution, waiting periods for handgun purchases, and tax and welfare programs that allegedly discriminate against mothers who stay home with their children. By maintaining a "scorecard" on each member of Congress, the Coalition keeps local constituents informed on how their representatives or senators vote on "family" and "moral" issues.

1990   In *Board of Education of Westside Community School Dis-*

1990
cont.

trict v. Mergens the Supreme Court upholds the Equal Access Act, thereby ensuring religious groups the same access as secular groups to public school facilities.

In *Oregon v. Smith* Justice Antonin Scalia, writing for the majority, holds that government need show only a "reasonable interest" as opposed to a "compelling interest" in order to limit the free exercise of religion. According to Scalia, the compelling interest doctrine, enunciated in *Sherbert v. Verner* (1963) and *Wisconsin v. Yoder* (1972), is a "luxury we can no longer afford." This prompts many in the religious community, including some on the right, to urge Congress to enact legislation "correcting" the High Court's decision.

1991

Paul Weyrich's National Empowerment Television (NET) hits the airwaves. The purpose is not only to make the public aware of what is wrong with the government, but also to offer prescriptions for change. Viewer call-ins consume much of the new network's airtime.

1992

The growing influence of the religious right within the Republican Party is evident at the national convention in Houston, Texas. The party's platform embraces the "profamily" positions of the Christian right.

1993

In November Congress passes the Religious Freedom Restoration Act and President Bill Clinton applauds the measure. Its purpose is to restore the compelling interest test previously set aside in *Oregon v. Smith*.

1994

Condemning President Bill Clinton's "liberal agenda," Pat Robertson's Christian Coalition mounts a vigorous attack on the president and the Democratic Party. The objective is to "reclaim America" by defeating liberal Democrats in the November congressional elections.

Former Marine Lieutenant-Colonel Oliver North, who attracted national attention because of his role in an illegal scheme in the mid-1980s to fund Nicaraguan "freedom fighters" by selling arms to Iran, an avowed enemy of the United States (known as the Iran-Contra scandal), wins the Republican Party's nomination for the U.S. Senate from Virginia. An avowed born-again Christian who appeals openly to the religious right, North has the endorsement of Pat Robertson. North eventually loses the bitterly fought race to the Democratic incumbent, Charles Robb.

The growing political influence of the religious right at the state level is apparent not only in Virginia, but also in Texas, Oklahoma, and Kentucky.

The Anti-Defamation League releases a report entitled *The Religious Right: The Assault on Tolerance and Pluralism in America,* which accuses evangelical and fundamentalist Christian leaders of playing upon fear and hatred in pursuit of political power. The report singles out the Christian Coalition, calling it exclusionist, a threat to American democracy, pluralism, and religious freedom, and hostile toward Jews. Pat Robertson dismisses the report as filled with half-truths and fabrications "reminiscent of the political style practiced by Joseph McCarthy in the 1950s."

L. Brent Bozell, chairman of the conservative Media Research Center, notes that such television programs as *Picket Fences, L.A. Law, Northern Exposure,* and *Christy* have begun to treat religious figures and subjects with more sensitivity.

Several prominent Roman Catholics and evangelical Protestants issue *Evangelicals and Catholics Together: The Christian Mission in the Third Millennium.* This cautious statement of cooperation between groups that in the past have quarreled bitterly over matters of doctrine dismays many evangelical Christians. So while conservative Protestants and Catholics often share common positions on abortion and school prayer, ancient theological differences continue to hamper political cooperation.

Candidates beholden to the religious right score major victories in the November elections, as the Republicans obtain a majority in the House of Representatives for the first time in forty years and regain control of the Senate.

1995 More than thirty Jewish and conservative Christian leaders hold a five-hour meeting in Washington in an effort to stem the angry rhetoric prompted by last year's Anti-Defamation League report on the Christian right. In essence, the two sides agree to disagree without rancor. Jerry Falwell describes the gathering as positive, and Ralph Reed hopes to avoid such hostility in the future, but Abraham Foxman of the Anti-Defamation League declares that "the report stands." Foxman acknowledges that the report has caused Christian conservatives "pain," but hastily adds that Jews are also pained by the seeming anti-Semitism of some of Pat Robertson's remarks and the religious right's constant reference to the United States as a "Christian" nation.

Encouraged by the recent national elections, leaders of eight conservative and evangelical Christian groups prepare a constitutional amendment that would allow student-led prayers in public schools. Asked about school prayer on *This Week with David Brinkley*, a weekly ABC television program, House Speaker Newt Gingrich (R-GA) replies that a religious freedom bill of some sort, one that would go beyond merely school prayer, probably would come before the House after the Easter recess.

Speaking to the Conservative Political Action Conference, Ralph Reed serves notice that the Christian Coalition will not support the Republican ticket in 1996 unless the party's presidential and vice presidential candidates oppose abortion. This appears to be a departure from Reed's effort to expand the base of the Christian Coalition by toning down harsh rhetoric on moral issues.

Two prominent Southern Baptist leaders, Larry Lewis, president of the Southern Baptist Home Mission Board, and Richard Land, executive director of the convention's Christian Life Commission, come under attack for signing *Evangelicals and Catholics Together*. Critics consider the document heretical, making too many concessions to Catholic doctrine, while defenders counter that theological differences should not deter evangelicals and Catholics from working together on such issues as abortion and school prayer.

Speaking from convention headquarters in Nashville, Tennessee, Jim Henry, president of the Southern Baptist Convention, and Richard Land, head of the convention's Christian Life Commission, declare their opposition to the nomination of Henry Foster as U.S. surgeon general. The two Baptist leaders object to Foster's stand on abortion. This brings a stern rebuke on NBC *Nightly News* from journalist and fellow Baptist Bill Moyers, who asserts that the Southern Baptist Convention has been "captured by a political posse allied with the Republican Party." Concludes Moyers: "The irony is that Henry Foster, M.D., himself a Baptist, has been a lifelong crusader against teenage pregnancy and probably more successful at preaching abstinence than a dozen doctors of theology. But when God becomes partisan, religion becomes unforgiving and all subtlety excommunicated."

1996   The Christian Coalition is accused of racism for mailing out sample voter guides that use a black man to portray issues that the organization opposes and a white man to represent matters it supports. Ralph Reed apologizes, claiming a printer error, but Julian Bond, a board member of the National Association for the Advancement of Colored People, hints at hypocrisy, suggesting that Reed's lofty preachments "about racial equality and Christian morality" are "tossed aside in favor of racial wedges and voter manipulation" at election time.

Congress passes and President Clinton signs the welfare reform act, which contains a little-noticed provision on "charitable choice," championed by Senator John Ashcroft (R-MO). This allows faith-based organizations to receive federal tax money for providing various services to the needy, such as drug rehabilitation and job training. Significantly, the legislation does not require those faith-based organizations either to divest their social programs of religious content or to comply with federal statutes regarding equality of treatment for all citizens regardless of race, gender, or sexual preference.

1996 *cont.*	By a margin of 342 to 67, Congress passes the Defense of Marriage Act, a measure that appeals to religious and social conservatives. The law defines marriage in traditional terms as a union between a man and a woman and allows states not to recognize same-sex marriages performed in other states and to withhold benefits from the domestic partners of homosexuals. Thrice-married Bob Barr (R-GA), one of the freshmen elected in 1994, sponsors the legislation.

Over the opposition of the religious right, President Bill Clinton defeats Republican challenger Robert Dole of Kansas. At the same time, twelve of the seventy-three Republican freshmen elected in 1994 are defeated for reelection, suggesting some public weariness with the Newt Gingrich–led Republican "Revolution of '94." |
| 1997 | Ralph Reed announces he will step down as executive secretary of the Christian Coalition on September 1 to organize a political consulting firm, Century Strategies. He plans to work for the election of conservative politicians in upcoming elections.

The U.S. Supreme Court declares the Religious Freedom Restoration Act unconstitutional, but leaves the door open to such legislation from the states. Split six to three, the Court rules in *City of Boerne v. Flores* that Congress had exceeded its authority in the Religious Freedom Restoration Act, for that law "is not a proper exercise of Congress's . . . enforcement power because it contradicts vital principles necessary to maintain separation of powers and the federal-state balance."

Randy Tate, one of the staunchly conservative first-year Republicans elected to the U.S. House in 1994 who was defeated for reelection in 1996, assumes leadership of the Christian Coalition. |
| 1998 | Appearing on *NBC Today* with Mat Lauer, First Lady Hillary Clinton defends her husband and attributes his troubles to a "vast right-wing conspiracy."

Efforts to impeach President Bill Clinton gain momen- |

tum when it becomes apparent that his unequivocal denial on national television of a sexual relationship with a White House intern, Monica Lewinsky, is false. For many on the religious right, the president's misbehavior is symptomatic of the nation's moral decline.

Reflecting the reservations of some Americans about such legislation, Republican Governor Pete Wilson vetoes the California Religious Freedom Protection Act, a measure that would have sharply restricted state authority regarding religion.

As the midterm elections approach, Ralph Reed, now an independent political consultant, advises Republicans to tone down their rhetoric. It makes Republicans look mean-spirited, he observes, when they accuse others of "having the wrong values."

Republicans suffer serious setbacks in the midterm elections, as Democrats gain five seats in the House and hold their own in the Senate. Democrats interpret their success as a signal from the American public to end the impeachment investigation of the president.

Criticized for his party's poor performance in the midterm elections, House Speaker Newt Gingrich announces he will resign from the House and not seek the speakership in the forthcoming congressional term.

Ralph Reed's first outing as an independent political strategist produces mixed results. While many of his candidates win, Reed loses a high-profile contest in Alabama, where Fob James, the Republican incumbent, is defeated.

Randy Tate of the Christian Coalition praises the House for its vote in favor of impeachment and calls on President Bill Clinton to resign, this in the face of national polls showing continuing public support for the beleaguered president.

1999   With the public showing little support for impeachment, Pat Robertson announces that Republicans

1999
cont.

should call off the effort to remove President Clinton. Polls in late December 1998 and January 1999 show that a majority of Americans disapprove of the House's vote to impeach and object to the Senate's effort to remove Clinton. Indeed, 72 percent of Americans support the president's handling of his office.

Pat Robertson's announcement on impeachment bewilders many of his followers. One of the kinder responses comes from Andrea Sheldon, executive director of the Family Values Coalition, who remarks simply that friends sometimes disagree.

The Senate, divided along partisan lines, fails to convict the president.

As the state's legislative session begins, Texas Governor George W. Bush sides with social and religious conservatives on a parental notification law on abortion, a pilot program to test vouchers in private schools, and passage of the Religious Freedom Restoration Act. Even so, hardliners on the religious right, suspicious of the governor's commitment to their agenda, dub him "Conservative Lite."

Jerry Falwell arouses controversy when he asserts that the Antichrist is a Jewish man who probably is alive now. In the face of protest, Falwell backtracks: "I apologize to my Jewish friends here and around the world, and I apologize to the Christians here for having created any kind of rift. I apologize not for what I believe, but for my lack of tact and judgment in making a statement that served no purpose whatsoever."

To the bemusement of some and the ire of others, Jerry Falwell declares that Tinky Winky, the oldest and biggest of television's psychedelic quartet of "Teletubby" children's characters, is a symbol of gay pride.

Although acknowledging that "there is no easy solution to the violence and depravity that has swept America's schools," Randy Tate offers "the timeless values of faith and morality" as a potential remedy. Predictably,

Tate supports school prayer, asserting: "When kids come together to pray, they more than likely will not come together to fight."

Reflecting growing disenchantment within the religious right, two former aides to Jerry Falwell and the Moral Majority, Cal Thomas, now a nationally syndicated newspaper columnist, and Ed Dobson, now a Michigan pastor, conclude in a new book, *Blinded by Might*, that "religious conservatives are best served by preaching the Christian gospel—not by preaching organized political involvement." Religious people should certainly continue to vote and run for office, assert the authors, but the "ordained clergy, left and right, from Jesse Jackson to Jerry Falwell should withdraw from partisan politics." This advice, coming from two of their own, does not set well with many on the religious right.

Prone to intemperate remarks, Pat Robertson, on his television program *The 700 Club*, criticizes Scotland for its tolerance of homosexuals, declaring "you can't believe how strong homosexuals are" in that "dark land." This prompts the Bank of Scotland to cancel a planned business venture with the televangelist.

After acknowledging that she believes in God, seventeen-year-old Cassie Bernall is slain along with eleven other classmates and a teacher at Columbine High School in Littleton, Colorado. She quickly becomes a martyr to many evangelical Christians.

Craig Scott, sixteen-year-old brother of Rachel Scott, one of the twelve Columbine shooting victims, tells the Southern Baptist Convention: "I definitely think if we had prayers in school, this would never have happened."

The attack at Columbine High School sparks renewed interest in religion in public schools, such as posting the Ten Commandments and allowing school prayer.

Former House Speaker Newt Gingrich tells a Republican Women Leaders Forum that teachers' unions bear

1999
cont.

responsibility for the Littleton shootings. "We have had a thirty-five-year experiment in a unionized, bureaucratic, secular assault on the core values of this country. . . . God has been driven out of the classroom. We have seen the result in a secular, atheistic system in which God is not allowed to exist."

Representative Bob Barr (R-GA), in a House debate, suggests that the Littleton shootings would not have occurred if the Ten Commandments had been posted in the school.

The U.S. House votes to allow the posting of the Ten Commandments in schools and other public buildings. Tom Flynn, a former Roman Catholic and the current director of the First Amendment Task Force for the Council of Secular Humanism, calls the vote not only an insult to millions of Americans, but also "a piece of legislative grandstanding that will almost certainly be ruled unconstitutional."

Representative Robert Aderhalt (R-AL) attaches a provision regarding the Ten Commandments to a juvenile crime bill designed to decrease school violence. Aderhalt believes the Commandments will promote "the right values" in children and calm violence.

Governor Jeb Bush of Florida, brother of Governor George W. Bush of Texas, signs legislation creating the nation's first statewide education voucher program. The law permits students in poor-performing public schools to attend private schools, including sectarian ones, of their choice at taxpayer expense. Fifty-eight students promptly enroll in the program, thereby receiving what Jeb Bush calls "opportunity scholarships" of $3,389 from the state.

Jerry Falwell's newspaper, *National Liberty Journal*, asserts that the all-female Lilith Fair concert tour is named for a demon. According to ancient Jewish literature, Lilith was created by God as Adam's first wife, but she left Eden and dwelled with demons after refusing to be submissive to Adam.

Governor George W. Bush signs the Texas Religious Freedom Restoration Act, which forces the state to show a compelling interest, such as the protection of public health or safety, before restricting the free exercise of religion. Says Bush: "Texas will not stand for government interference with the free exercise of religion."

Pat Robertson's Christian Coalition loses its tax-exempt status, concluding a suit begun in 1996 when the Federal Election Commission sued the Coalition, claiming it was little more than an arm of the Republican Party.

The Eleventh U.S. Circuit Court of Appeals in Atlanta unanimously agrees that public school students in Alabama may pray on the public address system and at graduation exercises so long as they do not proselytize and so long as school personnel have no direct role in such activity. To prohibit students from engaging in any kind of prayer at school, reasons the appellate court, would be to foster atheism. "Permitting students to speak religiously signifies neither state approval nor disapproval of that speech," the judges declare.

Federal District Judge Joyce Green takes issue with the Federal Election Commission, dismissing many of the charges brought against the Christian Coalition in 1996. Pat Robertson calls the decision a "decisive victory for First Amendment freedom."

By a six-to-four vote, the Kansas Board of Education stuns the scientific community by making it optional to teach evolution in the public schools and deleting questions about evolution from state assessment tests.

Some Kansans believe the decision on evolution makes the state look backward, a sentiment confirmed when a subsequent study commissioned by the Thomas B. Fordham Foundation and released in September 2000 ranks Kansas dead last with regard to the teaching of science.

Pat Robertson endorses political assassinations, reasoning that it makes more sense to "take out" someone like

1999
cont.

Yugoslav president Slobodan Milosevic or Iraqi President Saddam Hussein than to spend "billions of dollars on a war that harms innocent civilians." Sarcastically, Washington, D.C., columnist Marianne Means wonders if political assassination is Robertson's idea of "a good family value."

A Gallup Poll discloses that 68 percent of Americans favor the teaching of creationism alongside evolution. This is not surprising, given that 44 to 50 percent of Americans since the late 1970s have consistently affirmed the belief that God created humans in their present form no more than 10,000 years ago.

Whether aware of such statistics or not, presidential aspirants for 2000 are careful not to offend the religious right on evolution. Vice President Al Gore says "localities should be free to teach creationism as well" as evolution; Governor George W. Bush believes youngsters "ought to be exposed to different theories about how the world started"; Steve Forbes dismisses evolution as "a massive fraud"; and Gary Bauer categorically rejects the notion that humans descended "from apes."

Quietly following the lead of Kansas, the Kentucky Education Department substitutes the phrase "change over time" for the word "evolution" in its new science guidelines. This concerns many science teachers, given the periodic efforts in Kentucky to teach creationism.

Republican leaders in the U.S. House introduce a voucher bill, the Academic Emergency Act, allowing students in failing public schools to attend private schools at government expense.

Pat Robertson offers his assessment of potential presidential candidates for 2000. He dismisses Gary Bauer, with whom he agrees on numerous issues, as a "lost cause"; Elizabeth Dole is just "a Southern Belle"; and Jesse Ventura, the Reform Party governor of Minnesota, is "off his rocker." Perhaps chastened by recent Republican setbacks, a more pragmatic Robertson supports George W. Bush, believing the Texas governor has the best chance of winning in 2000.

In a document titled *Faithful Citizenship: Civic Responsibility for the New Millennium,* the National Conference of Catholic Bishops calls for a "new kind of politics." The bishops urge all Americans to be more civil in political debate, more concerned about impoverished children, and more alert to a "growing culture of death" (abortion, capital punishment, and euthanasia).

Responding to a ruling by the Fifth U.S. Circuit Court of Appeals that went against the Santa Fe Independent School District, near Galveston, Texas, the U.S. House approves a resolution urging the Supreme Court to approve prayer before high school football games.

In October Mel White, a Christian minister who cofounded SoulForce, Inc., a California-based organization that fights for gay rights, and 200 of his followers meet with Jerry Falwell and 200 of his followers in Lynchburg, Virginia. The meeting changes few minds, but Falwell apologizes for his harsh antigay rhetoric of the past and declares that it is time that "we love the sinner more than we hate the sin," a modification of his usual stand that God hates both the sin and the sinner. Before revealing his homosexuality, White had assisted Falwell and Pat Robertson in writing their autobiographies.

A federal judge in Ohio declares Cleveland's school voucher program unconstitutional because it uses public tax money to send children to religious schools.

President Bill Clinton encourages public schools to invite churches and faith-based organizations to assist in programs during and after school that are designed to advance student literacy, improve discipline, and enhance school safety. "I have never believed the Constitution required our schools to be religion-free zones," declares the president, "or that our children must check their faith at the schoolhouse door."

2000   The Family Research Council, an evangelical Christian lobby in Washington, D.C., calls its effort to persuade lawmakers to permit the posting of the Ten Commandments in public schools "Hang Ten." Legislatures in Colorado, Florida, Illinois, Kentucky, Mississippi, Missouri, Oklahoma, and South Dakota are considering such legislation, and Minnesota and North Carolina are expected to follow suit.

Senator John McCain easily defeats presumed front-runner Governor George W. Bush in the New Hampshire Republican primary. This makes the approaching South Carolina primary suddenly crucial to the Bush campaign.

Gary Bauer abandons the presidential race after a poor showing in New Hampshire and endorses John McCain just prior to the hotly contested South Carolina primary.

With the Republican contest heating up, George W. Bush delivers an address at Bob Jones University, a staunchly fundamentalist and anti-Catholic institution in South Carolina. The McCain campaign exploits Bush's action, hinting in Michigan, a state with a large Catholic populace and the next Republican battleground, that the Texas governor is anti-Catholic.

Bush subsequently apologizes to Catholics for his appearance at Bob Jones University, explaining: "On reflection, I should have been more clear in disassociating myself from anti-Catholic sentiments and racial prejudice."

George W. Bush remarks that Jesus is his "favorite political philosopher."

With the religious right taking the initiative, an all-out smear campaign is begun against John McCain in South Carolina. By telephone, e-mail, and other means voters are "informed" about the senator's first wife, alleged marital infidelities, his usage of profane language, and his "softness" on the gay issue. Pat Robertson, in a recorded telephone message sent to thousands, accuses McCain of being allied with "vicious" anti-Christian bigots.

The Bush campaign at first denies any knowledge of efforts to tarnish McCain in South Carolina, but later admits to funding some of Robertson's calls.

Campaigning in Virginia, McCain levels a stinging attack at Pat Robertson and Jerry Falwell. Declares McCain: "Neither party should be defined by pandering to the outer reaches of American politics and the agents of intolerance, whether they be Louis Farrakhan or Al Sharpton on the left or Pat Robertson and Jerry Falwell on the right." It is unfortunate, McCain suggests, that George W. Bush has linked himself to those who practice the "political tactics of division and slander."

George W. Bush handily wins the Republican primaries in South Carolina and Virginia, "but at what cost?" asks columnist Cal Thomas, who concludes that the South Carolina contest shows that "people who are supposed to serve a higher kingdom . . . can get down and dirty with the best of the pagans."

Although Cal Thomas concedes that when preachers "get down and dirty with . . . politicians they can expect to be treated as . . . politicians," he nevertheless believes that John McCain "has gone too far in denouncing Pat Robertson and Jerry Falwell as 'agents of intolerance.'"

George W. Bush's appearance at Bob Jones University draws attention to that institution's ban on interracial dating. In the wake of sharp criticism, Bob Jones III, president of the school since 1991, announces on CNN's *Larry King Live* that, "as of today, right now, we're dropping" the ban. Bush remarks that "the university has made the right decision."

Judge L. Ralph Smith, Jr. of the Circuit Court of Florida rules that the use of tax money for private school education is a violation of the state constitution. This derails Florida's new voucher program, but Governor Jeb Bush vows that "this is the first inning of a long, drawn-out legal battle."

The Republican Party primary in Texas allows voters to

2000
cont.

express their position on student-initiated prayers at school sporting events. Statewide, 94 percent of Republican voters approve the proposition. Because the resolution is nonbinding, critics accuse Texas Republicans of grandstanding.

George Bush meets in Austin, Texas, with a dozen gay Republicans, assuring them that a Bush administration would hire qualified people who shared his political views, regardless of sexual preference. This allays somewhat the perception of Bush as intolerant of homosexuals.

Jerry Falwell introduces "People of Faith 2000," a plan to register at least ten million voters with the help of local pastors. Falwell's claim of nonpartisanship to the contrary, critics insist that the Virginia preacher's real intention is to advance the presidential fortunes of George W. Bush.

Cal Thomas chides Jerry Falwell for his "People of Faith 2000," claiming his friend "has again succumbed to the temptation of politics and its illusion of power." Asserts Thomas: "'People of Faith 2000' will raise some money and make noise, but it will change little."

Thirteen years after removing the title "Reverend" from his name to run for president in 1988, Pat Robertson renews his ordination vows and once again attaches "Reverend" to his name. The Virginia pastor, now seventy years old, announces that he intends to devote his remaining years to missions and soul winning.

By a vote of two to one, the Sixth U.S. Circuit Court of Appeals strikes down Ohio's state motto, "With God, all things are possible." Adopted in 1959 and inscribed on state stationery, reports, and tax returns, the motto, according to the court, amounts to a government endorsement of Christianity. Taken from Matthew 19:26, the motto presumably expresses a sentiment not shared by Muslims, Jews, and others. This prompts the dissenting judge to wonder about the inscription on U.S. coins, "In God We Trust," which has been upheld by federal appeals courts.

House Majority Whip Tom DeLay contends that if George W. Bush wins the presidency there will be "a very aggressive counterattack on the antireligious crusade of the news media and the entertainment industry."

On NBC's *Meet the Press* Pat Robertson warns George W. Bush not to pick John McCain as his vice presidential running mate. Robertson accuses McCain of intemperance.

Emerging as something of a celebrity to the religious right, Marian Ward, the Santa Fe Independent School District student who challenged the restriction on prayer before football games, gives the invocation at the Texas Republican Party's convention in Houston.

Divided six to three, the Supreme Court upholds the Fifth U.S. Circuit Court of Appeals regarding the Santa Fe Independent School District and prayer before sporting events. Says Justice John Paul Stevens, such prayer "has the improper effect of coercing those present to participate in an act of religious worship." Taking place on government property at a school-sponsored event, pregame prayer, Stevens continues, gives the impression of having the state's "seal of approval."

George W. Bush attacks the *Santa Fe* decision for preventing devout students from expressing their faith, but Cal Thomas, while disagreeing with the Court's majority, concludes that pregame prayer actually "trivializes the act of prayer." Conservative Christians, he asserts, are "fooling themselves" if they think such prayers either signify that "all must be right with the world," improve the quality of the game, or contribute to fewer injuries.

Linda Holloway, who chaired the Kansas Board of Education and supported the new standards on evolution, is defeated for reelection.

Al Gore picks Connecticut Senator Joseph Lieberman, an Orthodox Jew, as his vice presidential running mate,

2000
cont.

the first Jew put forth in a presidential campaign by a major party. By selecting a man of such devout faith, one who had rebuked President Clinton for his sexual misbehavior, the vice president blunts the ability of the Republican Party to use the Clinton scandals against him in the upcoming presidential campaign.

On the campaign trail Joseph Lieberman talks openly about religion. Invoking the authority of George Washington, he tells audiences in Chicago, Detroit, and South Bend, Indiana, that religion reinforces morality. "There must be a place for faith in America's public life," he declares, and he hopes his nomination will encourage people "to feel more free to talk about their faith." On another occasion Lieberman hails America as "the most religious country in the world" and proclaims all Americans the "children of the same awesome God."

Disclosing divergent attitudes within the American Jewish community, Abraham H. Foxman, national director of the Anti-Defamation League, urges Lieberman to stop making "overt expressions" of religious belief on the campaign trail. Foxman believes such religious emphasis in the political arena "becomes inappropriate and even unsettling in a religiously diverse society such as ours."

As appeals to the divine become more frequent, George W. Bush tells a B'nai B'rith convention in Washington of his support for Israel and admiration of social programs initiated by faith-based organizations. Adds Bush: "Our nation is chosen by God and commissioned by history to be a model to the world of justice and inclusion and diversity without division. Jews and Christians and Muslims speak as one in their commitment to a kind, just, tolerant society."

Not to be outdone, Vice President Al Gore, a Southern Baptist, reveals that before making any decision he asks, "What would Jesus do?"

In an obvious appeal to religious and social conservatives, Reform Party nominee Pat Buchanan vows to "make America God's Country again" by appointing only antiabortion judges and kicking gays out of the military.

Although a lifelong Southern Baptist, Jimmy Carter withdraws from the Southern Baptist Convention because of that body's continuing move to the political and religious right. The final straw for the former president is a revision of the convention's statement of faith, the Baptist Faith and Message, which calls on women to be submissive to their husbands, rejects women as pastors, and uses language Carter finds objectionable regarding biblical inerrancy.

The Food and Drug Administration's approval of the abortion pill, RU-486, draws sharp criticism from many on the religious right. Reverend Flip Benham, director of Operation Save America (formerly Operation Rescue), warns that any doctor who "thinks he can prescribe this and have any degree of anonymity . . . is mistaken." He adds that if doctors "want to put their practice in jeopardy, they can start prescribing this pill."

George W. Bush criticizes the Food and Drug Administration, calling the decision mistaken, but gives no pledge to ban RU-486 if elected president. Al Gore favors the decision.

Putting pragmatism above morality, Pat Robertson remains noticeably silent about RU-486, explaining that he does not want to put Bush on the spot with the presidential election so near.

For Pat Robertson, Lieberman poses a dilemma. Although admiring the senator for his high moral values, the televangelist worries he will pull voters away from Bush.

In a document titled *The U.S. Supreme Court and the Culture of Death,* some 300 U.S. Catholic bishops accuse the High Court of bringing "our legal system to the brink of endorsing infanticide." In unusually strident lan-

2000
cont.

guage, the bishops blame the Court for helping "to create an abortion climate, in which many Americans turn to the destruction of innocent life as an answer to social and personal problems." Particularly upsetting to the bishops is a recent Supreme Court ruling overturning Nebraska's ban on so-called partial birth abortions.

With the presidential race dragging on without resolution due to the close vote count in Florida, some on the religious right suspect the Democrats of trying to steal the election. The Christian Coalition warns of "an unfolding miscarriage of justice," while Jerry Falwell contends that Al Gore's efforts are "now being viewed by grassroots people everywhere as an attempt to steal the White House."

The diversity of President-elect George Bush's cabinet nominees elicits a favorable response, but the selection of the staunchly conservative and intensely religious John Ashcroft for attorney general draws fire.

2001

Civil rights leader Reverend Jesse Jackson promises to mobilize national opposition to John Ashcroft. "You cannot very well go to a Martin Luther King celebration on January 15 and vote for an Ashcroft," says Jackson, who contends that the Bush appointee would "unravel fifty years of civil rights law."

Soon after taking office President Bush acts on two issues dear to religious conservatives. He prohibits U.S. funding to foreign family planning agencies that sanction abortion, and his proposed educational reforms include a voucher program. Students in poor-performing schools would be eligible to receive $1,500 to attend another public school or a private, parochial, or charter school.

Consistent with his view of compassionate conservatism, President Bush proposes the creation of a White House Office of Faith-Based and Community Initiatives that would manage some $8 billion in federal grants and tax breaks over the next decade. The office's purpose would be to assist the Bush administration in dealing with the country's social ills. "We in government must not fear faith-based programs," the president asserts, but Barry Lynn, director of Americans United for the Separation of Church and State, calls the proposal "a terrible idea." Admittedly, religious organizations such as Catholic Charities and Lutheran Social Services have for years accepted federal funds to operate homeless shelters and soup kitchens and to provide literacy classes and adoption services, but only on the condition that those social activities were secularized. The worry is that the president's proposal requires no such secularization, thus permitting churches, synagogues, and mosques to receive public tax dollars without divesting their social programs of religious content. In fact, Jim Harrington, director of the Austin-based Texas Civil Rights Project, accuses Bush of "winking at this mixture of federal money and religion, and that's the problem."

A Gallup survey in early February discloses that 48 percent of Americans approve of the president's "initiative that will use government funds to help religious organizations provide social services"; 44 percent disapprove.

Ironically, several prominent figures on the religious right, notably Pat Robertson and Jerry Falwell, usually strong supporters of the president, express opposition to the faith-based initiative. Their objection is twofold: government interference in religious matters, and federal financial assistance to certain non-Christian groups.

3

Biographical Sketches

Most of the individuals covered here have risen to prominence since World War II. Intellectually and theologically,
however, much of the contemporary religious right is
rooted in the late nineteenth and early twentieth centuries. To
provide some sense of continuity, therefore, several figures from
the earlier era, such as John Nelson Darby and J. Gresham
Machen, have been included. Other individuals, such as Robert
Welch and Paul Weyrich, more political conservatives than fundamentalist Christians, have been included because their goals
have much in common with those of the religious right. Inasmuch as people on the religious right are often associated with
organizations, and in fact organizations often have been built
around particular personalities, readers should consult Chapter 5
with these biographies.

Gary L. Bauer (1946–)

Gary Bauer was one of the more conservative Republican presidential candidates in 2000, but his campaign experience represents the often complex and personally risky combination of
religion and politics. For many years Bauer worked for conservative Christian causes, serving as a congressional lobbyist for
James Dobson's organization, Focus on the Family (FF). Until
2000 Bauer headed the Family Research Council (FRC), an off-
shoot of FF formed in 1988. Before leaving the organization to
campaign for the presidency, he had raised the annual budget to
$14 million and established a mailing list of 400,000 people. The
organization became not only a conduit for fund raising, but also
a source of committed volunteers to work in campaigns and loyal
voters to go to the polls on election day. In 1997 Bauer created the

Campaign for Working Families, a political action committee that raised over $2 million from 90,000 donors, a group to which he turned to raise funds for his bid for the presidency.

Raised in Newport, Kentucky, Bauer received a B.A. in 1968 from Georgetown College in Kentucky and a J.D. in 1973 from Georgetown University. After working for a trade association, he joined Ronald Reagan's presidential campaign in 1980 as a senior policy analyst and served the Reagan administration in various capacities, including deputy undersecretary for planning, budget and evaluation; chairman of the president's Special Working Group on School Discipline; assistant to the president for policy development; and undersecretary in the Department of Education. In 1988 and 1996 Bauer expressed displeasure with the Republican presidential candidates—George Bush and Robert Dole—concluding that their credentials were insufficiently conservative. This dissatisfaction undoubtedly influenced his decision to seek the Republican nomination in 2000 despite advice to the contrary from fellow religious right leaders Pat Robertson and James Dobson.

During his brief campaign for the Republican nomination, Bauer advocated policy positions supportive of conservative Christian values. He avidly opposed legalized abortion and objected to the push for a "right to die," which, he warned, would result in a "duty to die." Bauer advocated additional reforms of the welfare system, arguing for an end to cash entitlements that he claimed encouraged irresponsibility. Any assistance should be tied to changing the behavior of recipients, he believed. He called for tax cuts for families, rather than increased spending on government programs. Bauer opposed any special legislative action to protect gay rights. He promised to tie any foreign policy actions to the willingness of foreign governments to recognize their citizens' freedom of religion. These orthodox conservative positions notwithstanding, Bauer raised eyebrows among those on the religious right by advocating positions, such as a patients' bill of rights and campaign finance reform, more characteristic of a moderate or liberal candidate. Bauer's accidental fall from a New Hampshire stage while flipping pancakes foreshadowed his disappointing showing in that state's primary.

After dropping out of the race, he endorsed Senator John McCain for the nomination, thus gaining the further disapproval of many on the religious right. An even greater heresy, Bauer was present when McCain publicly denounced Pat Robertson and Jerry Falwell as "agents of intolerance." His own Family Research Council and his longtime ally, James Dobson, publicly criticized his support for McCain. Although the religious right's disaffection with Bauer may be interpreted as a reaction to someone moderating his conservative views in order to broaden political support, the source of Bauer's difficulties with former allies may be due in part to his idealism. For instance, Bauer was critical of Pat Robertson for supporting trade with China and not mentioning his own broadcast interests in that country.

Although Bauer no longer has ties to the Family Research Council, he still operates his political action committee. He plans to continue an active public life, writing speeches and expressing his opinions in the media, and will perhaps write a book about his campaign experiences. Bauer may also work for reform in the Republican Party, which he believes is too closely tied to corporate interests.

Robert J. Billings (1926–1995)

A major supporter of Christian schools, Robert Billings was a member of the Department of Education during President Ronald Reagan's administration. He graduated from Bob Jones University and served as a high school principal, but left that position because of what he considered excessive government interference and the dominance of humanist values in public education. He and his wife began establishing Christian schools across the nation. He also served as president of Hyles-Anderson College in Crown Point, Indiana. In 1976 he ran an unsuccessful campaign for Congress. Billings founded the National Christian Action Coalition in 1978, a successor to Christian School Action. One of the Coalition's major goals was to oppose government involvement in Christian schools. Consequently, Billings directed the effort against the Internal Revenue Service when that agency in 1978 sought to deny tax exemptions to Christian schools for alleged racial discrimination. In 1979 he helped to persuade Jerry Falwell to form Moral Majority and assisted in rallying support for Falwell among influential people in the religious right. He became the organization's first executive director.

Billings left Moral Majority in 1980 to serve as a religious adviser in Ronald Reagan's campaign for the presidency. After Reagan became president, Billings was named the director of regional offices in the Department of Education. In this post he played a major role in fending off Internal Revenue Service proposals to tax religious schools. Even so, in 1983 the Supreme

Court reversed the Reagan administration's decision to grant tax-exempt status to Billings's alma mater, Bob Jones University. Like other leaders of the religious right in 1988, Billings supported a Republican candidate for president, backing Senator Robert Dole's unsuccessful attempt to gain the nomination. Billings was quoted as saying that people do not wish to think for themselves, but desire leadership and want to be told what to think by those who are more closely involved with politics.

Bill Bright (1921–)

Founder and leader of Campus Crusade for Christ for nearly fifty years, Bill Bright has patterned a conservative Christian message intended to appeal to contemporary Americans. Still attached to fundamentalist beliefs such as biblical inerrancy and the blood atonement of Christ, Bright nonetheless introduced alternative techniques for "selling" Christianity consistent with modern consumer culture and the hope for financial success, using athletes and popular music stars to attract young people on college campuses. In the late 1960s, during youth protests against the war in Vietnam, Bright stated his support for student radicals, using such phrases as "revolution now" and commenting that dissent was an important ingredient in society. However, Bright remained committed to a conservative agenda, including preservation of family values, personal initiative, and the capitalist system.

Bright, who was born in Coweta, Oklahoma, had a conversion experience at age sixteen. His participation in the Hollywood Presbyterian Church, which had a relaxed atmosphere, mixing evangelizing with social interaction, undoubtedly had a later influence on Bright's choice of professions. In 1946 he entered Princeton Seminary, but transferred after a year to the more conservative Fuller Seminary in Pasadena, California. In his final year at the seminary the idea of the Campus Crusade came to him, and so he left the school and rented a house near the University of California at Los Angeles and began his campaign for religious conversion. Billy Graham, who in 1955 recommended a more friendly approach to spreading the gospel message, confirmed Bright's belief that personal religious commitment, especially among youth, was necessary to combat the trend toward secularism in the United States and the advance of communism around the world. Thus, Bright's approach emphasized the need for personal conversion, but never unequivocally condemned American materialist culture.

Bright combined entrepreneurial skills with a pragmatic approach to the Christian faith, claiming that spiritual laws governed people's relationship with God and treating biblical accounts as rationally founded and empirically verifiable. He presented a simple message to potential converts—although God loves each person, sin separates that person from God. Therefore, because Jesus Christ was the only path to God, each person must individually accept Christ as savior. Bright developed straightforward methods that are used by Crusade participants for approaching students. Training seminars were offered at Crusade headquarters at Arrowhead Springs, California. In the 1960s Bright formed Athletes In Action (AIA), an adjunct to Campus Crusade. The AIA basketball team played exhibition games with college teams, taking the opportunity to witness to the audience during halftime.

In 1972 Bright initiated EXPLO events, public rallies intended to motivate high school and college students to use Campus Crusade methods to create converts in their homes, churches, and schools. At EXPLO '74, held in South Korea, Bright's political naivete became evident when he announced his support for President Park Chung Hee's regime. Billy Graham, who had worked with Bright's Campus Crusade, disapproved of Bright's support for the repressive regime. Of concern to others have been Bright's tight organizational control and seeming intolerance of differing opinions and criticism. Others have indicated their concern for his ties to wealthy donors such as Nelson Bunker Hunt. Some critics expressed concern for Bright's acceptance of contemporary American economic values, fearing his movement would be compromised by the very secular world he hopes to transform.

These reservations notwithstanding, in the 1990s Bright's campus ministries continued to expand. In 1996 Bright won the Templeton Prize in Religion for advancing the understanding of God and spirituality, which included an award of over $1 million. Bright's Campus Crusade organization had expanded to nearly 13,000 full-time workers and over 101,000 volunteers in 165 countries. Among his projects was an attempt to mobilize millions of Christians around the world to fast and pray for spiritual revival. Bright hoped to extend his conservative Christian message worldwide, expressing the intention of converting one billion people and establishing one million churches by the year 2000.

William Jennings Bryan (1860–1925)

William Jennings Bryan's influence on the development of the religious right stems largely from his participation as a prosecutor in the 1925 Scopes trial in which John T. Scopes was charged with violating a state law forbidding the teaching of evolution in the public schools of Tennessee. At issue in this trial was the conflict between a literal interpretation of the Bible and scientific explanations of natural events, a conflict in which fundamentalists disclosed deep suspicions toward a modern society seemingly at odds with their religious beliefs. Despite his association with fundamentalist opposition to evolution theory, Bryan's political life involved the pursuit of objectives that cannot readily be associated with a religious right ideology, then or now.

Bryan, a native of southern Illinois, graduated as class valedictorian from Illinois College in 1881. He entered Union Law School in Chicago and received his law degree in 1883. He moved to Lincoln, Nebraska, in 1887, immediately became active in politics, and was elected to the U.S. House of Representatives in 1890. In 1896 he captured the Democratic Party's nomination for the presidency. The American people rejected him at the polls in 1896, again in 1900, and yet again in 1908, giving Bryan the dubious distinction of having been defeated in three presidential elections. After Woodrow Wilson was elected president in 1912, he chose Bryan as his secretary of state. Bryan attempted to maintain a basically pacifist stance and opposed American involvement in World War I. Wilson's policy of "neutrality," which in fact favored Great Britain and France, led Bryan to resign from the Wilson cabinet.

Unlike many fundamentalists, Bryan did not find premillennialism an attractive doctrine. He supported many progressive policies and causes: women's suffrage, direct popular election of the president, a national minimum wage, direct election of U.S. senators, a graduated income tax, and the use of government to control the power of corporations. On other issues, such as Prohibition and Sabbatarianism, Bryan took more conservative positions closer to the hearts of fundamentalists.

Bryan opposed the teaching of evolution, an issue to which he devoted increasing attention as his influence in politics faltered. He argued that state legislatures had the right to restrict the teaching of evolution, at least to the extent that such instruction must label evolution a mere hypothesis or "guess" as to the origin of humankind. Evolution was not only a poorly founded conjecture, but also represented a serious threat to society, in Bryan's view. Acceptance of the social Darwinian view of the survival of the fittest, which to Bryan was the essence of evolution, would weaken God's presence in people's lives. He regarded the teaching of evolution to be an issue best decided democratically: the people have the right to control their own schools and can do so through the institutions of representative democracy. This view gained new popularity in some state legislatures in the 1980s.

Bryan was ill equipped to criticize the theory of evolution and a scientific method about which he knew virtually nothing. He had generally limited his reading to the Bible and such other sources as the classics and the writings of Thomas Jefferson. Except for the daily newspaper, he inquired little into developments of the modern world. Although the World's Christian Fundamentals Association had asked him to prosecute Scopes, prominent fundamentalists deserted him to face the crafty Clarence Darrow alone. Bryan and Darrow, Scopes's defense attorney, confronted each other directly at the 1925 trial. When he unwisely agreed to be cross-examined by Darrow, Bryan's ignorance of the theory he so strongly criticized became apparent. Due to Bryan's nationally reported humiliation, the jury's guilty verdict against Scopes was a pyrrhic victory. Bryan died within a week of the trial's conclusion.

Edgar C. Bundy (1915–)

During the 1950s and 1960s Edgar Bundy, executive director of the Church League of America, played a leading role in the anticommunist movement. After receiving a B.A. from Wheaton College in 1938, he enlisted in the army in 1941 and served for six years, ultimately reaching the rank of major. In 1942, still in the army, he became an ordained Southern Baptist minister. After World War II Bundy served as chief of research and analysis in the Intelligence Section of the Alaskan Air Command. He left the military in 1948 to become the city editor of the Wheaton, Illinois, *Daily Journal*. The following year the Senate Appropriations Committee invited him to testify on the communist threat in the Far East. Numerous invitations to speak at meetings of various political and patriotic groups soon followed, and for a time he worked with Carl McIntire in public relations and as a researcher.

Bundy became active in the Illinois American Legion, playing a role in condemning the *Girl Scout Handbook* for containing "un-American" material and writing a resolution for the Legion's 1955 national convention declaring the United Nations Educational, Scientific, and Cultural Organization subversive. In 1956 the Church League of America named him its executive director. He edited the organization's *News and Views*, which became an important source of information on anticommunism for the religious right. Bundy recorded lectures with titles such as "The Perils of the Social Gospel" and "The Perversion of the Bible," for use by organizations conducting countersubversion seminars. His book, *Collectivism in the Churches* (1958), described the way in which various elements in American society, including those supporting the social gospel, were subverting American liberty. After the 1950s the Church League declined in prominence and Bundy's fellow anticommunists in the religious right receded into the background of American politics.

Charles E. Coughlin (1891–1979)

The controversial "radio priest" of the 1930s and precursor of contemporary televangelism, Charles Coughlin had an estimated radio audience of forty million listeners during the height of his fame. If not a major player, he was a considerable irritant in American politics of the 1930s. Coughlin studied theology at St. Michael's College at the University of Toronto and, after teaching at Assumption College in Windsor, Ontario, for six years, entered the diocese of Detroit in 1923. Possessing a rich baritone voice, Coughlin early on made occasional radio broadcasts. In 1925 he was appointed priest in a parish in Royal Oak, a suburb of Detroit. Coughlin began a radio program in order to raise funds to remedy the financial problems of the parish. By 1930, broadcasts from his church, the Shrine of the Little Flower, were carried over several Columbia Broadcasting System (CBS) stations. After CBS dropped his program, Coughlin established his own network that ultimately included twenty-six independent stations. With the start of the Great Depression, he focused on the international monetary crisis and assailed those groups, particularly the big banks, allegedly responsible for America's economic plight. Although initially a Roosevelt supporter, Coughlin soon became a severe critic of New Deal policies and a fierce opponent of communism.

In the mid-1930s Coughlin entered more directly into politics. In 1935 persistent rumors circulated that he and Governor Huey Long of Louisiana were gravitating toward one another, and in 1936 he supported third-party candidate William Lemke for the presidency. That same year Coughlin founded the National Union for Social Justice and the magazine *Social Justice*. The magazine became controversial for publishing such things as the discredited *Protocols of the Elders of Zion*, which prompted charges of anti-Semitism. Partially due to his opposition to American involvement in World War II, Coughlin came under federal grand jury investigation. In 1942 he ceased publication of his magazine and ended his radio program after it came increasingly under review by church authorities. Although Coughlin occasionally wrote about political issues, he remained out of the public limelight, devoting his energies to priestly duties in his Detroit parish until his retirement in 1966.

John Nelson Darby (1800–1882)

This Anglican minister, who left the Church of Ireland to become a leader of the Plymouth Brethren, found in post–Civil War America fertile soil for his dispensational premillennial beliefs. Between 1859 and 1877 he toured this country at least six times, winning numerous converts to his views, particularly among Baptists and Presbyterians. Through the likes of James Brooks, Cyrus Scofield, and J. Frank Norris, Darby's influence on American fundamentalism has been substantial. Born in London, Darby was educated at Trinity College, opened a law practice in Ireland, became a minister upon conversion to Christianity, soon declared Anglicanism bankrupt, and joined the Brethren in 1828 because of their simple ways, congregational autonomy, and adherence to scripture. When the Brethren split in the 1840s, Darby became the leader of the more rigid faction, called the Darbyites.

For the most part, Darby's dispensational premillennialism was rather conventional. He divided history into distinct epochs, or dispensations, each of which differed with regard to God's plan of redemption. The crucifixion and the Jewish rejection of Jesus marked the end of one dispensation and opened another, the church age. This era in turn would end with the rapture, followed swiftly by the seven-year reign of the Antichrist, a period of tribulation during which Jews would be horribly persecuted. The eventual defeat of the Antichrist at the Battle of Armageddon and the triumphal return of Christ would initiate the millennium. The most distinctive aspect of Darby's thought centered on the reestablishment of a Jewish nation. Indeed, Darby's end-of-time scenario was tied closely to the fate of the Jews, a surviving remnant of whom supposedly would come to recognize Jesus as the long-awaited Messiah.

Several factors account for the acceptance of Darbyism in this country. First, Darby vigorously defended and zealously promoted his variant of dispensational premillennialism. Second, in an age when Darwinism and liberal theology undermined confidence in the scriptures, Darby's emphasis upon biblical authority and literalism appealed to many conservatives. And, third, the Niagara Bible Conferences initiated by Brooks, the success of the Scofield Reference Bible, and the prominence of Norris among fundamentalists ensured a wide audience.

James C. Dobson (1936–)

A psychologist and former professor of pediatrics at the University of Southern California School of Medicine, James Dobson heads Focus on the Family, an organization concerned with social issues affecting the "traditional" family structure. His popular thirty-minute weekday radio program, *Focus on the Family*, has a daily audience of four million. By radio and television combined, he reaches approximately twenty-eight million people every week, giving him a larger reach than either Jerry Falwell or Pat Robertson at their height. Although Dobson gives advice about problems people face in contemporary family life and emphasizes traditional Christian values, he does not present the explicitly Christian message of other radio evangelists and seldom refers directly to biblical texts. His book on child rearing, *Dare to Discipline* (1970), became a popular evangelical alternative on the subject, criticizing permissive parents and emphasizing the need for discipline within a loving child-parent relationship. To date, his books have sold over sixteen million copies, and his tracts and pamphlets have sold additional millions. With an annual budget of $116 million and a staff of some 1,300, including several licensed family counselors who deal with emergency situations and other trained staff members who deal with less urgent cases, Dobson's enterprise in Colorado Springs, Colorado, dwarfs Pat Robertson's Christian Coalition.

Dobson's involvement in national politics has come as a result of his concern for the family as an institution. He was selected to attend a White House conference on the family during President Jimmy Carter's administration, and he served on six government panels during President Ronald Reagan's administration, the most notable of which was the Commission on

Pornography headed by Attorney General Edwin Meese. Believing his views, as well as those of his followers, were not receiving enough attention in Washington, Dobson in 1988 merged his organization with a heretofore small think tank in the nation's capital, the Family Research Council, headed by Gary Bauer. This arrangement not only elevated Bauer's profile considerably, but also enabled Dobson to advance his hard-right positions on matters like abortion, homosexuality, and teen sex without jeopardizing his fatherly image as an advocate of the family. In essence, Bauer deflected the heat away from Dobson. Since the FRC was so blatantly political, however, Focus on the Family, so as not to endanger its tax-exempt educational status, cut its legal tie to Bauer's group in 1992.

The son, grandson, and great-grandson of Nazarene preachers, Dobson has been a moralist in the political arena, a visionary who expects the process to yield swift, transforming results. After the fashion of Old Testament prophets, Dobson proclaims justice, as he interprets it, giving no consideration to practical consequences. "It's either God's way," he insists, "or it is the way of social disintegration." This mind-set has made Dobson quick to rebuke his more pragmatic political and spiritual kinfolk, people who share his objectives but understand more clearly the necessity of compromise. Thus, in 1996 Dobson faulted Ralph Reed for not attacking more aggressively Colin Powell's position on abortion, and in 1998 he threatened to wreak havoc on Republicans unless the party delivered on the issues of importance to religious and social conservatives. Dobson illustrates the dilemma faced by the Republican Party. If it meets the demands of the popular and influential radio and television host, it runs the risk of alienating Americans of more moderate persuasion.

Colonel V. Doner (1949–)

Colonel Doner, who headed the Christian Action Council in Santa Rosa, California, was one of the cofounders of Christian Voice, a religious right organization that became active in national politics in the 1980s. Doner and his colleagues in Christian Voice claimed that, through their campaign activities, they were responsible for defeating President Jimmy Carter and thirty incumbent congressmen in the 1980 election. Christian Voice published moral report cards on congressional Democrats and ran controversial campaign ads, including one that identified President Carter with the homosexual rights movement. Doner was noted for his combative style in his appearances on such television programs as *60 Minutes* and *Phil Donahue.*

In his book, *The Samaritan Strategy* (1989), Doner pondered the political activities of the religious right movement of the 1980s. He described the movement's association with the Republican Party and revealed the extent of Republican financial support in 1984 in establishing the American Coalition for Traditional Values. Doner claimed that by 1986 Republican leaders had begun to fear the expanding influence of the Christian right and therefore halted financial assistance. Doner left Washington in 1986, having decided that the religious right had failed to achieve its objectives. After leaving Washington, Doner, reflecting on past political involvement, concluded that the religious right neglected to demonstrate sufficient concern for those in need, such as the homeless and abused children. Altering strategy, Doner began to seek contacts with more liberal evangelical Christians to try to work together in achieving common service goals. He claimed that Christians will merit the opportunity for leadership in their communities by caring for those in need.

Doner's recent thoughts on religion and politics have appeared in the *Chalcedon Report,* a publication of the Chalcedon Society, a reconstructionist Christian organization. He expressed his deep disappointment with the Republican party in the 1990s for failing to maintain faith with its basic principles, being out of touch with average Americans, failing to mobilize the "Moral Majority," and demonstrating moral bankruptcy in not restoring the nation's Christian heritage. Doner also faulted evangelical Christians for not recognizing the authority of the Old Testament and its relevance to contemporary society.

Jerry Falwell (1932–)

The religious right's most prominent spokesman by the early 1980s, Jerry Falwell demonstrated that fundamentalist Christians could be effectively involved in the political process. Raised among rowdy bootleggers in the hill country of central Virginia, his formative years gave no hint of later religious stature. After becoming a Christian in 1952, he attended Bible Baptist College in Missouri. Four years later he returned home to Lynchburg, established an independent Baptist church in a vacant bottling plant, promptly took to the airwaves with a thirty-minute radio program, and within six months aired his first telecast. The smoothly articulate pastor quickly became an institution. From only thirty-five members in 1956, his Thomas Road congregation numbered almost 20,000 by the early 1980s and his Sunday service, *The Old-Time Gospel Hour,* was carried to an estimated twenty-one million faithful listeners via 681 radio and television stations. Falwell's fund-raising capacity was impressive. By 1980 he was generating about $1 million per week, enough to sustain a college, Liberty University in Lynchburg, Virginia, with approximately 3,000 students, a home for alcoholics, a children's day school, a seminary, sixty-two assistant pastors, and 1,300 employees.

As noteworthy as these church-related achievements were, Falwell was becoming better known to the American public because of his venture into politics. Assisted by such conservative political strategists as Paul Weyrich, Howard Phillips, and Edward A. McAteer, the popular preacher launched Moral Majority, Inc., in 1979. The purpose was to give a political voice to a growing tide of disenchanted Christian fundamentalists, religionists who, like Falwell himself, had traditionally abstained from the political process. By the late 1970s Falwell was convinced that America's moral decline, as presumably exemplified by Supreme Court decisions on prayer in the public schools and abortion, the pervasiveness of "smutty" television, the assertiveness of the gay community, and the push for the Equal Rights Amendment, could be reversed only by vigorous political activism from the religious right. Ironically, it was disappointment with another "born-again" Christian, President Jimmy Carter, a Southern Baptist layman, that prompted Falwell to political action.

The extent to which Moral Majority contributed to the success of conservative Republicans in the 1980s is open to debate, but there is no denying the organization's efforts. It hastily established local chapters in all the states, conducted voter registration campaigns and educational seminars, and targeted liberal Democrats for defeat. Claims of nonpartisanship notwithstanding, Moral Majority clearly was more at ease with a conservative Republican agenda. The organization was never very successful in attracting nonfundamentalists, and so in an effort to broaden its support, Falwell renamed it Liberty Federation in 1986. That same year Falwell's ministries, like those of many other televangelists, suffered serious economic losses in the wake of the Praise The Lord (PTL) scandal, in which PTL leader Jim Bakker was tried and convicted of misappropriation of funds. A Gallup Poll disclosed that 62 percent of the American public viewed the preacher unfavorably. Consequently, in 1989 he dissolved Moral

Majority, devoted more attention to his local congregation and college, and assumed a lower profile.

In the late 1990s Falwell continued to be the lightning rod for attacks on the religious right for his comments on alleged threats to the American Christian culture. For instance, in early 1999 he announced that the Antichrist was a Jewish man who probably was alive now, thereby angering many American Jews, and he declared that Tinky Winky, one of the "Teletubbies" characters, was gay and therefore a menace to American youth. His vocal opposition to homosexuality led to a meeting in Lynchburg in October with Christian supporters of gay rights. Although Falwell agreed with them that violence against homosexuals must cease, he did not alter his opposition to policies geared to eliminate discrimination based on sexual orientation. Falwell maintained a relatively low profile in the 2000 presidential race, but nonetheless worked behind the scenes during the Republican primaries to assist with George W. Bush's bid for the nomination and defeat John McCain. For this he and Pat Robertson came under severe attack from McCain during the Virginia primary. Perhaps Falwell's most overt role in the campaign was his effort to register at least ten million voters for the November election, called "People of Faith 2000."

William ("Billy") Franklin Graham (1918–)

Although less active politically than other key figures in the religious right, Billy Graham can be credited with practicing a biblically based and passionate style of evangelism that set the standard for many others. He helped to make evangelical Christianity acceptable once again to the general American public. Graham attended Bob Jones University in 1936 and the Florida Bible Institute from 1937 to 1940, where he was ordained a Southern Baptist minister in 1939, and graduated from Wheaton College in 1943. He assumed the duties of pastor at the First Baptist Church in Western Springs, Illinois, in 1943 and the following year became a preacher for the Youth for Christ organization. From 1947 to 1952 Graham served as president of Northwestern Schools in Minneapolis, Minnesota. During the early postwar years he began holding highly successful revival meetings in anticipation of the televised "crusades" and in 1950 formed the Billy Graham Evangelistic Association to help coordinate his activities. In 1952 Graham resigned from Northwestern Schools and moved to Montreat, North Carolina. In 1955, believing that the journal *Christian Century* was too liberal, he assisted in establishing the more conservative *Christianity Today*.

In 1952 President-elect Dwight Eisenhower asked for Graham's advice about an inaugural prayer, and thus began the evangelist's long association with national political figures. He gave the opening prayer at President Lyndon Johnson's 1965 inauguration and led President Richard Nixon's Sunday worship services at the White House. Not surprisingly, Graham became known as the "friend to presidents." After Nixon's resignation under the shadow of the Watergate scandal, Graham showed less enthusiasm for such political associations.

In the 1950s and 1960s Graham, in accord with other religious right leaders, was a strong anticommunist. During the American involvement in Vietnam, he was an uncritical supporter of government policy. On other public policy issues, Graham took conservative stands, such as opposing the school prayer ban and criticizing the Supreme Court for being too lenient with criminals. Although he emphasizes a decidedly conservative theology and focuses primarily on the need for personal conversion, Graham has been willing to express his concern for social justice. This willingness first became apparent in the early 1950s when he ended segregated seating at his crusades. In the 1980s he unexpectedly began to raise questions about the dangers of the arms race. Although some elements of the religious right have criticized Graham's more moderate, essentially nonpolitical evangelism, attitude surveys over the years indicate that he has consistently remained one of the more esteemed Americans.

In the 1990s the aging evangelist publicly supported ecumenism, expressing the belief that not only Roman Catholics but also members of other faiths, such as Muslims and Buddhists, and even nonbelievers could receive God's grace. Many on the religious right objected to this apparent compromise with the fundamentals of Christianity. By the late 1990s Graham's failing health resulting from Parkinson's disease, prostate difficulties, and high blood pressure prevented him from pursuing an active work schedule. He delegated many responsibilities within the Billy Graham Evangelistic Association to his son Franklin. In January 2000 health problems prevented Graham from attending the National Prayer Breakfast in Washington, one of the few he had missed since the tradition began in 1953, and in July he was unable even to present a message via satellite to Amsterdam 2000, a conference attended by 10,000 evangelists.

Robert Grant (1936–)

One of the leading figures in the religious right during the 1980s, Grant was one of the founders of Christian Voice in 1978 and of the American Freedom Coalition (AFC) in 1987. He remains president of AFC. He graduated from Wheaton College and Fuller Theological Seminary and was the founding dean of the California Graduate School of Theology. In 1975 he established American Christian Cause, a California organization that opposed gay rights and pornography. Christian Voice, originally named Citizens United in 1976 and briefly called American Christians United, became well known for constructing moral report cards that rated congressional and presidential candidates on a variety of issues, including foreign policy. For instance, Grant and his organization considered support for the Reagan administration's Strategic Defense Initiative, known as "Star Wars," to be probiblical. He also agreed with Reagan administration attempts to provide aid to the Nicaraguan contras.

After a poor showing of his candidates in the 1986 congressional elections, Grant decided that Christians must cooperate with other groups, including non-Christians, to achieve common objectives. The religious right had become fragmented, having failed to build an effective coalition. Grant became one of the founders of the American Freedom Coalition and assumed the title of president. In establishing the new organization, he reportedly accepted financial assistance from Sun Myung Moon's Unification Church. In addition, a number of administrative officers were said to be members of the Unification Church. Because of rumors that he was a new messiah, as well as some of his church's practices, such as the mass marriage ceremonies, the Korean-born Moon has been a controversial figure. And in 1982 he was tried and convicted of conspiracy to evade taxes. Grant stated that he did not agree with the Unification Church's theology and claimed that no one religious group dominated AFC. In order to achieve a just cause, Grant concluded, sometimes money had to be accepted from those who have it and are willing to contribute. In the 1990s Grant, along with the organizations he helped to establish, ceased playing a major role in religious right politics.

John Hagee (1940–)

Over the last twenty-five years John Hagee, senior pastor at Cornerstone Church in San Antonio, Texas, and president of Global

Evangelism Television, has developed a nationwide broadcast ministry. In addition to his daily and weekly television and radio programs, Hagee sells audio- and videotapes of his sermons and has published several popular books. He has consistently supported the religious right agenda, preaching on social and political topics such as abortion, environmentalism, feminism, the homosexual movement, and American foreign policy in the Middle East. During President Bill Clinton's administration, Hagee's sermons often contained ill-chosen humor critical of the president, such as suggesting the nation would be better off if the president and first lady perished in an accident.

Born in Baytown, Texas, Hagee attended Trinity University in San Antonio, Texas, on a football scholarship and received a bachelor's degree in 1964. He continued his studies at North Texas State University, earning a master's degree in 1966, and at Southwestern Bible Institute near Dallas, obtaining theological training. Subsequently he was granted an honorary doctorate from Oral Roberts University. The son of a Baptist minister, Hagee began his career as an evangelist in 1958. In 1966 he became the founding pastor of what would ultimately become Trinity Church, a charismatic congregation in San Antonio. In the mid-1970s Hagee divorced his wife and married a member of the congregation. He left Trinity in 1975 to become pastor of the twenty-five-member Church of Castle Hill in San Antonio, and within two years built a new sanctuary seating 1,600 people. In 1987 the church, renamed Cornerstone, dedicated another sanctuary with a seating capacity of 5,000.

Hagee's influence among evangelicals has increased with the dissemination of his fundamentalist message through the sale of audiotapes and videotapes. His church services are broadcast on 110 individual television stations as well as the Trinity Broadcasting Network (TBN) and the Inspirational Network. In Canada, Hagee's program is carried by the Vision Network. His speaking style is highly appealing to many fundamentalist Christians. Although rotund, he is very animated, presents his scriptural interpretations in a highly confident and uncompromising manner, and offers applications of scripture for listeners' daily lives. Hagee is a best-selling author, having written books on the end times and the millennium (*Beginning of the End* [1996] and *Final Dawn over Jerusalem* [1999]), and alleged conspiracies in American government and society (*Day of Deception* [1997]). In addition, the Cornerstone pastor distributes a bimonthly magazine, *John Hagee Ministries,* to which he contributes articles.

Hagee sells videotapes of his talks, such as *Take America Back*, a three-tape series including the subjects "Back to the Bible," "Back to Basics," and "Back to the Future"; and "America Under Judgement," a tape in the *Curses: Their Cause and Cure* series.

Hagee's support for the religious right notwithstanding, he has been criticized by many evangelical Christians for claiming that Jews have a separate covenant with God from that of Christians and therefore need not be converted to Christianity to achieve salvation. Contrary to a common stereotype of fundamentalist Christians, Hagee is an avid opponent of anti-Semitism. He has received accolades from Jewish organizations for his support of the Jewish people and the Israeli nation, having raised over $1 million to assist Soviet Jews wishing to resettle in Israel. In response to criticisms of his apparent adherence to a "dual covenant" theory of salvation, Hagee has charged those who challenge him on this theological point with encouraging anti-Semitism. Some fundamentalists have also expressed concern about Hagee's attachment to the so-called faith movement, including adherence to the prosperity doctrine, which is the claim that wealth can be achieved through obedience to God's laws and through giving to the church, and positive confession, which is the belief that Christians can speak certain states of affairs into reality if they have enough faith.

Hank Hanegraaff (1950–)

President of the Christian Research Institute (CRI), Hank Hanegraaff is both highly revered and avidly attacked by those in the evangelical Christian community. Hanegraaff has taken stands strongly opposing abortion and supporting creationism, positions that correspond closely to the religious right. However, he has attacked certain individuals and movements in the evangelical community that he claims depart from orthodox Christian beliefs. On his nationally broadcast daily radio program, *The Bible Answer Man*, Hanegraaff responds to the questions of callers, which often deal with movements that Hanegraaff severely criticizes. He also travels the country as a guest speaker at church conferences and gatherings. The CRI's major objective is to expose cults that allegedly distort the Christian message. Examples of movements the CRI brands as cults are the Mormon Church, the Jehovah's Witnesses, and the Masons. The Trinity Broadcasting Network and its owner, Paul Crouch, as well as various personalities who appear on the network, such as Benny

Hinn and Kenneth Copeland, come under attack for their presumed departure from the true faith and descent into cultic behavior.

Raised as an adherent of the Christian Reformed Church, Hanegraaff states that he became a true Christian after investigating scientific evidence for creation, the resurrection of Jesus, and the inspiration of the Bible. He served as a staff member in D. James Kennedy's Evangelism Explosion and participated in other church programs. Hanegraaff later associated with Walter Martin, then head of the CRI. When Martin died, Hanegraaff assumed the presidency of the organization.

Hanegraaff has written several books dealing with topics relevant to contemporary Christianity in the United States. Two that have raised controversy among evangelicals are *Christianity in Crisis* (1997) and *Counterfeit Revival* (1999). In *Christianity in Crisis* Hanegraaff attacks various televangelists who present what he considers unbiblical messages, such as adherents of the so-called faith movement and the health and wealth gospel, the belief that God rewards people who demonstrate adequate faith. In *Counterfeit Revival* he investigates evangelists who encourage emotional displays at public meetings and claim that such behavior is a sign of God's presence. A case in point is Rodney Howard Brown, originally from South Africa, whose preaching of "holy laughter" rouses audiences into uncontrollable bouts of laughter and strange behavior. Hanegraaff objects to the recent trends of the health and wealth gospel and holy laughter not only because he considers them unbiblical, but also because they defy rationality and calm consideration of the facts. Similarly, in *The FACE That Demonstrates the Farce of Evolution* (1998), Hanegraaff does not pit science against religious belief, but instead accuses supporters of evolution theory of being unscientific, dishonest, and unwilling to admit that a conscious designer is at work in the universe. An instructor who teaches methods of improving the memory, Hanegraaff often uses acronyms. The acronym "FACE" in the title of this antievolution book means Fossil Follies; Ape-Men Fiction, Frauds, and Fantasy; Chance; and Empirical Science. The "Farce" in the title stands for "Fossil record: an embarrassment for evolutionists"; "Ape-men are fraud, fiction, and fantasy"; "Recapitulation—the theory that the human fetus repeats, or recapitulates, stages in human evolution, has been discredited"; "Chance renders evolution not just improbable, but impossible"; and "Empirical science supports intelligent design and the creation of fully formed, complex organisms." During the period of widespread anticipation prior to January 1, 2000, of a computer-related disaster, Hanegraaff published *The Millennium Bug Debugged,* in which he criticized the sensational journalism surrounding so-called Y2K. His most recent work, *The Resurrection* (2000), offers what Hanegraaff considers definite proof that Jesus rose from the dead.

Billy James Hargis (1925–)

In the depths of the Cold War in the 1950s, Billy James Hargis represented the propensity of evangelists of the religious right to combine a fundamentalist Christian message with an extreme patriotism and anticommunism. In 1943 Hargis began his studies for the ministry at Ozark Bible College in Bentonville, Arkansas, but remained there only a year. He ultimately received a Bachelor of Arts degree from Pikes Peak Bible Seminary in 1957 and a Bachelor of Theology degree from Burton College in Colorado Springs, Colorado, in 1958. He was awarded an honorary Doctor of Laws degree from Bob Jones University in 1961. Hargis founded the Christian Crusade organization to save America from communism. To this day, each issue of his *Christian Crusade Newspaper* contains the quote, "All I want to do is preach Jesus and save America."

Hargis gained notoriety in 1953 by participating with Carl McIntire in the Bible Balloon project, a plan to float balloons carrying Bible messages to Iron Curtain countries. In the early 1960s Hargis became more actively involved in politics, urging his followers to work for conservatives in election campaigns. During the tumultuous times of the late 1960s and early 1970s, Hargis identified campus radicals, antiwar protesters, and advocates of black power with communism and a general decline of moral values in America.

In 1974 Hargis announced that, due to health problems, he was giving up much of his work in the Christian Crusade and was resigning as president of the American Christian College in Tulsa, which had been founded just five years earlier. He also intended to stop his tours around the country and cease his weekly syndicated television programs. A strong opponent of sexual transgressions, Hargis in 1976 found himself accused of sexual misconduct by one female and three male students at his college. He emphatically denied the charges. The accusations came on the heels of Hargis's final separation from the American Christian College. Since that time, Hargis has maintained his Christian

Crusade ministry in Neosho, Missouri, and conducts yearly Bible conferences that include a good deal of political commentary. More recent issues of *Christian Crusade Newspaper* continue to warn against the dangers of communism and celebrate conservative Republican victories in congressional elections. However, Hargis has never regained his earlier fame and influence.

Gary Jarmin (1949–)

As one of the religious right's more active leaders during the 1980s, Gary Jarmin played a key role as a legislative lobbyist. By the late 1980s he was instrumental in refocusing part of the movement away from explicitly Christian lobbying efforts in Washington and toward a more secular, grassroots orientation. Jarmin was the legislative director of Christian Voice and the administrator of the organization's Moral Government Fund, a political action committee that made donations to congressional campaigns in the 1980s. Christian Voice began the controversial practice of issuing moral ratings of congressional and state officials. The organization grew out of antigay rights and antipornography campaigns in California in the late 1970s. Jarmin became field director for the American Coalition for Traditional Values in 1984 and also became the political director for the American Freedom Coalition (AFC) when the new organization was established in 1987. A major objective for AFC, Jarmin believed, was the building of local organizations, called precinct councils, to concentrate on local issues. Among the reasons for the new emphasis were an increasing awareness of social needs and the desire to avoid theological divisions, along with the emerging realization that increased religious tolerance was necessary in order to build alliances with other organizations that shared the AFC's goals.

The general ineffectiveness of the religious right in the 1986 congressional elections convinced Jarmin and others that Christians by themselves could not alter the political mood of the country. Others in the religious right were troubled by Jarmin's apparent willingness to accept support from, and work with, representatives of the controversial Reverend Sun Myung Moon's Unification Church. Moon's unorthodox religious practices and conviction for tax evasion were especially embarrassing for religious right supporters.

In the mid-1980s Jarmin characterized the Republican Party as an instrument to be used to achieve the objectives of the Christian right. As Reagan's presidency drew to a close, Jarmin noted that the Christian right had not achieved all that it had sought, but that involvement with the administration had provided valuable experience in government and politics.

Jarmin has remained active politically. In 1996 he took part in writing the Republican party's national platform and insisted that the party maintain its uncompromising stand against abortion rights. Jarmin has been involved in the Council for National Policy, a coalition of conservative political leaders who meet to formulate strategies for furthering their political agendas. He heads the Parents' Day Council, which each year recognizes model parents. In partnership with his wife, Gina Mondres, Jarmin operates Jar-Mon Consultants, Inc., a Washington lobbying firm. He heads the U.S.-Cuba Foundation, an organization that favors lifting the American embargo against Cuba.

Bob Jones, Sr. (1883–1968)

No family perhaps has been more vigorous in the battle against modernism than that of Bob Jones, Sr. And perhaps there has been no family trio more alike in fundamentalist temperament and theology than the Joneses—Senior, Junior (b. 1911), and Bob Jones III (b. 1939). An Alabama native, Bob Jones, Sr., was converted in a Methodist church at age eleven, preached his first revival at twelve, had a brush-arbor church with fifty-four members at thirteen, was a licensed minister at fifteen, became a circuit rider at sixteen, and was orphaned at seventeen. Although an eager student, Jones enjoyed limited opportunities for schooling. In December 1900 he enrolled at Southern University in Greensboro, Alabama, but left after two years to become a full-time evangelist. An effective pulpiteer, he was compared by many observers to Billy Sunday, a popular evangelist in the early twentieth century. Although best known in the South, Jones preached in much of the North, from Illinois to New York.

Bob Jones, Sr., accepted the Bible literally, as do his son and grandson, and any deviation from this narrow approach was heresy. Accordingly, he abandoned Methodism, convinced that the denomination had embraced modernism, and devoted himself to fundamentalist causes. He was active in the World's Christian Fundamentals Association, founded in 1919; served on the Moody Bible Institute's continuing education faculty; and in 1926 established his own college, Bob Jones University, which has been located in Greenville, South Carolina, since 1947. The presidency of the school has passed from father to son to grandson.

Despite many common interests with other religious fundamentalists, the Joneses represent a separatist variety of fundamentalism. They therefore have nothing to do with either unbelievers or those who associate with unbelievers. In the 1950s and 1960s, for instance, they denounced Billy Graham for allowing nonfundamentalists to participate in his local crusades and for not directing converts to fundamentalist congregations. Likewise, in the 1980s they scorned Jerry Falwell for allowing Catholics and other "infidels" into Moral Majority. Carl McIntire was the kind of fundamentalist most admired by the Joneses, and like McIntire, the Joneses have been unwilling to play down theological differences for the sake of political cooperation.

D. James Kennedy (1938–)

D. James Kennedy's sermon messages of spiritual and cultural renewal are televised nationwide from the 9,500-member Coral Ridge Presbyterian Church in Fort Lauderdale, Florida. Kennedy was born in Augusta, Georgia, and was raised in Chicago. While in high school, he moved with his family to Florida. He earned his B.A. from the University of Tampa and his master of divinity degree from Columbia Theological Seminary. He has also received a master of theology degree from the Chicago Graduate School of Theology and a Ph.D. from New York University. Among Kennedy's many publications are *Evangelism Explosion,* 4th ed. (1996), *What If Jesus Had Never Been Born? The Positive Impact of Christianity in History* (1997), and *The Gates of Hell Shall Not Prevail* (1997).

In 1962 Kennedy founded Evangelism Explosion International, a training program for laypeople to convert nonbelievers to Christianity. This program now operates worldwide to increase the membership of church congregations. In 1989 Kennedy began the Knox Theological Seminary, which trains pastors dedicated to the reformed tradition. The seminary is committed to a belief in the inerrancy of the Bible. In addition to his weekly television program (*The Coral Ridge Hour*), a daily half-hour radio program (*Truths That Transform*), and a daily sixty-second radio commentary (*Reclaiming America*), Kennedy's Coral Ridge Ministries include the Center for Christian Statesmanship, which attempts to minister to people in government and political positions in Washington, D.C. The Center for Reclaiming America, another segment of the Coral Ridge Ministries, strives to inform Americans about issues considered crucial to the Christian faith and to motivate them to support biblical principles on which Kennedy claims the nation was founded. The Center is geared to help citizens "reclaim their communities for Christ." In 1971 Kennedy founded the Westminster Academy, a Christian school in Fort Lauderdale that provides instruction from kindergarten through the twelfth grade.

Beverly LaHaye (1930–)

Wife of religious right leader Tim LaHaye, Beverly LaHaye has played a major role in organizing conservative Christian women in support of the religious right's political agenda. LaHaye, whose father died when she was young, grew up in Missouri and Michigan during the Great Depression. With her husband, she first gained national attention in the 1970s by offering seminars that advocated greater sexual gratification for Christian married couples. She and her husband Tim published *The Act of Marriage: The Beauty of Sexual Love,* rev. ed. (1998), which within a few years had sold more than one million copies. The book is essentially a sex manual for Christians. She began her own ministry in the late 1970s, publishing such books as *The Spirit-Controlled Woman* (1976) and *How to Develop Your Child's Temperament* (1977). Although LaHaye regards women as individuals in their own right who should engage actively in politics, she advises them to remain subordinate to their husbands and to household duties.

In 1979 she formed Concerned Women of America (CWA) with only nine members. By 1987 she claimed a membership of more than 500,000 women organized into 1,800 local chapters. In 1985 LaHaye moved with her husband to Washington, D.C., where she established the new national office of CWA. In 1987 she was given life tenure as president of the organization. LaHaye has gained a well-deserved reputation for effective political advocacy on behalf of conservative Christian causes. In September 1987 she testified in favor of Robert Bork, President Ronald Reagan's unsuccessful nominee to be the next chief justice of the Supreme Court.

LaHaye has concentrated efforts as much on local as on national issues. For instance, CWA was given credit in 1986 for the defeat of an equal rights amendment to the Vermont state constitution. LaHaye hosts *Beverly LaHaye Today,* a daily radio program, and, following her husband's lead, has published two novels— *Seasons under Heaven* (1999) and *Showers in Season* (2000)—having conservative Christian themes.

Tim LaHaye (1926–)

Tim LaHaye first gained national prominence for his Family Life Seminars and workshops on Christian marriage, which he conducted with his wife, Beverly. The LaHayes coauthored *The Act of Marriage: The Beauty of Sexual Love*, rev. ed. (1998), in which they claim that Christians can experience great sexual enjoyment.

LaHaye attended Western Conservative Baptist Seminary and in 1956 moved to San Diego, California, to become the pastor of Scott Memorial Baptist Church. His book *The Battle for the Mind* (1980) focused on "secular humanism" as a major threat to Christianity. He defined "humanism" as a religion that places sole confidence in human beings and acknowledges no need for God. In *The Coming Peace in the Middle East* (1984), LaHaye identified philosophies and philosophers he considered harmful to humankind.

One of the founders of Moral Majority, LaHaye started a branch of that organization, Californians for Biblical Morality, in 1980. That same year he created the Council for National Policy, a coalition of religious right leaders. In 1983 LaHaye established the American Coalition for Traditional Values (ACTV), which conducted a voter registration campaign for the 1984 election. After the election, LaHaye announced that the organization had registered two million voters, although other sources claimed a much lower number. One of LaHaye's objectives was to acquire more government appointments for born-again Christians in President Ronald Reagan's second administration. LaHaye moved ACTV headquarters to Washington, D.C., in 1985, and in January 1986 reports surfaced that he had received financial support for ACTV from a representative of Sun Myung Moon's Unification Church, an embarrassing revelation in the evangelical community because of Moon's 1982 conviction for tax evasion. The following year LaHaye became an honorary national cochairman of U.S. Representative Jack Kemp's campaign for the presidency, but resigned from that position when news reports disclosed statements in his published works critical of Roman Catholics and Jews. In the 1994 elections he was actively involved in a nationwide voter drive to get conservative Christians to the polls.

LaHaye, along with Jerry Jenkins, began to publish the best-selling series *Left Behind* in 1996. As of 2000, they had completed eight books in the series. Audiotape versions of the book are also available, and a movie of the same title has been released.

Hal Lindsey (1930–)

The most successful spinner in recent years of apocalyptic scenarios, Hal Lindsey has fueled the Christian right's belief that Armageddon is nigh. The Houston, Texas, native attended the University of Houston for two years, but dropped out, served a stint in the Coast Guard, and later worked as a tugboat captain on the Mississippi River. An avowed agnostic, he was converted as a result of reading a Gideon New Testament Bible, and soon thereafter was absorbed by the biblical prophecies of Ezekiel and Revelation. From 1958 to 1962 he attended Dallas Theological Seminary, earning a master's degree in theology. The next ten years he spent with the Campus Crusade for Christ, speaking to audiences throughout the United States and in Mexico and Canada.

In 1970 Lindsey published *The Late Great Planet Earth*. The astonishing success of this work, which reportedly sold twenty million copies in fifty-two languages worldwide and was made into a movie in 1978, demonstrated the appetite for the visionary genre, and Lindsey capitalized on the hunger. He churned out in rapid succession a string of apocalyptic thrillers, such as *Satan Is Alive and Well* (1972), *The Terminal Generation* (1976), and *The 1980s: Countdown to Armageddon* (1980). Typical of this kind of literature, which tends to flourish during eras of national and international stress, Lindsey's works saw in current events a fulfillment of biblical prophecies about the end of time. The restoration of Israel in 1948, along with Israel's control of Jerusalem in 1967, convinced Lindsey that the "terminal generation" was at hand, although he wisely avoided precise dates. And until the 1980s, when he espoused a strong military to resist communism abroad and endorsed capitalist values to counter socialist tendencies at home, he had also generally avoided identification with a specific political agenda. Lindsey obviously was at ease with the religious right, and figures on the religious right, such as Pat Robertson and Jerry Falwell, were just as happy with his vision of doom, evidence of which they, too, saw in American society. Lindsey continues to present his interpretations of biblical prophecy in published works and in the broadcast media. He has become a regular presence on the Trinity Broadcasting Network.

J. Gresham Machen (1881–1937)

This strong-willed and querulous Presbyterian professor who was schooled at Johns Hopkins University, Princeton Theological

Seminary, and in Germany could be regarded as the theological and ideological grandfather of contemporary fundamentalists. As a teacher at Princeton Seminary from 1906 to 1929, he raised issues that still excite the religious right, from biblical inerrancy to open hostility toward all forms of liberalism. Typical of his unbridled attack upon modernism was *Christianity and Liberalism* (1923), a work in which he asserted that it was impossible to be a Christian and a liberal at the same time.

Increasingly intolerant of the more liberal sentiments of other denominational and seminary leaders, a disgruntled Machen left Princeton and founded Westminster Theological Seminary in Philadelphia in 1929. Continuing his attack, Machen now accused the Presbyterian USA's missionaries of doctrinal infidelity. Eventually defrocked in 1936 over this dispute, he promptly established the rival Presbyterian Church of America. Even this new group was soon torn by schism, giving substance to the claim that if Machen had lived long enough, he ultimately would have been the denomination's only member. Machen's student, Carl McIntyre, would go on to influence the direction of the religious right in post–World War II America.

Clarence E. Manion (1896–1979)

After leaving a twenty-five-year career in academics, Clarence Manion established the Manion Forum of the Air, a popular political broadcast in the 1950s and 1960s. A Roman Catholic, Manion received a B.A. in 1915 from St. Mary's College in St. Mary, Kentucky. He attended the Catholic University of America, receiving his M.A. in 1916 and a Master of Philosophy in 1917. He went on to the University of Notre Dame, where he received his law degree in 1922. In 1925 Manion was appointed professor of constitutional law at Notre Dame, and in 1941 he began serving as dean of the College of Law, a position he held until 1952. The following year he became head of President Eisenhower's Inter-Governmental Relations Commission.

Soon becoming dissatisfied with the Eisenhower administration, Manion resigned his position after one year to found the *Manion Forum*, a weekly radio series consisting of conservative commentary. First broadcast over sixteen radio stations, by 1965 the Manion Forum was being carried by more than 300 radio and television stations. The program included Manion's own commentaries as well as interviews with political, educational, business, and military personalities. In the late 1950s Manion joined the John Birch Society, becoming one of its original directors. Although he supposedly did not always agree with the organization—for example, he did not support its claim that President Dwight Eisenhower was an agent of the Communist Party—he refused to resign from the society. Known for his often extreme public statements, Manion demonstrated cordiality and personal warmth in his private life. He published several books, including *Let's Face It* (1956), *The Conservative American* (1964), and *Cancer in the Constitution* (1972). In addition to his own publications, Manion inspired and published Barry Goldwater's *Conscience of a Conservative* (1960), the book that helped launch the Arizona senator's successful bid for the Republican presidential nomination in 1964.

Edward A. McAteer (1927–)

Along with Paul Weyrich and Howard Phillips, Edward McAteer has worked tirelessly to involve the religious right in the political process. Formerly a marketing specialist from the Colgate-Palmolive Company, he is an active Southern Baptist layman whose pastor in Memphis, Tennessee, contributed significantly to the fundamentalist takeover of the Southern Baptist Convention. The Religious Roundtable, established in 1979 with a council of fifty-six, the same number that signed the Declaration of Independence, was McAteer's primary organizational contribution to the religious right. And just as Weyrich worked to enlist Jerry Falwell for Moral Majority, McAteer sought just as diligently to bring James Robison to the Roundtable. Indeed, in 1979 McAteer recruited a quintet of notable fundamentalists—Robison, Falwell, Pat Robertson, James Kennedy, and Charles Stanley—to serve on the board of this new organization.

Bringing people from the religious and political right together, McAteer's group sponsored the National Affairs Briefing (NAB) in Dallas, Texas, in August 1980. Nonpartisan billing notwithstanding, this was a fundamentalist and conservative Republican affair. Of the 1980 presidential candidates, Ronald Reagan was the only one to attend the gathering. The national attention this meeting attracted was not altogether beneficial to either McAteer or the Christian right. The stridency of some of the speakers, along with hints of anti-Semitism, disturbed many Americans. And following McAteer's unsuccessful race for the U.S. Senate in 1984, the Roundtable's influence declined sharply. Although his support of conservative causes remained as fervent as ever, McAteer did not support Weyrich's effort to recast the Christian right's social objectives in terms of a secular "cultural revolution." He was too much of a Baptist fundamentalist to embrace a political strategy that deliberately omitted the God of Judeo-Christianity, however desirable the ends.

McAteer continues as president of the Religious Roundtable, although his political profile has shrunk considerably. However, he still maintains close ties to the fundamentalists who seized control of the Southern Baptist Convention in the 1980s. In 2000 McAteer appealed to supporters to join a long distance telephone company, LifeLine, which would contribute 10 percent of receipts to the Roundtable.

Carl McIntire (1906–)

A virulent anticommunist crusader, Carl McIntire reached the height of his influence during the Cold War era of the 1950s. As a student at Princeton Theological Seminary in the 1920s, he had come under the sway of fundamentalist J. Gresham Machen. Accordingly, when Machen left Princeton and founded Westminster Theological Seminary in 1929, McIntire followed. Upon graduation in 1931, the intelligent and energetic young Presbyterian became the pastor of a major fundamentalist congregation, the Collingswood, New Jersey, Presbyterian Church. Proving to be rigidly doctrinaire, autocratic, self-righteous, and intolerant of opposing views, McIntire subsequently disrupted almost every religious agency he touched. Continuing as pastor of the New Jersey church into his early nineties, McIntire further divided the congregation by refusing to step down.

In 1936 McIntire, along with Machen, was expelled from the Presbyterian Church (USA), and for a brief time thereafter affiliated with Machen's Presbyterian Church of America. But the mixture of these two strong-willed Calvinists was volatile at best, and an eruption was not long in coming. In 1937 McIntire forged his own denomination, the Bible Presbyterian Church, and upon this foundation erected his own religious empire. He kept the faithful informed through the columns of the *Christian Beacon,* begun in 1936, and *The Twentieth Century Reformation Hour,* a thirty-minute radio broadcast begun in 1955, and he trained loyal disciples at his Faith Theological Seminary in Philadelphia and at colleges in Cape Canaveral, Florida, and Pasadena, California.

Unfortunately, McIntire's ability to create was matched by a proclivity for disruptive controversy. His autocratic methods and dogmatic beliefs invariably spawned dissent. In 1956 he was un-ceremoniously expelled from the American Council of Christian Churches, a body that he had founded in 1941, and in 1971 a bit-ter schism occurred at Faith Theological Seminary. The school's president, most faculty members, and approximately half the students left in protest of McIntire's high-handed leadership and outspoken support of complete military victory in Vietnam.

Both prone to conspiratorial thinking, McIntire and Senator Joe McCarthy of Wisconsin easily gravitated together. The asso-ciation was symbiotic. The cleric gave the politician a touch of di-vinity, whereas the politician enhanced the quarrelsome Presbyterian's national stature. McCarthy paid attention to McIn-tire, and therefore the preacher's charges of religious and politi-cal apostasy in high places received more extensive press coverage. A young minister whose own career as an anticommu-nist crusader received a boost from McIntire was Dr. Billy James Hargis.

Until the late 1990s McIntire continued to serve as pastor of the Bible Presbyterian Church in Collingswood, New Jersey, a congregation that had declined to fifty people meeting in a build-ing that seated over a thousand. Concluding that McIntire, then in his nineties, was no longer competent, the congregation asked him to retire. Demonstrating the querulousness that character-ized most of his professional life, McIntire appealed to the pres-bytery of New Jersey after two divisive congregational meetings. When the presbytery ruled against him, the aging leader of the religious right withdrew from the synod and vowed to continue the fight in court.

Dwight Lyman Moody (1837–1899)

A noted nineteenth-century revivalist, Dwight L. Moody estab-lished the standard for highly organized evangelism campaigns in twentieth-century America. Born in Northfield, Massachu-setts, Moody moved to Boston while still a teenager to become a boot and shoe salesman. While in Boston, he became active in the Young Men's Christian Association (YMCA) and the Congrega-tional Church. He moved to Chicago in 1856 to continue his suc-cessful business ventures and there renewed his association with the YMCA. In 1860 he began to work exclusively for that reli-gious organization and during the Civil War was involved in ef-forts to evangelize wounded soldiers.

In 1872 Moody traveled to Great Britain and began a popular revivalist campaign in Scotland, Ireland, and England, ending with a four-month stay in London in 1875. Returning to the United States, he conducted well-organized revival meetings in such large cities as Philadelphia, New York, and Boston. The popularity of these evangelistic efforts can be attributed to Moody's uncomplicated presentation of a loving and merciful God. Along with fellow evangelist Ira Sankey, Moody produced collections of gospel hymns that added to the enthusiasm of audiences at revival meetings. After another tour of Great Britain from 1881 to 1884, Moody began organizing annual student Bible conferences. He founded three schools: the Northfield Academy for Young Women in 1879, the Mount Hermon School for Young Men in 1881, and the Chicago Bible Institute for Home and Foreign Missions (now the Moody Bible Institute) in 1889. The latter schools served as a training ground for urban evangelists and as the source of inexpensive religious publications.

Moody's major accomplishment was to tailor traditional evangelical Protestantism for urban residents in a newly emerging industrial America. As a conservative evangelical, however, Moody found it difficult to deal with the conflicts beginning to arise between liberal and conservative wings of American Protestantism.

Cardinal John O'Connor (1920–2000)

Cardinal John O'Connor, the outspoken Roman Catholic Archbishop of New York for sixteen years, took vocal stands on such issues as abortion, contraception, and homosexuality, and was highly criticized for politicizing his church office. O'Connor used the pulpit as well as a regular newspaper column to publicize controversial positions on a variety of issues. Although often labeled a conservative, O'Connor might better be called a communitarian, for his concerns included the welfare of the less well-to-do and the moral values of the entire community. He was outspoken on many subjects, strongly believing the church should be a guide in everyday life. In 1990 O'Connor declared that Catholic politicians who took a pro-choice position on the issue of abortion risked excommunication from the church. In 1998 the cardinal announced his boycott of professional baseball because the Yankees and the Mets played games on Good Friday.

O'Connor was born in Philadelphia to a working-class family. He attended public schools until his junior year in high school, when the Christian Brothers at West Catholic High School

sparked his ambition to become a missionary. After his ordination as a priest in 1945, O'Connor worked with disabled children
and pursued degrees in ethics, clinical psychology, and political
science. He served as a chaplain during the Korean War, beginning a twenty-seven-year career as a chaplain in the navy and
marine corps. In 1965 O'Connor served in Vietnam, receiving the
Legion of Merit Award. He wrote a book defending American involvement in Vietnam, a work he later came to regret. He ultimately became chaplain at Annapolis and chief of navy
chaplains. In 1979 O'Connor left military service with the rank of
rear admiral; became bishop in Scranton, Pennsylvania, in 1983;
and was appointed archbishop in New York in 1984. In 1985 Pope
John Paul II made him a cardinal. His close relationship with
John Paul increased O'Connor's influence within the church hierarchy.

O'Connor was most often considered politically conservative, largely due to his vocal opinions on such social issues as
abortion and homosexuality. He became a major advocate for the
pro-life forces, heading the bishops' Committee on Pro-Life Activities in the early 1990s. To O'Connor, gay and lesbian lifestyles
were equivalent to biblical sin, and he objected to gay Catholics
marching in New York's St. Patrick's Day parade. Believing that
"good morality is good medicine," he criticized health care pro-
fessionals for what he considered a failure to deal with the moral
aspects of AIDS, including "sexual aberrations" and drug abuse.
However, O'Connor served on the President's Commission on
AIDS, initiated several programs for AIDS victims, and worked
personally to assist those afflicted with the virus. Despite fervent
opposition to abortion rights, he strongly opposed the bombing
of abortion clinics. Responding to such bombings in 1995, the
archbishop offered himself as the target to anyone who wished to
kill someone at an abortion clinic.

Although O'Connor was closely associated with many conservative Christian causes, he worked to improve the condition
of workers and the poor, supporting the causes of organized
labor and advocating improved health care. In the early 1990s he
intervened in the labor-management controversy in the New
York newspaper industry, meeting with labor leaders in an effort
to end strikes. He opposed the death penalty, a position consistent with his antiabortion stand in support of the preservation of
human life. In the 1980s O'Connor criticized the Reagan administration's support for counterrevolutionary guerrillas in Central
America and the proposal to build a missile defense system.

Marvin Olasky (1950–)

To some observers Marvin Olasky is the "godfather of compassionate conservatism"; to others, "a leading thinker and propagandist of the Christian right" or, more harshly, an overly zealous Presbyterian fundamentalist whose "historical judgements are so crude and pinched" (*New York Times Magazine*, September 1999) they will most likely "buttress the stereotypes of those who are prejudiced against religious conservatives" (*New York Times Book Review*, February 28, 1999). One thing is certain, Olasky has the ear of President George W. Bush, who said of the University of Texas at Austin journalism professor: "Marvin offers not just a blueprint for government, but also an inspiring picture of the great resources of decency, caring, and commitment to one another that Americans share." One detects in this remark the nebulous outlines of the president's compassionate conservatism. So, who is Olasky?

An intellectual vagabond, Olasky has embraced at different times sharply divergent philosophical and religious expressions. His search for a worldview governed by explicit and discernable laws led him from Judaism to atheism to Marxism-Leninism to Christian fundamentalism. Born in Massachusetts of second-generation Russian Jewish immigrants, Olasky, as he put it, "was bar mitzvahed at thirteen and an atheist at fourteen." Entering the American Studies program at Yale in 1968, coincidentally just as Bush was leaving, he was soon immersed in left-wing politics, protesting the war in Vietnam and championing the causes of labor. He graduated from Yale in 1971, and from that point to late 1973 his life veered radically from one direction to another. He married his first wife, took a job as a reporter in Oregon, joined the Communist Party, and made a pilgrimage to Russia. By the end of 1973 he had divorced his wife, abandoned communism, and entered the graduate program at the University of Michigan in American Culture. Not long afterward he met Susan Northway, an undergraduate at Michigan, who would become his second wife in 1976. From 1973 to 1976 Olasky moved to the political and religious right. Since his doctoral dissertation, "Clean Pictures with Red Blood? American Popular Film and the Adversary Intention," dealt with politics and American films, he studied the classic westerns and was impressed by their strong sense of right and wrong. He prepared a course on early American literature, reading numerous Puritan sermons in the process. And he studied the Christian existentialists. In 1976 Olasky became a Christian. John Wayne and Jonathan Edwards had displaced Marx and Lenin.

A one-year stint as a lecturer at San Diego State University in 1976–1977 was followed by five and a half years in public relations for the DuPont Corporation in Delaware. By 1983, when Olasky arrived at the University of Texas as an assistant professor of journalism, he had matured as a Calvinist, a Presbyterian fundamentalist, and an outspoken critic of abortion and welfare. A prolific writer, authoring some 200 articles and numerous books, Olasky perhaps would have remained an obscure journalism professor and right-wing polemicist but for the opportune publication of *The Tragedy of American Compassion*. Released in 1992 on the cusp of the Republican "Revolution of '94," this work expressed the sentiment of many conservatives. Specifically, Olasky offered a rationale for slashing welfare and downsizing government, and doing it all in the name of family values and compassion. Instead of the "false compassion" of the existing welfare state, which doled out material aid without providing spiritual guidance or imposing discipline on the poor, true compassion nourished the soul as well as the body. And "faith-based" institutions, presumably having proved their superiority to secular governmental agencies, should receive tax support to advance programs for the needy.

Former Secretary of Education William Bennett pronounced *The Tragedy of American Compassion* the "most important book on welfare and social policy in a decade" and sent a copy to Republican Newt Gingrich, the new Speaker of the House. Addressing the nation as Speaker for the first time in 1995, Gingrich proclaimed: "Our models are Alexis de Tocqueville and Marvin Olasky. We are going to redefine compassion and take it back." That was a heady moment, and all of a sudden Olasky was a celebrity to the religious and political right, a frequent guest on television talk shows, and a favorite of newspaper reporters. Of course, critics—and there were many—argued that it would be impossible for private, religious-based charities to meet all the needs of destitute Americans. After all, government programs to help the poor had emerged earlier in the century in part because of the inability of private charity to meet such vast needs. Critics therefore believed Olasky's ideas were being used by cynical conservative politicians primarily to dismantle various social programs. If such censure bothered him, it was not apparent in Olasky's most recent book, *Compassionate Conservatism* (2000), for which Bush wrote the foreword. Although Olasky is much more intensely evangelistic than Bush, always seizing the opportunity to proselytize, the two men hold comparable views on welfare and the relative importance of religion and government in helping the poor. That alone ensures Olasky's continued prominence for the near future.

Ralph Reed (1961–)

Ralph Reed was born in Portsmouth, Virginia, only a short distance from Pat Robertson's first broadcast studio. His early years were interrupted by frequent moves. His father was a navy doctor, and by the time Reed entered high school the family had lived in seven towns in five states. Upon graduation from high school in Toccoa, Georgia, he entered the University of Georgia. In summer 1981 a U.S. Senate internship took him to Washington, D.C., where he remained through the fall working with the National College Republicans. He returned to the University of Georgia in spring 1982, completed his degree, then resumed his efforts in the nation's capital with the National College Republicans. With the approach of the 1984 senatorial race in North Carolina between Jim Hunt and Jesse Helms, the outspoken Republican incumbent whose political and religious conservatism made him a favorite of the religious right, Reed left Washington for Raleigh. He promptly founded Students for America and joined the fray in behalf of the North Carolina senator. Reed unquestionably loved politics; even so, he entered the graduate program at Emory University on a scholarship, obtained a Ph.D. in history in 1986, and anticipated a career in academia. Three years later he was the executive secretary of Robertson's new Christian Coalition.

Reed's fondness for conservative politics and causes was long-standing. As a child he read biographies of the presidents, as well as William L. Shirer's *The Rise and Fall of the Third Reich*, which impressed upon him the power of politics. At the University of Georgia he was a College Republican, debater, and columnist for the school paper, *Red and Black*. Reed eventually lost this journalistic position because he plagiarized a story. Always on the political right of every issue, Reed was a leader among campus conservatives by 1982. Shortly thereafter he discovered religion. This nominal Methodist smoked and drank until the early 1980s, whereupon he promptly put away cigarettes and John Barleycorn and became a born-again, charismatic Christian. God and Caesar now became allies, as Reed discovered the "true" meaning of politics. "I now realize," said the new convert, "that politics is a noble calling to serve God and my fellow man." Appropriately, his dissertation at Emory, which focused on the early history of church-related colleges, criticized some sectarian schools for sacrificing their religious heritage for endowments.

Although Reed supported Jack Kemp over Robertson in the 1988 presidential primaries, the Virginia televangelist admired the young man's organizational talent and religious commitment. When Robertson formed the Christian Coalition in 1989, Reed became its executive secretary. Despite his affable nature and disarming good looks, Reed is a shrewd political strategist. One admirer aptly described him as "the Christian Lee Atwater," recalling that skilled adviser who gained a reputation for being ruthlessly competitive during President George H. W. Bush's 1988 presidential campaign. Winning was everything to Reed, but he also recognized that the road to victory took many turns. Accordingly, Reed sought to broaden the Christian Coalition, to make it more ecumenical. He therefore occasionally downplayed such issues as abortion, homosexuality, and prayer in the schools, emphasizing instead taxes, crime, and education. This kind of flexibility, foes acknowledged, made Reed a formidable opponent. Still, this was a risky strategy, and it was difficult for the Christian Coalition to attract moderate conservatives without offending its hard-core base.

In summer 1997, following Republican setbacks in the 1996 elections, Reed left the Christian Coalition to found his own political consulting firm, Century Strategies. He has since offered his talents to conservative Republican candidates, and he played a significant, albeit behind-the-scenes, role in George W. Bush's victory in the bitter Republican presidential primary in South Carolina in winter 2000.

Marion Gordon "Pat" Robertson (1930–)

Perhaps the religious right's most successful television entrepreneur, Pat Robertson was born and reared in Lexington, Virginia. The son of a prominent politician, Senator A. Willis Robertson, and a devoutly religious mother, the intelligent and charming Robertson seemed marked for success. A Phi Beta Kappa graduate of Washington and Lee University, he subsequently studied at the University of London, served as a noncombatant with the marines in Korea (1951–1952), and enrolled in Yale Law School, graduating in 1955. Although reared a Baptist, the youthful Robertson was not particularly religious, as evidenced by a fondness for women, whiskey, and poker. In 1956 this all changed.

Following a religious experience that was helped along by a staunch fundamentalist whom his mother respected, Robertson promptly entered The Biblical Seminary, later rechristened the New York Theological Seminary, in New York City. And it was here at this conservative enclave from 1956 to 1959 that he became a charismatic evangelical. In 1959 Robertson returned to Virginia, purchased a television station in Portsmouth, and launched the Christian Broadcasting Network (CBN) in January 1960. Three years later, seeking to raise funds to cover monthly costs of $7,000, he sought to enlist 700 listeners who would pay $10 per month. From this emerged The 700 Club and later *The 700 Club Program*, which deliberately copied the format of *The Johnny Carson Show*. Jim Bakker, a religious fund raiser par excellence who later established the Praise The Lord (PTL) complex at Charlotte, North Carolina, joined CBN in 1965. Bakker deserves considerable credit for the success of Robertson's telethons. By 1975 CBN had an estimated 110 million viewers, and in 1979 Robertson opened an impressive international headquarters building and CBN University at Virginia Beach. By 1987 his empire sprawled over 380 acres and employed over 4,000 people.

Robertson's social concerns were virtually identical to those of other figures on the religious right. He opposed abortion, homosexuality, pornography, and the Equal Rights Amendment, and he encouraged prayer in the public schools and tuition tax credits for private schooling. Failing miserably in the 1988 presidential campaign to translate television celebrity status into political success, Robertson quickly regrouped. In 1989 he founded the Christian Coalition, heir to Jerry Falwell's Moral Majority, and thereby institutionalized his profamily, "values-oriented" politics. Quickly becoming the most powerful political body of religious conservatives, the Coalition pursued an aggressive grassroots campaign to defeat politicians, from school board elections on up, whose values were not sufficiently profamily. Although the organization continues to wield considerable influence, it reached its climax about 1996–1997, declining significantly thereafter. In spring 2000 Robertson, who had dropped the title "Reverend" just prior to his 1988 presidential run, reaffirmed his ordination vows, attached the title once again to his name, and announced that his heart was "on missions" and "getting people into the kingdom of God." This did not mean, however, that the televangelist was leaving the political playing field.

Indeed, there is every indication that he intends to keep one foot planted squarely in Caesar's world, the other in God's.

James Robison (1943–)

Often billed as "God's Angry Man" because of a belligerent pulpit style and rigid dogmatism, James Robison was second in prominence only to Jerry Falwell in calling America to repentance for its "wicked" ways. Destitute and abandoned by her alcoholic husband, Robison's mother advertised him at birth in a Houston, Texas, newspaper and subsequently gave him to a Baptist minister and his wife in Pasadena, a Houston suburb. When Robison was five, his mother reclaimed him, headed to Austin, Texas, and over the next decade went through a series of marriages and divorces. At age fifteen Robison returned to his foster parents in Pasadena, experienced conversion, and at age eighteen resolved to become an evangelist.

Robison attended East Texas Baptist College and San Jacinto Junior College, but he dropped out and embarked upon full-time evangelism in late 1963. At six feet three inches and over 200 pounds, he was a commanding presence in the pulpit. In 1965 he established the James Robison Evangelistic Association and five years later aired his first thirty-minute television program. By 1980, with headquarters at Hurst, near Fort Worth, Texas, he employed 150 full-time staff members and his television show, *James Robison, A Man with a Message,* was carried by 100 stations in twenty-eight states. Many observers saw the young evangelist as an eventual successor to Billy Graham.

Casting himself as pro-life, promoral, profamily, and pro-America, Robison quickly became a major voice on the religious right. He denounced abortion, homosexuality, premarital sex, the Equal Rights Amendment, and "secular humanism" with as much passion as, and much more stridency than, Falwell, with whom he was closely associated in the 1980s. Along with Edward A. McAteer, he helped organize the Religious Roundtable in 1979, and in August the following year the Roundtable's National Affairs Briefing (NAB) at the Reunion Arena in Dallas brought him to the attention of a national audience. Despite its nonpartisan billing, the NAB turned into a love feast for presidential candidate Ronald Reagan. Typical of so many on the religious right in the 1980s, Robison found in Reagan a knight to carry the banner for God and country.

In the 1990s Robison changed the name of his organization

from the James Robison Evangelistic Association to Life Out-reach International. This organization was established to provide humanitarian assistance to the needy in the United States and around the world. Two of its ministries are Mission Feeding and Water for Life. In addition, the organization trains new believers to spread the gospel. Robison also changed the format of his tele-vision program, now called *Life Today*, introducing a talk show setting in which he and his wife Betty interview guests and take calls from the television audience.

Hugh Ross (1945–)

Hugh Ross is president of Reasons To Believe, a California-based organization that attempts to provide Christians with scientifi-cally valid reasons for their religious faith. Ross's defense of Christian belief coalesces well with a conservative perspective that Christian beliefs are compatible with a modern scientific un-derstanding of the world and that events described in the Bible can be scientifically verified. Ross hosts the weekly television program *Reasons To Believe*, on which he discusses various scien-tific subjects in the context of Christian faith. Although he admits that the universe is billions of years old, thus disagreeing with the "young earth" theologians, he contends that there is clear ev-idence of design in the universe. Ross elicits mixed reactions from fundamentalist Christians who agree with his claim for de-sign, but are uncomfortable with his conclusions about the age of the universe. Nonetheless, when referring to the early chapters of the Book of Genesis, Ross sometimes speaks as though he takes literally the stories of Adam and Eve, the Garden of Eden, and the fall into sin as the cause of human death.

A native of Canada, Ross received a bachelor of science de-gree in physics from the University of British Columbia in 1967, and M.S. and Ph.D. degrees in astronomy from the University of Toronto. He received a grant from the Canadian National Re-search Council for postdoctoral study at the California Institute of Technology, where he investigated distant quasi-stellar objects, called quasars. Ross claims scientific studies and historical exam-ination of scripture convinced him that the Bible was the true word of God. He argues that believers should check the evidence for their beliefs, evidence he contends consistently confirms the existence of the Christian God.

From 1973 to 1978 Ross served as a research fellow in radio astronomy at the California Institute of Technology. It was during this period that he became actively involved in Christian ministry, becoming minister of evangelism at the Sierra Madre Congregational Church, a position he held from 1976 to 1987. He continues to serve that church as minister of apologetics. In 1986 he established Reasons To Believe. In 1997 he became a lecturer in the Simon Greenleaf Institute of Apologetics at Trinity Law School in Santa Ana, California.

Ross has published several books on science and the Christian faith, including *The Fingerprint of God: Recent Scientific Discoveries Reveal the Unmistakable Identity of the Creator* (1991), *Creation and Time: A Biblical and Scientific Perspective on the Creation-Date Controversy* (1994), *Beyond the Cosmos: What Recent Discoveries in Astronomy and Physics Reveal about the Nature of God* (1996), and *The Genesis Question: Scientific Advances and the Accuracy of Genesis* (1998). In addition, Ross has produced several videotapes on science and religious belief that are available through his organization.

Francis Schaeffer (1912–1984)

If J. Gresham Machen was the intellectual grandfather of contemporary fundamentalism, Francis Schaeffer certainly was the father. These spiritual kinsmen both believed that America had drifted far from its Christian moorings. For Machen, the "villain" was liberalism in the nation's churches; for Schaeffer, it was secular humanism in Western culture. In 1929 Machen, certain that Princeton Theological Seminary had succumbed irretrievably to liberalism, left the Presbyterian school and established Westminster School of Theology in Philadelphia. Even this conservative haven soon proved too liberal for one of Machen's strong-willed disciples, Carl McIntire, who subsequently founded Faith Theological Seminary in Wilmington, Delaware, in 1937. Amid the controversy between these two doctrinaire Presbyterians, Schaeffer's theological pilgrimage began. He entered Machen's school in 1935, but finished with McIntire in 1937.

Schaeffer was born in Philadelphia. His working-class parents were nominal Lutherans. Set on a career in engineering, he went to Drexel Institute, but soon switched to Hampden-Sydney College, a Presbyterian institution in Virginia. From this liberal arts school he journeyed to Westminster Seminary, where Machen and McIntire already were feuding over matters of eschatalogy, Christian liberty, and denominational sectarianism. For a decade, 1937 to 1947, Schaeffer pastored in St. Louis, ministering primarily to blue-collar workers and children. Sponsored by the Independent Board of Presbyterian Missions, Schaeffer was sent to Europe in 1947, and over the next few years he traveled and preached extensively across the continent. In 1954 he bought a chalet in Huénoz, Switzerland, named it L'Abri, "The Shelter," and became a guru of sorts to his neighbors, students, and spiritual travellers of all types. Joining an anti-McIntire group in founding Covenant College and Seminary and the Evangelical Presbyterian Church, he severed ties with his old mentor in 1956. Diagnosed with cancer in 1978, Schaeffer returned to the United States, where his attention turned increasingly to the debate on abortion.

Schaeffer's evangelistic endeavors had made him well known by the early 1960s. A torrent of well-received tapes, films, and books made him a household name in much of the English-speaking Christian world by the 1970s. In many of his twenty-five books Schaeffer gave the positions of the religious right a scholarly gloss. His *No Final Conflict* (1975) was a defense of biblical literalism. To question the historicity of Genesis, he argued, was to raise doubts about the reliability of all scripture. Originally conceived as a Christian response to *Civilization*, a popular PBS series by Kenneth Clark and Jacob Bronowski, Schaeffer's most sweeping assessment, *How Should We Then Live? The Rise and Decline of Western Thought and Culture* (1976), dealt with the bête noire of the religious right, secular humanism. From the Greeks and Romans to the Renaissance to the Enlightenment, Schaeffer contrasted the "weaknesses" of human-centered cultures to the "strengths" of Christianity, which was rooted in God's absolute truth. The result of humanism could be seen in the ovens of Auschwitz and the abortion clinics of the United States. Tim LaHaye's popular work, *The Battle for the Mind* (1980), owes much to Schaeffer's treatise. Written with C. Everett Koop, *Whatever Happened to the Human Race?* (1979) was an unsparing indictment of abortion. This cheapening of life Schaeffer attributed to the erosion of the Christian view of humanity. Intended as a guide for Christian activism, *A Christian Manifesto* (1981) called the righteous to battle. Schaeffer applauded Jerry Falwell's Moral Majority, for it had boldly entered the political arena in behalf of divine law. Other Christians should not only follow suit, but also, as a last resort, engage in civil disobedience. To Schaeffer, the use of state funds for abortion certainly justified such resistance. Significantly, Randall Terry, leader of Operation Rescue, one of the more militant antiabortion groups, readily acknowledges his debt to Schaeffer. Indeed, in Schaeffer all of the religious right had found a spokesman of intellectual vigor and sophistication.

Frederick Charles Schwarz (1913–)

A fervent anticommunist crusader, Fred Schwarz came to the United States from Australia in the early 1950s at the invitation of Carl McIntire and the American Council of Christian Churches. Schwarz received a medical degree from the University of Queensland and practiced as a psychiatrist in Sydney until 1953, when he came to the United States. He joined W. E. Pietsch, a radio evangelist, in Waterloo, Iowa, where he became one of the founders of the Christian Anti-Communism Crusade. Although initially tied to McIntire's American and International Councils of Christian Churches, Schwarz placed less emphasis on spreading a Christian message than on disseminating a doctrine of anticommunism. In 1958 Schwarz moved his organization to Long Beach, California. He ultimately de-emphasized association with McIntire's two councils, did not appeal directly to Christian fundamentalists for their support, and showed little concern for such fundamentalist positions as the premillennial return of Christ. Although he presented no clear theological position, Schwarz nonetheless saw conservative Christianity as the only possible alternative to communism.

In the 1950s Schwarz used the airwaves to disseminate his message, but increasingly thereafter he travelled the nation, offering "schools" on anticommunism. His presentations stressed the nature of the world as divided into good and evil forces. In 1957 Schwarz received increased attention when he appeared before the House Un-American Activities Committee to testify as an expert on communism. His book *You Can Trust the Communists (To Be Communists)* (1960) portrayed communists as well-organized and exceptionally intelligent individuals whose behavior was very predictable once people understood their very logical, but ultimately insane, thought. He also characterized as mental illness the belief that negotiations with communists could bring peace. In the 1970s Schwarz and his organization were active in presenting an anticommunist message in many countries, including El Salvador and the Philippines. Now in his late eighties, Schwarz has retired and returned to Australia. The Christian Anti-Communism Crusade, meanwhile, continues under new leadership and distributes a newsletter renamed *The Schwarz Report*.

Cyrus Ingerson Scofield (1843–1921)

Cyrus Scofield is considered one of the more important figures to influence the character of premillennialist thought in the twentieth century. Born in Tennessee, he fought on the Confederate side in the Civil War and subsequently set up a law practice in Kansas. Accused of stealing political contributions from a candidate for public office, he left Kansas in 1877, abandoning his wife and two children. She divorced him in 1883. Scofield moved on to St. Louis, Missouri, where he was arrested and imprisoned on charges of forgery. While in prison Scofield was converted to Christianity and in 1882 became pastor of the First Congregational Church in Dallas, Texas. He also edited *The Believer,* a monthly publication, and directed a Bible correspondence course.

In 1895 Scofield moved to Massachusetts to become a faculty member at Dwight L. Moody's Northfield Bible School and began work on a project to provide notes for the King James Version of the Bible. The result was the *Scofield Reference Bible,* considered by many observers to be one of the more important popularizations of premillennial dispensationalism. The nontechnical presentation gained wide popularity among laypersons. Scofield believed that anyone could interpret biblical prophecy. Formal learning and theological training were unnecessary. Sales of the reference Bible from its first publication in 1909 to 1967 are estimated at between five and ten million copies, and a revised edition in 1967 so far has sold nearly three million copies. Some have argued that because of the special format of Scofield's Bible, in which notes are presented on the same page with scriptural text, many readers accord as much authority to the annotations as to the scriptures. In any event, many twentieth-century Bible students have embraced Scofield's scriptural notes, unaware perhaps of the author's specific interpretation.

Scofield divided history into distinguishable time periods, indicating that God's relationship with human beings is progressing from one age to the next. Beginning with Innocence, the world proceeds to the ages of Conscience, Human Government, Promise, Law, and Grace, the time period from Christ to the present. The final stage, called the Kingdom Age, would occur after the prophesied Battle of Armageddon. Christ would govern the world as a theocracy for one thousand years, followed by the final judgment and the end of all ages. Scofield, like subsequent premillennialists, doubted the prospects for peace and human improvement before Christ's direct intervention. At the end of World War I Scofield claimed that any attempt to establish a world order would only hasten the coming of the Antichrist. Asserting that Christ and the Apostles were not reformers, Scofield argued that the church should prepare for the end of time rather than becoming involved in social reform. Only in the millennial age would humans turn away from their corrupted natures. Christ's rule would lead to the defeat of selfishness and the elimination of inequalities in worldly goods.

Contemporary writers such as Hal Lindsey reflect Scofield's influence. Scofield emphasized the importance of Israel as a nation, for instance, and claimed in 1916 that Russia would invade the Holy Land in the end time. Although his contemporaries tended to hold the same view, Scofield put special emphasis on such an invasion in his Bible and elsewhere.

Jay Alan Sekulow (1956–)

As chief counsel for the American Center for Law and Justice (ACLJ), Jay Sekulow has proved an articulate advocate for the right of Christians to proselytize to the general public. He has presented his case on such television programs as *Good Morning America*, *Nightline*, *CNN Crossfire*, and *Larry King Live*. Sekulow appears regularly on Pat Robertson's *The 700 Club*. One of his primary areas of activity is defending parents and students who challenge local school districts' interpretations of Supreme Court rulings on school prayer.

Sekulow earned his B.A. and J.D. degrees from Mercer University. In 1990 he established the ACLJ in Virginia Beach, Virginia. He has published several books that provide advice for Christians concerned about expressing their beliefs in the public realm. In *And Nothing but the Truth* (1996), Sekulow and coauthor Keith Fournier relate their experiences fighting legal battles on church-state issues. The authors describe situations that proved to their satisfaction that religious expression is being suppressed in the public realm and Judeo-Christian values are being displaced as a vital ingredient of our society. In *Knowing Your Rights* (1993), Sekulow explains the rights, especially freedom of speech, that Christians have and the framework within which they can exercise those rights. In *From Intimidation to Victory* (1990), he deals with several issues involving the right of Christians to freedom of speech, including the rights of parents to speak out against such evils as abortion and to employ the strategy of civil disobedience.

In his booklet *Christian Rights in the Workplace* (1998), he emphasizes that the law does not prohibit religious employees or employers from speaking about their faith in the workplace.

Sekulow has served as lead counsel and presented oral arguments before the Supreme Court in several cases. In *Board of Airport Commissioners v. Jews for Jesus* (1987) the Court invalidated an airport regulation restricting the distribution of religious literature in airport terminals. In *Board of Education of Westside Community Schools v. Mergens* (1990) the Court ruled that the Equal Access Act was constitutional, thus providing high school students with the right to establish Bible and prayer clubs. In *Lamb's Chapel v. Center Moriches School District* (1993), the Court ruled that a school district inappropriately prohibited the showing of the James Dobson film *Turn Your Heart toward Home* in a school facility.

R. C. Sproul (1938–)

R. C. Sproul is best known in Christian circles as the founder of Ligonier Ministries, described as a teaching fellowship to educate Christians about their faith. Sproul is the principal teacher, having written over forty-five books and produced dozens of video- and audiotaped lectures dealing with such biblical and theological themes as predestination and election, the providence of God, biblical inerrancy, the Holy Spirit, church creeds, and the doctrine of justification by faith. He has produced longer lecture series, including *Dust to Glory* (1997), fifty-seven presentations on the Bible; *The Consequences of Ideas* (1998), a series on Western philosophy, including treatments of such philosophers as Plato, Aristotle, Augustine, Hume, Kant, and Nietzsche; and most recently *Foundations: An Overview of Systematic Theology* (2000), which includes sixty presentations on such topics as angels and demons, the creation of human beings, the nature of sin, election and reprobation, and the end of the age and the return of Christ. These presentations, as well as a half-hour daily radio program, *Renewing Your Mind,* and regular appearances at weekend seminars around the country, have attracted a devoted following to Sproul's fundamentalist theology.

Sproul is the editor of *Tabletalk,* a monthly magazine that serves as a daily devotional. Each issue has a theme, which, although not explicitly political, often deals with a social issue, such as homosexuality or marital fidelity. For instance, the March 1997 issue, titled "Homosexuality: Unnatural Selection," contained articles condemning homosexuality; the August 2000 issue was titled "Liberalism: Spiritual Adultery," claiming that the term "liberal Christian" is an oxymoron; and the September 2000 issue dealt with "Defiling the Body," sexual infidelity among clergy and laypeople. Issues have theological themes such as preserving the fundamental beliefs of the Christian faith in the contemporary church against advocates of secularism.

After earning his Ph.D. from the Free University of Amsterdam at the age of twenty-five, Sproul began teaching theology and philosophy at various colleges and seminaries. He is a Presbyterian and holds to the Calvinist roots of the denomination. Presently he is a professor of theology and apologetics at Knox Theological Seminary in Fort Lauderdale, Florida, and also conducts seminars at Westminster Theological Seminary. However, Sproul's primary interest for thirty years has been lay teaching, a task for which his organization is geared.

Sproul is the intellectual descendant of such conservative American theologians as J. Gresham Machen and Francis Schaeffer. He has continued their strong objections to the liberal trends in Christian theology begun in the late nineteenth century and their reaffirmation of traditional Christian beliefs such as the inerrancy of scripture, some form of creationism, and the historicity of Christ's birth, death, and resurrection. Like Schaeffer, Sproul believes that secular humanism represents a major threat to the Christian roots of Western culture. Among Sproul's concerns is an alleged "anything goes" attitude in mainstream churches. Although Sproul's preference for conservatism might be interpreted as a political stand, he tends to remain aloof from any explicit statement of political preferences. Nonetheless, his social conservatism and preference for a fundamentalist theology coincide with the religious right's more overtly political stands.

Randy Tate (1965–)

Critics once described Randy Tate, an intensely religious political conservative and successor to Ralph Reed as executive director of the Christian Coalition, as "the poster boy of the radical right," a perception seemingly bolstered by the ratings of several special-interest groups. Whereas Tate's congressional voting record earned a "zero" from the Sierra Club and League of Conservation Voters, it scored a "100" from the Christian Coalition and National Rifle Association. Born in Puyallup, Washington, Tate attended Tacoma Community College and in 1988 obtained a baccalaureate from Western Washington University. Something of a political junkie, he was elected to the state legislature while in his senior year at the university, and in 1988 he supported the presidential bid of televangelist Pat Robertson. After three terms in the state legislature, where he became the Republican caucus chairman, Tate was elected to the U.S. House, swept into office by the so-called Republican revolution of 1994.

Tate only narrowly defeated his Democratic opponent in 1994, but he acted as though he had won by an overwhelming majority and thus had the wholehearted support of his district to pursue the objectives of religious and social conservatives. He was a true believer who quickly caught the eye of House Majority Whip Tom Delay (R-TX), as well as Speaker Newt Gingrich. He worked to restrict abortion rights, eliminate the National Endowment for the Humanities and the Corporation for Public Broadcasting, repeal the assault weapons ban, prevent any increase in the minimum wage, establish English as the nation's official tongue, prohibit flag burning by a constitutional amendment, provide vouchers for students to attend private schools, and weaken environmental restrictions. Tate made the mistake of attempting to impose a narrow agenda that lacked broad public support. Most Americans, whether Republicans or Democrats, did not want a woman's right to an abortion eliminated, or environmental regulations rolled back, or the ban on assault weapons repealed. Opposed by labor unions and environmental groups, Tate, despite strong backing from the Christian Coalition and other conservative organizations, was defeated in 1996. The assessment of Tate's Democratic opponent, David Adam Smith, was discerning: "Randy Tate will do a very good job of representing the Republican Party in the Ninth District. I'll do a good job of representing everybody in the district."

In August 1997 Tate, prematurely bald and looking older than his thirty-one years, took the helm of the Christian Coalition. Another run for Congress was an option, Tate explained, but "after much prayer" he concluded that "this position affords an even greater opportunity to shape the future of America." Making family issues a top priority, the Coalition under Tate has opposed late-term abortions, sought the repeal of the marriage tax penalty, objected to legislation according "special rights based on sexual behavior," urged the defeat of state gay adoption laws, and supported efforts to allow inner-city parents to send their children to the schools of their choice. In 1998 Tate praised the U.S. House for its vote to impeach President Bill Clinton, then urged the president to spare the country more turmoil by resigning. Polls in late 1998, as well as the outcome of the midterm elections, showed that most Americans did not share Tate's opinion on impeachment and resignation.

Cal Thomas (1940–)

Cal Thomas is the best-known evangelical Christian journalist on the contemporary scene, one whose conservative judgments emanate from a deeply rooted Judeo-Christian moral code. A native of Washington, D.C., the lanky six-foot-seven-inch Thomas played basketball for his alma mater, American University. Interested in broadcast journalism at an early age, he became a disc jockey and news reader at sixteen, and two years later joined NBC News in Washington, D.C., as a copy boy. Rising through the ranks, he worked as a radio and television reporter for the network in the 1960s. Thomas has also been associated with PBS television and, while in the army, Armed Forces Radio and Television in New York City. His column with the Los Angeles Times Syndicate began in 1984 and today is carried by over 450 newspapers, making Thomas one of the nation's more widely read commentators.

A religious conservative, Thomas was influenced by Richard Halverson, former chaplain of the U.S. Senate, and Francis Schaeffer, the prestigious philosopher-theologian of the religious right. As with many other religious conservatives, he was dismayed by the feminist and gay rights movements, as well as the increased rates of abortions and divorces, developments seen by people of Thomas's persuasion as the ill-favored results of liberalism. Consequently, Thomas joined Jerry Falwell and served as a vice president of the Moral Majority in the early 1980s. Through the political process he and his spiritual kinfolk intended to stem the nation's perceived moral and cultural decline. Given such active involvement in the religious right, Thomas's recent "awakening" was highly significant. The religious right, according to Thomas in *Blinded by Might* (1999), written in collaboration with Edward Dobson, had little to show for twenty years of political activism. Indeed, Thomas believed "the moral landscape of America" had gotten worse and concluded: "Two decades after conservative Christians charged into the political arena, bringing new voters and millions of dollars with them in hopes of transforming the culture through political power, it must be acknowledged that we have failed."

Although religious conservatives should remain active as voters, they should no longer expect politics to transform the moral climate of America. Virtue, or morality, cannot be imposed from above by government, but rather must be chosen from below by the people themselves. Thomas thus argued that the time had come to return to the traditional evangelical pursuit of saving individual sinners. The strength of religious conservatives lay in the transforming power of the gospel, not the coercive power of the state. As an example of how religious conservatives could effect constructive change, Thomas cited the establishment of crisis pregnancy centers across the nation. More than anything in the political arena, this, thought Thomas, had contributed to a reduction in abortions.

Although still in agreement with their objectives, Thomas, true to the sentiments expressed in *Blinded by Might*, frequently took issue with religious conservatives during the 2000 presidential campaign. The nastiness of the South Carolina Republican primary, for instance, proved that people supposedly committed to a higher calling could "get down and dirty with the best of the pagans." As for the excuse "The left does it," Thomas retorted: "I wasn't aware that the pagan left had replaced biblical principles in setting the agenda for the Christian church." Thomas also chided Falwell, whose "People of Faith 2000" was supposed to register ten million new voters. The effort, said Thomas, would "raise some money and make noise," but would "change little." And at times there was humor, as in his characterization of Joseph Lieberman as an "itinerant Jewish evangelist." This last remark suggests that while Thomas faults his religious brethren for their continuing faith in politics, he nonetheless remains a partisan. He opposed Al Gore and Lieberman during the 2000 presidential campaign, and he takes issue now with those who consider George W. Bush too dumb and inexperienced to be president. Thomas is convinced that Bush has the wisdom, a virtue apparently paramount to knowledge, to surround himself with able people.

Robert H. W. Welch, Jr. (1899–1985)

The founder of the John Birch Society and its leader for twenty-five years, Robert Welch dedicated himself to fighting what he saw as a communist conspiracy to capture American government and society. He received a degree from the University of North Carolina and attended the U.S. Naval Academy and Harvard University Law School, but failed to graduate from either. In 1921 he started a successful candy business. He left the company in

1956 and devoted himself thereafter to fighting the communist conspiracy that he fervently believed was enveloping America.

In 1958 Welch met with eleven other businessmen to form the John Birch Society, named for a Baptist missionary to China who had been killed by Chinese communists at the end of World War II. Welch considered Birch to be the first casualty of World War III. The transcript of Welch's lengthy presentation at that meeting was published as *The Blue Book* (1959). Representing the basic philosophy and objectives of the society, this book called for three things: "less government, more individual responsibility, and a better world." In *The Politician*, a biographical manuscript first published in 1958, Welch stated that communists had infiltrated the highest levels of American government. He believed Dwight Eisenhower had not only become president through communist maneuverings, but was also a knowing agent of the communist conspiracy. Welch charged other noted Americans, including Presidents Franklin Roosevelt and Harry Truman, Secretary of State John Foster Dulles, and General George C. Marshall, with varying levels of complicity in the communist plot to gain control of the American government.

Although he came from a fundamentalist Baptist background, Welch did not maintain formal ties to that tradition. His beliefs have been described as universalistic; he selected no particular brand of Christianity as the one true faith. His writings demonstrated a belief in the individualistic liberalism of the nineteenth century, as well as a suspicion of democracy, which he described as demagoguery and a fraud. After the mid-1960s Welch's fame declined. Maintaining his strong anticommunist stance, he once referred to President Ronald Reagan as a "lackey" of communist conspirators. Welch stepped down as president of the John Birch Society in 1983.

Paul Weyrich (1942–)

Sometimes described as the religious right's point man, Paul Weyrich not only enunciated conservative positions in the 1970s and 1980s in an extreme way, but also labored diligently to politicize the religious right. Behind his cherubic exterior lurks a pugnacious temperament. A Roman Catholic of blue-collar origins, he was born in Racine, Wisconsin. Strictly speaking, Weyrich was not a member of the religious right, but rather a shrewd political strategist who saw Protestant fundamentalists as an untapped pool of voters for conservative causes. The trick was to bring them into the political process and to unite them with conservative Roman Catholics. Weyrich saw in certain social issues an opportunity to achieve precisely this goal. Little if any difference, he believed, separated many Protestant fundamentalists from Catholics on such matters as abortion, prayer in the public schools, and anticommunism. Jerry Falwell and Pope John Paul merely represented different sides of the same coin.

Out of headquarters in Washington, D.C., Weyrich operated the Committee for the Survival of a Free Congress, basically a training school for conservative political candidates. Along with Edward A. McAteer and Howard Phillips, he not only courted Falwell but also minted the phrase "Moral Majority." As conceived by Weyrich, Moral Majority was to bring religious fundamentalists of whatever stripe together for common political ends. Meanwhile, the Religious Roundtable, headed by McAteer, was seen by Weyrich as an umbrella organization designed to coordinate the political efforts of several religious right groups, including Moral Majority and Christian Voice. Weyrich even attempted to unite religious and secular conservatives in the cause of "cultural conservatism," meaning basically political objectives that Christians, Jews, and even atheists could pursue without abandoning their respective theological positions. Given his continued association with the Free Congress Research and Education Foundation and prominence on the religious and secular right for such a long time, it came as a shock when Weyrich in February 1999 declared "the culture war" lost and "politics" a failure. A disillusioned Weyrich believed the time had come for religious and social conservatives to pursue their objective by means other than politics.

Donald Ellis Wildmon (1938–)

Television programming has been the primary concern of this mild-mannered but determined Methodist minister from Tupelo, Mississippi. In the belief that most television programs undermine "traditional" family values, he encouraged his congregation one Sunday in December 1976 to turn off the tube for a week. Convinced by resulting coverage in the national press that he had hit upon an idea whose time had come, Wildmon promptly organized the National Federation for Decency in 1977, renamed the American Family Association (AFA) in 1987. Headquartered initially in Wildmon's family dining room, the new organization boldly set out to purify the airwaves. By 1992 the AFA operated out of a new building, had a staff of thirty-five, claimed to have 450,000 members in 640 chapters nationwide, and conducted state-of-the-art direct-mailing operations that raised over $6 million annually.

Wildmon's strategy was twofold: first, to monitor network shows for sexual content, profanity, and violence; and, second, to threaten with boycotts the corporate sponsors of offensive programs. In this way he would punish not only the networks, but also the businesses that funded unacceptable shows. Accordingly, Pepsi, Dr. Pepper, Wendy's, Domino's Pizza, Ralston Purina, General Mills, Honda, Mazda, AT&T, and others have all incurred the preacher's wrath. The extent to which such pressure tactics have succeeded is debatable. If AT&T, as Wildmon believed, discontinued its advertisements on *Saturday Night Live* because of his threats, Holiday Inn, Johnson & Johnson, Waldenbooks, and others have ignored the television censor with apparent impunity. During the 1980s Wildmon, a member of Moral Majority, worked closely with Jerry Falwell to make the airwaves "safe" for family viewing.

Wildmon continues to serve as president of the AFA and contributes a brief column to the organization's monthly newsletter, *American Family Association Journal*, expressing opposition to homosexuality, support for prayer in the schools, and the need to strengthen moral values. He also distributes a monthly "Action Letter" informing supporters about AFA activities. Wildmon joined other religious right leaders in criticizing President George W. Bush for appointing two openly homosexual men to his administration.

4

Survey Data and Quotations

A Survey of Conservative Christian Attitudes

This study focuses primarily on the "elite" of the religious right—organizations and their leaders. If the religious right ended there, it would be of little consequence to the social and political fabric of America. Millions of ordinary Americans, however, agree with the religious right's conservative interpretation of American society and politics. This agreement not only adds significantly to the perceived moral force of the movement, but also accounts for the generous financial support of many conservative Christians. Multitudes of evangelical Christians, awakened by charismatic leaders and mobilized by grassroots organizations, have become a force to be reckoned with on election day.

Religion and the American Population

To illuminate some of the religious attitudes of Americans, attitudes that help in understanding the appeal of the religious right, this chapter employs a data analysis of the National Opinion Research Center's 1998 General Social Survey. Over 90 percent of Americans questioned in Gallup surveys since 1944 consistently express some belief in God.[1] Table 4.1 summarizes the results of the 1998 General Social Survey, in which respondents were asked to select the category, ranging from "I don't believe in God" to "I know God really exists and I have no doubts about it," that best expresses their belief about God. These results are consistent with the Gallup Polls, for if the four categories indicating some level of belief are combined, over 90 percent of those surveyed express belief in God or a "higher power."

Table 4.1
Belief in God (percentage)

Don't believe	3.3
Don't know, no way to find out	4.9
Believe in higher power	9.5
Believe sometimes	4.7
Believe with doubts	14.7
Believe without doubts	62.8
Don't know	0.1

Source: 1998 General Social Survey, N=1165.

The 1996 report from the Princeton Religion Research Center's Religion in America Study discloses additional characteristics of self-reported born-again (or evangelical) Christians. A 1995 Gallup Poll question asked respondents if they would describe themselves as "born-again" or evangelical Christians.[2] Table 4.2 summarizes the results. Born-again or evangelical Christians tend to be female, older (over fifty), residents of the South and the Midwest, from small towns, with no college education, lower-income, and Protestant. Although a larger proportion of black respondents identified themselves as born-again than did whites, African Americans tend not to play an active role in the religious right.

In analyzing the 1998 General Social Survey (GSS) data, we have taken the GSS methodology for categorizing Protestant denominations into three categories, fundamentalist or evangelical, moderate, and liberal, and collapsed the last two categories into one: mainline Protestant. Therefore, in our analysis we divide respondents' church affiliation into two categories: "evangelical Protestant" and "mainline Protestant." For example, respondents indicating their church affiliation as Missouri Synod Lutheran, Wisconsin Synod Lutheran, Southern Baptist, Churches of Christ, or Assemblies of God were categorized as "evangelical Protestant." Respondents stating their church membership as Congregationalist, Methodist, Episcopalian, Presbyterian, Disciples of Christ, Evangelical Lutheran Church in America, American Baptist, Unitarian, or Friends were categorized as "mainline Protestant." Table 4.3 presents the number of adherents (including children and regular participants in addition to church membership) to each of the Protestant denominations and the percentage each represents of the respective evangelical or mainline Protestant group (derived from Bradley 1992).

The following tables, drawn from the 1998 General Social

Table 4.2
Born-Again or Evangelical Christians (percentage)

	Yes	No	Number
Nationally	41	55	3,017
Gender			
Male	38	55	1,493
Female	43	51	1,524
Age			
Under 30	36	56	623
30–49	42	53	1,334
50–64	39	55	547
65 and older	46	48	333
Region			
East	38	67	682
Midwest	39	51	780
South	56	39	936
West	36	58	619
Community			
Urban	38	55	1,324
Suburban	36	58	997
Rural	53	41	684
Race/Ethnicity			
White	39	55	2,568
Black	61	32	276
Hispanic	41	52	178
Education			
Attended college	35	60	1,828
Did not attend	47	45	1,176
Household income			
$50,000 and over	30	65	884
$30,000–$49,999	44	52	763
$20,000–$29,999	43	50	467
Under $20,000	46	46	736
Religious Preference			
Protestant	41	53	1,665
Roman Catholic	23	69	859

Note: Percentages exclude missing cases.
Source: Gallup, George H., Jr. 1996. *Religion in America, 1996 Report.* Princeton, NJ: Princeton Religion Research Center, p. 45.

Survey, compare the views of evangelical and mainline Protestants. Table 4.4 presents the regional distribution of those respondents indicating an evangelical Protestant church affiliation in contrast to those who state an affiliation with nonevangelical, or mainline, churches.

As expected, southern states have a disproportionately higher number of evangelical Protestants compared to the rest of the nation, with over half of those so identified residing in this re-

Table 4.3
Evangelical and Mainline Protestant Church Adherents

	Number	Percent
Evangelical Protestant		
Assemblies of God	1,280,760	7.8
Churches of Christ	3,674,472	13.2
Lutheran–Missouri Synod	2,603,725	9.4
Southern Baptist Convention	18,940,682	68.1
Wisconsin Evangelical Lutheran	419,928	1.5
Total	26,919,567	100.0
Mainline Protestant		
Congregationalist	135,789	0.5
Methodist	11,091,032	43.0
Episcopalian	2,445,286	9.4
Presbyterian	3,774,727	14.5
Disciples of Christ	1,037,757	4.0
Lutheran (ELCA)	5,226,798	20.2
American Baptist	1,873,731	7.2
Unitarian	190,193	0.7
Friends	130,484	0.5
Total	25,905,797	100.0

Source: Bradley, Martin B., Norman M. Green Jr., Dale E. Jones, Mac Lynn, and Lou McNeil. 1992. *Churches and Church Membership in the United States, 1990: An Enumeration by Region, State and County Based on Data Reported for 133 Church Groupings*. Atlanta, GA: Glenmary Research Center.

Table 4.4
Religious Preference by Region (percentage)

	Evangelical Protestant	Mainline Protestant
Region		
Northeast	9.4	25.5
Midwest	25.3	23.9
South	54.8	28.4
West	10.5	22.2
Total	100.0	100.0

Source: 1998 General Social Survey, N=2640.

Table 4.5
Church Adherence by Region (percentage)

	Evangelical Protestant	Mainline Protestant
Region	(N=27,800,417)	(N=25,905,797)
Northeast	4.7	19.0
Midwest	19.0	32.6
South	67.5	38.0
West	8.8	10.4
Total	100.0	100.0

Source: Bradley, Martin B., Norman M. Green Jr., Dale E. Jones, Mac Lynn, and Lou McNeil. 1992. *Churches and Church Membership in the United States, 1990: An Enumeration by Region, State and County Based on Data Reported for 133 Church Groupings*. Atlanta, GA: Glenmary Research Center.

gion. These survey results can be compared with actual church adherence in the two religious groups in the four regions, as presented in Table 4.5. The table indicates a fairly close relationship between the respondents' report of religious preference and actual percentage of church adherents (derived from Bradley 1992).

Political Preferences

Recent campaigns and elections suggest a close relationship between the religious right and the Republican Party. The religious right provides campaign resources and voters for the Republicans, while the party supports evangelicals on issues such as abortion, pornography, prayer in the schools, and "family values." Therefore, we expect a larger proportion of evangelicals to support the Republican Party than mainline Protestants. Table 4.6 presents a cross-tabulation of religious preference by political party identification.

Given sampling error, there is no significant difference between the party loyalties of evangelicals and mainline Protestants. Party identification in the United States, while a good indicator of voter preference, is a far from perfect predictor. Many evangelical Protestants, while identifying with the Democratic Party, may vote for Republican candidates more consistent with their religious preferences. A comparison of Tables 4.6 and 4.7 indicates that while the party identification of evangelical Protestants favors the Democratic Party, 1996 voter preferences show a greater level of voter support for the Republican Party among evangelical Protestants. Although both groups questioned in this survey reported greater support for the Democratic than the Republican Party, a larger proportion of evangelical Protestants supported the Republican candidate than did mainline Protestants.

Of special note, Table 4.6 indicates that approximately one-third of both evangelical and mainline Protestants claim to be Independents. Therefore, neither party has an especially strong hold on either religious group.

Perhaps ideological preference rather than party identification is the factor that distinguishes evangelicals from mainline Protestants. Table 4.8 furnishes some support for this alternative expectation. A larger proportion of evangelical Protestants report being conservative than do mainline Protestants (41 percent versus 32 percent). These findings are consistent with the common understanding of the religious right. Therefore, to the extent that

Table 4.6
Party Affiliation and Religious Preference (percentage)

	Evangelical Protestant	Mainline Protestant
Republican	22.0	25.2
Democratic	45.9	41.1
Independent	32.1	33.7
Total	100.0	100.0

Source: 1998 General Social Survey, N=1318.

Table 4.7
Voter Preference for President, 1996 (percentage)

	Evangelical Protestant	Mainline Protestant
Candidate		
Clinton	49.5	55.4
Dole	39.9	33.0
Perot	10.6	11.6
Total	100.0	100.0

Source: 1994 General Social Survey, N=1595.

evangelical Protestants become more politically active, one would expect conservative candidates of either party to fare better than liberal candidates.

Policy Preferences

In addition to ideological self-identification, opinions about specific policy issues are informative. For instance, the General Social Survey asked whether too little money, about the right amount, or too much money was being spent in various policy areas. Table 4.9 indicates the percentage of evangelical and mainline Protestants who thought "too little" money was being devoted to these areas. Overall, on socioeconomic issues, there is little difference between evangelical and mainline Christians. Only slight differences were found, and in some categories the proportion of evangelical Protestants exceeded that of mainline Protestants responding "too little." Spending for big cities is the only category in which a majority of both evangelicals and mainline Protestants failed to say too little money is being spent. We speculate that responses in this category reflect fiscal conservatism rather than religious viewpoints. Mainline Protestants were only somewhat less likely to say too little money is being spent on the poor, which, in addition to sampling error, may be attributable to fiscal conservatism and higher socioeconomic sta-

Table 4.8
Religious Affiliation and Ideological Preference (percentage)

	Evangelical Protestant	Mainline Protestant
Ideology		
Liberal	21.3	31.2
Conservative	41.2	31.9
Moderate	37.5	36.9
Total	100.0	100.0

Source: 1998 General Social Survey, N=2507.

Table 4.9
Religious Preference and the Support of Public Spending (percentage)

	Evangelical Protestant	Mainline Protestant
Issue		
Health	68.4	67.3
Education	72.3	74.0
Big Cities	17.8	19.0
Environment	51.8	64.8
Poor	65.5	64.8

Source: 1998 General Social Survey, N=2507.

tus among mainline Protestants (see Table 4.2 for an indication of household income among the two groups).

Social and Moral Issues

Social and moral issues that leaders of the religious right have often used in their criticisms of contemporary American society were also surveyed. Respondents were asked, for instance, if they thought marijuana should be made legal. The results are summarized in Table 4.10. The distribution is in the expected direction. Both groups oppose legalization by large margins, but a larger percentage of evangelicals (79.5 versus 60.7 percent) are in opposition.

Respondents were asked their opinion of a married person who has sex with someone other than his or her marriage partner. Table 4.11 provides a summary of the results. Once again, although large proportions of both evangelicals and mainline Protestants objected to extramarital sex, a larger proportion of evangelicals expressed disapproval. Combining the alternatives that such behavior is "always wrong" and "almost always wrong," 94 percent of evangelical responses fall in these two categories, compared with 89 percent of mainline Protestants.

132 Survey Data and Quotations

Table 4.10
Religious Preference and Attitude toward Legalizing Marijuana (percentage)

	Evangelical Protestant	Mainline Protestant
Legalize	16.0	32.3
Don't legalize	79.5	60.7
Don't know	4.5	7.0
Total	100.0	100.0

Source: 1998 General Social Survey, N=1765.

Table 4.11
Attitude toward Extramarital Sex by Religious Preference (percentage)

	Evangelical Protestant	Mainline Protestant
Attitude		
Always wrong	85.7	75.1
Almost always wrong	8.7	14.0
Sometimes wrong	2.8	6.5
Not wrong	1.9	2.6
Don't know	0.9	1.8
Total	100.0	100.0

Source: 1998 General Social Survey, N=1758.

Another issue of great concern to the religious right is homosexuality, particularly the assertiveness of the gay community in pursuit of civil rights. Table 4.12 reports the results of a General Social Survey question asking respondents their attitude toward homosexuality. A large difference in attitudes is expressed on this issue, with nearly 76 percent of evangelical Protestants stating that homosexuality is always wrong, and 45 percent of mainline Protestants holding this position. Responses to a question in the 1994 General Social Survey coincide with these findings. Respondents were asked whether they regarded homosexuality as a choice or something that cannot be changed. Although 63 percent of evangelical Protestants responded that homosexuality is a choice, just 37 percent of mainline Protestants held this position. Religious right groups tend to regard sexual preference as something that can be changed and have recommended religious therapies that allegedly convert "gays" into "straights."

In addition to homosexuality, the religious right expresses strong opposition to pornography. Table 4.13 indicates the opinions of respondents regarding the legal status of pornography. Although nearly one-half of evangelical respondents expressed a preference for laws making pornography illegal for all, only one-

Table 4.12
Religious Preference and Attitude toward Homosexuality

	Evangelical Protestant	Mainline Protestant
Always wrong	75.8	44.5
Almost always wrong	5.1	5.6
Sometimes wrong	3.4	7.8
Not wrong at all	12.3	33.9
Don't know	3.4	8.2
Total	100.0	100.0

Source: 1998 General Social Survey, N=1755.

Table 4.13
Attitudes about the Legality of Pornography

	Evangelical Protestant	Mainline Protestant
Illegal to all	49.7	32.7
Illegal to those under 18	46.4	62.0
Legal	2.5	4.5
Don't know	1.4	0.8
Total	100.0	100.0

Source: 1998 General Social Survey, N=1764.

third of mainline respondents supported that option. Sixty-two percent of mainline Protestants, but just 46 percent of evangelical Protestants, were willing to restrict the prohibition against pornography to those under eighteen years of age, while having no restrictions on the access to pornography of those over eighteen. A very small proportion in both groups was willing to accept no limitations on pornography at all.

Religious right organizations have emphasized their strong opposition to both homosexuality and pornography; therefore, it is not surprising to discover that the opinions of evangelical Protestants coincide with this opposition.

Abortion is perhaps the most important issue unifying religious right groups that, due to doctrinal differences, would otherwise likely have little to do with one another. A number of questions in the 1998 General Social Survey deal with the issue of abortion and the circumstances under which respondents would not object to the procedure. These circumstances include ones in which the baby may have a serious defect, the woman is married and does not want any more children, the woman's health is seriously endangered by the pregnancy, the woman cannot afford any more children, the pregnancy resulted from rape, the woman is not married and does not want to marry the man, and the

Table 4.14
Religious Preference and Conditions under Which an Abortion Should Be Legal (percentage)

| | Evangelical Protestant | | | | Mainline Protestant | | | |
	Yes	No	Don't Know	Total	Yes	No	Don't Know	Total
Birth defect	65.4	30.1	4.5	100	79.6	16.6	3.8	100
Unwanted	23.5	72.3	4.2	100	47.2	48.1	4.7	100
Health	78.1	16.8	5.1	100	86.3	9.7	4.0	100
Can't afford	26.2	68.7	5.1	100	48.4	46.5	5.1	100
Rape	66.1	28.3	5.6	100	81.1	15.1	3.8	100
Not married	23.7	72.5	3.8	100	46.9	47.9	5.2	100
Any reason	24.1	71.7	4.2	100	44.4	49.7	5.9	100

Source: 1998 General Social Survey, N=1761.

woman wants an abortion for any reason at all. Table 4.14 reports respondents' opinions about the permissibility of abortion in these circumstances.

Generally, evangelicals are less likely than mainline Protestants to approve of the legal right to an abortion. The greater willingness of mainline Protestants to give weight to nonreligious factors when considering an abortion would be viewed by many on the religious right as a "humanist" perspective. In some circumstances, however, a large majority of evangelicals are willing to support this legal right. These conditions include the strong chance of a birth defect, the health of the pregnant woman is seriously endangered, and the pregnancy resulted from rape.

If these survey results truly reflect the attitudes of most evangelicals, the more militant antiabortion groups do not represent accurately the opinions of evangelical Americans, a large majority of whom is willing to accept legal abortion in some of the above-mentioned circumstances. Both religious groups, however, are much less willing to sanction legal abortions under other conditions. Less than 50 percent of both religious groups are willing to approve of abortions if the mother does not want or cannot afford any more children or if the mother is not married. The complexity of opinions on this question leads to the conclusion that there is no easy solution to the abortion issue.

The religious right has made prayer in public schools one of its major causes and advocates a constitutional amendment to allow for at least voluntary prayer. Table 4.15 summarizes the results of a question that asked respondents their opinion of the U.S. Supreme Court's ruling that no state or local government may require the reading of the Lord's Prayer or Bible verses in

Table 4.15
Supreme Court Decision on Lord's Prayer and Bible Reading

	Evangelical Protestant	Mainline Protestant
Approve	28.5	49.1
Disapprove	68.9	45.5
Don't know	2.6	5.4
Total	100.0	100.0

Source: 1998 General Social Survey, N=1746.

public schools. The responses suggest that conservative Christian leadership has strong backing from evangelical Protestants, over two-thirds of whom register disapproval. In addition, 45 percent of mainline Protestants also disagree with the Court's decision.

Religious right leaders and organizations, by providing unambiguous positions on many social issues, may be an important influence in creating characteristically unambiguous attitudes among evangelicals. These leaders and organizations, along with conservative politicians, stand to benefit in the political arena. Therefore, it may prove informative to examine the percentage of persons surveyed who responded "Don't know" in each of the religious groups for Tables 4.10, 4.11, 4.12, 4.13, 4.14, and 4.15. This comparison is presented in Table 4.16. Although the differences are not always significant, evangelical Protestants have the smallest percentage of "Don't Know" responses in four of the six tables. In Table 4.13 (Attitudes about the Legality of Pornography) the percentage of "Don't Know" responses for both evangelical and mainline Protestants is very low (1.4 and 0.8 respectively). For the seven items in Table 4.14, evangelical and mainline Protestants have the same average proportion of "Don't Know" responses, perhaps indicating that evangelical as well as mainline Protestants face genuine dilemmas when considering the appropriateness of abortion in difficult circumstances, such as when the pregnancy results from rape or presents a danger to the health of the woman. Nonetheless, the overall pattern of responses suggests that evangelical Protestants are more likely to form opinions on social issues, and, as already noted, these opinions are more likely to be conservative.

Holding an opinion on an issue does not necessarily spur action in support of that opinion. One of the main objectives of religious right organizations has been to activate evangelical Protestants politically. Accordingly, General Social Survey reports were examined to determine the extent to which evangeli-

Table 4.16
Percentage of "Don't Know" Responses from Tables 4.10–4.15

Table	Evangelical Protestant	Mainline Protestant
4.10	4.5	6.9
4.11	0.9	1.8
4.12	3.4	8.2
4.13	1.4	0.8
4.14	4.6 (average)	4.6 (average)
4.15	2.6	5.7

cals participate in the electoral process. Given sampling error and assuming that overreporting of voter turnout applies equally to each group, evangelical voting levels (61.1 percent voting) compare favorably with mainline Protestants (65.1 percent voting) for the 1996 election. Inasmuch as evangelical Protestants traditionally have tended to remain aloof from the political arena, this finding suggests that the efforts of religious right organizations have been successful in getting growing numbers of the faithful to the polls.

Potential for Success

The proportion of the American public expressing a belief in God remains high. The Religion in America Study reports that majorities of Americans polled respond that they pray to God, read the Bible, and consider the Bible to be inerrant (Gallup 1990, 48–49). Further survey results indicate that Americans hold religion to be an important part of their lives. For more than forty years the Gallup organization has asked Americans, "How important would you say religion is in your own life— very important, fairly important, or not very important?" (Gallup Poll News Service 1994, 1). The percentage of those interviewed who responded that religion is either "very" or "fairly" important remains consistently high, falling in the 85–90 percent range over the forty years the question has been asked. The preceding discussion suggests that, with a few exceptions, large proportions of evangelical Protestants hold conservative views on many social and moral issues consistent with the religious right.

Although these findings bode well for the religious right, disclosing the possibility of directing American politics away from perceived secular trends, one should be wary of glib conclusions.

Table 4.17
Marital Status and Religious Preference (percentage)

	Evangelical Protestant	Mainline Protestant
Married	49.5	46.1
Widowed	11.0	10.1
Divorced	17.3	15.4
Separated	3.1	3.1
Never married	19.1	25.3
Total	100.0	100.0

Source: 1998 General Social Survey, N=2639.

Many students of the religious right have serious doubts about the movement's ability to impose its influence more widely on what they perceive to be an essentially secularized American society. Some limited evidence for this reservation can be found in survey results on marital status, as found in Table 4.17. In a fundamental area of moral life and "family values," no significant differences are evident between evangelical and mainline Protestants with regard to the percentage in each group reporting being divorced.

Responses to questions dealing with abortion, summarized in Table 4.14, indicate the willingness of both evangelical and mainline Protestants to acknowledge situations in which abortion appears to be a reasonable alternative, despite efforts of the religious right to invoke biblical mandates against the practice.

These observations suggest that contemporary social conditions may be deeply at odds with certain of the goals of the religious right. Social changes resulting from the improving economic status of women and advancing technology (such as the RU-486 abortion pill and the "morning after" pill) make possible what previously would have been unthinkable. And such changes, when combined with the presupposed value of individual choice that underpins classical liberal ideology, permit a freedom often at odds with the "traditional values" that the religious right advocates. To attempt to limit such developments can be compared with trying to put the proverbial genie back in the bottle. Nonetheless, we recognize the genuine concern of those evangelical Christians who wish to achieve what they perceive to be a better world for themselves and their children. Therefore, we expect the religious right to remain active, but not necessarily to consistently achieve major victories in the American political arena.

Quotations

The following quotations express the positions of individuals in the religious right on issues of major concern to the movement. No quotation is necessarily representative of all leaders. Quotations from analysts and critics, who offer an evaluation of the movement, are also included.

America's Christian Heritage

The Constitution, as far as we're concerned, is a Christian document.

—Gary Jarmin, *Christian Century* (April 16, 1980)

You find that anytime America was on its knees, both our economy and our security and our spiritual temperature rose at the same time, and whenever we got off our knees all three have deteriorated.

—Robert J. Billings, *Christian Century* (October 8, 1980)

The critical issue of our day is the relationship of Christ and His Word to our political and legal system in the United States. Who has jurisdiction over every aspect of American society, Jesus Christ or the State? Is this to be a Christian nation or a humanistic nation? The only faithful answer that a Bible-believing Christian can give is this: "Blessed is the nation whose God is the LORD" (Psalm 33:12). "For the LORD is our judge, the LORD is our lawgiver, the LORD is our king; He will save us" (Isaiah 33:22).

—Gary DeMar, *God and Government: A Biblical and Historical Study* (1982)

I believe our nation was chosen by God and commissioned by history to be a model of justice and inclusion and diversity without division.

—Governor George W. Bush, speaking to the Simon Wiesenthal Center Museum for Tolerance (March 2000)

Today my belief in the dream that is America is stronger than it has ever been. But I am also convinced that the American dream is at risk. It is at risk for families who must spend more and more hours working just to make ends meet. It is at risk for children who grow up without fathers. It is at risk for a generation of young people trapped in a system of public education that neither challenges their minds nor sharpens their character. It is at risk for the unborn, the aged, and the infirm. And it is at risk for millions of Americans trapped in poverty unable to find hope, uncertain about finding opportunity.

—Randy Tate, Statement on becoming executive director of the Christian Coalition (August 1997)

Antiabortion

Beliefs have no credibility when unaccompanied by sacrifice. We must stubbornly refuse to remain silent in the face of the holocaust of God's unborn children. Not all of us in the church will be called upon by our Lord to do the same thing in the same way. All of us can, however, be supportive of sacrificial intervention that gives credibility to our words. This must involve much more than peaceful civil disobedience at abortion clinics to save the lives of unborn children. But surely it can include it.

—Randy C. Alcorn, *Is Rescuing Right?* (1990)

What we must change is not our message, but our behavior. Babies are dying whose lives could be saved if pro-life advocates were equipped to argue their case persuasively. We can win if we force abortion advocates to defend killing babies. The battle over partial-birth abortion indicates this.

—Scott Klusendorf, "The Vanishing Pro-Life Apologist: Putting the 'Life' Back into the Abortion Debate," *Christian Research Journal* (vol. 22, no. 1, 1999)

Anticommunism

For not only is this loss of reinforcing faith in the cement of our morals a weakness in itself of immense significance, but like all of our weaknesses it has been pounced upon by the Communists, and used and made worse by them with great skill and determination for their own purposes. . . . The Communists are able to use this lack of moral stamina among their enemies in a thousand ways to make their own progress easier and the conquest of those enemies more rapid.

—Robert Welch, *The Blue Book of the John Birch Society* (1961)

Make no mistake about it. The Communists are winning. Hitler died; Nazism died with him. Mussolini died; Fascism died with him. Tojo died; Japanese militarism died with him. Stalin is dead; COMMUNISM LIVES ON. Lenin is dead; COMMUNISM LIVES ON. Why? Because Communism is a *satanic* weapon more powerful than the atom bomb, hydrogen bomb, cobalt bomb, or all of them combined, to bring about the seven-year Tribulation Period in which the whole world will worship Satan and his son, the anti-Christ, who will be the leader of a godless world government, and his religious counter-part, the "false prophet," the false Messiah.

—Billy James Hargis, *Communist America: Must It Be?* (1986)

Emerging from its lair of godless materialism, dressed in garments of science, Communism seduces the young and utilizes their perverted religious enthusiasm to conquer the world. Building on the doctrines of godless materialism, Communism has completely reversed the meaning of our basic moral terms. When we, in our ignorance of this fact, insist on interpreting their phraseology as if they believed the Christian philosophy from which we have derived our basic concepts, we aid and abet them in their program for our conquest and destruction.

—Fred C. Schwarz, "Love: Communist Style," *The Schwarz Report* (December 1999)

Biblical Inerrancy

No one, as far as I know, holds that the English translation of the Bible is absolutely infallible and inerrant. The doctrine held by many is that the Scriptures *as originally given* were absolutely infallible and inerrant, and that our English translation is a *substantially accurate* rendering of the Scriptures as originally given. We do not possess the original manuscripts of the Bible. These original manuscripts were copied many times with great care and exactness, but naturally some errors crept into the copies that were made. We now possess so many good copies that by comparing one with another, we can tell with great precision just what the original text was. Indeed, for all practical purposes the original text is now settled. There is not one important doctrine that hangs upon any doubtful reading of the text.

—Reuben A. Torrey, *Difficulties and Alleged Errors and Contradictions in the Bible* (1907)

If Paul is wrong in this factual statement about Eve's coming from Adam [1 Cor. 11:8], there is no reason to have certainty in the authority of any New Testament factual statement, including the factual statement that Christ rose physically from the dead.

—Francis A. Schaeffer, *No Final Conflict: The Bible without Error in All That It Affirms* (1975)

Being wholly and verbally God-given, Scripture is without error or fault in all its teaching, no less in what it states about God's acts in creation, about the events of world history, and about its own literary origins under God, than in its witness to God's saving grace in individual lives. . . . This authority of Scripture is inescapably impaired if this total divine inerrancy is in any way limited or disregarded, or made relative to a view of truth contrary to the Bible's own; and such lapses bring serious loss to both the individual and the Church.

—Chicago Statement on Biblical Inerrancy, Norman L. Geisler, ed., *Inerrancy* (1979)

Compassionate Conservatism

I've described myself as a compassionate conservative, because I am convinced a conservative philosophy is a compassionate philosophy that frees individuals to achieve their highest potential. It is conservative to cut taxes and compassionate to give people more money to spend. It is conservative to insist upon local control of schools and high standards and results; it is compassionate to make sure every child learns to read and no one is left behind. It is conservative to reform the welfare system by insisting on work; it is compassionate to free people from dependency on government. It is conservative to reform the juvenile justice code to insist on consequences for bad behavior; it is compassionate to recognize that discipline and love go hand in hand.

—Texas Governor George W. Bush, in an address at the Austin Convention Center (March 7, 1999)

Compassionate conservatism is neither an easy slogan nor one immune from vehement attack. It is a full-fledged program with a carefully considered philosophy. It will face in the twenty-first century not easy acceptance but dug-in opposition. It will have to cross a river of suspicion concerning the role of religion in American society. It will have to get past numerous ideological machine-gun nests. Only political courage will enable compassionate conservatism to carry the day and transform America.

Marvin Olasky, *Compassionate Conservatism* (2000)

The "compassionate conservative" candidate for public office wants you to see him as a person who wants to cut your taxes while at the same time raising your benefits. "Compassion" speaks to the benefits, "conservative" to the taxes, and in all the confusion we forget that we're talking about only one pile of money. Place your bets on "compassion" not on "conservative," and remember, they're compassionate with *your* money.

—R. C. Sproul, Foreword to James R. White, *The Potter's Freedom* (2000)

Culture

If you look at the cultural war that's going on, most of what those who disagree with us represent leads to death—abortion, euthanasia, promiscuity in heterosexuality, promiscuity in homosexuality, legalization of drugs. There are only two choices. It really is that clear. It's either God's way, or it is the way of social disintegration.

—James Dobson, *U.S. News & World Report* (May 4, 1998)

Economics and Capitalism

When men are taught that the capitalist system is rigged against them, that they have a legal and moral right to welfare payments, and that those who live well as a result of their own labor, effort, and forecasting skills are immoral and owe the bulk of their wealth to the poor, we must recognize the source of these teachings: the pits of hell.

—Gary North, *The Sinai Strategy: Economics and the Ten Commandments* (1986)

The Bible promotes free enterprise. The book of Proverbs and the parables of our Lord clearly promote private property ownership and the principles of capitalism. We therefore are strong free-enterprisers.

—Jerry Falwell, *Houston Chronicle* (April 5, 1987)

Work is the heart and soul, the cornerstone of Biblical charity. In fact, much of the outworking of Biblical charity is little more than a subfunction of the doctrine of work. Its operating resources are the fruit of work: the tithe, hospitality, private initiative, and voluntary relief. Its basic methodologies are rooted in the work-ethic: gleaning, training, lending, and facilitating. Its primary objectives revolve around a comprehension of the goodness of work: productivity, rehabilitation, and entrepreneurial effort.

—George Grant, *Bringing in the Sheaves: Transforming Poverty into Productivity* (1988)

Education

When a student reads in a math book that there are no absolutes, every value he's been taught is destroyed. And the next thing you know, the student turns to crime and drugs. . . .

Crime, violence, immorality and illiteracy . . . the seeds of decadence are being taught universally in schools.

—Mel and Norma Gabler, *Texas Monthly* (November 1982)

It's not surprising that Harry [Potter] has suddenly soared to the peaks of popularity in schools across the country. His story fits right into the international program for multicultural education. . . . The envisioned global community calls for a common set of values that excludes traditional beliefs as intolerant and narrow—just as the Harry Potter books show. . . .

The biblical God simply doesn't fit into his world of wizards, witches, and other gods.

—Billy James Hargis, "Bestseller Harry Potter Teaches Wrong Lessons," *Christian Crusade Newsletter* (January 2001)

The popularity of Harry Potter is evidence that our dull, materialistic educational system is starving children's imaginations. The main problem with the Potter series is its positive spin on "witchcraft," though the series also retains elements of good fantasy. . . . The best antidote for Christian families to the negative effects of fantasy is to ground their children in positive literature and, above all, in the wonders of the Word of God.

—Gene Edward Veith, "Good Fantasy and Bad Fantasy," *Christian Research Journal* (vol. 23, no. 1, 2001)

Evolution and Creationism

Perhaps the most difficult doctrine which evolution has yet to reconcile to religion is the position that man, by the supposition that he evolved into a higher organism from a man-like ape (or

ape-like man), is no more than a specialized primate. The implication, of course, is that *all* physical, intellectual and social traits
in man can be observed in a rudimental state in apes. While
there are some who speak of the social behavior of apes; the
human-like mannerisms of dogs; the intelligence of chim-
panzees, dolphins, or whales; true religion teaches that man is a
unique being in all creation.

—Dean R. Zimmerman, *Evolution: A Golden Calf* (1976)

Darwinism is a theory of empirical science only at the level of
microevolution, where it provides a framework for explaining
phenomena such as the diversity that arises when small popu-
lations become reproductively isolated from the main body of
the species. As a general theory of biological creation Darwinism is not empirical at all. Rather, it is a necessary implication
of a philosophical doctrine called scientific naturalism, which is
based on the nonscientific assumption that God was always absent from the realm of nature. Evolution in the Darwinian
sense is inherently antithetical to theism, although evolution in
some entirely different and nonnaturalistic sense could con-
ceivably (if not demonstrably) have been God's chosen method
of creation.

—Phillip E. Johnson, "What Is Darwinism?" *Christian Research Journal*
(July–August 1997)

Homosexuality

Unless homosexuality be understood fundamentally as a trans-
gression of God's Law, no further deliverance and recovery can
be made. And not only must the Law of God be pressed upon
the conscience, but God's forgiveness must also be offered. The
repenting homosexual's only hope—his eternal security—is in
the uncompromised message of the Scriptures.

—Charles McIlhenny, "Pointing the Way Home: A Pastor's Perspective," *Tabletalk* (March 1997)

The gay and lesbian agenda is gaining a head of steam across
the nation. California and other states are in the process of establishing homosexuals as a bona fide minority, with all the
privileges pertaining thereto. Minority status for homosexuals
will guarantee them an equal place at the table with women,
Hispanics and African-Americans in matters like affirmative action, job quotas, financial benefits for same-sex partners and

much more. For the first time in American history, it appears we will soon be rewarding persons for their misbehavior. For Christian schools, churches and other ministries, tax-exempt status could eventually be denied to those who do not hire a quota of gays and lesbians as teachers, pastors and workers.

—Jerry Falwell, "My Open Letter to Mel White" (July 1999)

In our post-modern world if a word still carries the scent of goodness, all the baddies will claim it for their own. Thus the homosexual crowd lobbies for gay marriage, even though marriage has *always* been defined as a union between a man and a woman.

—R. C. Sproul, Foreword to James R. White, *The Potter's Freedom* (2000)

Liberalism

Liberalism agrees with Satan . . . . The God of the Bible does not have good intentions for us, Satan said, and liberals agree. The God of the Bible is against premarital sex, against homosexual behavior, against the lust for money, against the things human beings want to do. The God of the Bible, they say, is a bad God, a false God. This is what all the "mainstream churches" today teach. It is the viewpoint of most social and political liberals, who hate the so-called "Christian Right" because they hate the teaching of the Bible. For them, the God of the Bible is an evil god.

—James B. Jordan, "Hath God Said?" *Tabletalk* (August 2000)

Moral Law

Without the connection to a higher law, it becomes more and more difficult for people to answer the important day-to-day questions that test us: Why is it wrong to lie or cheat or steal? Why is it wrong to settle conflicts with violence? Why is it wrong to be unfaithful to one's spouse, or to exploit children, or to despoil the environment, or defraud a customer, or demean an employee?

—Senator Joseph Lieberman, Democratic vice presidential candidate, addressing an audience at the University of Notre Dame, *Houston Chronicle* (October 25, 2000)

Patriotism

We are not a perfect nation, but we are still a free nation because we have the blessings of God upon us. We must continue to follow in a path that will ensure that blessing. We must not forget that it is God Almighty who has made and preserved us as a nation.

—Jerry Falwell, *Listen, America!* (1980)

It's sad to think of the school children of the past who cringed at the thought of their flag touching the ground while being removed from the school flagpole. It's grim to remember the price paid for her raising at Iwo Jima. It's distressing to think of tears shed by wives and mothers who have seen her draped over the coffin of a loved one. But it's a marvel that no one has figured out why she can now be publicly burned. What further sign does God need give us as proof we have been conquered?

—Pastor Pete Peters, *America Conquered* (1991)

Political Activism and Strategy

I realize that it is "popular" to be a born-again Christian. But for some strange reason it is "unpopular" to stand up and fight against the sins of our nation. Will you take a stand and help me Clean Up America? How would you answer these questions: Do you approve of pornographic and obscene classroom textbooks being used under the guise of sex education? Do you approve of the present laws legalizing abortion-on-demand that resulted in the murder of more than one million babies last year? Do you approve of the growing trend toward sex and violence replacing family-oriented programs on television? . . . If you are against these sins, then you are exactly the person I want on my team. I have put together a Clean Up America campaign that is going to shake this nation like it has never been shaken before. I cannot do it alone. Together we must awaken the moral conscience of our nation. The battle has just begun.

—Jerry Falwell, quoted in Gerald Strober and Ruth Tomczak, *Aflame for God* (1979)

I had never actively solicited candidates for political office. Then, in the providence of God, I was subjected to a painful educational experience, when the church attempted to get a zoning variance passed by the city council. After three years of effort, we lost, 6 to 2. For the first time, I realized that men and women largely hostile to the church controlled our city.

—Tim LaHaye, quoted in Kathleen C. Boone, *The Bible Tells Them So: The Discourse of Protestant Fundamentalism* (1980)

Friends, we are in real trouble right now, and it is time to take a stand and tell the authorities: "We can not and will not obey you when it means to surrender the lordship of Christ." Then we should be ready to defend ourselves in court and go to jail if necessary for our convictions. After all, we would be in pretty good company since much of the New Testament was penned in prison!

—Don Boys, *Christian Resistance: An Idea Whose Time Has Come—Again* (1985)

If the religious right is ever to accomplish its stated goal of returning our nation to moral sanity and spiritual stability, it must humbly but determinedly *set its own course* according to the wind of the Spirit of God. It must no longer be the pawn of powers and principalities, of godless men and institutions be they left or right. In short, the religious right must not compromise.

—George Grant, *The Changing of the Guard: Biblical Blueprints for Political Action* (1987)

Everyone wants to be in the "big time" politically. Everyone wants to run for governor. *Let them.* Meanwhile, we take over where today's politicians think that nothing important is happening. We should get our initial experience in ruling on a local level. We must prepare ourselves for a long-term political battle. We start out as privates and corporals, not colonels and generals. We do it God's way.

—Gary North, *Inherit the Earth: Biblical Blueprints for Economics* (1987)

You wait until the Sunday before the election and you distribute [moral report cards] all in one day. The election is held on Tuesday. Now why do we distribute them the Sunday before? It needs to be fresh in the voter's mind. Voters do not have a particularly long retention period. Number two, it does not give the liberal candidate that we're opposing time to go run back to all the churches screaming that he's not really that way, which is what they try to do if you give them a chance. Thirdly, when that liberal National Council of Churches minister stands in

front of the pulpit and denounces the report card in the church
service, it's too late because you've distributed it on Sunday, the
election was held on Tuesday, and the minister denounces it the
next Sunday, you see.

—Colonel Doner, quoted in Sara Diamond, *Spiritual Warfare: The Politics of the Christian Right* (1989)

The most urgent challenge for pro-family conservatives is to develop a broader issues agenda. The pro-family movement has
limited its effectiveness by concentrating disproportionately on
issues such as abortion and homosexuality. These are vital
moral issues, and must remain an important part of the message. To win at the ballot box and in the court of public opinion,
however, the pro-family movement must speak to the concerns
of average voters in the areas of taxes, crime, government
waste, health care, and financial security.

—Ralph Reed, "Casting a Wider Net," *Policy Review* (Summer 1993)

I guess it irritates me when people who know what is right put
self-preservation and power ahead of moral principle. That is
more offensive to me, in some ways, than what Bill Clinton
does with interns at the White House.

—James Dobson, *U.S. News and World Report* (May 4, 1998), on his refusal to compromise for political gain.

Prayer in the Schools

Supporters of prayer in school seek to restore traditional values.
They call for a constitutional amendment to reaffirm and reestablish the original intent of the religious freedom clause of
the First Amendment, that which has been stolen, twisted, and
used against them. The issue, they insist, is the guaranteed
preservation of religious liberty.

—Rus Walton, *Biblical Solutions to Contemporary Problems: A Handbook*
(1988)

We cannot allow an out-of-control, activist judiciary to sacrifice
our freedoms at the altar of politically correct, modern-day liberalism.

—Susan Weddington, chair of the Texas Republican party, expressing
anger at the U.S. 5th Circuit Court of Appeals for disallowing prayer at
school-sanctioned sporting events (January 2000).

Opponents of prayer . . . contend that if it is allowed to take place openly, such as at a football game, someone who doesn't share the same faith will have to decide between not going to the game or feeling uncomfortable. But the government's primary responsibility should be to protect the freedoms of all the students rather than force a national practice of atheism so that some might be spared having to hear something they don't agree with.

—Sean R. Tuffnell, *Houston Chronicle* (January 2000)

Reconstructionism

God has a plan for the conquest of all things by His covenant people. That plan is His law. It leaves no area of life and activity untouched, and it predestines victory. To deny the law is to deny God and His plan for victory.

—Rousas John Rushdoony, *God's Plan for Victory* (1977)

Christianity has given birth to the greatest prosperity, stability, and liberty known in history. To the extent that the Christian view is also the biblical view (contrary to liberalism, which attempts to separate the two), we may expect God's objective blessings upon that people whose God is the Lord, as evidenced in their law code.

—Kenneth L. Gentry Jr., *God's Law in the Modern World: The Continuing Relevance of Old Testament Law* (1993)

Religious Equality Amendment (proposed)

Section 1. Neither the United States nor any State shall abridge the freedom of any person or group, including students in public schools, to engage in prayer or other religious expression in circumstances in which expression of a nonreligious character would be permitted; nor deny benefits to or otherwise discriminate against any person or group on account of the religious character of their speech, ideas, motivations or identity.
Section 2. Nothing in the Constitution shall be construed to forbid the United States or any State to give public or ceremonial acknowledgement to the religious heritage, beliefs, or traditions of its people.
Section 3. The exercise, by the people, of any freedoms under the First Amendment or under this Amendment shall not constitute an establishment of religion.

—*Traditional Values Report* (May–June 1995)

Right to Bear Arms

The right to defend one's life, family, liberty and property is a God-given right, supported by Scripture and illustrated in God's Law as seen in Nature. Any person, group or government which would attempt to deprive one of this right, or attempt to persecute, prosecute or punish one for exercising this right, violates God's Law and is an enemy of God's people. Weapons are essential for self-defense and Jesus admonished His followers to purchase a sword. A firearm is the modern equivalent of a sword, thus gun control in any form or manner is in opposition to God's Law.

—*Remnant Resolves* (1988)

Secular Humanism

If the atheistic, amoral, one-world humanists succeed in enslaving our country, that missionary outlet [America] will eventually be terminated. As a Christian and as a pastor, I am deeply concerned that this ministry be extended. The eternal souls of millions of people depend on us to supply them with the good news. In addition, I am concerned that the 50 million children who will grow up in America during the next generation will have access to the truth, rather than the heresies of humanism.

—Tim LaHaye, *The Battle for the Mind* (1980)

A humanist is a humanist is a humanist! That is, he believes as a humanist, thinks as a humanist, acts as a humanist, and makes decisions as a humanist. Whether he is a politician, government official, or educator, he does not think like a pro-moral American, but like a humanist. Consequently, he is not fit to govern us or to train our young.

—Tim LaHaye, *The Battle for the Mind* (1980)

The humanistic ideas of moral relativity and individual divinity are destructive in and of themselves. But, when combined, this philosophical mixture has proven disastrous to the American culture: when everything is relative, pleasing yourself becomes the most important thing. When right and wrong do not exist, good and evil are viewed as concepts. As such, neither is based on truth, but on individual perception. If every individual is his own god, there is no Judge, so each is free to do what he pleases; no reward will be gained for good works, and no consequences paid for evil.

—Lynn Stanley, *The Blame Game: Why Society Persecutes Christians* (1996)

Taxation

Communism is a system of private property confiscation and control. Any means of property control and confiscation used in the U.S.A. today *against* the consent of the individual is a communist practice. . . . The graduated income tax is one of the strongest planks of the Communist Manifesto. Every Christian should be opposing it with all his strength. . . . But, lo, most Christians and pastors criticize those brave persons who are participating in Godly resistance. In fact, many pastors and Christians preach against sodomy and abortion; but at the same time they are supporting the practice of those very sins through the graduated income tax.

—Everett Sileven, *The Christian and the Income Tax* (1986)

Should we pay taxes to the government of the United States of America? Christ did not say to pay what Caesar demanded, nor did He say that God demanded anything. The individual must decide who he wishes to serve. If Caesar has a return due him for services rendered, then that which is Caesar's should be paid. But what about your God and His just dues? Did Caesar bring the sun and rain and the growth of crops and livestock? What does your government do with the tax money which you pay? Are they not paying for the murder of the unborn in abortion clinics? Are they not teaching the diabolical, satanic lie called humanism in the schools with your taxes paying the bills? Have you been taking that which is God's and paying for evil and wicked government? Did not our government lie to us about Pearl Harbor, Korea, Viet Nam, Watergate, energy shortage and social security? Your government is a liar and Satan is the father of lies and our churches are teaching that you must render unto our wicked government whatever they demand.

—M. J. "Red" Beckman, *Born Again Republic* (1988)

By the use of various methods of taxation, we have been deprived of the right to property contrary to God's Law against theft. Therefore, we, God's Covenant People, call for a repentance by our Government of all unscriptural methods of taxation as outlined in His Law.

—*Remnant Resolves* (1988)

It is conservative to cut taxes and compassionate to give people more money to spend.

—Governor George W. Bush, *The Texas Observer* (May 1999)

Responses to the Religious Right:
Scholarly and Polemical

At least within the twentieth century, and especially since the Second World War, American fundamentalism has commonly been strongly aligned with extreme political conservatism. Christianity is, in these circles of the far right, understood to give complete sanction to the capitalist system and to a *laissez-faire* approach to society, and government intervention in social arrangements, the welfare state, mildly reformist attitudes, liberalism and socialism are all alike seen as forms of communism masquerading under another name. In such a milieu, though accusations of communism may be common coin (and even Billy Graham is said to have been called a communist by such extremists, or at least to have been accused of being "soft on communism"), an actual socialist Christian, even a mild one, is as inconceivable among conservative evangelicals as a man with two heads.

—James Barr, *Fundamentalism* (1978)

In the eighties, America has given birth to a new form of terror, a campaign of fear and intimidation aimed at the hearts of millions. It is in two great American arenas—religion and politics—that this new terror has raised its head. In the past few years, a small group of preachers and political strategists has begun to use religion and all that Americans hold sacred to seize power across a broad spectrum of our lives. They are exploiting this cherished and protected institution—our most intimate values and individual beliefs—along with our civil religion—our love of country—in a concerted effort to transform our culture into one altogether different from the one we have known. It is an adventurous thrust: with cross and flag to pierce the heart of America without bloodshed. And it is already well under way.

—Flo Conway and Jim Siegelman, *Holy Terror: The Fundamentalist War on America's Freedoms in Religion, Politics and Our Private Lives* (1984)

In attempting to discover if the majority of Americans actually subscribe to the New Christian Right definition of public morality, scholars have conducted a multitude of opinion surveys based on local, state, and national samples. With an unusual degree of accord, these surveys have challenged the most enthusiastic claims about the extent of broad public support for the profamily agenda. In fact, support for the core items making up

the "profamily" agenda has been limited to a minority of the population and apparently has declined over the course of the 1970s and 1980s. . . . In the face of New Right efforts to the contrary, the public apparently has become more liberal on issues like abortion, tolerance for homosexuality, and women's rights.
—Kenneth D. Wald, *Religion and Politics in the United States* (1987)

It should be recalled that conservative Christianity began to flourish at the very moment when the more sedate and rational branches of Protestantism were floundering. In the 1970s the United Presbyterian Church lost 21 percent of its members. The Episcopal Church lost 15 percent. The United Church of Christ and the United Methodists both lost 10 percent. As these moderate and liberal denominations, which recognized the complexities of modern life and resisted biblical simplification, declined, many of their former members defected . . . to conservative, born-again Christianity. They filled the thousands of new conservative churches and schools that were founded as the revival spread to every corner of the country and eventually claimed 60 million adherents. The revival became so successful that by 1980, despite the complaints of mainline Protestants and Catholics, the very word "Christian" had come to mean a born-again conservative.
—Michael D'Antonio, *Fall from Grace: The Failed Crusade of the Christian Right* (1989)

For the Religious Right, the close of the century will be a time of unprecedented evangelistic activity and preoccupation with the second coming of Christ. Adherents of the "pre-tribulation rapture" theory are anxiously packing their spiritual bags as they await departure from the planet. "Post-millenialists" [sic] who believe that they themselves are destined to usher in the Kingdom of God on earth will escalate their drive to transform secular institutions. Evangelicals of all stripes hope that the spiralling technological advances, political turmoil and economic instability expected in the 1990s will help them attract millions of "lost sheep" seeking answers to life's most profound questions.
—Sara Diamond, *Spiritual Warfare: The Politics of the Religious Right* (1989)

At times it has seemed that if evangelicals were to wake up as citizens of an African or Asian nation, their identity as followers of Christ would be profoundly shaken. Why? Not simply because of the differences in language, food, and culture, but because many American evangelicals have been truly more American than Christian, more dependent on historical myths than spiritual realities, more shaped by the flag than the cross. . . . These tendencies came to a climax in the eighties with the rise of the religious Right. What began as an appreciation of the contribution faith made in our nation turned into a false reliance on evangelicals' social standing in America. The evangelical identity shifted from being grounded in the source of blessing to being grounded in the blessing itself. Their status as pilgrims in search of the heavenly kingdom was less important than being citizens of a "Christian America." Following the pattern of most idolatry, something to be appreciated became a point of overattachment, a source of reliance, and finally an idol that led to public pride and self-deception.

—John Seel, "Nostalgia for the Lost Empire," in Os Guinness and John Steel, eds., *No God but God* (1992)

Rooted in the past, connected to the political context of its times, the Christian right has demonstrated a distinctive approach to politics characterized by alternating strains of accommodation, activism, and alienation, continuing tensions between movement members, and a paradoxical synthesis of piety and protest. Far from short-lived, its redemptive approach to politics is cyclical and recurrent.

—Michael Lienesch, *Redeeming America: Piety and Politics in the New Christian Right* (1993)

The handful of losses suffered by its candidates in the November 1998 federal elections hasn't changed the Right's state-by-state plan to impose its agenda on local communities: first, infiltrate school boards where the line between church and state can be obliterated with the most impact and least resistance; second, work stealthily to win control of state and local Republican parties and then, in turn, local elective offices and state legislative seats. Indeed, Radical Right leaders now claim to have taken control of up to 31 state Republican parties—to say nothing of the Impeachment-obsessed Republican leadership in Congress.

—Carole Shields, President, People for the American Way (June 1999)

This [the posting of the Ten Commandments in public schools] is all driven by looking for some kind of magic fix to school violence. If the mere presence of religious material stopped sin, the presence of Gideons [sic] Bible in hotel rooms would have stopped adultery long ago.

—Barry Lynn, executive director of Americans United for the Separation of Church and State, *Houston Chronicle* (February 20, 2000)

[John] Aschroft's positions on abortion and the right of women to control their own bodies are so far removed from those of most Americans as to raise significant doubts about his fitness to serve as the nation's chief legal officer.

—People for the American Way (December 2000)

Notes

1. Bezilla, Robert, ed. 1993. *Religion in America 1992–1993*. Princeton, NJ: Princeton Religion Research Center, p. 20.

5

Directory of Organizations

The organizations listed here vary considerably in basic ideology and political influence. They differ politically from extreme right stances to more traditional conservative positions. Members of some organizations would undoubtedly object strongly to being categorized with other groups that appear here. Many of these groups presently engage actively and successfully in politics; others, influential at one time, have lost their prominence, and several never did gain wide public attention. Several organizations that were significant in the evolution of the contemporary religious right but that no longer exist are also included. Despite the wide variation, we believe these groups all share a family resemblance. They all profess a more traditional Christian faith and advocate minimal government interference in people's lives, except, of course, with regard to specific objectives of their own, such as restricting abortion and pornography. In order to provide a more complete landscape, we have also included some organizations whose principles and objectives collide with those of the religious right.

Organizations on the Religious Right

Alliance Defense Fund (ADF)
P.O. Box 54370
Phoenix, AZ 85078-9948
(602) 953-1200
http://www.alliancedefensefund.org
Alan E. Sears, President

The Alliance Defense Fund was established in 1994 with the support of the evangelical Christian leaders Bill Bright, Larry Burkett, James Dobson, D. James Kennedy, Marlin Maddoux, and Donald Wildmon. Intended to counter the influence of the American Civil Liberties Union, the ADF provides financial and legal assistance to those involved in lawsuits that have the potential for establishing legal precedents in the areas of the free exercise of religion, family values, and opposition to abortion. The organization claims credit for obtaining a favorable Supreme Court decision in *Rosenberg v. Rector and Visitors of the University of Virginia* (1995), in which a Christian, student-run publication won the right to receive student activity funds. The ADF claims to have had a hand in nearly 130 lower court victories involving what the organization calls Christian values, including opposition to legal recognition of homosexual marriages.

PUBLICATIONS: *ADF News Alerts,* monthly newsletters that report on ADF legal activities, pending legal cases, and prayer requests.

American Association of Christian Schools (AACS)
4500 Selsa Road
Blue Springs, MO 64015
(816) 795-7709
(816) 795-7709 (fax)
http://www.aacs.org
Dr. Carl Herbster, President

Founded in 1972, this organization focuses on two major goals. First, AACS assists in the maintenance and improvement of the quality, both academic and spiritual, of Protestant Christian schools. It offers a number of services, including teacher placement and teacher certification programs, and acts as a source for instructional materials. Second, AACS provides interest-group representation in protecting the integrity of Christian schools against government interference at both the state and national levels.

PUBLICATIONS: *AACS Capitol Comments,* a monthly newsletter; the annual *AACS Directory; The Builder,* an occasional publication.

American Center for Law and Justice (ACLJ)
1000 Centerville Turnpike
P.O. Box 64429
Virginia Beach, VA 23467
(804) 523-7570
(757) 226-2836 (fax)

http://www.aclj.org
Jay Sekulow, Executive Counsel

In 1990 Pat Robertson formed the ACLJ, a public-interest law firm concerned with defending traditional family values and the religious and civil liberties of Americans. Believing secularism in America has led to attempts to restrict the preaching of the gospel in public places, the organization offers legal advice and supports attorneys in cases in which the rights of Christians are challenged. The ACLJ objects to legalized abortion and what it sees as the harmful effects of social welfare agencies on the traditional family unit.

PUBLICATIONS: *Law & Justice Journal,* quarterly.

American Christian Action Council
See Council of Bible Believing Churches

American Coalition of Unregistered Churches (ACUC)
2711 South East Street
Indianapolis, IN 46206
(317) 787-0830
(317) 781-2775 (fax)
http://home.inreach.com/dov/unregchs.htm
Greg Dixon, National Chair

Founded in 1983 in Chicago by a group of fundamentalist ministers, the ACUC represents a group of fundamentalist pastors and churches that oppose government interference in the activities of pastors, churches, and Christians generally. The organization follows a strict policy of separation of church and state, including resistance to government regulation in such areas as building codes and permits, legally required registration or incorporation of churches, licensing of pastors, and Social Security tax payments for church employees.

PUBLICATIONS: *The Trumpet,* a bimonthly newspaper.

American Council of Christian Churches (ACCC)
P.O. Box 5455
Bethlehem, PA 18015
(610) 865-3009
(610) 865-3003 (fax)
http://www.amcouncilcc.org
Richard Harris, President

This organization was established in 1941 by Carl McIntire as a reaction to the National (then Federal) Council of Churches

(NCC), which McIntire considered too liberal. The ACCC required its members to maintain complete separation from the NCC. The ACCC has opposed communism and other beliefs that it considers a threat to American religious, economic, and political freedom. Because of dissension between McIntire and other leaders of the ACCC, in 1969 the organization dropped McIntire from the executive council. In 1970 it left the International Council of Christian Churches, another organization created by McIntire. The ACCC holds to a fundamentalist doctrine, advocates the inerrancy of the Bible, supports dissemination of the "historic Christian faith" in America and around the world, and opposes liberal, socialist, and communist doctrines. The organization, which claims a membership of 1.5 million, is affiliated with the Council of Bible Believing Churches.

PUBLICATIONS: *Fundamental News Service,* a bimonthly newsletter that discusses social and political issues of concern to Christians.

American Family Association (AFA)
P.O. Box 2440
Tupelo, MS 38803
(601) 844-5036
(601) 842-6791 (fax)
http://www.afa.net
Donald E. Wildmon, Executive Director

Founded by Donald Wildmon in 1977, this organization promotes what it terms the "biblical ethic of decency in American society" and focuses its attention on the perceived immorality, profanity, and violence on television and in the other mass media. The organization encourages the television networks to broadcast family-oriented entertainment. The AFA compiles data on televised programming it deems objectionable and encourages boycotts of the offending networks and their sponsors. The AFA also employs petition campaigns. Prior to 1988 the AFA was known as the National Federation for Decency.

PUBLICATIONS: *AFA Journal,* which is published monthly, and pamphlets dealing with the organization's opposition to pornography and sex education in the public schools.

American Freemen Association
See Christian Patriot Association

American Life League (ALL)
P.O. Box 1350
Stafford, VA 22555
(540) 659-4171
(540) 659-2586 (fax)
http://www.all.org
Judie Brown, President

Begun in 1979 by five families as the American Life Education and Research Trust, the American Life League considers the pro-life movement a moral crusade to protect human life. Thus, it objects to the compromising of politics. To the ALL, life is a gift from God, and so there can be "no exceptions and no compromises" on the question of abortion. The group contends that the survival of the United States depends upon "securing for the pre-born the guarantee of being born as honored citizens of a country that practices, under God, liberty and justice for all."

PUBLICATIONS: *Celebrate Life,* a bimonthly magazine.

**American Society for the Defense of Tradition,
Family and Property (TFP)**
P.O. Box 1868
York, PA 17405
(717) 225-7147
(717) 225-7479 (fax)
http://www.tfp.org
Raymond E. Drake, President

A civic organization founded in 1974 and based largely on Roman Catholic doctrine, the TFP defends traditional values, the family, and the right to property. It opposes what are considered socialist and Marxist positions on these subjects. The Society is concerned with what it perceives as a crisis in morality, politics, and religion and works toward educating Americans in ways to defend traditional values and free enterprise.

PUBLICATIONS: *Crusade Magazine,* bimonthly; *TFP in Action,* a monthly newsletter.

Americans United for God and Country (AUGC)
P.O. Box 183
Merion Station, PA 19066
(215) 224-9235
Leslie Harris, Executive Director

Begun in 1977, this organization, claiming a membership of 10,400, supports tuition tax credits for private schools as a means of furthering the Judeo-Christian tradition. According to the organization, because religious citizens provide tax funds to operate public school systems, their principles deserve attention in the curriculum. These principles include patriotism and the basic governing concepts listed in the Constitution and the Bill of Rights. The AUGC holds an annual conference on July 4.

PUBLICATIONS: None.

Associates for Biblical Research (ABR)
1313 Orchard Way
Frederick, MD 21703
(301) 898-9358
(301) 668-3000 (fax)
http://www.christiananswers.net
Gary Byers, Executive Director

Founded in 1969, this association conducts research on biblical archaeology and promotes creationism as a scientifically legitimate approach to the origins of human life. The organization conducts an educational program and sponsors an annual archaeological excavation in Israel.

PUBLICATIONS: *Bible and Spade,* quarterly; *ABR Newsletter,* bimonthly.

Campus Crusade for Christ International (CCC)
100 Lake Hart Drive
Orlando, FL 32832
(407) 826-2000
http://www.ccci.org
William R. (Bill) Bright, President

Bill Bright began the CCC in 1951 on the University of California–Los Angeles campus. In addition to college and university ministries, including Bible study groups, faculty groups, and student, family, and pastoral conferences, Campus Crusade has programs to reach high school students, military personnel, and prisoners. The organization is active in 152 countries around the world "to help fulfill the Great Commission of Christ . . . and to work with other members of the Body of Christ."

PUBLICATIONS: *Worldwide Challenge,* a bimonthly magazine.

Center for Christian Statesmanship
214 Massachusetts Avenue, NE
Washington, DC 20002
(202) 547-3052
http://www.statesman.org
Frank Wright, Director

Established by D. James Kennedy, pastor of Coral Ridge Presbyterian Church in Fort Lauderdale, Florida, the Center for Christian Statesmanship has three goals: "to minister the Gospel of Jesus Christ to leaders in our nation's capital," "to equip our nation's leaders for ministry and service," and "to reestablish the principles and practices of Christian statesmanship." The Center conducts Bible studies on Capitol Hill for elected officials and government workers, and holds Politics and Principle luncheons at which members of Congress and others present views about the relationship between personal faith and public service. Each year the Center presents the Distinguished Christian Statesman award to a public official. Past winners include Senators John Ashcroft and Sam Brownback and House Majority Leader Dick Armey.

PUBLICATIONS: None.

Center for Reclaiming America
P.O. Box 632
Fort Lauderdale, FL 33302
(877) 725-8872
http://www.reclaimamerica.org
Janet Folger, National Director

Claiming that the United States has fallen away from its appropriate place as a Christian nation, the Center for Reclaiming America works to "inform the American public and motivate people of faith to defend and implement the biblical principles on which our country was founded." National director Janet Folger, formerly legislative director for the Ohio Right to Life Society, lobbies for passage of legislative proposals important to the religious right, such as a ban on "partial-birth" abortions. Folger has a daily sixty-second broadcast, *Reclaiming America with Janet Folger,* which is carried on more than 300 radio stations and over 200 television stations.

PUBLICATIONS: *Fastfacts,* an occasional newsletter.

Chalcedon Foundation (CF)
P.O. Box 158
Vallecito, CA 95251
(209) 728-3510
Mark R. Rushdoony, President

This organization seeks to reconstruct government and society according to biblical principles. The CF issues grants to scholars conducting research into the relevance of biblical law and faith to contemporary life.

PUBLICATIONS: A monthly newsletter, the *Chalcedon Report,* and the semiannual *Journal of Reconstruction.*

Christian Anti-Communism Crusade (CACC)
P.O. Box 129
Manitou Springs, CO 80829
(231) 437-0941
David Noebel, President

Founded in 1953 by Fred Schwarz, originally an Australian physician, this anticommunist religious and educational group has a long history of providing information regarding the evils of communism. Lectures and forums coordinated by the organization for citizen groups, college students, and churches stress communist strategy and philosophy in order to prepare individuals to resist more effectively the communist threat. In explaining its objective, the organization employs a medical analogy, with communism as the disease, the Crusade the pathologist, and politicians, educators, and voters the physicians. The CACC has been active not only in the United States, but also in several foreign nations, including India, the Philippines, Korea, Taiwan, Malaysia, El Salvador, and Chile. In 1998 Schwarz retired as president, but the organization continues under Noebel's leadership.

PUBLICATIONS: *The Schwarz Report,* a monthly newsletter; Fred Schwarz's books and booklets, including *You Can Trust the Communists (To Be Communists)* (1960), *Why Communism Kills* (1984), *Beating the Unbeatable Foe* (1996), and David Noebel's *Understanding the Times: The Religious Worldviews of Our Day and the Search for Truth* (1995).

Christian Coalition of America (CCA)
499 South Capitol Street, SW, Suite 615
Washington, DC 20003
(202) 479-6900

(202) 479-4260 (fax)
Randy Tate, Executive Director

The Christian Coalition of America, which was founded in 1989 by Pat Robertson as the Christian Coalition, is a grassroots political organization concerned with an alleged lack of morality in government. The Christian Coalition was reorganized in 1999 into two separate organizations: the Christian Coalition of America, which is involved in "voter education," and the Christian Coalition International, a political action committee. The organization seeks the election of legislators who have high moral values and supports legislation of concern to the Christian right, especially profamily measures. The CCA has opposed homosexuals in the military, taxpayer-funded "abortion-on-demand," condom distribution in the public schools, "socialized medicine," legal recognition of homosexual marriages, and increased government spending and taxation. Although it does not support specific candidates, the organization distributes Congressional Scorecards, revealing candidates' positions on issues and voting records on measures considered important to Christian voters. In 1993 and 1994 the CCA claimed to have distributed twenty-nine million Congressional Scorecards and forty million voter guides (candidates' stands on key issues) in an effort to affect election outcomes and government policy.

PUBLICATIONS: *Christian American*, a bimonthly newsletter.

Christian Crusade
P.O. Box 977
Tulsa, OK 74102
(918) 665-2345
(918) 438-4235 (fax)
Billy James Hargis, President

Founded in 1948, the Christian Crusade has had a long history of opposition to communist and socialist ideologies, as well as to what the organization believes were attempts by supporters of such ideologies to infiltrate American government and society. The Christian Crusade (formerly Christian Echoes National Ministry) works to preserve the conservative Christian ideals upon which it believes America was founded. In addition to opposing communism, the organization has objected to American participation in the United Nations, government interference in the economy, and federal involvement in areas such as education that it believes are constitutionally reserved to the states. After the 1994 congressional elections, Christian Crusade strongly supported the Republican policy agenda in Congress. The organization strongly criticized Bill Clinton during his presidency.

PUBLICATIONS: *Christian Crusade Newspaper*, a monthly publication with a circulation of 55,000 that treats current events from a conservative Christian standpoint. Billy James Hargis authors many of the front-page items.

Christian Defense League (CDL)
P.O. Box 449
Arabi, LA 70032
(504) 277-5940
(504) 277-5626 (fax)
http://home.inreach.com/dov/cdl.htm
James K. Warner, Executive Officer

Launched in 1964, the CDL supports the perpetuation of traditional Christian values and fosters the development of Christian leaders in the public realm. The organization offers educational programs.

PUBLICATIONS: Two monthly magazines, *CDL Report* and *Christian Vanguard*.

Christian Echoes National Ministry
See Christian Crusade

Christian Family Renewal (CFR)
P.O. Box 73
Clovis, CA 93613
(209) 297-7818
(800) 345-7646 (toll-free)
Dr. Michael Norris, President

Established in 1970, this organization focuses on problems related to the family. The CFR attempts to offer Christians ways to resolve social problems in politics, business, and education. Among the issues of concern to the organization are abortion, homosexuality, and pornography.

PUBLICATIONS: *Jesus and Mary Are Calling You*, an annual newsletter; a report on homosexuality, satanism, and abortion.

Christian Heritage Center (CHC)
1941 Bishop Lane, Suite 810

Louisville, KY 40218
(502) 452-1592
(502) 452-1593 (fax)
Dr. N. Burnett Magruder, Executive Director

A Christian patriotic organization founded in 1964, the CHC advocates a return to the basic faith and liberties of the American founding. The organization supports the introduction of prayer, Bible reading, and the teaching of the Ten Commandments in the public schools, and it assesses the influence of atheism, humanism, and communism in American government and society. The organization produces the daily radio broadcast *Liberty Radio Program.*

PUBLICATIONS: *Awake and Alert,* monthly.

Christian Law Association (CLA)

P.O. Box 4010
Seminole, FL 33775
(727) 399-8300
(727) 398-3907 (fax)
http://www.christianlaw.org
David Gibbs, President

The CLA began in 1977 with David Gibbs's successful defense of a couple who had been arrested and jailed for refusing to send their children to public school, preferring instead home schooling in a religious atmosphere. Attached to the Gibbs and Craze law firm, the CLA uses litigation to defend members' religious rights. The organization receives monthly dues from churches and individuals who, if they require legal assistance regarding their religious rights, will receive representation at no additional cost.

PUBLICATIONS: *Teacher's Forum,* monthly.

Christian Patriot Association (CPA)

P.O. Box 596
Boring, OR 97009
(503) 668-4941
(503) 668-8614 (fax)
Richard G. Flowers, Founder

Founded in 1982 as the American Freeman Association, this patriotic Christian organization concerns itself with what members believe to be unconstitutional abuses of government power. The organization attempts to restore to American citizens the sovereignty that government abuses have threatened. Information relevant to such abuses is gathered from mass media reports and compiled for distribution.

PUBLICATIONS: *The Patriot Review,* monthly.

Christian Research (CR)
P.O. Box 385
Eureka Springs, AR 72632
(501) 253-7185
Daniel Gentry, Director

This organization, founded in 1958, offers itself as an alternative to the secular media and the American educational system. Although the CR calls for upholding the American Constitution, as the organization interprets its original meaning, and encourages patriotism and nationalism, major emphasis is placed on obeying God's commands over any human law. The CR informs Christian Americans of their biblical heritage and responsibilities and warns them of threats to "our theocratic republic." The organization supports a revisionist history of the Holocaust. Christian Research was formerly Pro-American Books.

PUBLICATIONS: *Facts for Action,* a quarterly newsletter.

Christian Research Institute (CRI)
P.O. Box 7000
Rancho Santa Margarita, CA 92688-2124
(949) 858-6100
http://www.equip.org
Hendrik (Hank) Hanegraaff, President

The CRI, established in 1960, opposes perceived threats to the Christian faith. It provides information about the direction of events in the secular world relevant to Christianity. The institute advocates "orthodox" Christianity and critically evaluates groups it considers to be heretical cults, such as the Jehovah's Witnesses and Mormons. The CRI has focused critical attention on such popular televangelists in the so-called faith movement as Benny Hinn, Kenneth and Gloria Copeland, Oral Roberts, and Trinity Broadcasting Network founder Paul Crouch and his wife Jan. Former president Walter Martin was noted for engaging in debates with religious leaders having opposing views. The CRI sponsors the *Bible Answerman,* a syndicated radio program hosted by Hanegraaff.

PUBLICATIONS: *Christian Research Journal: Examining Today's Religious Movements/Giving Reasons for Christian Faith,* a quarterly journal that examines various religious cults and the occult; a quarterly, *Christian Research Newsletter,* that deals with cults and the occult.

Christian School Action
See National Christian Action Coalition

Christian Voice (CV)
This Christian right organization, founded in 1978, became virtually nonexistent after the formation of the American Freedom Coalition in 1987. The CV grew out of the movement opposing civil rights for gays and lesbians in California and was expanded through direct-mail appeals. In 1980 the organization created an associated group, Christians for Reagan, which concentrated on voter registration. The CV focused on such issues as abortion, gay rights, pornography, a school prayer amendment, and the Equal Rights Amendment. It gained publicity through the controversial use of "moral report cards" for members of Congress. In the 1980s, when the religious right concentrated its efforts on influencing the national legislative process, Gary Jarmin served as the major congressional lobbyist for the organization.

Church League of America
George Washington Robnett, an advertising executive, formed the Church League in 1937 to combat the perceived communist threat in America. The organization sought to advance "Christian Americanism" and to oppose centralization of political authority. It opposed President Franklin Roosevelt's "court packing" plan in 1937 and campaigned against his bid for reelection in 1940. In 1956 Edgar C. Bundy succeeded Robnett as the organization's leader. The Church League collected data on individuals and organizations suspected of having communist affiliations and maintained a library of publications the organization considered subversive. One section of the library focuses on John Dewey, whose works were believed to be sympathetic to communism. The organization distributed literature to ministers, informing them of the dangers of communism and socialism, and published a monthly newsletter, *News and Views,* that alerted readers to the activities of leftist organizations. The Church League never attracted a large following and by the mid-1960s had declined into obscurity.

Coalition for Religious Freedom (CRF)
5817 Dawes Avenue
Alexandria, VA 22311-1114
(703) 823-7582
Dan Holdgreiwe, Executive Director

Founded in 1984, reportedly with assistance from Sun Myung Moon's Unification Church, this nondenominational organization, formerly the Committee for Religious Freedom, assists religious groups in dealing with the various levels of government on questions involving freedom of religion. Many of the top religious figures of the 1980s, including Tim LaHaye, Jerry Falwell, Ben Armstrong, Pat Robertson, Rex Humbard, D. James Kennedy, and Jimmy Swaggart, served on the original executive board. The CRF offers advice and information to churches regarding the activities of all branches and levels of government that have an impact on religious institutions. The organization has dealt with such issues as the licensing of ministries, tax laws as applied to religious groups, government health and safety codes for private religious schools, and accreditation controversies.

PUBLICATIONS: *Religious Freedom Alert* (approximately ten issues per year), a tabloid that provides information and commentary on church-state relations.

Committee for Religious Freedom
See Coalition for Religious Freedom

Concerned Women for America (CWA)
1015 15th Street, NW, Suite 1100
Washington, DC 20005
(202) 488-7000
(202) 488-0806 (fax)
http://www.cwfa.org
Beverly LaHaye, President

Beginning in the late 1970s with just nine members, the CWA currently claims a membership of over a half million women. It reports an annual budget of $8 million. The organization conducts educational programs that emphasize the theme of traditional American values and lobbies the national and state legislatures on issues of concern to members. The organization has backed a number of religious right positions, including support for religious freedom, antiabortion legislation, required AIDS testing for marriage license applicants, and a strong national defense. It has opposed the Equal Rights Amendment, pornography, sex and violence in the mass media, condom advertising on television, unisex insurance rates, violence in families, and communism in the Western Hemisphere. The CWA supported President Reagan's efforts to aid the Nicaraguan contras. The CWA, along with Phyllis Schlafly's Eagle Forum, received credit in 1986 for defeating a Vermont equal rights amendment. The CWA has had success as a legal defense foundation, providing legal representation to Christian parents who have challenged local public school policy. The organization has attempted to increase religious right influence at the local level by organizing its members in congressional districts to campaign for favored candidates and to maintain contact with public officials. Members can receive training on how to run for political office, organize a campaign for board of education, and influence public school policy.

PUBLICATIONS: *Family Voice,* a magazine with eleven issues per year.

Council of Bible Believing Churches in the U.S.A. (CBBC)
8442 Cook Way
Thornton, CO 80229-4222
Ovid M. Hepler, President

Founded in 1968 as the American Christian Action Council and later known as the National Council of Bible Believing Churches, this organization was established to assist the International Council of Christian Churches in promoting fundamentalist Christian beliefs based on the Bible and the traditional Christian faith.

PUBLICATIONS: *The Servant,* a monthly newsletter.

Creation Research Society (CRS)
P.O. Box 8263
St. Joseph, MO 64508-8263
http://www.creationresearch.org
Donald B. DeYoung, President

The CRS was founded in 1963 by a group of ten scientists who were unable to publish their research in scientific journals because it was conducted from a creationist perspective. Members of the organization are required to hold the following beliefs: "The Bible is the written word of God"; "All basic types of living things, including humans, were made by direct creative acts of God during the Creation Week described in Genesis"; "The great flood described in Genesis . . . was an historic event worldwide in its extent and effect"; and "We are an organization of Christian men and women of science who accept Jesus Christ as our Lord and Savior." The purpose of the organization is to encourage research and publication that recognizes creation as a valid explanation of the origin of the universe and humankind.

PUBLICATIONS: *CRS Quarterly*, a peer-reviewed journal of original research within the creationist framework.

Eagle Forum (EF)
P.O. Box 618
Alton, IL 62002
(618) 462-5415
(618) 462-8909 (fax)
http://www.eagleforum.org
Phyllis Schlafly, President

Founded in 1975 by Phyllis Schlafly, in part as a reaction to the Supreme Court abortion decision in *Roe v. Wade*, Eagle Forum is a profamily and conservative organization that is active at the local, state, and national governmental levels on issues concerning the family, education, and national defense. The EF supports "traditional morality," private enterprise, and a strong national defense, and opposes an equal rights amendment and sex education in public schools. The Forum focuses on tax policy, advocating an increase in tax exemptions for children and the elimination of what it considers discriminatory tax policy against the traditional family.

PUBLICATIONS: *Phyllis Schlafly Report*, a monthly newsletter containing information on such subjects as education, economics, social policy, and national defense and foreign policy.

Family Research Council (FRC)
801 G Street, NW
Washington, DC 20001
(202) 393-2100
(202) 393-2134 (fax)
http://www.frc.org
Kenneth L. Connor, President

Established in 1981 as the Family Research Group, this organization acquired its present name in 1988. The FRC is an affiliate of James Dobson's radio ministry, *Focus on the Family*. As a research-oriented group with a budget of $14,500,000 per year, it provides information to government agencies and members of Congress on issues such as parental autonomy, the problems of single parents, tax breaks for parents with preschool children, teen pregnancy, abortion, alternatives to public schools, welfare programs, and housing. Gary Bauer, who headed the organization until 2000, served as an aide to Education Secretary William Bennett and as a policy adviser to President Reagan.

PUBLICATIONS: *Washington Watch*, a monthly newsletter.

Family Research Group
See Family Research Council

Focus on the Family (FF)
8605 Explorer Drive
Colorado Springs, CO 80920
(719) 531-3400
(719) 548-4525 (fax)
http://www.family.org
James C. Dobson, President

Focus on the Family was founded in 1977 as the support organization for James Dobson's radio program of the same name that provides Christian guidance to troubled families. The organization encourages the development and maintenance of the family unit in unison with Christian values. Among its many activities, the FF provides information on such family-related topics as marriage and parenting, conducts educational and charitable programs, and provides child-related programs.

PUBLICATIONS: Several monthly magazines, including *Focus on the Family Citizen*, which evaluates legislative activities at all levels; *Teachers in Focus*, for educators in public and private schools; and *Parental Guidance*, a newsletter examining the media and popular culture; various magazines for youth, including *Breakaway* (for teenage boys), *Brio* (for teenage girls), *Clubhouse* (for children), and *Clubhouse Jr.* (for preschoolers).

Free Congress Research and Education Foundation (FCF)
717 Second Street, NE
Washington, DC 20002
(202) 546-3000
(202) 543-8425 (fax)
http://www.freecongress.org
Paul M. Weyrich, President

Founded in 1977, the Free Congress Research and Education Foundation, although not an explicitly religious organization, emphasizes cultural conservatism and the need to maintain traditional Judeo-Christian values. The organization claims that multiculturalism and "political correctness" are major threats to the American culture and has concluded that "activist" judges are a main enemy. During President Bill Clinton's administration, the FCF established the Judicial Selection Monitoring Project to oppose judicial appointments of liberal candidates. The organization also expresses concern about alleged attempts of the national government to eavesdrop on private telephone and e-mail communication. The views of the FCF are disseminated on such television programs as *Next Revolution, Endangered Liberties, Legal Notebook,* and *Taking Back Our Constitution,* which appear via America's Voice, a satellite network.

PUBLICATIONS: *Essays on Our Times* and *Policy Insights,* monthly series treating cultural and political issues; *Weyrich Insider,* a monthly newsletter; occasional books, special reports, and monographs.

Freedom Council (FC)
Pat Robertson began the Freedom Council in 1981 and terminated it in 1986. It was headquartered in Virginia Beach, Virginia. Focusing on freedom of religion, the FC attempted to educate Christians on religious and civil liberties. The organization supported litigation on such issues as school prayer and freedom of religion in the workplace. As a grassroots organization, the FC encouraged citizens to write to their representatives on issues related to freedom of religion. Before its termination, charges of financial irregularities arose involving the use of donations to the Freedom Council for Robertson's political activities. The organization was succeeded by the Christian Coalition.

Institute for Creation Research (ICR)
10946 Woodside Avenue North
Santee, CA 92071
(619) 448-0900
(619) 448-3469 (fax)
http://www.icr.org
John D. Morris, President

Established in 1970, the Institute for Creation Research is based on a belief in creationism and biblical inerrancy. Although originally the research arm of Christian Heritage College, the ICR became a separate entity in 1981. The Institute asserts that creation science should be taught along with the theory of evolution in the public schools and that scientific as well as biblical creationism should be a part of the curriculum at Christian schools. According to the ICR, among the postulates of scientific creationism are the following: each major kind of plant and animal was created functionally complete and did not develop from some other kind of organism; the first humans were originally created in their present form; scientific evidence exists for a relatively recent creation of the earth; and there is always the possibility of divine intervention in natural laws.

PUBLICATIONS: Various research monographs.

International Council of Christian Churches (ICCC)
P.O. Box 190
Collingswood, NJ 08108
(856) 858-0422
http://www.iccc.org.sg
Carl McIntire, President

The ICCC, formed in 1948 under the leadership of Carl McIntire, was the international version of his American Council of Christian Churches (ACCC). The organization was established as a direct response to the initiation of the World Council of Churches (WCC). McIntire objected to that organization's emphasis upon ecumenism among Protestant churches and its willingness to converse with Roman Catholics and Jews. In the 1950s leaders of the ICCC, along with the ACCC, cooperated with Senator Joseph McCarthy and the House Un-American Activities Committee in identifying possible communist influences in the clergy. The ICCC serves as a gathering point for fundamentalist churches worldwide and encourages a fundamentalist Christianity uncompromisingly opposed to all forms of modernism.

PUBLICATIONS: Regional papers.

John Birch Society (JBS)
P.O. Box 8040
Appleton, WI 54912
(920) 749-3780
(920) 749-5062 (fax)
http://www.jbs.org
John F. McManus, President

Founded by Robert Welch in 1958, the John Birch Society, although best known for what it opposes—communism, socialism, totalitarian government, the United Nations, and federal regulatory agencies—maintains a positive, though vague, image of a future world made better through the help of God. The organization professes a belief in the traditional moral values as found in the Judeo-Christian heritage and considers the family to be the most important element in society. Local chapters conduct letter-writing campaigns to public officials and distribute the society's literature. The organization supports a speakers' bureau and a seminar program.

PUBLICATIONS: *JBS Bulletin,* a monthly publication, and *The New American,* a biweekly newsmagazine.

Kingdom Identity Ministries (KIM)
P.O. Box 1021
Harrison, AR 72602
(870) 741-1119
http://www.kingidentity.com

Kingdom Identity Ministries is an extreme religious right organization that describes itself as "a politically incorrect Christian Identity outreach ministry to God's chosen (true Israel, the White, European peoples)." In 1998 the KIM assumed control of Your Heritage Ministry, which had been established in the 1950s by Bertrand Comparet, whom the organization describes as "the greatest Bible scholar of the twentieth century."

PUBLICATIONS: Several of Bertrand Comparet's writings as well as other books and tracts on such subjects as racial identity, biblical law, "God's Enemies," and the "Anti-Christ Conspiracy" are offered for sale.

Liberty Federation (LF)
P.O. Box 2000
Lynchburg, VA 24506
(804) 582-7310
P. Gilsman, President

Founded in 1979 as the Moral Majority Foundation by Jerry Falwell and given its present name in 1986, the organization never reached the prominence of its forerunner. The Liberty Federation has not been active since the Moral Majority was terminated in 1989. It still maintains an address and telephone number in Lynchburg, Virginia, claims a membership of 72,000 ministers and four million laypersons, and reports active engagement in persuading conservatives to register and vote for candidates that support traditional values as a way of responding to moral decline in America. The organization points to legalized abortion, pornography, and advocacy of homosexual rights as evidence of that moral decline.

PUBLICATIONS: None.

Moral Majority (MM)

Established in 1979 and finally terminated in 1989, three years after its activities had been shifted to the newly formed Liberty Federation, Moral Majority was the best known of the religious right organizations of the 1980s. It was established in order to activate the religious right politically. Moral Majority concentrated on the major religious right issues, including opposition to homosexuality, abortion, pornography, and the Equal Rights Amendment, and support for school prayer. The organization consisted of the Moral Majority Foundation, which claimed tax exemption; Moral Majority, Inc., which served as the political lobbying branch; and the Moral Majority Political Action Committee, the part of the organization responsible for raising campaign funds to support candidates for public office. The organization published the periodical *Moral Majority Report*. Although Moral Majority gained influence over the national political agenda during the early 1980s, it acquired a negative public image due in part to the aggressive lobbying activities of the organization and its leader, Jerry Falwell. Falwell resigned as president in November 1987.

National Association of Evangelicals (NAE)
P.O. Box 28
Wheaton, IL 60189
(708) 665-0500
(708) 665-8575 (fax)
http://www.nae.net
Dr. Billy A. Melvin, Executive Director

This interdenominational organization was founded in 1942 to provide an alternative to the National (then Federal) Council of Churches and to serve as a medium of cooperation among evangelical churches and organizations. Reporting a membership of fifteen million, the NAE includes 50,000 churches representing more than seventy-seven denominations. Such groups as Assemblies of God, Baptists, and evangelical wings of the Lutheran, Methodist, and Presbyterian denominations are represented in the membership. The organization sponsors various events, such as the Washington Insight Briefing and the Washington Student Seminar. The NAE has demonstrated explicitly conservative political preferences. For instance, in 1983 President Ronald Reagan chose an NAE meeting to make his well-publicized speech in which he referred to the former Soviet Union as the "evil empire." President Reagan spoke before the organization again in 1984, calling for a school prayer amendment to the Constitution. The NAE is associated with the Evangelical Fellowship of Mission Agencies and National Religious Broadcasters.

PUBLICATIONS: *NAE Washington Insight,* a monthly newsletter reporting on national government activities of concern to evangelical leaders; *National Association of Evangelicals—Dateline,* a quarterly newsletter providing a preview of events and meetings and information on state organizations; *National Evangelical Directory,* a biennial publication listing various evangelical organizations; and *United Evangelical Action: A Call to Action from the NAE,* a bimonthly reporting on organization activities and providing a calendar of future events.

National Christian Action Coalition (NCAC)
No longer in existence, this organization was established by Robert Billings in 1978. Billings left the organization after one year to become the first executive director of Moral Majority. He was succeeded at the NCAC by his son, William Billings. The NCAC was preceded by Christian School Action, an organization that Robert Billings formed in 1977. Billings initiated the NCAC in reaction to the Internal Revenue Service's attempts to withdraw the tax-exempt status of private schools that were judged racially discriminatory. The organization included the Christian Voter's Victory Fund (a political action committee), the Christian Education and Research Foundation, and the New Century Foundation (a publishing enterprise). Support declined during the early 1980s, and William Billings finally terminated the organization in 1985.

National Coalition for the Protection of
Children and Families (NCPCF)
800 Compton Road
Cincinnati, OH 45231
(513) 521-6227

(513) 521-6337 (fax)
http://www.nationalcoalition.org
Rick Schatz, President

In 1983 Reverend Jerry Kirk, concerned about the spread of pornography in the United States, established the National Coalition Against Pornography, now known as the National Coalition for the Protection of Children and Families (NCPCF), an ecumenical organization devoted to assisting religious, civic, and legal groups opposed to obscenity and child pornography. The organization calls for strict enforcement of obscenity and child protection laws and participates in efforts to strengthen those laws. The organization plays an educational role by distributing written materials and video- and audiotapes that give advice on how to combat pornography, and holds the annual National City Leaders Conference.

PUBLICATIONS: *NCPCF in Action,* a quarterly newsletter.

National Legal Foundation (NLF)

P.O. Box 64427
Virginia Beach, VA 23467
(757) 424-4242
(757) 420-0855 (fax)
http://www.nlf.net
Steven W. Fitschen, Executive Director

This public-interest law firm, founded in 1985 by Pat Robertson and originally financed by the Christian Broadcasting Network, offers legal services to defend constitutional liberties, especially religious freedom. The organization prepares legal briefs and educational materials dealing with church-state issues. Attorneys associated with the foundation choose to become involved in cases that are potentially precedent setting and that have national application. In the Supreme Court case *Westside Community Schools v. Mergens* (1990), Foundation attorneys successfully argued for the right of students to form a campus Bible club under the 1984 Equal Access Act.

PUBLICATIONS: *The Minuteman,* a quarterly newsletter; *Foundations of Freedom,* a booklet.

National Religious Broadcasters (NRB)

7839 Ashton Avenue
Manassas, VA 20109
(703) 330-7000

(703) 330-7100 (fax)
http://www.nrb.org
Brandt Gustavson, President

The membership of this organization includes religious radio and television producers, owners, and operators in the United States and worldwide. Founded in 1940, the NRB is a major data source about Christian broadcasting. The organization protects religious broadcasters' access to the airwaves and conducts meetings at which fund-raising techniques and new technology can be shared among members. The NRB provides religious programming to its members and operates religious radio and television stations. In 1988 the organization adopted a new financial code of ethics as a result of scandals involving television evangelists. The new code requires member organizations to provide annual income and expenditure statements to the NRB's executive committee. The organization's leaders have shown a preference for conservative political candidates. For instance, in 1988 all major Republican presidential hopefuls spoke at the NRB convention, while no Democratic candidates were invited. The NRB is associated with the National Association of Evangelicals.

PUBLICATIONS: *Directory of Religious Broadcasters,* an annual listing of those engaged in religious broadcasting, including radio and television stations and programmers; *NRB Magazine,* monthly.

National Right to Life Committee (NRLC)
419 Seventh Street, NW, Suite 500
Washington, DC 20004
(202) 626-8800
(202) 737-9189 (fax)
http://www.nrlc.org
David N. O'Steen, Executive Director

Formed in 1973 in reaction to the Supreme Court's *Roe v. Wade* abortion decision, this organization employs a wide variety of strategies, including testifying at congressional hearings, writing legislation, and litigating to protect "all innocent human life" threatened by abortion, euthanasia, and infanticide. The organization supports an amendment to the Constitution that would prohibit abortions. Due to the NRLC's willingness to compromise and its opposition to civil disobedience, this antiabortion organization is considered more moderate than other groups.

PUBLICATIONS: *National Right to Life News,* eighteen issues per year; books and pamphlets.

Operation Save America (OSA)
P.O. Box 140066
Dallas, TX 75374
(803) 821-8441
http://www.operationsaveamerica.org
Philip L. ("Flip") Benham, National Director

Operation Save America, which calls Americans to "repentance" for more than twenty-five million abortions since 1973, was originally founded as Project Life in 1984 by Randall Terry and his wife, who attempted to dissuade women from entering abortion clinics. The organization took on its present name in 1986 when it began the more confrontational tactic of blocking entrances to abortion clinics and conducting large demonstrations and sit-ins in order to "rescue" innocent children. Demonstrators often refused to leave, thus forcing police to arrest and carry them away. The OSA claims that over 50,000 arrests have resulted from such demonstrations and that nearly 1,000 abortions have been prevented. The organization has attempted to discourage doctors who perform abortions by publicizing their names and confronting them in public places, and has threatened similar treatment for physicians prescribing the abortion pill RU-486.

PUBLICATIONS: *William J. Murray Report,* a monthly newsletter.

Order of the Cross Society (OCS)
P.O. Box 7638
Fort Lauderdale, FL 33338-7638
(954) 564-5588
Reverend K. Chandler, Steward

Initiated in 1975, the OCS advocates the introduction of biblical principles into governmental organization and operation. Strong family ties and honest business practices are the organization's basic goals. The OCS encourages citizens not to accept government actions inconsistent with Christian principles. Unacceptable government policies include legalized abortion, government subsidies, and Social Security.

PUBLICATIONS: *Envoy,* an occasional publication.

Plymouth Rock Foundation (PRF)
1120 Long Pond Road

Plymouth, MA 02360-2626
(603) 876-4685
(603) 876-4128 (fax)
http://www.plymrock.org
Rus Walton, Executive Director

This organization, founded in 1970, wants to base American society and government on biblical principles. The foundation wishes to "restore" America as a Christian republic through the activities of Christians on an individual basis. Christian committees of correspondence have been established to promote action at the local level. The second week in November the Foundation holds America's Christian Heritage, an annual workshop and seminar for Christian leaders focusing on biblical understandings of government and education and the nation's Christian history.

PUBLICATIONS: *American Christian Heritage Series* and the *American Christian Statesmen Series,* books; *The Correspondent,* a monthly newsletter that provides information about local committee activities.

Pro-American Books
See Christian Research

Reasons To Believe (RTB)
P.O. Box 5978
Pasadena, CA 91117
(626) 335-1480
(626) 852-0178 (fax)
http://www.reasons.org
Hugh Ross, President

This organization, founded in 1986, strives for an explanation of creation that is compatible with the Bible and at the same time scientifically sound. It is affiliated with Campus Crusade for Christ International and the National Association of Evangelicals. Reasons To Believe seeks to answer skeptics and to offer Christians a stronger foundation for their faith.

PUBLICATIONS: *Facts and Faith,* published quarterly, deals with scientific issues relevant to the Bible; *Facts for Faith,* a quarterly magazine offering scientific evidence confirming Christian beliefs.

Religious Freedom Coalition (RFC)
P.O. Box 77511
Washington, DC 20013

(800) 650-7664
William J. Murray, Chairman

William Murray, the son of renowned atheist Madalyn Murray O'Hair who converted to Christianity in 1980, established the Religious Freedom Coalition in Fredericksburg, Virginia, in 1996. In 1998 the RFC organized religious leaders and conservative voters to support congressional passage of the Religious Freedom Amendment. Although the proposed amendment failed, the organization continues to lobby Congress to pass legislation supporting traditional family values. In addition, the RFC has supported a bill to allow the posting of the Ten Commandments in public places. The organization has supported various measures to place limitations on the right to an abortion and fetal tissue research. Murray and other members of the RFC go to atheist conventions, attempting to convert members to Christianity, and run advertisements in local newspapers.

PUBLICATIONS: *William J. Murray Report,* a monthly newsletter.

Religious Heritage of America (RHA)
1750 South Brentwood Boulevard, Suite 502
St. Louis, MO 63144
(314) 962-0001
Barbara J. Eichhorst, Executive Director

Religious Heritage of America, founded in 1951 as Washington Pilgrimage, seeks to preserve traditional American values and attempts to provide individuals with a clearer definition of those values. In 1954 the organization lobbied successfully for the inclusion of "under God" in the Pledge of Allegiance. Each year the RHA sponsors trips to religious, cultural, and historical sights.

PUBLICATIONS: *Religious Heritage of America,* a quarterly newsletter.

Religious Roundtable (RR)
P.O. Box 11467
Memphis, TN 38111
(901) 458-3795
Edward E. McAteer, President

Founded in 1979 by Ed McAteer to involve fundamentalist ministers and their congregations in politics, Religious Roundtable is concerned with the moral conditions of America, which the organization associates with the very survival of the Judeo-Christian tradition and Western civilization. James Robison was initially the organization's vice president. The Roundtable became active in the 1980 presidential campaign, organizing ministers in support of Ronald Reagan. After McAteer failed to win a U.S. Senate seat in 1984, the Roundtable became less prominent. The Religious Roundtable has emphasized such issues as child abuse, homosexuality, and pornography, and has lobbied to preserve a strong national defense through its affiliate, Roundtable Issues and Answers.

PUBLICATIONS: None.

Rutherford Institute (RI)
P.O. Box 7482
1445 East Rio Road
Charlottesville, VA 22906-7482
(804) 978-3888
(804) 978-1789 (fax)
http://www.rutherford.org
John W. Whitehead, President

John Whitehead began the institute in 1982, naming it after Samuel Rutherford, a seventeenth-century Scottish minister who argued that all persons, including royalty, must abide by the civil law. The Institute has experienced success using litigation and the threat of litigation to support individuals believed to have been denied their right to religious liberty. The Institute concentrates its efforts on such issues as freedom of speech, parental rights, family values, school prayer, home schooling, and abortion.

PUBLICATIONS: *Freedom under Fire,* a monthly newspaper.

Traditional Values Coalition (TVC)
P.O. Box 940
Anaheim, CA 92815-0940
(714) 520-0300
http://www.traditionalvalues.org
Reverend Louis P. Sheldon, Chairman

Formed in 1982 as the California chapter of Tim LaHaye's American Coalition for Traditional Values, the TVC is concerned with educating Christians about contemporary issues, with the intention that they will become politically active in support of traditional Christian and profamily values. The coalition focuses on such issues as public school prayer, abortion, sex education in the public schools, and gay rights legislation. It opposes any proposal to allow professed homosexuals in the military and has supported prohibiting them from taking part in the Boy Scouts. The TVC has reportedly succeeded in soliciting the support of African American conservative Christians, especially in California, on issues such as gay rights and condom distribution in public schools. Louis Sheldon's daughter, Andrea Sheldon Lafferty, serves as the TVC's executive director of lobbying activities in Washington, DC.

PUBLICATIONS: *Traditional Values Report,* an occasional newsletter.

Trinity Broadcasting Network (TBN)
P.O. Box A
Santa Ana, CA 92711
(714) 832-2950
http://www.tbn.org
Paul Crouch, President

Since Paul Crouch established the Trinity Broadcasting Network in 1973, it has become the largest Christian television network, broadcasting on more than 530 stations worldwide. The station has been successful at providing a wide range of programming as an alternative to the secular media, emphasizing "faith in God, love of family, and patriotic pride." Among the televangelists whose programs appear on TBN are Kenneth Copeland, Creflo Dollar, John Hagee, Marilyn Hickey, Benny Hinn, T. D. Jakes, Rod Parsley, Fred Price, James Robison, and Jack Van Impe. On TBN's "flagship production," *Praise the Lord,* Crouch, his wife Jan, and others interview guests on a lavishly furnished set. Striving to provide entertainment for Christians, TBN has opened Trinity Music City in Nashville, Tennessee, offering concerts, dramas, seminars, and other special events. Various movies intended for theater release have been produced, including *The Omega Code* (1999), a fictional treatment of the end-time events prophesied in Revelation.

PUBLICATIONS: None.

Woman's Christian Temperance Union (WCTU)
1730 Chicago Avenue
Evanston, IL 60201-4584
(847) 864-1397
http://www.wctu.org
Sarah Frances Ward, President

The oldest continuing women's organization in the United States, the WCTU was established in 1874 by a group of women who expressed concern about the dangers that alcohol posed for families and society. The organization advocates temperance, which it defines as "moderation in all things healthful" and "total abstinence from all things harmful." Membership involves signing a pledge of total abstinence. The WCTU achieved its greatest success in 1919 with ratification of the Eighteenth Amendment prohibiting the manufacture, sale, or transportation of alcoholic beverages in the United States. However, the obvious failure of this policy to control the use of alcohol resulted in ratification in 1933 of the Twenty-first Amendment repealing Prohibition. Nonetheless, the WCTU continued the campaign against the use of alcoholic beverages as well as drugs and tobacco. At times it issues statements on other issues. For instance, in 2000 the organization distributed a pamphlet disapproving of homosexuality.

PUBLICATIONS: *The Union Signal*, a quarterly journal.

World's Christian Fundamentals Association (WCFA)

The WCFA, founded in 1919 under the leadership of William Bell Riley and other noted conservative leaders such as J. Frank Norris and John Roach Straton, played a major role in forming the tenets of fundamentalist Christian belief. At its inaugural meeting in Philadelphia, the association adopted a nine-point Confession of Faith that included belief in the verbal inerrancy of the Bible, the premillennial return of Christ, the trinity, the deity of Jesus, the sinfulness of humanity, "substitutionary atonement," bodily resurrection of Jesus, justification by faith, and bodily resurrection of the just and the unjust. During the 1920s the association became embroiled in the question of evolution, supporting antievolution legislation in twenty states. The WCFA selected William Jennings Bryan to serve as its attorney at the famous Scopes trial in 1925. Riley resigned the presidency in 1929 and the organizational effectiveness of the association declined thereafter. A number of factors led to the WCFA's decline, including the extreme individualism of its leaders, the coming of the depression that diverted attention away from the concerns of the organization, and the ill-fated struggle over evolution. The association lingered on into the early 1950s.

Organizations Critical of the Religious Right

American Atheists (AA)
P.O. Box 5733
Parsippany, NJ 07053-6733
http://www.atheists.org
Ellen Johnson, President

Established by Madalyn Murray O'Hair in 1963, the AA works to achieve the civil liberties of atheists and a strict separation of government and religion. Formation of the organization resulted from the legal efforts of O'Hair to challenge instances of government support of organized religion. In 1995 she disappeared, and subsequently an associate was charged with her murder. When O'Hair disappeared, Ellen Johnson became head of the AA. The AA opposes religious right groups on several issues, including prayer in the public schools, religious accounts of creation, religious ceremony in government, and the claimed status of the Bible as the revealed word of God. In addition to regarding prayer in public institutions as unconstitutional, the AA insists that people cannot receive help through prayer but must rely instead on their own self-understanding and abilities.

PUBLICATIONS: *AANEWS*, an e-mail newsletter.

American Humanist Association (AHA)
7 Hardwood Drive
P.O. Box 1188
Amherst, NY 14226-7188
(716) 839-5080
(716) 839-5079 (fax)
http://www.infidels.org
Tony Hileman, Executive Director

The religious right finds many of the principles of this organization to be antithetical to its beliefs. The AHA holds that human beings are dependent on natural and social foundations alone and denies the relevance of any supernatural being. The organization encourages education in ethics as a substitute for religious training. Humanist counselors are certified with the same legal status as pastors or priests. Among the awards the AHA makes is the annual John Dewey Humanist Award.

PUBLICATIONS: *The Humanist,* a bimonthly magazine; *Free Mind,* a bimonthly newsletter. The organization also has a list of publications and audio- and videotapes critical of the religious right.

Americans United for Separation of Church and State (AU)
518 C Street, NE
Washington, DC 20002
(202) 466-3234
(202) 466-2587 (fax)
http://www.au.org
Barry W. Lynn, Executive Director

Americans United for Separation of Church and State monitors religious involvement in the public realm and takes part in lawsuits challenging such involvement. It has opposed efforts to introduce voluntary prayer in the public schools, establish school voucher programs, and post the Ten Commandments in public places. In election years the organization is especially concerned about religious groups intervening in partisan politics. For instance, in 2000 the organization mailed over 280,000 letters to churches across the nation, warning church leaders about the legal pitfalls of distributing Christian Coalition voter guides to their congregations. Americans United has asked the Internal Revenue Service to investigate the partisan political activities of churches.

PUBLICATIONS: *Church and State,* a monthly magazine.

Anti-Defamation League (ADL)
823 United Nations Plaza
New York, NY 10017
(212) 490-2525
(212) 867-0779 (fax)
http://www.adl.org
Abraham H. Foxman, Director

Founded in 1913, the ADL, also known as the Anti-Defamation League of B'nai B'rith, states as its goals the elimination of anti-Semitism and the achievement of justice for all individuals. The organization encourages better relations among differing religious faiths. The ADL supports democratic values and opposes extremist groups it considers threats to democracy. In recent years the organization has published materials, such as its 1994 report, *The Religious Right: The Assault on Tolerance and Pluralism in America,* that are critical of religious right groups and leaders.

PUBLICATIONS: *ADL on the Frontline,* a bimonthly newsletter; *Facts,* quarterly.

Council for Secular Humanism (CSH)
P.O. Box 664
Amherst, NY 14226-0664
(800) 458-1366
(716) 636-1733 (fax)
http://www.secularhumanism.org
Paul Kurtz, Chairman

The Council for Secular Humanism rejects any dependence on a transcendent being, emphasizing instead the force of reason and scientific inquiry, individual responsibility, human values and compassion, and the need for cooperation and tolerance. The organization accepts naturalism, the view that physical laws are not superseded by nonmaterial or supernatural entities. Claims about the occurrence of miracles are viewed with great skepticism. The Council conducts campaigns on ethical issues, holds conferences, offers educational courses, and distributes literature on secular humanism. The organization is often critical of the activities of religious right organizations, including their profamily stance, position on homosexuality, and attempts to proselytize.

PUBLICATIONS: *Free Inquiry,* a quarterly journal; *Secular Humanist Bulletin,* a quarterly newsletter.

Feminist Majority Foundation (FMF)
1600 Wilson Boulevard
Arlington, VA 22209
(703) 522-2214
(703) 522-2219 (fax)
http://www.feminist.org
Eleanor Smeal, President

Established in 1987 by five women, the Feminist Majority Foundation strives to improve the status of women and their role in making public policy by supporting research, education, and political action. It defines feminism as "the policy, practice or advocacy of political, economic, and social equality for women." The organization seeks to eliminate illegitimate forms of discrimination associated with sex, race, sexual orientation, age, religion, national origin, disability, and marital status. The FMF has come into conflict with the religious right particularly over issues relating to the role and status of women in society. It supported the introduction of the abortion pill RU-486 and backs the right of abortion clinics to operate unhindered by right-to-life groups. It has criticized the Southern Baptist Convention's boycott of the Walt Disney Company for "gay-friendly" policies.

PUBLICATIONS: *Feminist Majority Report*, a quarterly newsletter.

Freedom from Religion Foundation (FFRF)
P.O. Box 750
Madison, WI 53701
(608) 256-8900
http://www.ffrf.org
Anne Nicol Gaylor, President

Founded in 1978, this organization of atheists, agnostics, secularists, and humanists campaigns against fundamentalist religious beliefs, supports the separation of church and state, and opposes fundamentalist religious attacks on the rights of women and homosexuals. The organization has worked to end prayer in schools and at public events and investigates charges of sexual abuse made against the clergy. Films and public service announcements for television have been produced.

PUBLICATIONS: *Freethought Today*, a newspaper published ten times per year.

Institute for First Amendment Studies (IFAS)
P.O. Box 589
Great Barrington, MA 01230
(413) 528-3800
http://www.ifas.org
Skipp Porteous, National Director

Established in 1984 by former fundamentalist minister Skipp Porteous and attorney Barbara Simon, the IFAS attempts to counter the political activities of religious right groups largely through the dissemination of information. The organization gathers data and prepares reports about individuals and groups it considers a threat to First Amendment freedoms. The institute has a collection of hundreds of religious right publications. IFAS activities include attending religious right conferences and interviewing leaders.

PUBLICATIONS: *The Freedom Writer*, a bimonthly newsletter.

National Coalition Against Censorship (NCAC)
275 Seventh Avenue
New York, NY 10001

(212) 807-6222
(212) 807-6245
http://www.ncac.org
Joan E. Bertin, Executive Director

Founded in 1974, the NCAC is an alliance of fifty literary, artistic, religious, educational, professional, labor, and civil liberties organizations striving to defend the First Amendment values of freedom of speech and the press by opposing restraints on open communication and censorship. The coalition attempts to counter the activities of religious right organizations that are considered a danger to free speech. For instance, the NCAC has come to the defense of the *Harry Potter* series of children's books and opposed any outside censorship of Hollywood films, although it has called for movie executives to provide high-quality entertainment.

PUBLICATIONS: *Censorship News,* issued quarterly.

People for the American Way (PFAW)
2000 M Street, NW, Suite 400
Washington, DC 20036
(202) 467-4999
(202) 293-2672 (fax)
http://www.pfaw.org
Ralph G. Neas, President

Television producer Norman Lear established the PFAW in 1980 to counter the alleged antidemocratic and discordant effects on the American political process of religious right leaders and organizations such as Jerry Falwell and the Moral Majority. The religious right is seen as using religion to further its own political ambitions. According to the PFAW, traditional American values include cultural diversity, pluralism, the continuing importance of the individual, and freedom of expression. The organization works for tolerance and respect for diversity by monitoring religious right activities, opposing censorship, and supporting such rights as reproductive choice.

6

Selected Print Resources

Works about the Religious Right

The works listed in this section are divided into three categories. The biographical section presents a sampling of studies dealing with important figures in the development of the religious right. The section on general religious studies includes works that investigate more generally the relationship between religion and the social and political environment. The last section contains sources on the religious right and its activities in American society and politics.

Biography

Albert, James A. *Jim Bakker: Miscarriage of Justice?* Chicago: Open Court, 1997.

The scandal that forced Jim Bakker's resignation as head of the PTL organization and resulted in his conviction on fraud charges shook the public's confidence in televangelism. Albert details Bakker's rise and fall as a nationally known televangelist and reports on the trial that resulted in his imprisonment. The author concludes that although Bakker may have used PTL funds carelessly, he likely did not intentionally defraud contributors.

Boston, Robert. *The Most Dangerous Man in America?* Amherst, NY: Prometheus, 1996.

Robert Boston, assistant director of communication for Americans United for the Separation of Church and State, examines the objectives of Pat Robertson, the Christian Coalition, and the Coalition's American Center for Law and Justice. He criticizes Robertson's extremist politics, which, according to the author, involve an attempt to override the constitutional separation of church and state in order to establish a theocratic system. Boston accuses Robertson of attempting to manipulate the public through his media outlets, hypocritically changing political positions, and distorting the evidence on political issues.

Frady, Marshall. *Billy Graham: A Parable of American Righteousness.* Boston: Little, Brown, 1979.

Well researched and based on extensive interviews, this biography provides a largely sympathetic portrait of the famous evangelist. The author emphasizes Graham's basic innocence, which led to his failure to deal adequately with political events, especially during the turbulent 1960s.

Harding, Susan Friend. *The Book of Jerry Falwell: Fundamentalist Language and Politics.* Princeton, NJ: Princeton University Press, 2000.

Harding, an anthropologist, investigates the rise of religious right leader Jerry Falwell during the 1980s and the ways in which he altered the nature of fundamentalism in the United States. The author focuses on fundamentalists' use of language, shedding light on the continued success of religious right leaders such as Falwell in such areas as fund raising.

Harrell, David Edwin, Jr. *Pat Robertson: A Personal, Religious, and Political Portrait.* San Francisco: Harper and Row, 1987.

A political biography written shortly before Robertson's 1988 presidential bid, this book is a balanced and useful study of the Virginia televangelist. Divided into three parts, the work presents a biographical overview, a survey of Robertson's religious views, and a brief review of his political thinking on a variety of issues. Harrell also discusses Robertson's success in establishing the Christian Broadcasting Network.

Lippy, Charles H., ed. *Twentieth-Century Shapers of Popular Religion.* Westport, CT: Greenwood Press, 1989.

This biographical volume includes entries on over sixty people who have played important roles in the development of popular religious movements in the United States. Many of the biographical sketches are of religious right leaders.

Martin, William. *A Prophet with Honor: The Billy Graham Story.* New York: William Morrow, 1991.

This biography of Billy Graham offers insights into the well-known and respected evangelist, describing his youth, early adult years, and preparation for the ministry. Martin presents interesting details about Graham's early years, including his job as a successful Fuller Brush salesman before he entered the Florida Bible Institute. Graham first gained national attention when the media widely reported a meeting with President Harry Truman. Graham's association with Presidents Dwight Eisenhower and Richard Nixon kept him in the national limelight during the 1950s and 1960s. Martin explains the successful marketing techniques used by the Billy Graham Evangelistic Association and recounts Graham's evangelistic activities in various parts of the world.

Russell, Charles Allyn. *Voices of American Fundamentalism: Seven Biographical Studies.* Philadelphia: Westminster Press, 1976.

This exceptionally good study illustrates the diversity and complexity of fundamentalism through the careers of seven prominent fundamentalists: J. Frank Norris, John Roach Straton, William Bell Riley, Jasper C. Massee, J. Gresham Machen, William J. Bryan, and Clarence E. Macartney. Although a varied and colorful group, they were unified in their opposition to "modernism."

Simon, Merrill. *Jerry Falwell and the Jews.* Middle Village, NY: Jonathan David, 1999.

This reissue of Simon's book on Jerry Falwell and his public pronouncements regarding Judaism and Israel provides insights into the religious right leader's political stances, which mirror those of many conservative Christians. Simon, who died in 1997, was a political adviser in Israel and a research associate at the Tel Aviv University Center for Strategic Studies.

Straub, Gerard Thomas. *Salvation for Sale: An Insider's View of Pat Robertson's Ministry.* New York: Prometheus, 1986.

Straub, former producer for Pat Robertson's *The 700 Club* television program, writes of his increasing doubts about Robertson and television evangelism in general. Writing prior to Robertson's 1988 presidential bid, the author questions Robertson's media strategies.

Religious Studies

Ahlstrom, Sydney E. *A Religious History of the American People.* New Haven, CT: Yale University Press, 1972.

An extensive analysis of America's religious history, this book examines the moral development of Americans through the evaluation of varied religious movements, especially in the nineteenth and twentieth centuries. Ahlstrom examines such topics as regional beliefs, separation of church and state, and the relationship between religion and scientific progress. The book provides an excellent context for studying the Christian right.

Allen, Leslie H., ed. *Bryan and Darrow at Dayton.* New York: Russell and Russell, 1925.

Allen offers an account of the famous trial of John T. Scopes, who was prosecuted for violating a state law that forbade teaching evolution in the public schools of Tennessee. Published soon after the trial, the book provides portions of the official court record. In an attempt to be impartial, the editor includes an appendix in which appear excerpts from Genesis and a biology textbook of the times.

Ammerman, Nancy Tatom. *Bible Believers: Fundamentalists in the Modern World.* New Brunswick, NJ: Rutgers University Press, 1987.

A noted sociologist examines the conflict between "moderates" and "fundamentalists" within the Southern Baptist Convention, a conflict that by 1989 had been resolved in favor of the fundamentalists. According to Ammerman, a "gentlemanly consensus" among Southern Baptists of varying degrees of theological conservatism eroded as the South became more urban. Frightened by the changes inherent in urbanization, fundamentalists not only sought security in the "inerrant Word," but also outmaneuvered moderates for control of the convention.

Balch, David L. *Homosexuality, Science, and the "Plain Sense" of Scripture.* Grand Rapids, MI: Eerdmans, 2000.

These twelve essays written by biblical scholars, theologians, and psychologists present different interpretations of biblical statements (in Genesis, Leviticus, Romans, and I Corinthians) about the morality of homosexuality and evaluate scientific research on the subject. The book clarifies the viewpoints taken on the issue of homosexuality.

Balmer, Randall. *Mine Eyes Have Seen the Glory: A Journey into the Evangelical Subculture in America.* New York: Oxford University Press, 1993.

This highly readable religious travelogue through America's heartland focuses on fundamentalists, charismatics, and Pentecostals. Balmer illuminates the diversity of America's evangelical subculture. His journey took him from a holiness meeting in Florida to an Indian reservation in the Dakotas to a fundamentalist Bible camp in New York. This work is a must for anyone prone to easy generalization about evangelicalism.

———. *Grant Us Courage: Travels along the Mainline of American Protestantism.* New York: Oxford University Press, 1996.

In this sequel to *Mine Eyes Have Seen the Glory,* Balmer portrays his visits to twelve mainline Protestant churches that were originally the subjects of a series of articles published in *Christian Century.* Although the highly individualized treatments are not conducive to drawing generalizations, they do suggest possible explanations for the losses that such churches have suffered at the hands of more fundamentalist and evangelical movements.

Barr, James. *Fundamentalism.* Philadelphia: Westminster Press, 1978.

A British scholar, Barr has spent considerable time in America. This insightful study calls attention to links between British and American fundamentalism. According to Barr, fundamentalism has been more denominational in America than in Britain, resulting in bitter intradenominational splits in the United States. By contrast, fundamentalism in Britain has been nondenominational.

Baumgartner, Frederic J. *Longing for the End: A History of Millennialism in Western Civilization.* New York: Palgrave, 2001.

Baumgartner explores the history of various cults and sects that were established on the belief that the end of the world was imminent. Many of the groups, including some of recent origin, such as the Branch Davidians and Heaven's Gate, have led to violence, either against themselves or others.

Bawer, Bruce. *Stealing Jesus: How Fundamentalism Betrays Christianity.* New York: Crown, 1997.

Bawer argues that fundamentalist Christian movements, far too legalistic and lacking in compassion and a mission of loving service, fail to meet the requirements of Christianity. He investigates the rise of fundamentalism from the nineteenth century, focusing on John Nelson Darby, C. I. Scofield, and the rise of dispensational premillennialism, the belief that Christ will return to reign for a thousand years. Bawer investigates the work of more contemporary religious right figures such as Pat Robertson, Ralph Reed, Hal Lindsey, and James Dobson.

Bloom, Harold. *The American Religion: The Emergence of the Post-Christian Nation.* Hyattsville, MD: Daedalus, 1992.

Although he claims that America is not a Christian nation, but rather is dominated by a form of Gnosticism, Bloom nonetheless observes that the nation is "religion soaked." Americans tend to believe in a personal and loving God. The author examines a number of Christian movements, including Pentecostalism, the Jehovah's Witnesses, Seventh-Day Adventism, and the New Age movement, giving special attention to Mormons and Southern Baptists.

Boone, Kathleen C. *The Bible Tells Them So: The Discourse of Protestant Fundamentalism.* Albany: State University of New York Press, 1989.

Boone focuses on biblical inerrancy, a principle of utmost importance to fundamentalism and the doctrine of dispensational premillennialism. The author argues against the plausibility of inerrancy, referring to the lack of original texts and to the fact that interpreters tend to disagree over the meaning of biblical texts. Even inerrantists, Boone argues, have difficulty with words like "day" and "hour," resulting in questionable interpretations.

Boyer, Paul. *When Time Shall Be No More: Prophecy Belief in Modern American Culture.* Cambridge, MA: Belknap Press, 1992.

This study is the best available about the influence on contemporary American society of apocalyptic literature, a genre that reached fruition among the ancient Hebrews between the eighth and sixth centuries B.C. The post–World War II threat of nuclear destruction bred an intense concern about the end of time. According to Boyer, American foreign policy since the 1940s cannot be fully understood without some understanding of dispensational premillennialism. Such religious thinking helps explain President Ronald Reagan's reference to the Soviet Union as an "evil empire."

Bull, Malcolm, ed. *Apocalypse Theory and the Ends of the World.* Oxford, UK: Blackwell, 1995.

The scholarly essays contained in this work provide a broad overview of apocalyptic thought, covering the history of millenarianism (a belief in a future thousand-year period of universal peace and righteousness) from the ancient Greeks to the present. The authors examine the idea, persistent throughout recorded history, that the world must have a definite end. The essays provide an excellent basis for evaluating the many popular publications on the millennium that appeared at the close of the twentieth century.

Burgess, Stanley, and Gary McGee, eds. *Dictionary of Pentecostal and Charismatic Movements.* Grand Rapids, MI: Zondervan, 1989.

This reference work includes more than 800 entries on Pentecostal and charismatic movements primarily in the United States, but also in Europe. Individual entries focus on denominations, specific individuals within the movement, and varied topics such as the Healing Movement and Christian Perfection. The book includes entries on Jim Bakker and Jimmy Swaggart, detailing their fall from grace.

Caplan, Lionel, ed. *Studies in Religious Fundamentalism.* Albany, NY: State University of New York Press, 1987.

The contributors to this volume examine Islamic, Jewish, Sikh, Hindu, West African, and American Protestant fundamentalism in an effort to discover cross-cultural similarities. Although aware that fundamentalism in different parts of the world cannot be understood apart from its specific cultural context, the authors cautiously suggest several parallels. Interestingly, fundamentalists in many parts of the world tend to identify the erosion of male authority and the growing assertiveness of women with spiritual and national decline.

Carter, Stephen L. *The Culture of Disbelief: How American Law and Politics Trivialize Religious Devotion.* New York: Basic Books, 1993.

Carter deals with the dilemmas of religious involvement in the public arena that arise from an American society that is basically secular, despite the widespread expressions of religious belief. Though critical of the religious right, the author is concerned with establishing an appropriate balance in the principle of separation of church and state, recognizing that religion can strengthen those values Americans esteem.

Conkin, Paul K. *When All the Gods Trembled: Darwinism, Scopes, and American Intellectuals.* Lanham, MD: Rowman and Littlefield, 1998.

In a series of essays, Conkin discusses the controversy between fundamentalism and modernism over the status of religion and science in American society. The author focuses on the influence of modern scientific and philosophical naturalism, including Darwinist evolutionary theory, on American religious perspectives during the 1920s.

Cotton, Ian. *The Hallelujah Revolution: The Rise of the New Christians.* Amherst, NY: Prometheus, 1996.

Cotton, a British journalist, investigates the rise of evangelical and charismatic Christian movements during the twentieth century, predicting that such beliefs may become far more widespread in the twenty-first century. He associates such movements worldwide with a combination of irrationalist beliefs involving miracles, healings, and modern communications technology. He treats the political dimensions of the movement, which are not always conservative, and the possible psychological and neurological bases of religious experience.

Davis, Edward B., ed. *The Antievolution Pamphlets of Harry Rimmer.* Hamden, CT: Garland, 1995.

Volume six in the *Creationism in Twentieth-Century America* series (Ronald L. Numbers, general editor) contains sixteen of Henry Rimmer's works criticizing the theory of evolution. Rimmer, the most noted antievolutionist until his death in 1952, was a Presbyterian minister. Among the works included are "Modern Science, Noah's Ark, and the Deluge" (1925), "Modern Science and the First Fundamental" (1928), and "It's the Crisis Hour in Schools and Colleges" (no date).

Dayton, Donald. *Theological Roots of Pentecostalism.* Metuchen, NJ: Scarecrow, 1987.

This volume examines the history of Pentecostalism, tracing its Wesleyan roots to Great Britain. Dayton identifies four basic elements of this Christian belief: Christ as savior, Christ as baptizer in the Holy Spirit, Christ as healer, and Christ as the future king.

Dunn, Charles W., ed. *American Political Theology: Historical Perspective and Theoretical Analysis.* New York: Praeger, 1984.

This book provides an excellent selection of religious documents from the Mayflower Compact in 1620 to the Resolutions of the World Congress of Fundamentalists in 1980 and 1983. Dunn concludes with chapters on the theology of American presidents and theoretical propositions regarding American political theology.

————. *Religion in American Politics.* Washington, DC: CQ Press, 1989.

The contributors to this volume examine the conflicts that have arisen in the relationship between religion and politics in America. Individual articles deal with such topics as the First Amendment, the role of religion in maintaining community, religious right involvement in party politics, and religious lobbying efforts.

Edel, Wilbur. *Defenders of the Faith: Religion and Politics from the Pilgrim Fathers to Ronald Reagan.* Westport, CT: Praeger, 1987.

Edel's purpose is to expose the myths and misunderstandings about America's religious heritage, myths some groups and individuals exploit in order to gain political office. He explores the role of religion in public life throughout American history and observes that religious organizations have recently become significantly more involved in varied public policy issues. Edel notes with concern the desire of some political leaders to return to a relationship between church and state that existed in colonial times.

Fuller, Robert C. *Naming the Antichrist: The History of an American Obsession.* New York: Oxford University Press, 1995.

Fuller provides a detailed history of the use of the Antichrist theme in American religion and culture from the colonial period to the contemporary writings of such religious figures as Pat Robertson and Hal Lindsey. Various people and institutions have been identified as the "Antichrist," a term that appears only four times in the Bible. Among those suggested for the label included Native Americans, French Catholics, and the British king. More recently, many individuals and innovations have been associated with the Antichrist, including Pope John Paul II, the European Economic Community, the National Council of Churches, supermarket bar codes, and fiber optics. Fuller claims that Americans' tendency to speak of conflicts in terms of the battle of absolute good versus absolute evil has led to the preoccupation with identifying the Antichrist.

Gamwell, Franklin I. *The Meaning of Religious Freedom: Modern Politics and the Democratic Revolution.* Albany, NY: State University of New York Press, 1994.

This religious-philosophical-political work examines religious freedom in the context of First Amendment protections, over which there has been much disagreement. Gamwell argues that religious pluralism can lead to political agreement only through free discussion among the varying religious commitments.

Gasper, Louis. *The Fundamentalist Movement.* The Hague, Netherlands: Mouton, 1963.

This book is a historical treatment of fundamentalism, primarily from 1930 to the early 1960s. It contrasts two groups that developed during this time period: the militant American Council of Christian Churches and the more moderate National Association of Evangelicals. The author records the development of youth organizations and Bible institutes, the move toward nationalism, and the rise of evangelist Billy Graham.

Gatewood, Willard B., ed. *Controversy in the Twenties: Fundamentalism, Modernism, and Evolution.* Nashville, TN: Vanderbilt University Press, 1969.

Through this useful collection of documents, Gatewood shows that the modernist-fundamentalist conflict originated long before the 1920s and that its impact was more pervasive and enduring than other scholars suggest. The struggle within the churches was a reaction to processes, such as industrialization, urbanization, and scientific advancement, that had gradually undermined orthodox Protestantism and had raised moral issues for which orthodox Protestants had few relevant answers.

Hatch, Nathan O. *The Democratization of American Christianity.* New Haven, CT: Yale University Press, 1989.

This book is a good background for the study of contemporary conservative Christianity. The author examines the development of eighteenth- and nineteenth-century Protestant denominations, focusing on the emergence of the Baptist and Methodist denominations, as well as the Mormon church.

Hunter, James Davison. *American Evangelicalism: Conservative Religion and the Quandary of Modernity.* New Brunswick, NJ: Rutgers University Press, 1983.

Hunter investigates the tensions in the twentieth century between conservative American Protestantism and modern secularism. The book analyzes evangelicalism from a sociological and demographic perspective. Aspects of the evangelical view of the world, Hunter claims, have in fact been adjusted to modernity. Hunter employs survey data and the analysis of evangelical documents.

————. *Evangelicalism: The Coming Generation.* Chicago: University of Chicago Press, 1987.

Hunter bases this study on a survey of faculty and students at sixteen evangelical colleges and seminaries. The major focus is the encounter between religious beliefs and the modern secular world. The book is a good presentation of contemporary evangelical thought and culture.

Hutchison, William R. *The Modernist Impulse in American Protestantism.* Oxford: Oxford University Press, 1976.

Hutchison provides one of the better accounts of the development of liberalism, the intellectual foundation of the modernist impulse, within American Protestantism from the early 1800s through the 1920s. Like fundamentalism, modernism can be defined in varying ways. But as used by Hutchison, the term involves three ideas: the conscious adaptation of religious ideas to modern culture, the immanence of God in human cultural development, and the movement of human society toward the Kingdom of God.

Katloff, Mark A., ed. *Creation and Evolution in the Early American Scientific Affiliation.* Hamden, CT: Garland, 1995.

The tenth volume in the *Creationism in Twentieth-Century America* series contains forty-six articles written by various authors associated with the American Scientific Affiliation Society, a group founded in 1941 by evangelical scientists. Among the articles are "Biology and Christian Fundamentals" (R. L. Mixter 1950), "Why God Called His Creation Good" (William J. Tinkle 1950), and "The Origin of Man and the Bible" (J. Frank Cassel 1960).

Kurtz, Paul. *In Defense of Secular Humanism.* Buffalo, NY: Prometheus, 1983.

In this collection of papers written over a thirty-year period, Kurtz attempts to defend secular humanism, while acknowledging that most attention given the idea today originates with the religious right. Kurtz argues that much improvement can occur in morals and politics without religion.

Lawrence, Bruce B. *Defenders of God: The Fundamentalist Revolt against the Modern Age.* New York: Harper & Row, 1989.

This is an effort to place Islamic, Judaic, and Christian fundamentalism within a global context. Lawrence portrays fundamentalists as "moderns" who use science, technology, and the mass media to challenge the "heresies" of the modern age: rationalism, relativism, pluralism, and secularism. These "defenders of God" use modern means to uphold age-old transcendent values.

Marsden, George M. *Fundamentalism and American Culture: The Shaping of Twentieth-Century Evangelicalism, 1870–1925.* New York: Oxford University Press, 1980.

An excellent overview, this study traces fundamentalism from the latter nineteenth century through the 1920s. Marsden claims that fundamentalists underwent a drastic alteration in their relationship to culture. From respected evangelicals in the 1870s, they had become a laughingstock by the 1920s. This fine study furthers an understanding of that transformation.

————. *Reforming Fundamentalism: Fuller Seminary and the New Evangelicalism.* Grand Rapids, MI: Eerdmans, 1987.

This is an account of the Fuller Theological Seminary in Pasadena, California. Founded in 1947, this seminary soon became a focal point of sorts for an intellectual tug-of-war within fundamentalism itself. The Fuller fundamentalists, such as Charles Fuller, Harold Ockenga, Wilbur Smith, and Carl F. H. Henry, were determined to defend the supernatural aspects of Christianity, but they could not fully embrace the rigid separatism and dispensational premillennialism of the more intractable voices of the religious right, such as Carl McIntire. By the early 1950s the Fuller fundamentalists had begun to call themselves "evangelicals."

———. *Understanding Fundamentalism and Evangelicalism.*
Grand Rapids, MI: Eerdmans, 1991.

Marsden examines the historical roots of fundamentalism and
evangelicalism in the United States. Although diverse groups,
such as holiness churches, Pentecostals, traditional Methodists,
Baptists, Presbyterians, and Churches of Christ, compose the fundamentalist movement, the author identifies similarities. They
have to some extent separated themselves from modern culture,
but in recent years have experienced revitalization. Marsden focuses on fundamentalist views of science and politics. A final
chapter examines the fundamentalist legacy of J. Gresham
Machen.

Marsden, George M., ed. *Evangelicalism and Modern America.*
Grand Rapids, MI: Eerdmans, 1984.

Containing essays by thirteen scholars, this collection probes the
diversity and unity of fundamentalism. Arranged in two parts,
the essays first treat the rise of fundamentalism since World War
II more or less chronologically, then move on to topics such as
women, science, the arts, modernity, and biblical authority. The
book is an excellent guide for anyone interested in the emergence
and recent prominence of fundamentalism.

Martin, William. **With God on Our Side: The Rise of the Religious
Right in America.** New York: Broadway Books, 1996.

Martin describes the development of the religious right in seventeenth-century Massachusetts, and against that background presents a detailed account of the present positions of conservative
Christians. The author believes conservative fundamentalists
wish to impose their religious beliefs, including an insistence on
biblical inerrancy, on all Americans, and therefore pose a threat to
the constitutional doctrine of separation of church and state.
However, religious right leaders are weakened by their unwill-
ingness to compromise with those with whom they disagree.

Marty, Martin E. *Righteous Empire: The Protestant Experience in
America.* New York: Dial, 1970.

This treatment of Protestantism in America can be contrasted
with the later narratives that religious right authors have developed. Marty emphasizes the unfortunate results, including
racism and slavery, of the assumption of early settlers that they

were superior, God-chosen people with a special destiny. The author analyzes more recent changes in religious movements.

————. *Modern American Religion, Volume I, 1893–1919: The Irony of It All.* Chicago: University of Chicago Press, 1986.

This broad examination of American religion, including treatment of mainline churches, as well as evangelical and fundamentalist movements, emphasizes the difficulties Christians face when attempting to respond to change and modernization. Marty identifies the theological and political consequences of the resulting tension.

————. *Religion and Republic: The American Circumstance.* Boston: Beacon, 1987.

This series of articles by Marty looks to the achievement of consensus in a pluralistic society by discovering a common framework for diverse religious communities. The author examines what he considers the major characteristics of religion in America, such as the notion of civil religion and the perceived status of the Bible in Christian belief.

Marty, Martin E., and R. Scott Appleby. *Fundamentalisms Observed.* Chicago: University of Chicago Press, 1991.

This book is an excellent study of international movements of religious reaction in the twentieth century. Following a thematic approach, it examines the political, social, cultural, and religious context within which each movement emerges; its distinguishing beliefs; and the way each has responded to the modern world. This work demonstrates that American fundamentalism was part of a global phenomenon.

————. *The Glory and the Power: The Fundamentalist Challenge to the Modern World.* Boston: Beacon, 1992.

Codirectors of the Fundamentalism Project at the University of Chicago, Marty and Appleby focus on three religious movements in different countries. They examine Protestant fundamentalism in the United States; Israel's Gush Emunim, a small right-wing Jewish activist group; and Islamic fundamentalism, especially as it exists in Egypt. According to the authors, fundamentalist groups see history as a confrontation between good and evil, reject rationalism, and seek to maintain tradition.

Moen, Matthew C., and Lowell S. Gustafson, eds. *The Religious Challenge to the State.* Philadelphia: Temple University Press, 1992.

These essays provide a comparative view of the relationships between religion and politics. Individual essays treat topics such as religion in revolutionary Cuba, religion and politics in Israel, Islamic fundamentalism in Africa, and church-state relations in Mexico and Argentina.

Moore, R. Laurence. *Selling God: American Religion in the Marketplace of Culture.* New York: Oxford University Press, 1994.

This social history of religion in America investigates the use of commercial methods by religious leaders to advance religious causes. Moore also looks at business leaders who have employed religion to promote commercial interests. This book provides insightful background information for the study of the religious right and contemporary religion generally.

Nash, Robert J. *Faith, Hype, and Clarity: Teaching about Religion in American Schools and Colleges.* New York: Teachers College Press of Columbia University, 1998.

Nash presents four basic approaches (fundamentalist, prophetic, alternative spiritualities, and post-theist) to teaching religion. He defines and presents a brief history of fundamentalism (within Christianity as well as other religious traditions) and examines the fundamentalist worldview and the challenge of modernism. Referring to "the failure of the fundamentalist narrative," Nash describes the tendency of fundamentalists to claim that their beliefs and unimpeachable sacred texts explain every aspect of life.

Nelson, Paul, ed. *The Creationist Writings of Byron C. Nelson.* Hamden, CT: Garland, 1995.

The fifth volume in the *Creationism in Twentieth-Century America* series (Ronald L. Numbers, general editor) includes four works by Byron C. Nelson, a Lutheran supporter of creationism and a founder of the Religion and Science Association in 1935. Among the works are "Before Abraham: Prehistoric Man in Biblical Light" (1948) and "A Catechism on Evolution" (1937).

Neuhaus, Richard John. *The Naked Public Square: Religion and Democracy in America.* Grand Rapids, MI: Eerdmans, 1984.

This is a general treatment of the role of religion in American government and politics. The author's major theme is that politics and the Judeo-Christian faith are compatible, and that religion can play an important role in the American political process by helping to keep the public sphere viable.

Neuhaus, Richard John, ed. *Unsecular America*. Grand Rapids, MI: Eerdmans, 1986.

This group of essays is drawn from a 1985 conference on the relationship between religion and society conducted by the Center on Religion and Society. Among the topics discussed are the interdependence of capitalism, democracy, and religion; the ability of religion and modernization to coexist; secular humanism as a religion; and the American commitment to evangelicalism. Results of surveys of religious opinions are also included.

Noll, Mark A. *A History of Christianity in the United States and Canada*. Grand Rapids, MI: Eerdmans, 1992.

This book focuses on the rise and more recent decline of Protestantism in the United States. The author traces the development of a uniquely American brand of Christianity through the "Great Awakening" and the American Revolution. He associates the decline of evangelicalism with the emergence of modernism and the social gospel. Noll suggests that pluralism represents the future for religion in America.

Noll, Mark A., Nathan O. Hatch, and George M. Marsden. *The Search for Christian America*. Westchester, IL: Crossway, 1983.

This book contributes to the debate over the religious status of the Founding Fathers, which is an important issue for the religious right. Unlike many on the religious right who claim that the Founding Fathers based the nation on Christian principles, the authors, who are evangelical historians, argue that the notion of a Christian America is complex and difficult to demonstrate.

Numbers, Ronald L., ed. *Antievolution Before World War I*. Hamden, CT: Garland, 1995.

This first volume in the *Creationism in Twentieth-Century America* series (Ronald L. Numbers, general editor) includes four important critiques of evolution that were written prior to the antievolution movement of the 1920s. Authors are Alexander Patterson, Eberhard Denhert, Luther Tracy Townsend, and G. Frederick Wright.

————. *Creation-Evolution Debates.* Hamben, CT: Garland, 1995.

The second volume in the *Creationism in Twentieth-Century America* series (Ronald L. Numbers, general editor) contains seven debates between creationists and evolutionists during the 1920s and 1930s. One such debate between William Jennings Bryan and Henry Fairchild Osborn appeared in the *New York Times* in 1922.

————. *The Antievolution Works of Arthur I. Brown.* Hamden, CT: Garland, 1995.

This third volume in the *Creationism in Twentieth-Century America* series (Ronald L. Numbers, general editor) is composed of seven antievolution pamphlets by Arthur I. Brown, a surgeon whom fundamentalists in the 1920s regarded as a great scientist. Among the pamphlets are "Evolution and the Bible" (1920s) and "Men, Monkeys and the Missing Link" (1923).

————. *Selected Works of George McCready Price.* Hamden, CT: Garland, 1995.

Volume seven in the *Creationism in Twentieth-Century America* series (Ronald L. Numbers, general editor) includes four of George Price's works on creationism. Price is given credit for establishing a geology of the flood, which ultimately came to be known as scientific creationism. Among the works are "Q.E.D. or New Light on the Doctrine of Creation" (1917) and "Theories of Satanic Origin" (no date).

————. *The Early Writings of Harold W. Clark and Frank Lewis Marsh.* Hamden, CT: Garland, 1995.

This eighth volume in the *Creationism in Twentieth-Century America* series (Ronald L. Numbers, general editor) includes two works by Clark, "Back to Creation" (1929) and "The New Diluvialism" (1946), and one by Marsh, "Fundamental Biology" (1941). The authors, all students of creationist George McCready Price, were educated as biologists.

————. *Early Creationist Journals.* Hamden, CT: Garland, 1995.

The ninth volume in the *Creationism in Twentieth-Century America* series (Ronald L. Numbers, general editor) presents issues from three early creationist journals: *Creationist* (1937–1938), *Bulletin of Deluge Geology* (1941–1945), and its continuation, *Forum for the Correlation of Science and the Bible* (1946–1948).

Packer, J. I. *"Fundamentalism" and the Word of God.* Grand Rapids, MI: Eerdmans, 1958.

Written from a sympathetic viewpoint, this work is a good introduction to fundamentalism. With wit and humor, the author covers the usual territory of biblical authority and inerrancy and takes exception to the view of fundamentalists as obscurantists and unthinking biblical literalists.

Perry, Michael J. *Love and Power: The Role of Religion and Morality in American Politics.* New York: Oxford University Press, 1991.

This excellent, scholarly work examines the appropriate relationship between religious morality and politics in a morally pluralistic society. The author suggests that a more "ecumenical politics" might allow moral positions, especially about what is good for human beings, to contribute to political arguments.

Reichley, A. James. *Religion in American Public Life.* Washington, DC: Brookings, 1985.

This general treatment of religion and politics deals with historical interpretations of the First Amendment protection of religion and religious influence on policy making. Reichley examines topics such as the intentions of the constitutional framers and the positions denominations took on public issues during the Vietnam War era.

Robbins, Thomas, and Susan J. Palmer, eds. *Millennium, Messiahs, and Mayhem: Contemporary Apocalyptic Movements.* New York: Routledge, 1997.

Published as the interest in the "millennial myth" rose prior to the year 2000, this group of sixteen essays deals with variations on millennial movements, including economic, racist, environmental, and feminist groups, as well as organizations in more traditional churches. The authors investigate the tendency toward violence and confrontation with the established order. Individual essays deal with such topics as the more secular millennial movements of the survivalists and militias, technologically oriented groups, American Catholic apocalypticism, Mormon millenarianism (a belief in a future thousand-year period of peace and righteousness), and Christian reconstructionism.

Sandeen, Ernest Robert. *The Roots of Fundamentalism: British and American Millenarianism, 1800–1930.* Chicago: University of Chicago Press, 1970.

The author contends that fundamentalism may best be understood in the context of the history of millenarianism. The book traces the development of fundamentalism during the nineteenth and early twentieth centuries, discussing the importation of millenarianism from Great Britain to the United States and the development of dispensationalism. Whereas some scholars see publication of *The Fundamentals* and creation of the World's Christian Fundamentals Association as the beginning of the fundamentalist movement, one that climaxed in the 1920s, Sandeen argues instead that the unity of fundamentalism was already dissolving by about 1910. From that point on, divisive factionalism plagued the fundamentalists.

Schultz, Jeffery D., John G. West Jr., and Iain Maclean, eds. *Encyclopedia of Religion in American Politics.* Phoenix, AZ: Oryx, 1998.

This compendium of nearly 700 entries treats such topics as legal decisions, organizations, persons, and major events related to religion and politics. One essay presents a summary of religion and politics in the United States. Of major concern are the influences that religious considerations have had on politicians and the decisions they have made and the possible interaction between religion and politics in the future, especially over the issue of religious freedom.

Schultze, Quentin J. *Televangelism and American Culture: The Business of Popular Religion.* Grand Rapids, MI: Baker Book House, 1991.

Schultze argues that mass-media evangelism has strong ties to secular commercial broadcasting. Televangelists are portrayed as encouraging a religious belief related to a society of affluence and individualism, but the author moderates his conclusions by claiming that there are likely very few "charlatans" engaged in the enterprise.

Schultze, Quentin J., ed. *American Evangelicals and the Mass Media.* Grand Rapids, MI: Zondervan, 1991.

This collection of essays deals with how various aspects of the evangelical movement have been treated in the secular media.

Individual essays focus on televangelism and the response to it by the secular media. Additional essays cover other examples of the media, including books, magazines, and music.

Simmons, Paul D., ed. *Freedom of Conscience: A Baptist/Humanist Dialogue.* Amherst, NY: Prometheus, 2000.

The essays in this volume resulted from a conference at the University of Richmond in Virginia attended by liberal Baptist scholars and advocates of secular humanism. Among the issues discussed are academic freedom; social, political, and religious tolerance; separation of church and state; and the participants' mutual disapproval of the religious right and the conservative direction taken by the Southern Baptist Convention.

Smith, Christian. *American Evangelicalism: Embattled and Thriving.* Chicago: University of Chicago Press, 1998.

Basing his analysis on survey results, Smith takes exception to the common view of evangelicals as less educated, less affluent, and more fearful of contemporary culture than other Americans. He claims that evangelicals are better educated than most of those who could be labeled religious liberals and tend not to feel threatened by modern life. Yet, Smith concludes that evangelicals find themselves in a potentially stressful situation, perched between opposition to and integration into mainstream society.

Spong, John Shelby. *Rescuing the Bible from Fundamentalism: A Bishop Rethinks the Meaning of Scripture.* New York: Harper, 1992.

John Shelby Spong, the controversial Episcopal bishop of Newark, New Jersey, challenges the fundamentalist belief in the Bible as the inerrant word of God. He offers examples of claimed inconsistencies and contradictions. Spong argues that biblical literalism has been used to justify slavery, deny rights to minorities, subordinate women, and justify war.

———. *Here I Stand: My Struggle for a Christianity of Integrity, Love, and Equality.* San Francisco: Harper, 2000.

In this autobiography Spong outlines his efforts to offer American Christians an alternative to fundamentalism, discussing his opposition to the conservative views of such religious right leaders as Jerry Falwell and Pat Robertson. The author recounts his struggles within the hierarchy of the Episcopal church. He describes his defense of the rights of African Americans, women, and homosexuals within the church and argues for the need to make Christianity relevant to the realities of contemporary society.

Stone, Jon R. *On the Boundaries of American Evangelicalism: The Postwar Evangelical Coalition.* New York: Palgrave, 1999.

Stone traces the rise of a coalition of moderate Protestants in the 1940s and 1950s from the amorphous coalition called American Evangelicalism. This moderate coalition distinguished itself from both conservative fundamentalist and liberal factions. The author searches for reasons for the decline of this moderate group from the 1960s to the 1990s.

Trollinges, William Vance, and Edwin Grant Conklin, Jr., eds. *The Antievolution Pamphlets of William Bell Riley.* Hamden, CT: Garland, 1995.

The fourth volume in the *Creationism in Twentieth-Century America* series (Ronald L. Numbers, general editor) includes ten pamphlets by William Bell Riley, pastor of the First Baptist Church in Minneapolis, Minnesota. Riley was founder of the World's Christian Fundamentals Association, a major antievolution group in the 1920s. Among the pamphlets are "Are the Scriptures Scientific?" (no date), "Darwin's Philosophy and the Flood" (no date), and "The Scientific Accuracy of the Sacred Scriptures" (no date).

Tuveson, Ernest Lee. *Redeemer Nation: The Idea of America's Millennial Role.* New Haven, CT: Yale University Press, 1977.

This book provides an interesting and enlightening treatment of the background and consequences of millennial thought. Of particular interest is Tuveson's examination of the belief that America has been chosen as the instrument to achieve God's purposes in the final days.

Watt, David Harrington. *A Transforming Faith: Explorations of Twentieth-Century American Evangelicalism.* New Brunswick, NJ: Rutgers University Press, 1991.

This brief treatment of evangelicalism covers the period 1925 to 1976. The author focuses on recent cultural changes in politics, the status of the public and private realms, the role of women in society, and contributions in psychology. This approach illuminates the interaction of evangelicalism with the larger culture.

Weber, Timothy P. *Living in the Shadow of the Second Coming: American Premillennialism, 1875–1925.* New York: Oxford University Press, 1979.

This book is a good treatment of the rise of the premillennialist movement in America in the late nineteenth and early twentieth centuries. The author, a Baptist church historian, focuses on the social consequences of premillennialism, a doctrine that attempted to preserve orthodox beliefs against modernism and faith in social progress.

White, Ronald C., Jr., and Albright G. Zimmerman, eds. *An Unsettled Arena: Religion and the Bill of Rights.* Grand Rapids, MI: Eerdmans, 1991.

Written by a group of distinguished scholars, these essays confront the problem of maintaining a religious heritage in a pluralistic society. Such issues as prayer in public schools, public aid to parochial schools, the teaching of creationism, and the inclusion of religious ceremony in public events have led to nationwide debates about the meaning of the First Amendment and its applicability to contemporary America.

Wilcox, Clyde. *The Latest American Revolution? The 1994 Elections and Their Implications for Governance.* New York: St. Martin's, 1995.

This brief work discusses the importance of the religious right to the outcome of the 1994 elections. An appendix includes the House Republicans' "Contract With America," which discloses the influence of the religious right on that party's agenda. Among the promised measures are a "personal responsibility act" to discourage illegitimacy and teen pregnancy; a "family reinforcement act" that includes more stringent enforcement of child support, parents' rights in the education of their children, and stronger child pornography laws; and a stronger anticrime act.

Wills, Gary. *Under God: Religion and American Politics.* New York: Simon and Schuster, 1990.

With his usual grace, Wills explores American history from Roger Williams to Pat Robertson, focusing on those points of collision between religion and politics. Separation of church and state to the contrary notwithstanding, religion has always been a vital force in American society, and its influence has often been positive. As Wills writes, the abolitionist, women's, and civil rights movements derived considerable strength from the churches.

The Religious Right and Politics

Abraham, Ken. *Who Are The Promise Keepers? Understanding the Christian Men's Movement.* New York: Doubleday, 1997.

Abraham takes a sympathetic look at the Promise Keepers, an organization that schedules rallies for Christian men. The author examines the establishment of the Promise Keepers, its objectives, and many of the questions and criticisms that have been raised about the group, such as its relationship to women, minorities, the Republican Party, and other Christian groups.

Alexander-Moegerle, Gil. *James Dobson's War on America.* Amherst, NY: Prometheus, 1997.

Alexander-Moegerle, cofounder and former executive of James Dobson's Focus on the Family, presents a highly critical examination of Dobson and his organization. The author cohosted Focus on the Family's radio program and served on the organization's board of directors as a fund-raising consultant. He contrasts the "public" Dobson with the "private" individual who allegedly is motivated by competition, a desire for political power, and materialism. To the author, Dobson's conservative views could be a threat to civil liberties.

Alley, Robert S. *School Prayer: The Court, the Congress, and the First Amendment.* Amherst, NY: Prometheus, 1994.

Focusing on prayer in public schools, Alley investigates the historical background of the First Amendment's religion clauses, the courts' interpretations of these clauses for the past 200 years, and congressional debates over their application. The author makes a balanced presentation of views on both sides of the school prayer issue.

———. *Without a Prayer: Religious Expression in Public Schools.* Amherst, NY: Prometheus, 1996.

The U.S. Supreme Court, in *Engel v. Vitale* (1962) and *Abington Township School District v. Schempp* (1963), ruled that organized prayer and Bible reading in the public schools is unconstitutional. Alley explores subsequent court cases dealing with the First Amendment guarantee of separation of church and state.

He interviewed many of those engaged in such cases who objected to the continuing introduction of religious ceremony in the public schools. The author elaborates on the justifications that communities have used to reintroduce school prayer, including "nonpreferentialism," "toleration," and "accommodation."

Barkun, Michael. *Religion and the Racist Right: The Origins of the Christian Identity Movement.* Annapolis, MD: University of North Carolina Press, 1996.

Barkun analyzes white supremacist groups on the religious right, groups that hold beliefs referred to as Christian Identity. He examines the basic ideology and organizational development of the Christian Identity movement and traces the roles individuals in the movement played in activities such as the bombing of the federal building in Oklahoma City and the rise of militia movements across the country.

Blanchard, Dallas A. *The Anti-Abortion Movement and the Rise of the Religious Right: From Polite to Fiery Protest.* Old Tappan, NJ: Twayne, 1994.

Blanchard describes the history of the antiabortion movement in the United States, including the initial efforts primarily by Roman Catholic priests and laypersons in the 1960s; the court decisions, such as *Roe v. Wade*, that liberalized abortion policy; and the more extreme and sometimes violent antiabortion protests of the 1990s. An important trend in the antiabortion movement, the author concludes, has been its merging with a conservative political and cultural ideology and fundamentalist religious beliefs.

Boston, Robert. *Why the Religious Right Is Wrong about Separation of Church and State.* Amherst, NY: Prometheus, 1993.

Boston, assistant director of communications for Americans United for the Separation of Church and State, argues that the religious right poses a danger to the principle of separation of church and state. He believes that those on the religious right intend to create a theocratic system in the United States. Countering the arguments leaders in the religious right have made about the First Amendment guarantee of religious freedom, Boston examines the history of church-state relations and reviews court decisions on the issue.

———. *Close Encounters with the Religious Right: Journeys into the Twilight Zone of Religion and Politics.* Amherst, NY: Prometheus, 2000.

Boston attended religious right conventions, listened to speeches of the movement's leaders, and read their many mailings to gather information for this book about the conservative Christian political agenda. Subjects covered include the Christian Coalition, the Promise Keepers, the Rutherford Institute, Focus on the Family, and religious right leaders Pat Robertson, D. James Kennedy, Jerry Falwell, James Dobson, and Gary Bauer. Boston argues that although the religious right has suffered recent setbacks, it still remains a potent force in American politics.

Brasher, Brenda E. *Godly Women: Fundamentalism and Female Power.* Piscataway, NJ: Rutgers University Press, 1998.

Basing her findings on in-depth interviews with women in fundamentalist churches, Brasher identifies an interesting paradox: while fundamentalist women adhere to the traditional conservative view of the place of women in the family and church, they nonetheless often play active and influential roles in church and community affairs. Noting that the interaction between conservative religious beliefs and the contemporary society and culture are often complex, the author claims that women who hold fundamentalist beliefs adhere to a wide variety of positions regarding the role of women in church and society.

Bruce, Stephen. *The Rise and Fall of the Christian Right.* New York: Oxford University Press, 1988.

Employing a sociological perspective, Bruce examines the efforts of the Christian right in the 1970s and 1980s to organize politically and influence election outcomes. Although predictions of the religious right's downfall have proven premature, the problems involved in attempting to establish political coalitions are still relevant to the fortunes of the movement.

———. *Conservative Protestant Politics.* New York: Oxford University Press, 1998.

Bruce compares conservative Protestant political activity in the United Kingdom, the United States, South Africa, Australia, New Zealand, and Canada. The author emphasizes the limitations to success that those promoting a religiously motivated political agenda face in culturally diverse societies.

Bruce, Stephen, Peter Kivisto, and William H. Swatos Jr., eds. *The Rapture of Politics: The Christian Right as the United States Approaches the Year 2000.* New Brunswick, NJ: Transaction, 1994.

These essays examine the current influence of the religious right on American politics. The authors provide differing perspectives, from highly critical to sympathetic, on the efforts of this movement to combine religious and political concerns in the public arena.

Bull, Christopher, and John Gallagher. *Perfect Enemies: The Religious Right, the Gay Movement, and the Politics of the 1990s.* New York: Crown Publishing Group, 1996.

Bull and Gallagher trace the history of the religious right and the gay movement from the late 1960s, portraying them as groups bound to collide. The authors examine instances of the struggle, including state elections, the 1992 presidential election, and the congressional hearings on gays in the military. The authors appeal to both sides to jettison fierce rhetoric and accept greater civility.

Cantor, David. *The Religious Right: The Assault on Tolerance and Pluralism in America.* New York: Anti-Defamation League, 1993.

Cantor, senior research analyst at the Anti-Defamation League, provides a highly critical overview of the religious right in the early 1990s. He examines the major individuals and organizations on the religious right, their objectives and tactics, and their strengths and weaknesses. Cantor believes the religious right poses a major threat to American democracy and warns the reader of the danger he perceives emanating from a radical religious movement.

Capps, Walter H. *The New Religious Right: Piety, Patriotism, and Politics.* Columbia: University of South Carolina Press, 1990.

This is an excellent account of the better-known Christian right personalities of the 1980s. The author deals in depth with Jerry Falwell, interviewing him at the Thomas Road Baptist Church; Bob Jones, Jr., and Bob Jones III and their court battle over Bob Jones University; Francis A. Schaeffer, the famous theologian of the religious right; the rise and fall of Jim and Tammy Bakker; and Pat Robertson's failed bid for the Republican presidential nomination.

Carpenter, Joel A. *Revive Us Again: The Reawakening of American Fundamentalism.* New York: Oxford University Press, 1999.

Offering insights into the origins of the contemporary influence of the religious right in American politics, Carpenter traces the history of Christian fundamentalism from the Scopes trial in 1925 to the beginning of Billy Graham's crusades in 1949. Following the Scopes trial, which Carpenter considers an embarrassing debacle, fundamentalists continued to build a strong subculture through Bible schools, seminaries, small publishing houses, and use of the new technology of radio to spread their message across the country.

Clarkson, Frederick. *Eternal Hostility: The Struggle Between Theocracy and Democracy.* Monroe, ME: Common Courage Press, 1997.

Focusing on such groups as the Christian Coalition, the Unification Church, and the Promise Keepers, Clarkson claims that the religious right is subverting democracy in the United States. As evidence, the author cites the Christian Coalition's attempts to dominate the Republican Party, violence at abortion clinics committed by more radical antiabortion groups, and attacks on homosexuals.

Cromartie, Michael, ed. *Evangelicals and Foreign Policy: Four Perspectives.* Washington, DC: Ethics and Public Policy Center, 1989.

These essays examine the applicability of evangelical Christian beliefs to American foreign policy and international relations. The Bible is seen as establishing possible tenets for foreign-policy makers, including positions on terrorism and tyranny. Those on the political left are criticized for failing to separate political systems that are flawed from those that are fundamentally evil.

———. *No Longer Exiles: The Religious New Right in American Politics.* Washington, DC: Ethics and Public Policy Center, 1993.

This volume, drawn from a conference on the religious right, features four major chapters on the history of the religious right, future prospects for the movement, past failures, and evangelical voting patterns from 1976 to 1988.

———. *Disciples and Democracy: Religious Conservatives and the Future of American Politics.* Washington, DC: Ethics and Public Policy Center, 1994.

This volume of essays, originally presented at an Ethics and Public Policy Center Conference, examines the current status of the religious right, mostly from a sympathetic perspective. Individual essays deal with such topics as the religious right's impact on the 1992 presidential election, media treatment of the movement, and its relationship to the Republican Party.

D'Antonio, Michael. *Fall from Grace: The Failed Crusade of the Christian Right.* New York: Farrar, Straus & Giroux, 1989.

This book examines the Christian right through a series of interesting personal profiles of individuals committed to the movement. The book also deals with the fall of major television evangelists, such as Jim Bakker and Jimmy Swaggart, in the late 1980s, and recounts Pat Robertson's failed campaign for the presidency.

Diamond, Sara. *Spiritual Warfare: The Politics of the Christian Right.* Boston: South End Press, 1989.

In her highly critical account of the religious right, Diamond examines the various aspects of the movement, including religious broadcasting networks, extremist political activity such as bombing abortion clinics, and activities in foreign nations in support of a conservative American foreign policy.

———. *Roads to Dominion: Right-Wing Movements and Political Power in the United States.* New York: Guilford, 1995.

In this sequel to *Spiritual Warfare: The Politics of the Christian Right,* Diamond presents a more scholarly treatment of right-wing politics in the United States. The author analyzes the differences among the political right, the racist right, and the religious right and suggests connections among these groups. The book contains detailed information about the rise of right-wing political groups since World War II and speculates about their possible future rise to power.

———. *Facing the Wrath: Confronting the Right in Dangerous Times.* Monroe, ME: Common Courage Press, 1996.

Diamond presents a comprehensive view of the religious right's involvement in the political realm. Topics include organizations such as the Christian Coalition, conservative attacks on the Public Broadcasting System, the radio ministry of James Dobson's Focus on the Family, and "dominion theology." The author concludes that the religious right threatens secular education, has an antigay agenda, participates in aggressive antiabortion politics, and ultimately wishes to replace secular law with biblical law.

——. *Not by Politics Alone: The Enduring Influence of the Christian Right.* New York: Guilford, 1998.

In her continuing examination of the religious right, Diamond explores its cultural underpinnings and its deep roots within evangelical Christianity in order to shed light on the persistence of the movement as a force in American politics. Diamond claims that the major objective of the Christian right is to influence moral attitudes through cultural and political means, including a complex alliance with the Republican Party. The author details the proliferation of talk radio shows, publishing companies, law firms, and music studios—all a part of the continuing cultural influence of the religious right.

Durham, James R. *Secular Darkness: Religious Right Involvement in Texas Public Education, 1963–1989.* New York: Peter Lang, 1995.

Durham describes the increasing influence of conservative Christian individuals and organizations on public school policy in Texas during the 1960s, 1970s, and 1980s. Especially interesting is the rise of Norma and Mel Gabler as self-proclaimed experts on textbook selection who developed significant influence over the policies of the state board of education. In 1974 the Gablers pressured the board to issue a "proclamation" stating that "textbooks that treat the theory of evolution shall identify it as only one of several explanations of the origins of humankind and avoid limiting young people in their search for meanings of their human existence."

Dwyer, James G. *Religious Schools v. Children's Rights.* Ithaca, NY: Cornell University Press, 1998.

Dwyer takes a critical look at religious schooling, a sensitive area for fundamentalist Christians and Roman Catholics. He claims that religious schools are almost completely unregulated and may not serve the best interests of children. Therefore, public policy should focus not so much on the right of families and religious communities to raise children as they deem appropriate, but rather on what is best for the affected children from a secular perspective.

Edwards, Lee. *The Conservative Revolution: The Movement That Remade America.* New York: Free Press, 1999.

Edwards discusses those events and individuals, including those in the religious right, who contributed to the growth of conservatism as a major force in American society and politics.

Feder, Don. *Who's Afraid of the Religious Right?* Ottawa, IL: Jameson, 1998.

Feder examines the membership of the religious right and explores the movement's political and social agenda. The author analyzes the positions of the religious right on such topics as gays in the military, abortion, and prayer in the schools.

Foege, Alec. *The Empire God Built: Inside Pat Robertson's Media Machine.* New York: Wiley, 1996.

Foege, a contributing editor to *Rolling Stone* magazine, investigates the media empire behind Pat Robertson's political activity. The author describes the corporate structure of Robertson's empire, investigates the inner workings of the organization, and explains how it achieves its economic and political goals. According to Foege, Robertson has lessons for those who support as well as those who oppose him, especially regarding the effective use of mass media technology.

Green, John C., Mark J. Rozell, and Clyde Wilcox, eds. *Prayers in the Precincts: The Christian Right in the 1998 Elections.* Baltimore, MD: Georgetown University Press, 2000.

This book contains essays analyzing the role of the Christian right in the 1998 campaigns and elections in fourteen states. Although the authors generally conclude that the Christian right was not especially effective in recruiting like-minded candidates and raising campaign funds, they predict this religious coalition will continue to have significant influence on American politics.

Griffith, R. Marie. *God's Daughters: Evangelical Women and the Power of Submission.* Berkeley, CA: University of California Press, 1997.

This examination of Women's Aglow Fellowship, the largest women's international evangelical association, provides insights into the complex interaction of Christian women with contemporary culture. Griffith challenges the generally accepted view of evangelical Christian women, noting important connections between them and feminist causes they are often considered to oppose.

Guth, James L., and John C. Green, eds. *The Bible and the Ballot Box: Religion and Politics in the 1988 Election.* Boulder, CO: Westview, 1991.

The authors examine the wide variety of religious influences on the 1988 presidential campaign in which two Baptist ministers— Jesse Jackson, a liberal Democrat, and Pat Robertson, a conservative Republican—vied in their respective parties for the nomination. One suggestion is that the United States may be moving toward a party system similar to those in Europe, with a conservative religious party competing against a liberal secular one.

Hadden, Jeffrey K., and Anson Shupe, eds. *Secularization and Fundamentalism Reconsidered.* New York: Paragon House, 1989.

In the wake of renewed religious right activity in the 1980s, the contributors to this volume, who are sociologists of religion, examine the relationship between religion and politics in the United States and other nations. Of primary concern is the status of secularization theory in light of recent developments. Other topics include the role of the mass media in religious right successes, religious attitudes toward the capitalist system, and religious right involvement in presidential elections.

Herman, Didi. *The Antigay Agenda: Orthodox Vision and the Christian Right.* Chicago: University of Chicago Press, 1997.

Herman criticizes the positions of conservative Protestants on the issue of gay rights from the 1950s to the present. The author relies heavily on the periodical *Christianity Today* to discern religious right attitudes on this issue, describing how conservative Christians have used antihomosexual language in politics and journalism.

Hertzke, Allen. *Representing God in Washington: The Role of Religious Lobbies in the American Polity.* Nashville, TN: University of Tennessee Press, 1988.

The empirical research for this study includes interviews with policy makers and lobbyists. The analysis of lobbying activities of religious groups involves not only fundamentalist and evangelical organizations, but also Catholic and Jewish groups. Lobbyists' concerns vary from abortion to peace and world hunger.

Hofrenning, Daniel J. B. *In Washington but Not of It: The Prophetic Politics of Religious Lobbyists.* Philadelphia: Temple University Press, 1995.

Hofrenning provides a detailed examination of the activities of religious lobbyists at the national level. The author concludes that religious lobbyists, regardless of their ideological positions, are similar in that they all hold an antielitist position while pursuing their individual efforts to alter national policy.

Jelen, Ted G. *The Political Mobilization of Religious Beliefs.* New York: Praeger, 1991.

This book, based on an attitude survey Jelen conducted in fifteen churches in Greencastle, Indiana, contains a wealth of data on the political attitudes of those who support the Christian right. Of great interest is Jelen's discussion of the relation between the political activities of the religious right and opposition to other groups in society, including feminists, homosexuals, and atheists.

Jorstad, Erling. *The New Christian Right, 1981–1988: Prospects for the Post-Reagan Era.* Leiston, NY: Edwin Mellen, 1987.

Jorstad discusses the relationship between the Reagan administration and the new Christian right in the 1980s, focusing on such figures as Jerry Falwell, Pat Robertson, and Tim LaHaye and their assistance in Reagan's 1984 reelection campaign. The book also deals with the religious right's efforts leading up to the 1988 election, and adjustments in its agenda.

Judges, Donald P. *Hard Choices, Lost Voices: How the Abortion Conflict Has Divided America, Distorted Constitutional Rights, and Damaged the Courts.* Chicago: Ivan R. Dee, 1993.

The religious right has consistently employed the abortion issue to distinguish itself from what the movement considers secularizing influences in contemporary society. Treating pro-choice and pro-life movements equally, Judges criticizes both sides for misstating the nature of the conflict and demonstrating lack of knowledge and understanding of the choices women face. According to the author, the nature of the debate, characterized by distortion on both sides, has contributed to the polarization of American society.

Kintz, Linda. *Between Jesus and the Market: The Emotions That Matter in Right-Wing America.* Durham, NC: Duke University Press, 1997.

Although analysts often identify men as the major force within the religious right, Kintz notes the unique contribution women have made to the movement. The author observes that conservative Christian women have cultivated a unique power. They often stay home, where they can participate in furthering the political agenda of the religious right through phone calls, distribution of petitions, and use of e-mail. A source of the movement's strength is found in what Kintz calls "resonance," which the author identifies as appeal to the emotions.

Kintz, Linda, and Julia Lesage, eds. *Media, Culture, and the Religious Right.* Minneapolis: University of Minnesota Press, 1998.

Scholars from various academic fields, including media studies, sociology, religious studies, and political science, examine the increased significance of contemporary conservative Christian media, which coincides with attempts by those on the religious right to increase their social and political influence.

Kramnick, Isaac, and R. Laurence Moore. *The Godless Constitution: The Case against Religious Correctness.* New York: Norton, 1996.

The authors take issue with claims that the United States was founded as a Christian nation. They note that the Founders, hoping to avoid the severe religious conflicts of European nations, intentionally made no mention of God in the Constitution. The intellectual background and constitutional history of separation of church and state are examined, as well as contemporary attempts by religious groups to destroy the wall of separation between church and state by introducing a standard of "religious correctness" into American politics.

Larson, Edward J. *Summer for the Gods: The Scopes Trial and America's Continuing Debate over Science and Religion.* Cambridge, MA: Harvard University Press, 1998.

Larson presents a detailed account of the 1925 Scopes trial, held in Dayton, Tennessee, in which John T. Scopes was found guilty of teaching evolution to his pupils. The trial showcased the tug-of-war between evolutionists and creationists of the time. The author recounts the legal maneuverings of the prosecution, led by William Jennings Bryan, and the defense, led by Clarence Darrow, and investigates the event's broader religious, cultural, educational, and political consequences.

Lienesch, Michael. *Redeeming America: Piety and Politics in the New Christian Right.* Chapel Hill, NC: University of North Carolina Press, 1993.

This excellent work provides an in-depth view of social and political positions crucial to the religious right. Lienesch presents an intricate and fascinating analysis of conservative Christian writings. Among the topics included are the perceived social roles of men and women, defenses of capitalism, attitudes toward the political system, and the role of the United States as a redeemer nation.

Lugg, Catherine A. *For God and Country: Conservatism and American School Policy.* New York: Peter Lang, 1996.

Lugg offers a policy analysis of the influences that conservative groups, including the Christian right, had on federal school policies during President Ronald Reagan's first administration from 1981 to 1984. She focuses on the conservative social agenda that received renewed support following the 1980 Reagan election victory.

Menendez, Albert J. *Visions of Reality: What Fundamentalist Schools Teach.* Amherst, NY: Prometheus, 1993.

Even though a majority of those polled have consistently registered opposition to public support for nonpublic schools, Menendez notes that fundamentalist religious leaders have been pressuring Congress and state legislatures to initiate aid programs to such schools through such programs as vouchers and tuition tax credits. The author claims that history, English, and science textbooks used in fundamentalist private schools distort history, demonstrate prejudice against other religious faiths, question mainstream science, and generally indoctrinate children with "visions of reality" that should not be supported with public funds.

Moen, Matthew C. *The Christian Right and Congress.* Tuscaloosa, AL: University of Alabama Press, 1989.

This well-done empirical study examines the influence of the religious right in Congress, focusing on the years 1981 through 1984. Moen investigates the major legislative efforts (antiabortion legislation, a school prayer amendment, and tuition tax credits for parents with children in private schools) and the religious right's failure to achieve their objectives. The author notes the lesser successes of the movement.

———. *The Transformation of the Christian Right.* Tuscaloosa, AL: University of Alabama Press, 1992.

This examination of changes in the religious right during the 1980s is crucial to understanding the present status of the movement. Moen documents the religious right's shift away from uncompromising positions on the national level to a more politically sophisticated strategy that includes a greater regional and local emphasis.

Neuhaus, Richard John, and Michael Cromartie, eds. *Piety and Politics: Evangelicals and Fundamentalists Confront the World.* Lanham, MD: University Press of America, 1987.

This edited work provides a variety of views about, and from, the religious right. Articles feature the origins of evangelicalism and fundamentalism and the contemporary political significance of Christian conservatives. Articles by individuals within the movement provide assessments of the United States and the problems it faces.

Numbers, Ronald L. *The Creationists: The Evolution of Scientific Creationism.* Ewing, NJ: California Princeton Fulfillment Services, 1993.

After conducting many interviews and investigating various manuscripts, Numbers describes the formation of the creationist movement. The author investigates the origins of the debates between creationists and evolutionists, focusing on events in courtrooms, legislatures, and school boards.

Oldfield, Duane M. *The Right and the Righteous: The Christian Right Confronts the Republican Party.* Lanham, MD: Rowman and Littlefield, 1996.

Oldfield discusses the relationship between the Christian right and the Republican Party, analyzing the history and objectives of each organization. The author probes the significant influence the religious right has had on the Republican national platform and on the conservative political agenda, and examines the potential dilemmas this poses for the Republican Party in forging broader coalitions with other groups.

Peck, Janice. *The Gods of Televangelism: The Crisis of Meaning and the Appeal of Religious Television.* Cresskill, NJ: Hampton, 1993.

Although cautioning against exaggerating the media influence of the Christian right, Peck notes that the activist evangelicals, who compose one-fifth of the population, can be an influential force in American politics. The author focused her research on two televangelists: Jimmy Swaggart, who, prior to his fall due to personal indiscretions, employed a revivalist version of religious broadcasting, and Pat Robertson whose *700 Club* follows a talk show/news program format. Each represents a distinct way of combining conservative religious belief with contemporary media technology.

Porteous, Skipp. *Jesus Doesn't Live Here Anymore.* Amherst, NY: Prometheus, 1991.

Porteous, president and national director of the Institute for First Amendment Studies, recounts his personal experience with Christian fundamentalism. He became a "born-again" Christian at the age of eleven and came to believe that the Bible could provide the answer to any problem. The author spent many years in the Pentecostal ministry before finally deciding to leave. Why and how he left the ministry, which he describes as a liberating experience, and why he decided to fight against the fundamentalist movement constitute much of this study.

Rapp, Sandy. *God's Country: A Case against Theocracy.* Binghamton, NY: Haworth, 1991.

Rapp focuses on the religious right's role in sexual politics, describing the movement's emotional attacks on homosexuals and the right to privacy. She encourages readers to become politically active in opposition to the religious right and recommends effective strategies.

Ribuffo, Leo P. *The Old Christian Right: The Protestant Far Right from the Great Depression to the Cold War.* Philadelphia: Temple University Press, 1983.

The author places the new resurgence of the Christian right in the context of twentieth-century America from the 1930s to the 1950s. Ribuffo presents historical examples of religious right activity that are intended to trouble the reader.

Risen, James, and Judy L. Thomas. *Wrath of Angels: The American Abortion War.* Boulder, CO: Basic Books, 1999.

Risen and Thomas trace the history of the antiabortion movement as it expanded from a largely Catholic cause into a fundamentalist Protestant one. Although the antiabortion movement has not achieved the objective of banning abortion, the authors argue that it contributed to the rise of the religious right in American politics.

Rozell, Mark J., and Clyde Wilcox. *Second Coming: The New Christian Right in Virginia Politics.* Johns Hopkins University Press, 1996.

The authors investigate the influence of the religious right in Virginia politics since 1978 and analyze competition within the Republican Party between the centrists and the religious right activists. The book focuses on two candidates strongly supported by the religious right who gained Republican Party nominations: Michael Farris, who ran for lieutenant governor in 1993, and Oliver North, who ran for a seat in the U.S. Senate in 1994. Although neither was elected, their defeats by narrow margins may indicate further influence of the religious right in Virginia politics.

Shields, Carole. *Change the Hostile Climate.* Washington, DC: People for the American Way, 1999.

This publication, issued by People for the American Way, is an annual report on what the organization considers antigay discrimination by government, businesses, elected officials, and conservative religious groups across the nation. The 1999 edition reports on 300 such incidents.

Smidt, Corwin, ed. *Contemporary Evangelical Political Involvement: An Analysis and Assessment.* New York: University Press of America, 1989.

This edited volume contains both analytic and evaluative articles on the religious right. Contributors to the volume discuss such topics as the party identification of evangelicals, possible commonalities between evangelicals and secular humanists, the need for political sophistication among evangelicals, and possible limitations on the goals of a religious movement in a secular society.

Smith, Christian. *Christian America? What Evangelicals Really Want.* Berkeley, CA: University of California Press, 2000.

In a continuing analysis of evangelical Christians, Smith concludes from empirical studies that evangelicals are typically not extremists and do not believe in imposing their religious views of the world on the rest of society. The author indicates that evangelicals share with the rest of American society the same values of tolerance and individualism.

Snowball, David. *Continuity and Change in the Rhetoric of the Moral Majority.* Westport, CT: Praeger, 1991.

This study of the Moral Majority examines the history of the organization from 1979 to 1985, focusing on the rhetorical style its leaders employed to convey messages on such issues as abortion and pornography. The author investigates the interesting use of metaphor in organization statements and concludes with an evaluation of the Moral Majority, suggesting possible reasons for its termination.

Stacey, Judith. *In the Name of the Family: Rethinking Family Values in the Postmodern Age.* Boston, MA: Beacon, 1997.

Contrary to conservative and religious right positions regarding family breakdown and the consequent need to restore family values, including male authority, Stacey argues that alternative forms of family organization, including homosexual marriage, represent viable social groupings.

Stanton, Elizabeth Cady. *The Woman's Bible.* Northeastern University Press, 1993.

Originally published in the 1890s, this reworking of the Bible by one of the more noted figures of the women's movement challenges the commonly expressed conservative Christian view, still expressed in the religious right, that women should remain subservient to men. Focusing on scriptural passages involving women, Stanton claims that the Bible was a major cause of the suppression of women.

Wald, Kenneth D. *Religion and Politics in the United States.* 3d ed. Washington, DC: *Congressional Quarterly,* 1996.

Wald's overview of religion and politics in the United States extends beyond evangelical religious activity to include other religious influences. Although the author notes the secular nature of American society, he recognizes the importance of traditional interactions between religion and politics.

Wallis, Jim. *The Soul of Politics: Beyond "Religious Right" and "Secular Left."* Orlando, FL: Harcourt, 1995.

Relying on personal experiences with the problems of ghettos in Washington, D.C., Wallis contends that liberal and conservative emphases on social justice or individual values do not provide solutions. He calls for a reintegration of politics and spirituality.

Watson, Justin. *The Christian Coalition: Dreams of Restoration, Demands for Recognition.* New York: St. Martin's, 1997.

Basing much of his analysis on the writings of Pat Robertson and Ralph Reed, leaders of the Christian Coalition, Watson traces the conservative Christian organization from its founding in 1989 through its political successes, often based on accommodations with political allies. The author discusses the organization's objectives and offers explanations for its popularity among many Americans and its political influence. Although the vast majority of Americans profess to believe in a Christian God, the Coalition perceives itself as representing a minority beleaguered by a socially and politically liberal society.

Weber, Paul J., and W. Landis Jones. *U.S. Religious Interest Groups.* Westport, CT: Greenwood Press, 1994.

The authors present information on 120 national religious organizations in the United States. Although not limited to conservative groups, the volume includes a number of organizations on the religious right. The book contains a chapter on the history of religious interest groups in America.

Wilcox, Clyde. *God's Warriors: The Christian Right in Twentieth-Century America.* Baltimore, MD: Johns Hopkins University Press, 1992.

This study of religion and conservative politics provides a historical survey of the religious right through the twentieth century and examines previous efforts that used statistical analysis to explain religious activism. The book explores not only the Christian right and anticommunist movement of the 1950s, but also the more current fundamentalist and Pentecostal movements led by individuals such as Jerry Falwell and Pat Robertson.

———. *Onward Christian Soldiers? The Religious Right in American Politics.* Boulder, CO: Westview, 1996.

Wilcox describes the contemporary characteristics of the religious right, traces the movement's political history in the twentieth century, and analyzes its possible future effectiveness in influencing American public policy. The author ultimately investigates the appropriate role of religious groups in American politics and government, especially within the constitutional context of separation of church and state.

Works from the Religious Right

This section includes works on a wide variety of subjects relevant to the religious right: general worldview, political and economic issues, and personal and family concerns. We have added an additional section that includes several examples of the millennarian literature that flooded bookstores as the new millennium approached. There is, of course, unavoidable overlap among the various sections, as the topics range from personal accounts of the development of authors' beliefs to explorations of how those beliefs relate to the contemporary world.

The Religious Right Worldview

Ackerman, Paul D. *In God's Image after All: How Psychology Supports Biblical Creationism.* Grand Rapids, MI: Baker Books, 1990.

Ackerman relates psychological notions such as personality, self-will, perception, and self-image to biblical accounts. The author concludes that psychological data support the truth of scripture and the creation story.

Anderson, Leith. *Winning the Values War in a Changing Culture: Thirteen Distinct Values That Mark a Follower of Jesus Christ.* Minneapolis, MN: Bethany House, 1994.

Pointing to such phenomena as high rates of divorce and illegitimate births as signs of cultural collapse, Anderson argues that those in the Christian community too often act like the rest of society. To overcome what he considers the dangers of relativism, the author recommends that Christians adhere to thirteen biblically based values in order to win what he calls the values war.

Ankerberg, John, and John Weldon. *Darwin's Leap of Faith: Exposing the False Religion of Evolution.* Eugene, OR: Harvest House, 1998.

Ankerberg and Weldon examine the evolution versus creation

controversy, arguing that the Darwinian theory of evolution resembles a religion more than a scientific theory. The authors accuse Americans who adhere to the theory of evolution of persecuting those who do not.

Bakker, Jim. *Prosperity and the Coming Apocalypse.* Nashville, TN: Nelson, 1998.

Bakker, former head of the PTL ministry who was imprisoned for the misuse of donated funds, explains his beliefs about the end of the world. Bakker, who revealed in *I Was Wrong* (1997) his changed position on the place of wealth in a Christian's life, claims that contemporary Christians have developed a dependency on money, material things, and all the conveniences of modern society that have often become substitutes for God. Regarding eschatology, Bakker believes Christians will undergo at least part of the great tribulation prophesied in the Book of Revelation.

Ball, William B., ed. *In Search of a National Morality: A Manifesto for Catholics and Evangelicals.* Grand Rapids, MI: Baker Books, 1992.

These articles by Catholic and evangelical Protestant scholars present moderate religious right positions on issues about which it is hoped many Catholics and Protestants can agree. Among the topics covered are government and politics, secularization, abortion, education, family values, and morality.

Barton, David. *The Bulletproof George Washington: An Account of God's Providential Care.* Aledo, TX: Wallbuilders, 1990.

This brief book contends that God has granted special protection to the United States and focuses on God's alleged protection of George Washington during the French and Indian War. According to the author, Washington expressed appreciation for God's intervention in his life.

Behe, Michael J. *Darwin's Black Box: The Biochemical Challenge to Evolution.* New York: Free Press, 1996.

Behe, a biochemist and Roman Catholic, offers a scientific argument for the existence of God. Examining such examples as blood clotting and vision, the author observes an irreducible complexity at the micro level that science cannot explain. Arguing that Charles Darwin's gradualistic evolutionary theory is inadequate in explaining elaborate life processes, he posits an intelligent designer.

Blamires, Harry. *The Post-Christian Mind: How Should a Christian Think?* Ann Arbor, MI: Vine, 1997.

Taking a broad brush, Blamires criticizes contemporary society, claiming it is dominated by a "new paganism." Examining contemporary directions in such areas as human rights, morality, health, and politics, the author identifies secularism as a major threat to civilization and Christianity. He calls Christians to oppose what he considers cultural decadence encouraged by bad laws and a morally indifferent mass media.

Bright, Bill, and Ron Jenson. *Kingdoms at War: Tactics for Victory in Nine Spiritual War Zones.* San Bernardino, CA: Here's Life Publishers, 1986.

To Bright and Jenson, Christians are engaged in a war for the minds of Americans. The enemy is humanism. It is a war that requires commitment and sacrifice and does not allow for neutrality. This war entered a new phase when the Supreme Court in 1963 restricted Bible reading in public schools. The authors blame this decision for a series of evils, including political assassinations.

Brown, Walter T. *In the Beginning: Compelling Evidence for Creation and the Flood.* Phoenix, AZ: Center for Scientific Creation, 1995.

Brown defends creationism, employing geological, fossil, and biological data. The author employs traditional discussions of the worldwide flood recorded in the Book of Genesis and the purported resulting geological evidence to support creationism and to debunk evolution.

Colson, Chuck. *How Now Shall We Live?* Wheaton, IL: Tyndale House, 1999.

Colson, a White House official during the Richard Nixon administration who became a born-again Christian while serving time in prison for misdeeds committed during the Watergate scandal, diagnoses the flaws he sees in American culture and offers a religious-based solution. The author describes a culture characterized by disintegrating civility, violence, and moral indifference. He claims that although the culture presently dismisses and ridicules Christianity, only adherence to biblical principles can save the nation.

Crismier, Charles. *Preserve Us a Nation: Returning to Our Historical and Biblical Roots.* Sisters, OR: Multnomah, 1995.

Crismier views such problems as gangs, family dissolution, and unorthodox sexual practices as symptoms of a loss of moral character. He wants to return to a past time when biblical principles were practiced so that religious faith might be rekindled and moral character reestablished.

Davis, Percival, and Dean H. Kenyon. *Of Pandas and People: The Central Question of Biological Origins.* Dallas, TX: Haughton, 1989.

Davis and Kenyon present an argument for intelligent design as an alternative to Darwinian evolution. The work is made more attractive through the inclusion of seventy-five color photographs.

DeMar, Gary. *America's Christian History: The Untold Story.* 2d rev. ed. Powder Springs, GA: American Vision, 1993.

DeMar continues his argument, begun in earlier works, that the United States is, and always has been, fundamentally a Christian nation. The author examines events in American history, providing what he considers proof that Christianity shaped the basic character of the nation.

Dembski, William A. *Intelligent Design: The Bridge between Science and Theology.* Downers Grove, IL: InterVarsity, 1999.

Dembski, a supporter of the view that creation was the result of an intelligent force, deals with such topics as the perception of divine activity in nature, the importance of miracles, and criticisms of evolutionary theories.

Dembski, William A., ed. *Mere Creation: Science, Faith, and Intelligent Design.* Downers Grove, IL: InterVarsity, 1999.

The essays included in this work, written by nineteen scholars in the fields of mathematics, physics, astrophysics, biology, philosophy, and theology, explore possible weaknesses in, and question the foundations of, Darwinian theory.

Denton, Michael. *Evolution: A Theory in Crisis.* Portland, OR: Alder and Alder, 1997.

Denton, a self-proclaimed agnostic, challenges traditional theories of biological evolution. After an analysis of fossil records and biochemical data, he concludes that exclusively natural evolution cannot explain the biological diversity existing on earth.

DeParrie, Paul. *Dark Cures: Have Doctors Lost Their Ethics?* Lafayette, LA: Vital Issue, 1999.

DeParrie argues that since traditional ethical standards have been replaced by "pagan ethics," people can no longer assume that doctors and medical institutions hold in high regard the health and well-being of patients. The author laments the development of a medical profession that disregards human life, harvesting body parts of people considered less valuable, and using aborted fetuses for profit.

Devos, Dick. *Rediscovering American Values: The Foundations of Our Freedom for the 21st Century.* East Rutherford, NJ: Dutton, 1997.

Devos outlines twenty-four values, including honesty, compassion, initiative, self-discipline, and leadership, that he claims are the basis of liberty and will guide the country into the next century. The author believes that these values provide the foundation for American power and prosperity.

Drosnin, Michael. *The Bible Code.* New York: Simon and Schuster, 1998.

This book has the same popular appeal that Hal Lindsey's *The Late Great Planet Earth* had three decades ago. Both books foreshadow coming disasters for humankind. Drosnin's account is based on the claim that the Old Testament contains a secret code that, once deciphered through computer programs, reveals many past wars, famines, floods, assassinations, and wars as well as possible future catastrophes. Some argue that the appeal of this book and others like it is associated with a desire to believe in a divine order behind the apparent chaos of events.

Federer, William J. *America's God and Country: Encyclopedia of Quotations.* Coppell, TX: Fame, 1996.

This lengthy work (over 800 pages) presents inspirational quotes from prominent early Americans, presidents, statesmen, court decisions, military heroes, scientists and inventors, religious leaders, educators, and artists. Federer attempts to demonstrate that national leaders have relied on God for their inspiration and that they built the nation on biblical principles.

Guiness, Os, and John Seel, eds. *No God but God: Breaking with the Idols of Our Age.* Chicago: Moody Press, 1992.

This group of essays deals with the perceived problems of contemporary evangelicalism. An overreliance on marketing and management techniques, psychology, and politics has created idols that threaten the true Christian mission. The authors ask American evangelicals to recall their long past, confront modern idolatry, and campaign for religious freedom for all.

Hagee, John C. *The Revelation of Truth: A Mosaic of God's Plan for Man.* Nashville, TN: Nelson, 2000.

Taking a dispensational perspective popularized by C. I. Scofield, Hagee outlines the seven time periods from creation to the end time and the creation of a new heaven and a new earth. He argues that the time of Jesus' return is drawing near.

Ham, Kenneth. *The Lie: Evolution.* Green Forest, AR: Master Books, 1996.

Ham seeks to discredit Charles Darwin's theory of evolution, challenging the veracity of evolution theorists. Referring to scripture, the author employs arguments developed earlier in the twentieth century, contending that the theory of evolution is a serious threat to moral values. Ham associates biological evolution with the social philosophy of Social Darwinism developed by Herbert Spencer.

Ham, Kenneth, Andrew Snelling, and Carl Wieland. *The Answers Book.* Colorado Springs, CO: Master Books, 1991.

The authors attempt to answer questions of concern to supporters of the biblical creation thesis. They tackle such topics as dinosaurs and their extinction, the ice ages, the origin of different races, and the origin of animals in Australia.

Hanegraaff, Hank. *Christianity in Crisis.* Eugene, OR: Harvest House, 1993.

Hanegraaff, president of Christian Research Institute, offers an evangelical warning against the "faith movement" and its leaders, among whom are Kenneth Copeland, Charles Capps, and

Paul Crouch. Those in the faith movement, by emphasizing such things as physical healing and financial prosperity, stray from the orthodox Christian understanding of God. The book demonstrates the sort of disagreements that arise within conservative Christianity.

———. *The FACE That Demonstrates the Farce of Evolution.* Nashville, TN: Word, 1998.

Hanegraaff, president of the Christian Research Institute, argues that the evolutionary theory of human existence cannot be correct. Citing racist quotes from Charles Darwin, the author attempts to associate evolution with racism. Contending that the theory of evolution depends on the working of random chance, Hanegraaff asserts that the probability is extremely small that complex biological systems could have developed randomly.

Hayward, Alan. *Creation and Evolution.* Minneapolis, MN: Bethany House, 1995.

Using biblical references regarding creation, scientific data about evolution, and an investigation of the age of the universe, Hayward concludes that, statistically, the Darwinian theory of evolution is defective.

Huse, Scott M. *The Collapse of Evolution.* Grand Rapids, MI: Baker, 1998.

Examining the evidence for the theory of evolution and using the Bible as a source of information, Huse contends that evolution and creationism are incompatible. Noting examples of design in the natural world, the author concludes that evolution is fatally flawed. An appendix titled "Scientific Facts That Prove Evolution" is left blank.

Jakes, T. D. *The Great Investment: Faith, Family and Finance.* New York: Putnam, 2000.

T. D. Jakes, the popular television minister, discusses the relevance of the Christian faith to the maintenance of the family and achieving economic prosperity. Jakes states that God calls Christians to prosper so that their wealth can be used to spread the gospel. He advises people to act wisely in financial matters, distinguishing between needs and wants and avoiding gambling and lotteries.

Johnson, Phillip. *Darwin on Trial.* Washington, DC: Regnery, 1991.

This book offers an interesting analysis of Darwin's theory of evolution conducted by a legal expert. Johnson charges that scientists inappropriately accept Darwin's theory and have unsuccessfully attempted to establish supporting evidence. The author examines the problem of fossils and other topics relevant to a creationist response to evolution.

————. *Defeating Darwinism by Opening Minds.* Downers Grove, IL: InterVarsity, 1997.

Attempting to turn the tables on proevolution arguments, Johnson claims that clear thinking about the issues involved in the creation-evolution debate will result in greater skepticism about the validity of Darwinian theory.

————. *Objections Sustained: Subversive Essays on Evolution, Law and Culture.* Downers Grove, IL: InterVarsity, 1998.

In this volume of collected essays, Johnson criticizes what he calls the "idolatry of Darwin." Topics include American pragmatism, postmodernism, "pop" science, and religious freedom.

————. *Reason in the Balance: The Case Against Naturalism in Science, Law, and Education.* Downers Grove, IL: InterVarsity, 1998.

Johnson challenges naturalism, the belief dominating the contemporary worldview that holds that the material world is all that has existed or ever will exist. According to the author, this belief has had adverse moral consequences for science, law, and education.

————. *The Wedge of Truth: Splitting the Foundations of Naturalism.* Downers Grove, IL: InterVarsity, 2000.

Johnson argues that naturalism, which he states has been the dominant perspective of contemporary science, will no longer hold its preeminent place. The author believes the message of Christianity offers a new beginning for consideration not only of science and religion but of all meaningful human activity.

Kennedy, D. James, ed. *The Gates of Hell Shall Not Prevail: The Attack on Christianity and What You Need to Know to Combat It.* Nashville, TN: Nelson, 1997.

Noting that Christianity has often been the subject of attack throughout its history and presently is the subject of a culture war, the authors insist that the church always has, and always will, prevail. They contend that the church continues to grow despite such attacks and that opponents are historically destined to lose.

Klicka, Christopher J., and Gregg Harris. *The Right Choice: The Incredible Failure of Public Education and the Rising Hope of Home Schooling.* Rev. ed. Gresham, OR: Noble Books, 1994.

Klicka sets forth for parents considering home schooling the cultural beliefs supposedly being inculcated in the public schools. D. James Kennedy, a major religious leader, has written the foreword, and Gregg Harris of Christian Life Workshops offers practical advice about how to begin home schooling.

Knight, Robert H. *The Age of Consent: The Rise of Relativism and the Corruption of Popular Culture.* Dallas, TX: Spence, 1998.

With a foreword by 2000 religious right presidential candidate Gary Bauer, this book focuses on the dangers of philosophical relativism. Knight investigates what he considers the indications of cultural decline in such areas as film, television, popular music, architecture, and even religion.

LaHaye, Tim. *The Race for the 21st Century.* Nashville, TN: Thomas Nelson, 1986.

The race referred to in the title is the competition between Christians and humanists for control of American culture into the twenty-first century. The Christian must not only guard his family against humanist pressures, but also work to defeat the humanistic forces that are distorting society. Although LaHaye accepts political pluralism among religious groups, he rejects any legitimate political role for secular humanists.

LaHaye, Tim, and David Noebel. *Mind Siege: The Battle for Truth in the New Millennium.* Nashville, TN: Word, 2001.

LaHaye, coauthor of the popular *Left Behind* series, and Noebel, president of the Christian Anti-Communism Crusade, expose the alleged dangers of secular humanism. They claim that mainline churches have accepted many of the tenets of humanism, including evolution, socialism, higher criticism of the Bible, moral relativism, liberation theology, and world government.

Lightner, Robert P. *The Last Days Handbook: A Comprehensive Guide to Understanding the Different Views of Prophecy.* Nashville, TN: Thomas Nelson, 1990.

This is a good source for understanding an issue important to many on the religious right. Lightner discusses the premillennial, amillennial, and postmillennial approaches to biblical prophecy, acknowledging that sharp disagreements sometimes emerge over these various positions. The author encourages evangelical Christians to recognize basic agreements over biblical prophecy.

Lindsey, Hal. *Planet Earth—2000 A.D.* Palos Verdes, CA: Western Front, 1994.

Lindsey discounts any inherent significance to the year 2000 but does suggest that the "seven-year countdown" to Christ's return could begin before that date. Lindsey refers to a variety of occurrences, including political events in Asia and the Middle East, the formation of the European Community, the increased popularity of occultism, an increasing crime rate, the spread of AIDS, and more severe natural disasters such as earthquakes and floods to support his argument that the end times are near.

MacArthur, John. *Reckless Faith: When the Church Loses Its Will to Discern.* Wheaton, IL: Crossway, 1994.

MacArthur expresses a common concern among more fundamentalist Christians about the moral health of American churches. He believes modern secular society, in which no limits on behavior seem to exist, has had too great an influence on the church. Using biblical prescriptions, MacArthur suggests ways in which Christians can discern the authentic from the inauthentic in the church.

Machen, J. Gresham. *Christianity and Liberalism.* Grand Rapids, MI: Eerdmans, 1997.

Originally published in 1923, this book presents an "orthodox" Christian response to a more liberal theology that became popular in the early twentieth century. Machen deals with distinctions between liberalism and orthodoxy in such areas as the relationship between God and man, the authority of the Bible, the person of Christ, the meaning of salvation, and the institution of the church. Machen's views influenced the development of more recent positions taken by the religious right.

Marshall, Peter, and David Manuel. *Sounding Forth the Trumpet.* Grand Rapids, MI: Baker, 1998.

In this third volume examining American history from a conservative Christian perspective, the authors investigate the events preceding the Civil War. The book begins with John Quincy Adams's administration and closes with the 1860 election, focusing on those people the authors believe were used by God to shape the history of the nation.

Matrisciana, Carly, and Roger Oakland. *The Evolution Conspiracy.* Eugene, OR: Harvest House, 1991.

Defending the Christian fundamentalist position on creationisn, the authors portray the conflict between creationism and evolution theory as one between two religions. The authors emphasize what they consider the moral consequences of a complete victory for evolution theory.

McDowell, Josh, and Bob Hostetler. *The New Tolerance: How a Cultural Movement Threatens to Destroy You, Your Faith, and Your Children.* Wheaton, IL: Tyndale, 1998.

The authors argue that tolerance, often considered a positive virtue, in fact threatens the maintenance of a Christian society. They object to a permissive attitude toward what they consider threats to Christian beliefs, such as homosexuality, feminism, and alternative religious beliefs.

Moreland, J. P., ed. *The Creation Hypothesis: Scientific Evidence for an Intelligent Designer.* Downersgrove, IL: InterVarsity, 1994.

The authors of these essays argue that explanations for the existence of the universe and of life must include God. Contributors deal with the beginnings of life, the source of organic groupings, explanations of language, and the origins of the universe, with emphasis placed on the "Big Bang" theory.

Moreland, J. P., and Scott B. Rae. *Body and Soul: Human Nature and the Crisis in Ethics.* Downers Grove, IL: InterVarsity Press, 2000.

Holding the traditional doctrine of Christian dualism, Moreland and Rae argue that ethical questions of abortion, fetal research, cloning, and euthanasia must be informed by the religious view that human beings possess a soul.

Noebel, David A. *Understanding the Times: The Religious Worldviews of Our Day and the Search for Truth.* Eugene, OR: Harvest House, 1994.

Noebel compares and contrasts four major contemporary worldviews: Christianity, Marxism/Leninism, secular humanism, and the New Age movement. According to the author, a worldview includes beliefs about theology, philosophy, ethics, biology, psychology, sociology, law, politics, economics, and history. Noebel, who asserts the superiority of Christianity over the other worldviews, has been criticized for failing to consider other religious faiths.

North, Gary. *Is the World Running Down? Crisis in the Christian Worldview.* Tyler, TX: Institute for Christian Economics, 1988.

North urges the religious right to accept pluralism. Those on the religious right should be willing to strive within the existing governmental structure, a strategy that has already brought some success. Nonetheless, North does not lose sight of conservative Christian values that are ultimately hostile to a pluralist perspective.

Oakland, Roger, with Dan Wooding. *Let There Be Light.* Santa Ana, CA: Oakland Communications, 1993.

This work contrasts the moral and religious effects of evolution and creation theories. The authors contend that the teaching of evolution has been deceitful and has taken God out of people's lives, while creationism restores humankind's relationship with God.

O'Hear, Anthony. *Beyond Evolution: Human Nature and the Limits of Evolutionary Explanation.* New York: Oxford University Press, 1999.

Although not writing from a Christian perspective, O'Hear contends that the Darwinian theory fails to account for crucial aspects of human existence, including human consciousness, the search for knowledge, a sense of morality, and the perception of beauty.

Parks, Jerald. *False Security: Has the New Age Given Us a False Hope?* Lafayette, LA: Huntington House, 1992.

Parks examines the New Age claim that humankind is being transformed into a higher level of civilization and compares it to biblical notions of the last days and the collapse of civilization. Humanity may be faced with a time of darkness not seen since the fall of the Roman Empire and the beginning of the Middle Ages.

Pearcy, Nancy, and Charles B. Thaxton. *The Soul of Science: Christian Faith and Natural Philosophy.* Wheaton, IL: Crossway, 1994.

Pearcy and Thaxton distinguish between a period when scientists and people generally accepted Christianity publicly and more recent times in which science has become hostile to Christian belief. The authors relate the accomplishments of scientists such as Robert Boyle, Isaac Newton, and Carl Linnaeus, whose scientific achievements occurred in the context of the Christian faith.

Peretti, Frank E. *The Oath.* Nashville, TN: Word, 1996.

This best-selling fictional account of a small town's struggle with sinister forces is relevant to the cultural views of the religious right, portraying a battle between the forces of good and forces of evil in this world.

Pierce, Alfred R. *It Is Finished.* Rev. ed. Camden, NJ: Radiant Publications, 1993.

A lawyer, former mayor of Camden, New Jersey, former chairman of the Delaware River Port Authority, and student of the Bible, Pierce claims that the United States is the Babylon of the Book of Revelation and will be destroyed. He argues that Satan is now in control of the world.

Pitts, F. E. *The U.S.A. in Bible Prophecy: Two Sermons Preached to the U.S. Congress in 1857.* Baltimore, MD: J. W. Bull, 1862.

These two sermons, "The United States of America Foretold in the Holy Scriptures" and "The Battle of Armageddon," delivered prior to the Civil War, are notable for their inclusion of the United States in biblical prophecy. Pitts identifies the United States and Russia as those powers described in Ezekiel 38 that will be involved in the final battle of Armageddon.

Quayle, Dan. *Worth Fighting For.* Nashville, TN: Word, 2000.

Former Vice President Dan Quayle argues that scandal in government and unwise policies have led the United States in the wrong direction. To set the country on the right track, Quayle believes, will require a return to faith in God and a willingness to take responsibility for one's own actions. The author offers his position on such subjects as social security, abortion, and gay marriage.

Robertson, Pat. *The New Millennium.* Dallas, TX: Word, 1990.

Robertson examines the history of Christianity, its present situation in the world, and its prospects for the twenty-first century. He claims that the United States is the strongest Christian nation since the fall of the Roman Empire and the "last great expression" of Christianity's victory.

Ross, Hugh. *Creation and Time: A Biblical and Scientific Perspective on the Creation-Date Controversy.* Colorado Springs, CO: NavPress, 1994.

Ross attempts to resolve the apparent conflict between Christian and scientific views about the age of the earth and the beginning of the universe. He explores biblical texts and early church beliefs as well as scientific findings regarding these topics.

———. *The Genesis Question: Scientific Advances and the Accuracy of Genesis.* Colorado Springs, CO: NavPress, 1998.

Ross, a physicist and head of the organization Reasons To Believe, investigates the view that the biblical account of creation amounts to prescientific myth and attempts to demonstrate that the Book of Genesis coincides with scientific evidence supporting divine intervention in the natural world.

Russo, Steve. *Halloween: What's a Christian to Do?* Eugene, OR: Harvest House, 1998.

Russo expresses the discomfort that evangelical Christian parents feel when faced with the traditions of the larger secular culture. He offers advice to parents who wish to protect their children against what are perceived to be pagan observances.

Schaeffer, Francis A. *Escape from Reason.* Madison, WI: InterVarsity, 1968.

Written by perhaps the foremost conservative Christian political thinker, this brief volume investigates contemporary thought, tracing its development from Aquinas to the present. The author is highly critical of the present age, especially the "God is dead" movement, the rejection of rationality, and the turn toward non-rational experience. Evangelical Christians are urged not to separate Jesus from the content of scripture.

————. *The God Who Is There.* Downer Groves, IL: InterVarsity, 1968.

Schaeffer explores the nature of human despair in modern times. He investigates the origins of this condition of hopelessness and its evil consequences. Christianity is offered as the only means of combating despair.

————. *No Final Conflict: The Bible without Error in All That It Affirms.* Downers Grove, IL: InterVarsity, 1975.

This is a vigorous defense of biblical literalism based upon a rather traditional fundamentalist position. That is, Schaeffer argues that if one questions the historicity of Genesis, such as the actual existence of Adam and Eve, there is no reason to trust any factual statement in the Bible, including the resurrection of Jesus.

————. *How Should We Then Live? The Rise and Decline of Western Thought and Culture.* Old Tappan, NJ: Fleming H. Revell, 1976.

Schaeffer did not mint the term "secular humanism," but in this sweeping assessment of Western culture he certainly makes it the bête noire of conservative Christians in much of the English-speaking world. From the Greeks and Romans to the Renaissance and Enlightenment, he contrasts the "strengths" of Christianity, rooted in God's absolute truth, to the "weaknesses" of human-centered cultures whose moral relativism inevitably led to a cheapening of human life. Schaeffer admires the Reformation, for it represented the restoration of divine absolutes.

————. *A Christian Manifesto.* Westchester, IL: Crossway Books, 1981.

This work refutes socialism and humanism and calls Christians to organize against the trend toward immorality in our society. Schaeffer bases his arguments on the notion of a "form-free balance," an equilibrium between social responsibility and individual rights. With the antiabortion movement in mind, the author justifies civil disobedience when the government demonstrates its tyrannical nature by disobeying the law of God.

Schlossberg, Herbert. *A Fragrance of Oppression: The Church and Its Persecutors.* Wheaton, IL: Crossways, 1991.

Beginning with the supposition that American culture is in crisis and that humanism has become the dominant perspective, Schlossberg provides biblical guidance for Christian believers who want to have an impact on American cultural institutions by voicing their preference for a Christian worldview.

Scofield, C. I. *Scofield Study Bible.* New York: Oxford University Press, 1967.

First published in 1919, this King James version of the Bible contains extensive notes that present a fundamentalist perspective on such topics as dispensational premillennialism, scriptural inerrancy, and the distinction between Jews and Christians. This Bible became a major statement of belief for many conservative fundamentalist Christians. Oxford offers several versions of this still-popular Bible.

Spencer, James R. *Bleeding Hearts and Propaganda: The Fall of Reason in the Church.* Lafayette, LA: Huntington House, 1995.

Spencer criticizes popular church leaders for failing to maintain what he considers sound truth and principles of reason based on scripture. He faults some religious leaders for failing to maintain the tradition of biblical truth, compromising with contemporary secular beliefs, and participating in a general moral decline. He uses contemporary attitudes of some Christians toward homosexuality as an example of inappropriate compassion for what he considers a biblically unacceptable practice.

Stanley, Lynn. *The Blame Game: Why Society Persecutes Christians.* Lafayette, LA: Huntington House, 1996.

Stanley argues for absolute moral values, claiming that the United States was built on Christian principles. She attacks the mass media for alleged attempts to repress Judeo-Christian values, and she targets the National Education Association for using public funds and public classrooms to establish humanism as the national religion of the United States. According to Stanley, New Age religions and occultism are being disseminated in school classrooms. To combat such tendencies, the author urges members of Christian churches to maintain a biblically sound way of life.

Terrel, Steve. *The 90's, Decade of the Apocalypse: The European Common Market—The End Has Begun.* South Plainfield, NJ: Bridge Publishing, 1992.

This premillennialist treatment of biblical prophecy shifts attention away from the United States and Russia to the formation of the European Community as a sign of the end times. The Antichrist will be the first president of the United States of Europe, and this person supposedly will become the emperor of a new Holy Roman Empire and will begin wars of conquest.

Thompson, Bert. *Creation Compromises.* Montgomery, AL: Apologetics Press, 1995.

Thompson surveys the 200-year development of modern geology, paying particular attention to the belief that geological discoveries are incompatible with biblical claims of a recent creation and a worldwide flood. Some scientists and theologians, attempting to discover evidence of a much older earth in scripture, are considered to be parties to a compromise.

Torrey, Reuben A., and Charles L. Feinberg, eds. *The Famous Sourcebook of Foundational Biblical Truths.* Grand Rapids, MI: Kregel, 1990.

A set of twelve pamphlets each about 125 pages in length, these booklets not only assail modernism but also enunciate what came to be, and in essence still are, the key tenets of fundamentalism: the inerrancy of the Bible and the virgin birth, substitutionary atonement, bodily resurrection, and the second coming of Jesus. Along with these most frequently cited five fundamentals, the pamphlets, originally published between 1910 and 1915, emphasize the deity of Jesus, the sinful nature of humanity, salvation by faith, and the bodily resurrection of believers. They refute evolution and higher criticism, and they denounce Catholicism, Mormonism, Jehovah's Witnesses, Christian Scientists, and Spiritualism.

Van Bebber, Mark, and Paul Taylor. *Creation and Time: A Report on the Progressive Creationist Book by Hugh Ross.* Mesa, AZ: Eden Publications, 1994.

The authors criticize Hugh Ross, president of Reasons To Believe, for his advocacy of a "progressive creation" position. Although agreeing with Ross that life could not have arisen through natural processes, they point to his alleged erroneous biblical interpretations, such as the claim that the earth is billions of years old, that there was death before Adam's fall, and that the biblical flood was not worldwide.

Veith, Gene Edward, Jr. *Postmodern Times: A Christian Guide to Contemporary Thought and Culture.* Wheaton, IL: Crossway, 1994.

Veith associates postmodernism with a rejection of firm notions of truth, meaning, individual identity, and the value of human life. He argues that postmodernist ideas have proliferated among judges, writers, journalists, and teachers, and have had deep influences on film, television, art, literature, and politics. The author calls for a proclamation of the gospel in order to counteract the cultural consequences of postmodernist thought.

Walton, Rus. *Fundamentals for American Christians.* Nyack, NY: Parson, 1979.

Walton portrays an America based on fundamental biblical principles. The American revolution was influenced by the political thought of John Locke, who is described as a Christian thinker. The conservative Christian objective is to return the United States to its Christian roots, and to reject any attempt to combine Christianity with humanism.

Walvoord, John F. *Armageddon, Oil and the Middle East Crisis: What the Bible Says about the Future of the Middle East and the End of Western Civilization.* Rev. ed. Grand Rapids, MI: Zondervan, 1990.

This contribution to apocalyptic literature explains why the presence of oil in the Middle East makes that region the focus of biblical prophecies about the final battle of Armageddon. Walvoord establishes a chronology of events he claims will lead to the rapture and Christ's return.

Welch, Robert. *The Blue Book of the John Birch Society.* Appleton, WI: Western Islands, 1959, 1961, 1992.

This book is a transcript of the two-day presentation Robert Welch made at a meeting with eleven other men in 1958 that began the organization named for a fundamentalist Baptist missionary. Welch observes the loss of faith among fundamentalists of all religions and warns that this faith is being replaced by opportunism and hedonism. Communists are taking advantage of this loss. Though believing that fundamentalist faith cannot be restored,

Welch suggests a broader faith that will be acceptable to "the most fundamentalist Christian or the most rationalistic idealist."

Whitehead, John W. *The End of Man.* Westchester, IL: Crossway Books, 1986.

Although America still publicly expresses religious faith, Whitehead argues that the dissemination of humanist doctrines has become so extensive that discussion of what is right and wrong can no longer occur. The author advises Christians to maintain their values, avoid accommodation, and actively confront humanist beliefs.

Zacharias, Ravi K. *A Shattered Visage: The Real Face of Atheism.* Grand Rapids, MI: Baker Books, 1993.

The author contends America has proceeded toward atheism, both personally and institutionally. Christian civilization has been decimated by this atheism and citizens suffer the consequences of alienation, loneliness, and guilt. Zacharias claims that violence is a logical result of atheism.

———. *Deliver Us from Evil: Restoring the Soul in a Disintegrating Culture.* Nashville, TN: Word, 1998.

Zacharias argues that many contemporary popular ideas represent a threat to the traditional culture based on Christianity. Although humans have attempted to create an earthly utopia, the author contends they have ignored truth and the problem of evil and therefore have brought themselves close to social disintegration.

Political and Economic Issues

Alcorn, Randy C. *Is Rescuing Right? Breaking the Law to Save the Unborn.* Downers Grove, IL: InterVarsity, 1990.

Admitting that the rescuing strategy has been controversial within the Christian community, Alcorn nonetheless claims that the willingness of some to "make sacrifices" means "the lives of babies are being saved." Christians should do all they can to prevent abortions, the author concludes, even taking part in civil disobedience if necessary.

Bahnsen, Greg L. *By This Standard: The Authority of God's Law Today.* Tyler, TX: Institute for Christian Economics, 1991.

Instead of the moral relativism that dominates contemporary society, Bahnsen argues that individual Christians and society as a whole should be guided by both Old and New Testament laws and precepts.

Barton, Charles D. *America: To Pray or Not to Pray.* Rev. ed. Aledo, TX: Wallbuilders, 1989.

This work provides statistical evidence of an American decline ever since 1962, when the Supreme Court instituted the ban on school prayer and, according to the author, began to disallow religious principles generally in public affairs.

———. *Myth of Separation.* Rev. ed. Aledo, TX: Wallbuilders, 1991.

Taking quotes from the writings of the constitutional Founders and from Supreme Court decisions in the period 1795 to 1952, Barton argues that the separation of church and state is more myth than historical fact. In Barton's view, American history supports a close union between church and state.

Bolton, Richard, ed. *Culture Wars: Documents from the Recent Controversies in the Arts.* New York: New Press, 1992.

This volume contains documents dealing with the controversy over funding the National Endowment for the Arts (NEA), including congressional testimony, scholarly articles, opinion pieces, and personal correspondence. Individuals on the religious right, including Jerry Falwell, were major critics of the NEA.

Borst, W. A. *Liberalism: Fatal Consequences.* Lafayette, LA: Vital Issue, 1998.

Recounting the history of the liberal ideology in the United States, Borst exposes what he claims is the hypocrisy of liberalism. The author wants to empower the reader to resist cultural changes he attributes to liberal thinking.

Boys, Don. *Pilgrims, Puritans, and Patriots: Our Christian Heritage.* Maitland, FL: Freedom Institute Press, 1983.

Boys examines the history and beliefs of the early settlers on the North American continent in order to trace the nation's Christian heritage. He discusses the religious beliefs of Columbus and the

Puritans and the motivations of the colonists in coming to the New World. An additional topic is the meaning of the First Amendment and the role Christians have played in defending personal and religious freedom.

Carson, D. A. *The Gagging of God: Christianity Confronts Pluralism.* Grand Rapids, MI: Zondervan, 1996.

Carson, professor of the New Testament at Trinity Evangelical Divinity School, critically examines pluralism and pluralistic attitudes that he sees capturing American culture. The author rejects pluralistic perspectives, opting instead for what he considers the unique truth found in the New Testament account of Jesus.

Colson, Chuck, and Jack Eckerd. *Why America Doesn't Work: How the Decline of the Work Ethic Is Hurting Your Family and Future—and What You Can Do.* Dallas, TX: Word, 1991.

Colson, chairman of Prison Fellowship, and Eckerd, former head of the Eckerd drugstore chain, believe the spiritual foundation of the work ethic has eroded, thus causing many of the problems now facing the United States, including the decline of American competition in the world market, the deterioration of American schools, and the millions of unproductive people in prison and on welfare. The churches are given a major role in restoring the work ethic.

Colson, Chuck, with Ellen Santilli Vaughn. *Kingdoms in Conflict.* Grand Rapids, MI: William Morrow/Zondervan, 1987.

Colson, a former member of Richard Nixon's administration, was "born again" while serving time in prison because of Watergate misdeeds. This volume presents his views on the relationship between the Christian church and politics.

Dobson, Ed, and Ed Hindson. *The Seduction of Power.* Old Tappan, NJ: Fleming H. Revell, 1988.

The authors, each of whom formerly worked with Jerry Falwell, reflect on the flurry of religious right activity in the 1980s. The authors appear less optimistic about the results of this political activity, but recognize the need for continued, but possibly more subdued, involvement.

Domingo, Roger. *Orphans in Babylon: Abortion in America.*

Where Are We Now? How Did We Get Here? Where Should We Go? Sun City, CA: Turnstyle, 1998.

Presenting an overview of the pro-life movement, Domingo's purpose is to prepare readers for a ministry of saving "orphans" in what he considers the hostile world of American culture, which he refers to as "Babylon."

Doner, Colonel V. *The Samaritan Strategy: A New Agenda for Christian Activism.* Brentwood, TN: Wolgemuth and Hyatt, 1988.

Doner, a lobbyist for Christian Voice in the 1980s, evaluates religious right strategies in retrospect and concludes that the movement was far too negative in its objectives. The religious right was concerned primarily with blocking the objectives of more liberal groups. He suggests an overall change in tactics that includes the positive goal of helping the deserving poor as an alternative to the welfare state.

Eakman, B. K. *Cloning of the American Mind: Eradicating Morality through Education.* Lafayette, LA: Huntington House, 1998.

Recommended by Billy James Hargis's Christian Crusade, this book accuses those running the present public education system of employing psychological manipulation that is having devastating effects on children. The widespread use of psychological assessments, Eakman contends, has troubling implications for the maintenance of individual privacy.

Eidsmoe, John. *God and Caesar: Biblical Faith and Political Action.* Westchester, IL: Crossways Books, 1984.

The author focuses on a conservative economic interpretation of the Bible. He identifies the existence of private property in scripture extending from pre-Mosaic times to the millennium of Revelation. Eidsmoe highlights examples of private enterprise in several of Jesus' parables. Aspects of the Constitution, such as separation of powers, are viewed as rooted in the Christian tradition.

———. *Gays and Guns: The Case against Homosexuals in the Military.* Lafayette, LA: Huntington House, 1991.

Eidsmoe, proponent of a strong relationship between Christianity and the American political system, argues that admitting homosexuals openly into the military weakens combat effectiveness, creates risks to national security, and ends the traditional notion of the military as a rite of passage for young men.

———. *Columbus and Cortez: Conquerors for Christ.* Green Forest, AR: New Leaf, 1992.

Admitting that Indians suffered abuses at the hands of Columbus and other explorers, Eidsmoe nonetheless defends Christian intervention in the New World by arguing that many Native Americans who endured oppression under Native American traditions joined the explorers as liberators.

———. *Christianity and the Constitution.* Grand Rapids, MI: Baker, 1995.

Countering the position that the United States Constitution is neutral with regard to religious belief, Eidsmoe argues that the constitutional framers favored Christianity and wanted that religion to be sanctioned by the nation's governing document. The author summarizes the religious beliefs of some noted early Americans.

Feder, Don. *A Jewish Conservative Looks at Pagan America.* Lafayette, LA: Huntington House, 1993.

Feder claims abortion is not a right because it lacks any moral foundation. He traces America's problems to a lack of sexual inhibition that leads to the excessive display of other human passions. Suggestions for remedying the situation are offered.

Ferris, Michael. *Anonymous Tip.* Nashville, TN: Broadman and Holman, 1996.

Ferris, president of the Home School Legal Defense Association, wrote this novel to highlight his belief that government is attempting to prevent people of faith from caring for their own children. An anonymous and vindictive call to Child Protective Services, falsely charging mistreatment of a child, leads to a struggle between the government bureaucracy and a parent trying to exercise her parental rights.

Foreman, Joseph L. *Shattering the Darkness: The Crisis of the Cross in the Church Today.* Montreat, NC: Cooling Spring, 1992.

Foreman gives a biblical defense for Christians conducting "abortion rescues." The book includes a letter written from prison by antiabortion leader Randall Terry in which he justifies his actions.

Fries, Michael, and C. Holland Taylor. *A Christian Guide to Prosperity.* Oakland, CA: Communications Research, 1984.

This work offers investment and savings advice for Christians. The authors criticize the present system that allows people to prosper without working. To rectify this situation, they recommend a return to the gold standard and suggest keeping assets in gold and Swiss francs.

Gentry, Kenneth L., Jr. *God's Law in the Modern World.* Phillipsburg, NJ: Presbyterian and Reformed Publishing, 1993.

Focusing on "theonomy," the claim that Old Testament moral and civil laws remain applicable for Christians and society generally, the author discusses the role of law not only in preaching the gospel and personal Christian conduct, but also in the formation of national public policy.

Grant, George. *The Dispossessed: Homelessness in America.* Fort Worth, TX: Dominion, 1986.

Grant analyzes poverty from a conservative Christian perspective. Poverty and homelessness result from the sinfulness of Adam and Eve and therefore can be thought of as punishment. Christians can, through diligence, obedience to God, and the inspiration of the Holy Spirit, achieve prosperity. The responsibility for helping the poor and homeless falls not on government but the church, a responsibility that includes the need to admonish the idle.

————. *In the Shadow of Plenty: The Biblical Blueprint for Welfare.* Fort Worth, TX: Dominion, 1986.

Grant describes government welfare programs as wicked, biblically heretical, and administered by sinful people who have no genuine concern for the poor. Although the church has responsibility for charity, Grant argues that this is a limited role. The ultimate purpose of charity should be to make the poor more responsible and productive.

————. *The Changing of the Guard: Biblical Blueprints for Political Action.* Fort Worth, TX: Dominion Press, 1987.

Grant argues that Christian right successes result from a refusal to compromise religious principles. To return America to the theocratic status the Founders intended, he recommends a strategy of local, grassroots politics that includes activities beyond conventional participation. Churches should offer political education as well as opportunities for worship.

————. *Bringing in the Sheaves: Transforming Poverty into Productivity.* Brentwood, TN: Wolgemuth and Hyatt, 1988.

In this treatment of poverty, Grant contends that the objective of assistance to the poor is the return to productivity and independence. The author claims that the poor are often responsible for their own poverty, especially because of a lack of faith in God and the resulting sinfulness.

Hagee, John C. *Final Dawn over Jerusalem: Why Israel's Future Is So Important to Christians.* Nashville, TN: Nelson, 1999.

Hagee claims that Israel remains the chosen nation of God and discusses the history of Jerusalem and the Jewish people and nation. Attacking anti-Semitism, the author argues from biblical references that the Jewish people are the favored people of God and that anyone who attacks Israel will suffer God's wrath. The book coincides with a Christian right perspective that favors United States support for the state of Israel. Hagee believes Israel is the key to the end times prophesied in the Bible.

Hall, Verna M., and Rosalie J. Slater, eds. *The Bible and the Constitution of the United States of America.* Chesapeake, VA: Foundation for American Christian Education, 1983.

The authors have compiled a large number of historical documents, including sermons and public proclamations, that they claim demonstrate that the Bible was a fundamental influence in founding the United States.

Hargis, Billy James. *Day of Deception.* Tulsa, OK: Christian Crusade Books, 1991.

Hargis, leader of the Christian Crusade, focuses on the many ways in which Christians can be deceived. Marxists, "one-worlders," the New Age movement, religious liberals, supporters of theological heresies, and "enemies of the Christian home," such as the entertainment industry and amoral schools, are targeted for attack.

———. *The Federal Reserve Scandal.* Tulsa, OK: Christian Crusade Books, 1995.

Hargis argues that "liberals" are the cause of inflation, that the American economy is out of control, and that the value of money continues to fall. The author suggests ways for Christians to oppose these trends.

Heath, Charles C. *The Blessings of Liberty: Restoring the City on the Hill.* Lafayette, LA: Huntington House, 1991.

Heath reviews 200 years of American history during which he believes God has blessed Americans with liberty. Now we are in danger of losing this liberty, so Heath encourages the reader to return to Christianity and choose honest national leaders who will follow a conservative policy agenda that includes providing work for those on welfare, cutting federal government spending, and instituting term limits. The author considers this agenda the way to reestablish "God's city on the hill."

Hirsen, James L. *The Coming Collision: Global Law versus U.S. Liberties.* Lafayette, LA: Huntington House, 1998.

Distributed by Billy James Hargis's Christian Crusade, this book attacks "global activists," who are claimed to support everything from environmental extremism and radical feminism to New Age mysticism. Hirsen argues that international law is being used to spread this radical philosophy.

Hunter, Paul. *The Many Faces of Babylon: The Babylonian Influences upon Our Churches.* New York: Revelation Books, 1994.

Contrasting human and biblical systems of organization, Hunter claims God's plan as presented in the Bible must be followed. The New Age movement comes under attack, as do television, motion pictures, the recording industry, and the government, each of which is charged with deceiving and manipulating Christians.

Kah, Gary. *En Route to Global Occupation.* Lafayette, LA: Huntington House, 1991.

Kah, a trade representative for the state of Indiana, claims to have exposed a frightening secret plan to unite the nations of the planet into a godless New World Order.

Kincaid, Cliff. *Global Taxes for World Government.* Lafayette, LA: Vital Issue, 1997.

Expressing the fear many conservatives, including those on the religious right, have of the potential power of the United Nations, Kincaid claims that the international organization intends to tax American citizens and businesses trillions of dollars to support a host of spending programs around the world.

LaHaye, Tim. *Faith of Our Founding Fathers.* Brentwood, TN: Wolgemuth and Hyatt, 1987.

A leading figure in the Christian right provides his perceptions of the constitutional framers' religious beliefs. LaHaye stresses, in some cases beyond credibility, what he considers the Christian beliefs of the framers, concluding that the nation was founded on a general agreement regarding Christian principles.

Luksik, Peg, and Pamela Hobbs Hoffecker. *Outcome-Based Education: The State's Assault on Our Children's Values.* Lafayette, LA: Huntington House, 1995.

This is an indictment of outcome-based education (OBE), which the authors define as "education based on outcomes instead of time spent in class in specific disciplines." OBE focuses on skills that a student demonstrates rather than a body of knowledge that a student learns. The authors fear that students will be made to achieve academic as well as nonacademic outcomes, thus allowing the state to determine what are acceptable behaviors and beliefs. OBE is seen as a dangerous intervention by the state and national governments in the family's role in the determination of children's values.

Marshall, Peter, and David Manuel. *The Light and the Glory.* Old Tappan, NJ: Fleming H. Revell, 1977.

This survey of American historical events from Christopher Columbus's landing to the writing of the Constitution depicts God's benevolent intervention. The Puritans are given much of the credit for establishing a Christian nation. Ultimately, however, God's divine guidance is responsible for the successful revolutionary war and the Constitution. The authors argue that America is now suffering the consequences of straying from the spiritual path.

———. *From Sea to Shining Sea.* Old Tappan, NJ: Fleming H. Revell, 1986.

The authors offer a history of the United States from the writing of the Constitution to the Civil War from a conservative Christian perspective. Although many non-Christians took part in developing America, God is seen as guiding the entire nation according to His own plan.

McGuire, Paul. *Who Will Rule the Future? A Resistance to the New World Order.* Lafayette, LA: Huntington House, 1991.

McGuire argues that Christians must be willing to take a political stand in order to combat the political and spiritual forces confronting the United States. Christians must oppose the "New Age conspiracy," the move toward socialism, and the globalism of the United Nations.

McIlhenny, Chuck, Donna McIlhenny, and Frank York. *When the Wicked Seize a City: A Grim Look at the Future and a Warning to the Church.* Lafayette, LA: Huntington House, 1993.

When a father takes a biblical stand against homosexual rights, he and his family face a violent reaction. According to the authors, homosexuality is a threat to children, schools, and the Christian way of life.

Noll, Mark A. *Adding Cross to Crown: The Political Significance of Christ's Passion.* Grand Rapids, MI: Baker, 1996.

Noll originally presented these thoughts on the proper relationship between Christianity and politics as the inaugural Kuyper Lecture, an annual forum on religion and public life sponsored by the Center for Public Justice. James Bratt, Max Stackhouse, and James Skillen provide responses to the lecture. Noll urges Christians to concentrate on Christ when they think about, or engage in, political activity, asking them not to "forget the cross" and to take a "godlike stance" toward the world.

North, Gary. *Honest Money: The Biblical Blueprint for Money and Banking.* Fort Worth, TX: Dominion Press, 1986.

North observes that the reconstruction of an economy based on capitalism and Christian values may first require a total collapse of the economy. The author recommends that Christians prepare for hard times by purchasing gold and silver and storing up basic supplies.

———. *The Sinai Strategy: Economics and the Ten Commandments.* Tyler, TX: Institute for Christian Economics, 1986.

North argues for the compatibility of Christianity and capitalism, finding a basis for a free enterprise system beginning in Old Testament references. The Ten Commandments provide the religious, legal, and economic preconditions for the development of a free market.

———. *Inherit the Earth: Biblical Blueprints for Economics.* Fort Worth, TX: Dominion Press, 1987.

North recommends a religious right emphasis on local politics. Opting for a more long-term strategy, the author sees the importance of political struggles not at the national but at the local governmental level.

North, Gary, and Gary DeMar. *Christian Reconstruction: What It Is, What It Isn't.* Tyler, TX: Institute for Christian Economics, 1994.

North and Demar explain what is meant by Christian Reconstruction. It is a theological movement whose goal is to transform, or reconstruct, the world according to biblical principles. The authors argue that Christians have surrendered the public realm to the secular world, limiting themselves to the private world of the family and the church. Christians must enter public life and act to reform the world before Christ's second coming.

Olasky, Marvin. *The American Leadership Tradition: Moral Vision from Washington to Clinton.* New York: Free Press, 1999.

Olasky, adviser to George W. Bush during the 2000 presidential campaign, investigates the lives of thirteen prominent Americans, including ten presidents. Arguing that personal morality plays a significant role in political behavior, the author concludes that devotion to God and faithfulness in marriage are closely related to wise political decision making. Olasky concludes that the actions of presidents influence the behavior of future presidents and affect the public's trust in political leaders.

———. *Compassionate Conservatism: What It Is, What It Does, and How It Can Transform America.* New York: Free Press, 2000.

Olasky argues that government and religious groups, the so-called faith-based organizations, should cooperate more closely in providing assistance to the poor. This can be done by government partially funding the social welfare activities of private religious organizations. Olasky believes such organizations not only provide assistance for physical deficiencies but also minister to spiritual needs. President George W. Bush, who made "compassionate conservatism" a major theme in his 2000 campaign, wrote the introduction.

O'Leary, Dale. *The Gender Agenda: Redefining Equality.* Lafayette, LA: Vital Issue, 1997.

O'Leary examines the feminist movement, tracing its activities since the early 1970s. The author focuses on what he considers the destructiveness of the movement, claiming that it threatens the ideals of family, marriage, and motherhood. According to O'Leary, the feminist movement opposes the right of women to follow their traditional roles, seeking to alter the position of women in society through government adoption of a radical feminist ideology and spreading their doctrines worldwide through the United Nations.

Opitz, Edmund A. *Religion and Capitalism: Allies, Not Enemies.* Irvington-on-Hudson, NY: Foundation for Economic Education, 1992.

This book, originally published in 1970, examines differing forms of governing. Opitz concludes that a liberal ideology is conducive to strong government, whereas Christianity and capitalism mutually support one another.

Peters, Peter J. *America the Conquered.* LaPorte, CO: Scriptures of America Ministries, 1991.

Pastor Pete Peters argues that anti-Christian elements in society have conquered America. Evidence that the United States has been subdued is found in the Supreme Court's decisions on flag burning, the decline of sexual morality, the harassment of churches, an extensive increase in police powers, the secularization of schools, and the legalization of abortion. Peters advises Americans to turn to God in order to regain their freedom.

Rae, Debra. *The ABCs of Globalism: A Vigilant Christian's Glossary.* Lafayette, LA: Huntington House, 1999.

Rae presents definitions and discussions of terms related to a Christian interpretation of current economic and political trends, including what is considered a move toward a global social, economic, and political system.

Reed, Ralph. *Active Faith: How Christians Are Changing the Face of American Politics.* New York: Free Press, 1996.

Reed discusses his experience as head of the Christian Coalition, presents his own story of religious commitment, describes the importance of religious belief in the history of the United States, and analyzes the status of the Democratic and Republican Parties. The author outlines for religious conservatives a strategy of political activism.

———. *After the Revolution: How the Christian Coalition Is Impacting America.* Nashville, TN: Word, 1996.

Reed supports Christian involvement in the movement to improve American society, which he contends is in crisis. Christians must become aware of the nature of political and cultural problems, resist being placed by the secular world at the margins of public life, and cast ballots according to their Christian values.

———. *Politically Incorrect: The Emerging Faith Factor in American Politics.* Nashville, TN: Word, 1996.

Reed discusses the declining presence of religion in politics during the twentieth century and calls Christians to increase their participation at all levels, particularly local politics. He asks people to make their opinions known to government representatives. Although Reed admits that at times Christian involvement in politics has been detrimental, as with white resistance to integration and civil rights, he believes that organizations such as the Christian Coalition can have a beneficial impact on American society and politics.

Richardson, Stephen. *The Eagle's Claw: Christians and the IRS.* Lafayette, LA: Vital Issue, 1998.

Basing the discussion on his experience as a certified public accountant who represented Christians and Christian organizations before the Internal Revenue Service, Richardson describes what he considers the IRS's politically motivated intimidation of churches and how Christians can defend themselves against such attacks.

Remnant Resolves. LaPorte, CO: Scriptures for America Ministries, 1988.

This series of resolutions agreed to by "a remnant of God's people," meeting at the Rocky Mountain Family Bible Camp in Cederedge, Colorado, in July 1988, calls for self-government under God in both the family and the nation. The resolves promote the God-given right to defend life, liberty, property, and the family, and condemn abortion as murder and homosexuality as a sin against God.

Robertson, Pat. *America's Dates with Destiny.* Nashville, TN: Thomas Nelson, 1986.

Robertson presents various episodes in American history, emphasizing the importance of religious belief. The author attributes the nation's contemporary problems to acceptance of liberalism at the beginning of the twentieth century. A return to conservatism and evangelical Christianity represents the hope of reestablishing traditional values.

——. *The Turning Tide: The Fall of Liberalism and the Rise of Common Sense.* Nashville, TN: Word, 1993.

Robertson discusses the end of liberalism's dominance in America. He claims President Clinton and his wife Hillary were committed to an unacceptable radical and unbiblical political agenda.

Robertson, Pat, with Bob Slosser. *The Plan.* Nashville, TN: Thomas Nelson, 1989.

This book, published after Robertson's unsuccessful bid for the Republican presidential nomination, deals with the campaign and the reasons for Robertson's failure. God has a plan for everyone, and Robertson claims that despite his lack of success, the plan for him was to involve more Christians in politics and to spread the conservative Christian message.

Rushdoony, Rousas John. *Institutes of Biblical Law.* Nutley, NJ: Craig Press, 1972.

This book examines the Ten Commandments and other biblical laws. Rushdoony believes these laws provide a course for action when Christians follow the biblical command to achieve dominion over this world.

Satinover, Jeffrey. *Homosexuality and the Politics of Truth.* Grand Rapids, MI: Baker, 1996.

Coinciding with the religious right position, Satinover argues that behavioral studies are flawed and that an individual's homosexuality, a pattern of sexual behavior resulting from an interaction of psychological, biological, and habitual factors, is ultimately alterable. The author considers homosexuality a form of "soul sickness" that is inherent in the human race's "fallen nature."

Scheidler, Joseph M. *Closed: 99 Ways to Stop Abortion.* Westchester, IL: Crossway, 1988.

Scheidler, who heads the Pro-Life Action League, presents practical advice about stopping abortions, including fund-raising techniques, ways of coping with police during demonstrations, finding alternatives to abortion for women, and strategies for debate. The author advocates nonviolence.

Schenck, Paul, with Robert L. Schenck. *The Extermination of Christianity: A Tyranny of Consensus.* Lafayette, LA: Huntington House, 1993.

The authors contend that radical liberals are attempting to eliminate Christianity in America. American Christians are being subjected to slander and ridicule that represent the prelude to oppression rivaled only by the persecution of early Christians. To back their claim, the authors refer to what they consider the unfavorable depiction of the clergy in movies, on television, and in popular music, and to the perceived bias against Christians in the public schools.

Schweizer, Peter. *Disney, the Mouse Betrayed: Greed, Corruption, and Children at Risk.* Washington, DC: Regnery, 1998.

Schweizer echoes the criticisms of conservative Christian groups who charge that the Walt Disney Company, widely known as an organization providing family entertainment, has made too many compromises in order to increase profits. The author takes the Walt Disney Company to task for what he considers a betrayal of American values.

Sekulow, Jay. *From Intimidation to Victory: Regaining the Christian Right to Speak.* Lake Mary, FL: Creation House, 1990.

Sekulow, chief counsel for the American Center for Law and Justice, argues that Christians are winning against those forces that he believes are attempting to restrict the right of religious expression. The author deals with such issues as the separation of church and state, the rights of parents, abortion, censorship, and civil disobedience.

Sekulow, Jay, and Keith Fournier. *And Nothing but the Truth: Real-life Stories of Americans Defending Their Faith and Protecting Their Families.* Nashville, TN: Thomas Nelson, 1996.

Sekulow and Fournier discuss the First Amendment freedoms as applied to Christians, focusing on such issues as the right to display the Bible in the workplace or discuss religion with coworkers, the rights of churches under local zoning laws to be protected from such establishments as bars, and the right to show Christian-produced films in public buildings.

Sileven, Everett. *The Christian and the Income Tax.* Louisville, NE: Council for Religious Education, 1986.

Sileven holds that the Constitution limits public officials, not the people, who are subject only to God's law. Rules and regulations over the people, particularly the income tax, are unconstitutional, unscriptural, and contrary to the intentions of the Founding Fathers. Americans should refuse to go into debt, avoid credit cards, refuse to use FDIC banks, and, when on a jury, vote "not guilty" in cases concerning taxes. Sileven claims that anyone who supports such government programs as mass transit, public highways, and the public school system is a "practicing Communist."

Sproul, R. C. *Money Matters: Making Sense of Economic Issues That Affect You.* Wheaton, IL: Tyndale House, 1985.

This conservative evangelical look at economics praises the value of labor, claiming that God expected even Adam and Eve to work in the Garden of Eden. God has called us to be constructive managers of his creation, to subdue the earth, and to make it fruitful.

Terry, Randall A. *Operation Rescue.* Springdale, PA: Whitaker House, 1988.

Terry, organizer of sit-ins at abortion clinics, advocates the coerced closing of these clinics as a means of creating sufficient unrest to force government to outlaw abortion through passage of a Human Rights Amendment.

Thoburn, Robert L. *The Christian and Politics.* Tyler, TX: Thoburn Press, 1984.

Thoburn notes that as Christians retreated from the political realm, secular humanists captured the playing field, to the disadvantage of Christians. The author develops a biblical view of government, analyzes a number of issues—including education, welfare, taxation, and foreign policy—from a biblical stance, and discusses how Christians can involve themselves in politics more effectively.

Thomas, Cal, and Ed Dobson. *Blinded by Might: Can the Religious Right Save America?* Grand Rapids, MI: Zondervan, 1999.

Thomas, a former spokesperson for the Moral Majority, and Dobson, codrafter of the Moral Majority platform and former assistant to Jerry Falwell, express their apprehension about the participation of the Christian right in politics. Although adhering to many of the values advocated by the religious right, the authors argue that America cannot be made virtuous through political activity, but instead must depend for its salvation on individual Christians living moral lives and caring for the poor and the oppressed. Noting that politics inherently involves compromise, Thomas and Dobson indicate their concern for past cases of untruthfulness and violations of trust attributed to leaders in the religious right.

Turek, Frank S., and Norman L. Geisler. *Legislating Morality: Is It Wise? Is It Legal? Is It Possible?* Minneapolis, MN: Bethany House, 1999.

Turek and Geisler argue that a society cannot avoid legislating morality in order to support good and oppose evil. Such legislating can occur within a society characterized by religious diversity. The authors reject the standard position that law should not prohibit victimless crimes such as gambling and the usage of drugs, contending that such actions do have adverse effects on others.

Vernon, Robert. *L.A. Justice: Lessons from the Firestorm.* Colorado Springs, CO: Focus on the Family, 1993.

The author, a former assistant police chief in Los Angeles, discusses satanic influences in southern California that are responsible for such things as mob violence, racial conflict, and earthquakes. Vernon explains how the present situation developed and discusses whether there is a way to "save" Los Angeles.

Walton, Rus. *One Nation under God.* Nashville, TN: Thomas Nelson, 1987.

This work advocates an active political role for Christians, especially at the local level, in order to reestablish God's place in American government. Socialism and humanism are seen as destructive of biblical principles regarding government, economics, and education. The author supports a strong national defense, including nuclear deterrence. He expresses opposition to the United Nations, pointing to that organization's anti-American position and support of communism.

———. *Biblical Solutions to Contemporary Problems: A Handbook.* Brentwood, TN: Wolgemuth and Hyatt, 1988.

Walton looks to the Bible for solutions to a wide variety of political questions, including taxation, welfare, and economic growth. The author advocates a strong national defense as crucial to maintaining a Christian nation and cautions that the United Nations is a major humanist institution. Major aspects of the American constitutional order are claimed to be found in Old Testament accounts of the Hebrew people.

West, Jonathan. *Good-Bye America?* Bethesda, MD: Prescott, 1999.

Appalled by all that he finds wrong with the United States, including the failure of Congress to act effectively, the objectionable behavior of the president, the inadequacies of the judicial system, and an arbitrary bureaucracy, West calls for a rebirth of the nation as it enters the twenty-first century.

Whitehead, John W. *The Stealing of America.* Westchester, IL: Crossway Books, 1983.

Whitehead portrays the historical development of freedom and individualism in conjunction with responsibility, which he claims originated in Martin Luther's writings during the Reformation. This individualism, Whitehead argues, has been increasingly threatened in recent years by a growing governmental structure. The spread of collectivist influences originating in European thinkers is given some of the blame for the contemporary trend of limiting religious freedoms.

———. *An American Dream.* Westchester, IL: Crossway Books, 1987.

Whitehead, a legal scholar, is wary of the connection between religion and the state, noting that, except for Massachusetts, theocratic systems were rejected in colonial times. However, the author recognizes the historical importance of the clergy in establishing those rights and liberties so important to the "American dream." According to the author, it was through John Locke that Reformation thought was transmitted to America during the revolutionary era.

Whitemarsh, Darylann, and Bill Reisman. *Subtle Serpent: New Age in the Classroom.* Lafayette, LA: Huntington House, 1993.

The authors argue that the public school systems have allowed such evils as suicide, rape, drug use, violence, teen pregnancy, and a general disregard for authority. They identify the cause of these evils as attempts to introduce new moral codes without the permission or knowledge of parents.

Woods, Dennis. *Disciplining the Nations: The Government upon His Shoulder.* Phoenix, AZ: Vantage Group, 1998.

Woods, a political pollster, argues that in order to counter what he considers threats to the moral status of the nation, Christians must realize that scripture and the dissemination of the gospel concern all aspects of life, including government and social affairs.

Personal and Family

Bakker, Jim. *I Was Wrong.* Nashville, TN: Nelson, 1996.

Jim Bakker, former host of the popular *PTL* television show and head of Heritage USA and the Inspirational Network, recounts his personal fall from grace for misusing donated funds, a fall that shook the televangelism community. In 1989 Bakker, then forty-nine years old, received a forty-five-year prison sentence for misusing donated funds. While in prison Bakker claims that he had a change of heart, discovering fellowship among those in suffering. He now criticizes the "health and wealth gospel" he previously touted to his audience.

Dobson, James C. *The New Dare to Discipline.* Wheaton, IL: Tyndale, 1996.

Dobson, head of Focus on the Family, has revised his popular book about establishing parental authority through appropriate discipline. The author wrote the first edition, released in 1970, to counter what he believed were permissive child-rearing practices that fail to provide children with sufficient guidance for adulthood.

Falwell, Jerry. *Strength for the Journey: An Autobiography.* New York: Simon and Schuster, 1987.

Falwell begins with an account of family heritage and ends in the late 1980s after his stormy experience in the public sphere as leader of the Moral Majority. Of special note are accounts of his alcoholic father, his conversion experience in his mother's kitchen, subsequent preparation for the ministry, and his early days at Thomas Road Baptist Church.

———. *Falwell: An Autobiography.* Lynchburg, VA: Liberty House, 1997.

Jerry Falwell, the controversial religious right leader headquartered in Lynchburg, Virginia, offers insights into his life and the development of his conservative religious beliefs. He touches on such topics as sin, forgiveness, the importance of prayer, and the significance of the Bible to contemporary Christians.

LaHaye, Beverly, and Terri Blackstock. *Seasons under Heaven.* Grand Rapids, MI: Zondervan, 1999.

Beverly LaHaye followed her husband Tim into the field of fiction with this novel about love and Christian faith. This story about four women in different stages of life is intended to instruct women readers about issues of concern to conservative Christians, such as sex education in the public schools and the willingness to be a stay-at-home mother.

———. *Showers in Season.* Grand Rapids, MI: Zondervan, 2000.

A sequel to *Seasons under Heaven,* this novel continues the portrayal of the lives of families in a small town. Religious right issues are raised as the families face such difficulties as marital infidelity and the birth of a Down's syndrome baby.

LaHaye, Beverly, and Tim F. LaHaye. *The Act of Marriage: The Beauty of Sexual Love.* Grand Rapids, MI: Zondervan, 1998.

This revised edition of the LaHayes' best-selling book on sex and love in marriage adds reports on medical and social research findings gleaned since the book's original publication in 1976. The authors contend that married Christians can experience greater sexual satisfaction than non-Christians.

LaHaye, Tim. *Sex Education Is for the Family.* Grand Rapids, MI: Zondervan, 1985.

This is a conservative Christian view of sexuality. LaHaye identifies basic God-determined, biological differences between men and women, claiming that men are more capable of leadership while women are more passive. LaHaye denies any biological origin of homosexuality, attributing its development to the faults in child rearing of one or both parents. Advice is given to parents regarding the control of children, especially as they approach puberty.

————. *If Ministers Fall, Can They Be Restored?* Grand Rapids, MI: Zondervan, 1991.

Christian right leader LaHaye approaches the contemporary problem of ministers who have strayed sexually. He offers a formula for evading temptation and gives advice to churches that must deal with a minister who has fallen so that the minister might be returned to his position.

Robison, James. *Thank God, I'm Free: The James Robison Story.* Nashville, TN: Thomas Nelson, 1988.

Christian right leader Robison tells of his turn to Christianity after a difficult early life. Robison's mother, a single woman who was a victim of rape, took Robison from a foster home when he was five years old to live a fatherless and impoverished childhood. It was his foster mother, however, who was with him when he committed his life to God.

Schaeffer, Francis A. *Letters of Francis Schaeffer.* Westchester, IL: Crossway, 1985.

Schaeffer, the noted evangelical theologian, deals with a number of topics in this volume, including homosexuality, divorce, spirituality, sinfulness, and the role of the Holy Spirit in a Christian's life.

Schaffer, James, and Colleen Todd. *Christian Wives: Women Behind the Evangelists Reveal Their Faith in Modern Marriage.* Garden City, NY: Doubleday, 1987.

Schaffer and Todd portray the wives of the following television evangelists: Jim Bakker, Jerry Falwell, Billy Graham, Rex Humbard, Oral Roberts, Robert Schuller, and Jimmy Swaggart. The authors relate how each couple deals with the pressures of the evangelist's profession.

Schwarz, Frederick. *Beating the Unbeatable Foe: The Story of the Christian Anti-Communist Crusade.* Washington, DC: Regnery, 1996.

Schwarz, now retired from his leadership position in the Christian Anti-Communism Crusade (CACC), recounts his own Christian beliefs and the CACC's four-decade-long campaign to educate Americans about the dangers of communism. The author focuses on the communist goal of eliminating religious belief and reveals that evangelist Billy Graham urged him to form his anticommunist organization. A physician, Schwarz approached communism as a pathologist, portraying it as a spreading disease.

Millenarianism

Boys, Don. *Y2K.* Lafayette, LA: Huntington House, 1999.

Religious right organizations like Christian Crusade have hailed books that predicted devastation resulting from computers not recognizing the year 2000. Boys speculated about the possible effects of this computer problem on water supplies, the operation of automobiles, the rail system, and medical equipment. Such problems coincided with the fundamentalist Christian expectation of the great tribulation.

Byers, Marvin. *The Final Victory: The Year 2000.* 2d ed. Shippensburg, PA: Destiny Image, 1994.

This attempt to predict the end times based on biblical interpretation was published prior to much of the Y2K publicity. Using calculations based on the works of Isaac Newton, Byers argued that Christ would return in 2000.

Capps, Charles. *End Time Events: Journey to the End of the Age.* Lawrenceville, GA: Dake, 1999.

Capps explores what the Bible has to say about the possibility that the new millennium will bring the end of the world. He suggests how such biblical topics as Solomon's temple, Elijah's method of exiting the earth, and the transfiguration of Christ foreshadow the end times.

Coppes, Charles H. *Millennium Time Bomb: How to Prepare for and Survive the Coming Technological Disaster.* Lafayette, LA: Huntington House, 1998.

Sold by Billy James Hargis's Christian Crusade, this book deals with several possible catastrophes anticipated by many millennial thinkers. Coppes explores the possibility of martial law, global famine, and world government.

Crouch, Paul. *The Omega Code: Another Has Risen from the Dead.* Torrance, CA: Western Front, 1999.

Crouch, head of the Trinity Broadcasting Network, presents a fictional account, based on the Book of Revelation, of how the world might end. The novel, which became the popular movie of the same name, examines the possible political implications of end-times events.

Gentry, Kenneth L., Jr. *He Shall Have Dominion: A Postmillennial Eschatology.* Tyler, TX: Institute for Christian Economics, 1992.

In opposition to the belief of many contemporary Christians of a premillennial persuasion, Gentry contends that postmillennialism is the true biblical position: Christians will rule on earth for a thousand years, enforcing the laws of the Old Testament, before Christ returns.

Goetz, William. *The Economy to Come in Prophetic Context.* Camp Hill, PA: Christian Publications, 1999.

Goetz added to the Y2K question with this treatment of the possible global consequences of the American economy failing as a result of the computer crisis. Examining biblical prophecy, the author conjectured that a worldwide economic crisis could result in a global dictator coming to power, someone who looked suspiciously like the Antichrist.

Hagee, John C. *Beginning of the End: The Assassination of Yitzhak Rabin and the Coming Antichrist.* Nashville, TN: Nelson, 1996.

Hagee's book is an example of the attempt to interpret contemporary political events in the context of biblical prophecy. The author argues that the assassination of Israeli Prime Minister Yitzhak Rabin will lead Israel to agree to a peace process with Syria that will result in surrendering control of the Golan Heights to the United Nations. This is seen as the prelude to the war described in the Old Testament Book of Ezekiel, chapters 38–39, and the rise of the Antichrist.

———. *Day of Deception: Separating Truth from the Falsehoods That Threaten Our Society.* Nashville, TN: Nelson, 1997.

Continuing his theme that the end of the world is near, Hagee notes that Jesus, in Matthew 24, prophesied that deception would be the major indicator of the last generation. The author discovers deception in the U.S. government that is meant to destroy democracy. He identifies evil forces that are attempting to destroy the traditional family and the separate roles appropriate for men and women, property rights, patriotism, and individualism.

———. *From Daniel to Doomsday.* Nashville, TN: Nelson, 1999.

Hagee continues his examination of biblical prophecy, focusing on the Old Testament Book of Daniel. He attempts to place such contemporary events as the anticipated computer crisis after January 1, 2000, the Chinese theft of American military secrets, Saddam Hussein's aggressive intentions in the Middle East, and Israeli electoral politics into the anticipated end of the world.

Hart, Frank. *Revelation and the Rapture Unveiled! Ancient Hebrew Prophecies for the Year 2000 and Beyond.* Lafayette, LA: Prescott, 1999.

Hart presents his understanding of biblical prophecy, attempting to unravel the mysteries found in the Books of Revelation and Daniel. As have so many authors at the end of the twentieth century, Hart offers what he believes is the relevance of biblical prophecy to the new millennium.

Hayford, Jack. *E Quake.* Nashville, TN: Nelson, 1999.

Television minister Jack Hayford interprets the last days prophesied in the Bible, contending that an appropriate understanding of the mysteries cloaked in scripture can be found in events involving the series of earthquakes predicted in the Book of Revelation. The author suggests how Christians should set their priorities and live their lives in anticipation of the last days.

Hunt, Dave. *A Cup of Trembling: Jerusalem and Bible Prophecy.* Eugene, OR: Harvest, 1995.

In the context of Bible prophecy, Hunt examines the significance of Jerusalem, the capital of Israel. He investigates the origins of the Middle East conflict between Jews, Muslims, and Christians and speculates about the potential world consequences of the Israelis rebuilding the Jewish temple in Jerusalem, an event that supposedly will signal the beginning of the end times.

———. *Y2K: A Reasoned Response to Mass Hysteria.* Eugene, OR: Harvest, 1999.

Bible teacher Dave Hunt joined other students of biblical prophecy, presenting his own interpretation of the significance of the feared computer crisis. He advised Christians to rely on God's provision and to take steps to prepare for the inconveniences that might occur, warning them not to submit to the panic atmosphere alarmists had been generating.

Jeffrey, Grant R. *The Signature of God: Astonishing Biblical Discoveries.* Wheaton, IL: Tyndale House, 1997.

Jeffrey relies on historical, archaeological, and scientific documents to argue that the Bible was inspired by God. The author claims to have discovered Hebrew codes within scripture that prophesy events in the contemporary world.

———. *Millennium Meltdown: The Year 2000 Computer Crisis.* Belleville, MI: Spring Arbor Distributors, 1998.

Jeffrey provided a conservative Christian perspective on the Y2K frenzy that engulfed the nation prior to the turn of the century, thus combining worries about computers and biblical eschatology. Although giving advice on dealing individually with the possible problems associated with computers, the author speculated about the potential political consequences related to biblical prophecy, such as the formation of a world government and a cashless society.

Jeremiah, David. *Escape the Coming Night.* Nashville, TN: Word, 1999.

With the end of the twentieth century imminent, Jeremiah examined the Book of Revelation, indicating that predictions made in that book of prophecy were relevant to the contemporary world.

The author urged readers to be prepared for the events he claimed could soon be fulfilled.

Joyner, Rick. *A Prophetic Vision for the 21st Century: A Spiritual Map to Help You Navigate into the Future.* Nashville, TN: Nelson, 1999.

Joyner focuses on the prophesied reign of Christ on earth and provides practical advice to Christians for what he considers the uncertainties of the early twenty-first century.

LaHaye, Tim F. *Revelation Unveiled.* Grand Rapids, MI: Zondervan, 1999.

LaHaye explains his interpretation of biblical prophecy that undergirds the popular novel series, *Left Behind,* which he has been coauthoring with Jerry Jenkins. The author employs charts and diagrams in a simplified explanation of the Book of Revelation.

LaHaye, Tim F., and Jerry B. Jenkins. *Left Behind: A Novel of the Earth's Last Days.* Wheaton, IL: Tyndale, 1996.

In the first of a series of novels, LaHaye and Jenkins have created a fictional account of what might happen after the rapture that they believe is prophesied in the Book of Revelation. The authors alert readers to be prepared spiritually for the rapture, an event fundamentalist Christians believe will shortly occur. In the novel, people all over the world have disappeared, and various explanations are offered, from terrorists to extraterrestrial aliens. When Nicolae Carpathia, a popular Romanian politician, begins to establish a world government, those who are penitent establish the Tribulation Force to resist the Antichrist.

———. *Tribulation Force.* Wheaton, IL: Tyndale, 1997.

This sequel to *Left Behind* finds the main characters left behind after the rapture, struggling to resist the evil intentions of Nicolae Carpathia, the Antichrist who is becoming more powerful. Airline pilot Rayford Steele, his daughter Chloe, journalist Buck Williams, and Pastor Bruce Barnes join hands to study the Bible and resist the intentions of the Antichrist. Although Rayford and Buck become employees of Carpathia, they keep their faith a secret so that they can fight on the side of the Tribulation Force.

———. *Nicolae: The Rise of the Antichrist.* Wheaton, IL: Tyndale, 1997.

In this third novel of the *Left Behind* series, LaHaye and Jenkins focus on their fictional Antichrist, Nicolae Carpathia. In terms suggestive of the "New World Order" so feared by conservatives, Nicolae unifies nations into the "Global Community," consolidates the mass media into the "Global Community Network" and "Global Weekly," and establishes one religion, "Enigma Babylon One World Faith," with a spiritual leader appointed by Nicolae. The heroes, Rayford Steele and Buck Williams, come to a full realization of Nicolae's evil purposes. The sixth seal of the Book of Revelation is opened, bringing a huge earthquake, with the moon turning red, the sun becoming black, and the stars falling from the sky.

————. *Soul Harvest: The World Takes Sides.* Wheaton, IL: Tyndale, 1999.

In the fourth novel of the *Left Behind* series, LaHaye and Jenkins continue their fictional rendition of the events prophesied in the Book of Revelation. Having survived the devastation of the great earthquake, or the "wrath of the Lamb," portrayed in *Nicolae*, members of the Tribulation Force, including reporter Buck Williams, pilot Rayford Steele, and his daughter Chloe, continue their efforts to resist the evil intentions of the Antichrist, Nicolae Carpathia.

————. *Apollyon: The Destroyer Is Unleashed.* Wheaton, IL: Tyndale, 1999.

This fifth novel in the best-selling series on the tribulation prophesied in the Book of Revelation portrays the actions of Apollyon, the chief demon of the abyss, who leads a plague against the survivors of the tribulation. The drama of Nicolae Carpathia, the Antichrist, continues, as believers resist his political maneuvering. A divine plague of locusts is unleashed against those without the seal of God on their foreheads. The authors maintain the reader's interest with the characters' personal crises, including marital infidelity and pregnancies.

————. *Assassins.* Wheaton, IL: Tyndale, 1999.

LaHaye and Jenkins continue in this sixth volume their fictional account of the tribulation and the rise of the Antichrist. The authors describe the last half of the tribulation prophesied in the Book of Revelation.

———. *Are We Living in the End Times?* Wheaton, IL: Tyndale, 1999.

LaHaye and Jenkins, authors of the popular fiction series *Left Behind*, offer what they consider scriptural confirmation of their belief that the world is approaching the final days. They offer twenty reasons why they believe people now living will see the rapture, the event some Christians believe will signal the beginning of the end times when the true believers will be taken into heaven.

———. *The Indwelling: The Beast Possession.* Wheaton, IL: Tyndale, 2000.

This seventh book in the *Left Behind* series continues the end-times scenario, taking characters past the halfway point of the seven-year tribulation foretold in the Book of Revelation.

———. *The Mark: The Beast Rules the World.* Wheaton, IL: Tyndale, 2000.

In the eighth installment of the *Left Behind* series, Nicolae returns from the dead and plans to place the mark of the beast on all human beings. The Tribulation Force, evading the global security contingent, continues to preach the gospel in a disintegrating world.

Lindsey, Hal. *Apocalypse Code.* Torrance, CA: Western Front, 1997.

In a continuing effort to provide interpretations of Bible prophecy, Lindsey focuses on the Books of Daniel and Revelation, contending that biblical secrets about the final days have been revealed. The author claims he has deciphered Old Testament prophecies regarding what he considers the near future of the earth's present generation.

Lindsey, Hal, and Cliff Ford. *Facing Millennial Midnight: The Y2K Crisis Confronting America and the World.* Torrance, CA: Western Front, 1999.

Popular Bible prophet Hal Lindsey enlists the assistance of economist Cliff Ford to speculate about the potential effects on such structures as government, the monetary system, and utilities of the feared computer crisis. Lindsey is cautious in attempting to relate the anticipated crisis to biblical prophecy.

———. *The Late Great 20th Century: Prelude to Catastrophe.* Torrance, CA: Western Front, 1999.

Lindsey and Ford focus on what they consider the disintegration of the moral culture of the United States, examining events of the twentieth century that contributed to the precarious condition of the nation. The authors make recommendations for returning the United States to its former greatness.

Lockyer, Herbert. *All about the Second Coming.* Peabody, MA: Hendrickson, 1998.

Bible teacher Herbert Lockyer presents a detailed exposition of the Book of Revelation. The author treats such controversial eschatological issues among Christians as the battle of Armageddon, the tribulation and rapture, the return of Christ, and the millennium.

McGuire, Paul. *Countdown to Armageddon.* Lake Mary, FL: Creation House, 1999.

McGuire examines biblical prophecy of the end times, referring to such contemporary events as wars, famine, disease, and earthquakes to confirm his conclusion. The author looks to the establishment of Israel following World War II as a crucial sign of the final days.

Miller, Harland W. *Make Yourself Ready: Preparing to Meet the King.* Lafayette, LA: Vital Issue, 1998.

At the time of publication, interest in the millennium still raged in religious literature and film. Miller describes the signs of the end times—plagues, disasters, and wars—that the Bible predicts and places biblical prophecy in the context of events of the twentieth century.

Parsley, Rod. *On the Brink: Breaking through Every Obstacle into the Glory of God.* Nashville, TN: Nelson, 2000.

Parsley argues that the world is in a "fullness of time" period when "demon power" is leading humankind to devastation. The author provides advice about resisting the coming evil and the consequences of disaster.

Rawles, James Wesley. *Patriots: Surviving the Coming Collapse.* Lafayette, LA: Huntington House, 1998.

Sold by Billy James Hargis's Christian Crusade, this novel describes the collapse of modern civilization, exemplified by riots, looting, and the general breakdown of the technological infrastructure. Through this fictional account the author claims to be providing information about how to survive the predicted devastation.

Robertson, Pat. *The End of the Age.* Nashville, TN: Word, 1996.

Robertson, popular television evangelist and erstwhile presidential candidate, weighs in with his own fictional rendition of the end times as prophesied in the Book of Revelation. A series of natural disasters, including an asteroid that smashes into the sea between California and Hawaii, and a series of social and political upheavals, such as U.S. presidents who commit suicide and are murdered, lead to Antichrist Mark Beaulieu's world rule. Robertson takes the faithful through the hard times to the ultimate return of Jesus Christ, interspersing his conservative political commentary throughout.

Swindoll, Charles R., John F. Walvoord, and J. Dwight Pentecost, eds. *The Road to Armageddon.* Nashville, TN: Word, 1999.

Six Bible prophecy scholars—Charles Swindoll, John Walvoord, Dwight Pentecost, Charles Dryer, Ronald Allen, and Mark Bailey—discuss biblical prophecies regarding the return of Christ, intending to provide the reader with hope and confidence about the future.

Van Impe, Jack. *2001: On the Edge of Eternity.* Nashville, TN: Word, 1996.

For many years Van Impe has engaged in speculation about biblical prophecy in his published works as well as on a television program that he hosts with his wife. Here he discusses contemporary world events, claiming that they have significance in light of Bible passages prophesying the end of the world and the return of Jesus.

Van Kampen, Robert D. *The Rapture Question Answered: Plain and Simple.* Ada, MI: Fleming H. Revell, 1997.

Believing that the end times are near, Van Kampen offers his own biblical interpretation of the rapture of the church, when believers are to be taken into heaven. Not willing to accept the standard positions on the question, which include the pre-, mid-, and post-tribulation interpretations, the author develops a "pre-wrath" position, arguing that believers will endure the tribulation, or suffering, prophesied in the Book of Revelation, but will escape the "Day of the Lord," or the "Wrath of God," described in Daniel 12 and Matthew 24.

Walvoord, John F. *Every Prophecy of the Bible.* Colorado Springs, CO: Chariot Victor, 1999.

Walvoord, who previously wrote about the importance of oil and the Middle East to the fulfillment of biblical prophecy, offers in this book guidelines for interpreting scriptural prophecy, from Genesis to Revelation. The author reviews predictions he believes have already been fulfilled and considers those yet to occur.

Periodicals

The following periodicals and journals present the varied positions of, and examine questions relevant to, the religious right. Many of these publications are not available through libraries or the more popular distribution channels, but must be acquired directly from the organization.

The ACCC Report
American Council of Christian Churches
P.O. Box 5455
Bethlehem, PA 18015
Monthly. Free on request.

This newsletter reports on issues relevant to contemporary fundamentalist churches and comments critically on the National Council of Churches and the National Association of Evangelicals for their compromising attitude toward the faith. The publication also treats social and political issues of interest to conservative Christians.

American Family Association Journal
American Family Association
P.O. Drawer 2440
Tupelo, MS 38803
Bimonthly. $15 contribution suggested.

This monthly publication reports on cultural issues of concern to the religious right, including homosexuality and same-sex marriage, pornography and obscenity on television, and preservation of the traditional family.

Chalcedon Report
Chalcedon Foundation
P.O. Box 158
Vallecito, CA 95251-0158
Monthly. Donation requested.

This newsletter deals with issues involving the reconstruction movement and includes articles dealing with the application of Christian principles to contemporary society and culture.

Christian Beacon
Christian Beacon, Inc.
756 Haddon Avenue
Collingswood, NJ 08108-3712
Weekly. $12.

This newspaper, edited by Carl McIntire, deals with religious and social issues of concern to conservative fundamentalist Christians.

Christian Book Distributors Catalog
P.O. Box 7000
Peabody, MA 01961-7000
Bimonthly. Free on request.

This catalog of Christian reading, listening, and viewing resources often contains materials with themes that are of concern to the religious right.

Christian Century
Christian Century Foundation
407 South Dearborn Street
Chicago, IL 60605
Weekly. $30.

This moderate Christian publication comments extensively on religious right activities and personalities.

Christian Crusade Newspaper
P.O. Box 977
Tulsa, OK 74102-9979
Monthly. Free on request; donations accepted.

This publication of Billy James Hargis's Christian Crusade organization provides critical commentary on current political and economic issues, including American foreign policy. The newspaper still presents a strong anticommunist position.

Christian News
3277 Boeuf Lutheran Road
New Haven, MO 63068-9568
Weekly. $20.

Formerly *Lutheran News*, this newspaper provides a conservative perspective on events relevant to Christians, especially within, but not limited to, the Missouri Synod Lutheran Church, and national and international happenings of interest to conservative Christians.

Christian Reconstruction
Institute for Christian Economics
P.O. Box 6116
Tyler, TX 75711
Bimonthly. Free on request.

This newsletter, published in alternate months with *Biblical Economics Today,* provides scriptural discussions relevant to advancing the biblical reconstruction viewpoint.

Christian Research Book and Tape Catalog
Christian Research
P.O. Box 385
Eureka Springs, AR 72632
Yearly. Free on request.

This catalog lists a variety of books relevant to the religious right that can be ordered from Christian Research. In addition to Bibles and Bible reference works, many other categories of books are included, such as economics and money, evolution versus creationism, government, history, law and the Constitution, and taxes and taxation.

Christian Research Journal
Christian Research Institute
P.O. Box 7000
Rancho Santa Margarita, CA 92688-7000
Quarterly. $24.

This journal contains biblically based articles that deal with such current topics as cults, false doctrine, the New Age movement, and secular humanism. Techniques of evangelizing are presented and current literature on defending the faith is reviewed.

Christian Standard
Standard Publishing Company, Inc.
8121 Hamilton Avenue
Cincinnati, OH 45231-2396
Weekly. $18.

This magazine includes news, commentary, and essays dealing with the revival of the doctrines and rules of Christianity as set out in the New Testament.

The Christian Worldview
American Vision
P.O. Box 720515
Atlanta, GA 30328
Monthly. $20.

This newsletter holds that the Bible should be applied to all aspects of Christian life and provides instruction in the nature of government and the Christian's role in politics. A biblical view is provided for many current issues, such as secular humanism, the New Age movement, homosexuality, and government intervention in people's lives.

Christianity Today
Christianity Today, Inc.
465 Gunderson Drive
Carol Stream, IL 60188
Eighteen issues per year. $24.95.

This relatively moderate evangelical publication offers commentary on all aspects of the evangelical movement.

Church & State
Americans United for Separation of Church and State
518 C Street, NE
Washington, DC 20002
Monthly. $24 (including membership).

This magazine reports on the current relations between religious groups and government, including the political activities of religious right organizations and leaders.

Connections
Reasons To Believe
P.O. Box 5978

Pasadena, CA 91117
Quarterly. Free with contribution.

This newsletter includes articles on scientific subjects, arguing that scientific discoveries offer demonstrations of the existence of an intelligent creator. Also included are reports of the activities of Reasons To Believe, promotions of the organization's publications, and announcements of coming events.

The Correspondent
Plymouth Rock Foundation
Fisk Mill, Box 577
Marlborough, NH 03455
Monthly. $25.

This newsletter provides information about local Plymouth Rock Foundation (PRF) committee activities and reprints articles from these organizations. The prime concern is promoting biblical principles in local government.

Facts & Faith
Reasons To Believe
P.O. Box 5978
Pasadena, CA 91117
Quarterly. $24 donation.

This interdenominational newsletter reports on scientific discoveries that are believed to substantiate the biblical account of creation. The newsletter supports the view that science and religious faith are compatible.

Facts for Action
Christian Research
P.O. Box 385
Eureka Springs, AR 72632
Quarterly. $8.

This newsletter presents a fundamentalist Christian, highly patriotic, and conservative view of current events in American society and politics. The national government and its agencies are the focus of opposition and deep suspicion (for instance, the Internal Revenue Service is referred to as the "Gestapo" and the "Beast").

Facts for Faith
Reasons To Believe
P.O. Box 2269

Glendora, CA 91740-2269
Quarterly. $30.

Called "the Christian apologetics update," this magazine represents a branch of the Christian apologetics movement that is devoted to examining scientific advances in order to substantiate the truth claims of the Christian faith. The publication's major theme is that scientific investigation discloses intelligent design in the universe and demonstrates the existence of an intelligent creator.

First Things
Institute of Religion and Public Life
156 Fifth Avenue, Suite 400
New York, NY 10010
Ten issues per year. $24.

Edited by Richard John Neuhaus, this monthly journal of religion and public life includes articles that investigate public policy questions that stem from the intersection of religion and the political realm.

Focus on the Family
Focus on the Family, Inc.
801 Corporate Center Drive
Pomona, CA 91768
Monthly. Free on request.

This publication from James Dobson's organization focuses on public policy and issues related to traditional family values. Articles are intended to strengthen families and to support conservative Christian objectives such as limiting abortion and obscenity.

The Humanist
American Humanist Association
7 Hardwood Drive
P.O. Box 1188
Amherst, NY 14226-7188
Bimonthly. $24.95.

This magazine promotes the principles of humanism (the belief that human beings are interdependent and mutually responsible without any help from an acknowledged supreme being) so often considered by the religious right to be in direct opposition to Christian belief.

Journal of Christian Reconstruction
Chalcedon Foundation
P.O. Box 158
Vallecito, CA 95251
Twice annually. $14.

This journal presents articles dealing with the reestablishment of Christian intellectual and cultural standards, as found in the Old and New Testaments.

Lutheran Renewal
International Lutheran Renewal Center
2701 Rice Street
St. Paul, MN 55113-2200
Monthly. Free on request.

Growing out of the charismatic movement of the 1960s, this newsletter champions positions opposed to those of the mainline Evangelical Lutheran Church in America.

Midnight Call Magazine
P.O. Box 280008
Columbia, SC 29228
Monthly. $22.50.

This magazine deals with biblical prophecy and the end times, arguing that contemporary events have been predicted in the Bible. Articles focus on such topics as conflict between Israel and Arab nations, the New Age movement, the Antichrist, and the possibility of nuclear war.

NAE Washington Insight
National Association of Evangelicals
P.O. Box 28
Wheaton, IL 60189
Monthly. $14.95.

This newsletter reports on the various activities of the federal government and political issues at the national level that are of concern to the evangelical leadership.

The New American
The Review of the News Incorporated
P.O. Box 8040
770 Westhill Boulevard

Appleton, WI 54915
Bimonthly. $39.

This John Birch Society publication stands for traditional values, patriotism, independence, and the United States Constitution. The magazine's stated goal is "to educate and to activate Americans in support of God, family, and country." Articles focus on political science, social opinion, and economic theory and hold to a conspiracy theory regarding the influences on American culture and politics.

Phyllis Schlafly Report
Eagle Forum
P.O. Box 9683
Alton, IL 62002
Monthly. $20.

This newsletter provides reports and commentary in areas of interest to conservative Christians within education, politics, and social and economic policy.

Reason and Revelation
Apologetics Press, Inc.
230 Landmark Drive
Montgomery, AL 36117-2752
Monthly. $5 per copy.

This journal offers defenses of Christianity and presents evidence for its truth. A major emphasis is placed on creationism.

The Religion and Society Report
The Rockford Institute
934 North Main Street
Rockford, IL 61103-7061
Monthly. $24.

This newsletter of religious opinion presents conservative views on such topics as homosexuality, school prayer, and church-state relations. Articles have taken an especially strong stand against abortion.

The Rock
Plymouth Rock Foundation
6 McKinley Circle
P.O. Box 425

Marlborough, NH 03455
Quarterly.

This journal focuses on the responses that the Bible provides to secular humanism and to the perceived socialist-inspired alternatives in public policy.

The Schwarz Report
Christian Anti-Communism Crusade
P.O. Box 129
Manitou Springs, CO 80829
Monthly. Free on request.

This publication presents information about continuing communist activities around the world (referring to "lively communist corpses") and the efforts of the Christian Anti-Communism Crusade to counteract those activities. The newsletter also includes commentary on such issues as abortion, homosexuality, and AIDS, and a list of publications available for purchase from the organization.

Scoreboard Alert
National Citizens Action Network
P.O. Box 10459
Costa Mesa, CA 92627
Bimonthly. $14.

This periodical, dedicated to activating citizens for the preservation of American values, reports on legislative issues of concern to conservative Christians.

The Servant
Haven Baptist Church
P.O. Box 9562
Denver, CO 80209-0562
Monthly. Free on request.

This newsletter of the Council of Bible Believing Churches (United States affiliate of the International Council of Christian Churches) presents a conservative Christian perspective on current events in the United States and around the world. The publication opposes what are seen as liberal trends within the Christian church.

Tabletalk
Ligonier Ministries

P.O. Box 547500
Orlando, FL 32854
Monthly. $30.

A publication of R. C. Sproul's Ligonier Ministries, this devotional magazine includes daily Bible studies. Each month this conservative Christian periodical includes a theme such as adultery, homosexuality, or the "spiritual adultery" of liberal churches.

Traditional Values Report
Traditional Values Coalition
P.O. Box 940
Anaheim, CA 92815
Occasional. Individual issues provided on request.

This newsletter from the Traditional Values Coalition reports on current issues, such as perceived inroads of homosexuality in the educational system, sex education in the schools, and the relationship between church and state. Traditional family values are supported, and readers are encouraged to promote a constitutional amendment to protect the rights of religious persons.

Voice of Liberty
Voice of Liberty Association
692 Sunnybrook Drive
Decatur, GA 30033-5509
Semiannual. Donation.

This VLA newsletter provides a conservative Christian analysis of current events and focuses on biblical prophecy.

World
P.O. Box 2330
Asheville, NC 28802
Weekly. $49.95.

This weekly newsmagazine, edited by Marvin Olasky, reports on national and international news stories and analyzes current events from a biblical perspective. The magazine accepts the Bible as the inerrant word of God.

7

Selected Nonprint Resources

This chapter contains a variety of nonprint resources from and about the religious right, including video- and audiotapes, radio and television programs, computer software and databases, and website addresses. The listings include those resources that treat the major concerns of the religious right.

Audiotapes and Videotapes Presenting Religious Right Positions

This listing includes examples of the religious right's wide range of concerns. The topics include abortion, God's perceived role in American history and the founding of the Republic, creationism and evolution, the end times and the expected millennium, presidential politics, education, environmental issues, secular humanism, homosexuality, biblical inerrancy, American support for the state of Israel, the New Age movement, patriotism, anticommunism, and the political activism of conservative Christians.

Abortion: The American Holocaust
Type: 1/2-inch videocassette and audiocassette
Length: 45 min.
Date: 1992
Cost: $20 videocassette; $6 audiocassette
Source: John Hagee Ministries
P.O. Box 1400
San Antonio, TX 78295
(210) 494-3900

John Hagee presents an uncompromising argument against abortion based on the Bible and scientific claims that support the biblical position. He argues that Americans who support the right of abortion are no better than Germans who participated in the Holocaust.

Abortion: A Rational Look at an Emotional Issue
Type: 1/2-inch videocassette and audiocassette
Length: 180 min.
Date: 1994
Cost: $30 videocassette; $12 audiocassette
Source: Ligonier Ministries
P.O. Box 547500
Orlando, FL 32854
(800) 435-4343

R. C. Sproul, head of the Ligonier teaching ministry, discusses what he considers the deepest moral problem in our society. He argues that abortion is against God's law, against the laws of nature, and against reason.

Active Faith: How Christians Are Changing the Face of American Politics
Type: audiocassette
Length: 180 min.
Date: 1996
Cost: $18
Source: Simon and Schuster Audio
100 Front Street
Riverside, NJ 08075
(800) 943-9831

This tape is an audio version of Ralph Reed's book of the same title. Reed, who wrote the book while still director of the Christian Coalition, presents an overview of Christianity in American history, surveys recent American politics, and provides a guide to religious conservatives for becoming politically active.

AIDS: What You Haven't Been Told
Type: 1/2-inch videocassette
Length: 60 min.
Date: 1989
Cost: $19.95
Source: Jeremiah Films
P.O. Box 1710
Hemet, CA 92343
(714) 652-1006

Fundamentalists provide their perspective on AIDS, assess blame for its spread, and discuss possible protection against the disease.

All Rapped Up
Type: 1/2-inch videocassette
Length: 130 min.
Date: 1991
Cost: $39.95
Source: American Portrait Films
P.O. Box 19266
Cleveland, OH 44119
(800) 736-4567

A continuation of the "Hell's Bells" video, this program examines recent rock music, claiming to reveal the true nature of developments such as rap and hip-hop, and exposing what are considered the harmful effects of such music.

The American Covenant
Type: 1/2-inch videocassette
Length: 52 min.
Date: 1994
Cost: $19.95
Source: American Portrait Films
P.O. Box 19266
Cleveland, OH 44119
(800) 736-4567

Filmed at various historical sites around the nation, this tape examines the formation of the American Republic. Marshall Foster, a Christian historian, narrates ten events in the history of the nation, including the Pilgrims' *Mayflower* voyage and Patrick Henry's "Give me liberty or give me death" oration.

America's Godly Heritage
Type: 1/2-inch videocassette
Length: 60 min.
Date: 1993
Cost: $20
Source: Wallbuilders
P.O. Box 397
Aledo, TX 76008
(817) 441-6044

David Barton discusses the Christian beliefs and ideals he claims have guided America since the founding. Barton cites early Supreme Court decisions that affirmed the role of Christian principles in the public realm and criticizes more recent decisions that he considers to be ill conceived because they ignore the intentions of the Christian Founders.

Ancient Man: Created or Evolved
Type: 1/2-inch videocassette
Length: 58 min.
Date: 1994
Cost: $9.95
Source: Christian Book Distributors
P.O. Box 7000
Peabody, MA 01961-7000
(508) 977-5000

Roger Oakland investigates the creation versus evolution debate over the origin of human beings, tests each theory against the evidence, and expresses sympathy for the creationist position.

Apocalypse Planet Earth
Type: 1/2-inch videocassette
Length: 45 min.
Date: 1993
Cost: $19.95
Source: Jeremiah Films
P.O. Box 1710
Hemet, CA 92546
(800) 828-2290

Hal Lindsey, author of *The Late Great Planet Earth,* once again offers scriptural interpretations of current events. He reaches the expected dramatic conclusions regarding the end of history.

The Awesome Forces of God's Creation
Type: 1/2-inch videocassette
Length: 135 min. (3 tapes)
Date: Not available
Cost: $39.95
Source: Christian Book Distributors
P.O. Box 7000
Peabody, MA 01961-7000

(978) 977-5060
http://www.christianbook.com

This video presents stunning views of the forces of nature and interprets them as evidence of creation and the intelligent design of the world.

Battle for Our Minds: Worldviews in Collision
Type: 1/2-inch videocassette and audiocassette
Length: 90 min.
Date: 1994
Cost: $15 videocassette; $8 audiocassette
Source: Ligonier Ministries
P.O. Box 547500
Orlando, FL 32854
(800) 435-4343

R. C. Sproul examines three worldviews in Western culture: the classical/biblical perspective, the Enlightenment viewpoint, and post-Christian secularism. Sproul claims that secularism is now dominant and offers Christians advice for an effective defense of the Christian worldview.

Biblical Hermeneutics
Type: 1/2-inch videocassette
Length: 30 min.
Date: 1995
Cost: $35
Source: Creation Moments, Inc.
P.O. Box 260
Zimmerman, MN 55398-0260
(800) 422-4253

In this second program on the third video of the *Origins* series, Bob Walsh explains the basics of biblical interpretation from a creationist perspective. He answers charges that the Bible is not relevant to a scientific society. The first program on the tape is "New Age Movement."

Billy Graham: The Road to Armageddon
Type: 1/2-inch videocassette
Length: 47 min.
Date: 1990
Cost: $29.95
Source: Republic Pictures Home Video

12636 Beatrice Street
Los Angeles, CA 90006-0930
(213) 306-4040

In this presentation on contemporary society, the famous evangelist discusses signs of the coming conflagration predicted in the Bible.

Billy James Hargis' 90-Minute Video Tape Alert
Type: 1/2-inch videocassette
Length: 90 min.
Date: 1995
Cost: Contribution
Source: Christian Crusade Newspaper
P.O. Box 977
Tulsa, OK 74102
(918) 665-2345

A new tape under this title is available each month to those who contribute at least $15 to the *Christian Crusade Newspaper.* Each tape comments on contemporary national and international events from a religious right perspective.

The Biological Evidence for Design
Type: 1/2-inch videocassette
Length: 55 min.
Date: 1998
Cost: $19
Source: Reasons To Believe
P.O. Box 5978
Pasadena, CA 91117
(800) 482-7836
http://www. reasons.org

Michael Behe uses examples from biochemistry in an attempt to discredit the neo-Darwinian theory of evolution and examines evidence he believes indicates that human life resulted from intelligent design.

Biological Evidence of Creation
Type: 1/2-inch videocassette
Length: 28 min.
Date: Not available
Cost: $19.95
Source: American Portrait Films

P.O. Box 19266
Cleveland, OH 44119
(800) 736-4567

Challenging the view that human beings evolved from amphibians, Werner Gift, an information scientist, and Don Batten, a biologist, argue that biological change has definite limits. They conclude that the origins of life can be found in the creative activities of a deity.

Clinton's Circle of Power
Type: 1/2-inch videocassette
Length: 120 min.
Date: 1994
Cost: $43
Source: Liberty University
          1971 University Boulevard
          Lynchburg, VA 24506-8001

This controversial tape that Jerry Falwell promoted on his *Old Time Gospel Hour* includes interviews with Gennifer Flowers, who claimed to have had an affair with President Clinton when he was the governor of Arkansas, and Paula Jones, who charged Clinton with sexual harassment that allegedly occurred during that same period. The tape also suggests that the president was involved in killings in Arkansas as well as in the death of White House Deputy Counsel Vincent Foster.

Comparing Creation Accounts
Type: 1/2-inch videocassette
Length: 60 min.
Date: 2000
Cost: $19
Source: Reasons To Believe
          P.O. Box 5978
          Pasadena, CA 91117
          (800) 482-7836
          http://www.reasons.org

Hugh Ross, president of Reasons To Believe, investigates claimed discrepancies between the two creation accounts found in the first and second chapters of Genesis, arguing that Christianity provides the best explanation of creation.

Countdown to Eternity
Type: 1/2-inch videocassette
Length: 75 min.
Date: 1997
Cost: $16.95
Source: Christian Book Distributors
              P.O. Box 7000
              Peabody, MA 01961-7000
              (978) 977-5060
              http://www.christianbook.com

Bill Gallatin examines scripture, arguing that biblical prophecies are now being fulfilled. He points to such things as the advancement of technology, deterioration in moral standards, and the history of modern Israel as signs that the end is near.

Creation and Psychology!
Type: 1/2-inch videocassette
Length: 30 min.
Date: 1995
Cost: $35
Source: Creation Moments, Inc.
              P.O. Box 260
              Zimmerman, MN 55398-0260
              (600) 422-4253

In this second program on the second tape of the *Origins* series, Paul Ackerman explains the relationship between creation and psychology, examines the biblical view of the mind, and determines whether a person can be a faithful Christian and also a psychologist. The first program on this tape is "Has the Human Body Been Designed?"

Creation and the Last Days
Type: 1/2-inch videocassette
Length: 52 min.
Date: 1994
Cost: $14.95
Source: Creation Moments, Inc.
              P.O. Box 260
              Zimmerman, MN 55398-0260
              (800) 422-4253

Ken Ham argues for creationism and against evolution. He indicates that people in the "last days" will deny any evidence of biblical creation and the flood.

Creation and the Supreme Court
Type: audiocassette
Length: 120 min.
Date: 2000
Cost: $10 two tapes
Source: Reasons To Believe
P.O. Box 5978
Pasadena, CA 91117
(800) 482-7836
http://www.reasons.org

Dr. Hugh Ross discusses the 1987 U.S. Supreme Court decision on teaching creationism in public schools (*Edwards v. Aguillard*), explores the history of creation science, and suggests a way to present creationism appropriately in the classroom.

Creation Days
Type: 1/2-inch videocassette
Length: 60 min.
Date: Not available
Cost: $19
Source: Reasons To Believe
P.O. Box 5978
Pasadena, CA 91117
(800) 482-7836
http://www.reasons.org

This tape examines evidence for the belief that life began simply by chance, concluding that astronomy, physics, and other sciences offer proof that the appearance of life resulted from God's intentional design rather than happenstance.

Creation? Evolution? Resolving the Controversy
Type: audiocassette
Length: 9 hrs.
Date: 2000
Cost: $80
Source: Reasons To Believe
P.O. Box 5978
Pasadena, CA 91117
(800) 482-7836
http://www.reasons.org

In this series of nine lectures on eighteen tapes, Hugh Ross deals with questions regarding the issue of creation and the intelligent design of the universe. Among the lecture titles are "History of Creationism vs. Scientism," "Proofs for the Transcendence of the Creator," "Evidence of Design," "Resolving the Time-Scale Issue," and "Origin of Life." The tape set includes a thirty-nine-page booklet.

Creation or Evolution?
Type: 1/2-inch videocassette
Length: 58 min.
Date: Not available
Cost: $14.99
Source: Gateway Films/Vision Video
P.O. Box 540
Worcester, PA 19490-0540
(800) 523-0226
http://www.gatewayfilms.com

This video provides a Christian perspective on the controversy between creationism and evolution, asking whether the biblical account of creation is consistent with scientific findings. Such topics as the existence of differing life-forms and the geological record are treated.

Darwinism on Trial
Type: 1/2-inch videocassette
Length: 120 min.
Date: Not available
Cost: $30
Source: Reasons To Believe
P.O. Box 5978
Pasadena, CA 91117
(800) 482-7836
http://www.reasons.org

This video version of Phillip Johnson's book *Darwin on Trial* calls for a rethinking of Darwinism because many issues have not been resolved. Johnson, a law professor at the University of California at Berkeley, suggests that Darwin's theory may be incorrect.

Dawn's Early Light
Type: 1/2-inch videocassette
Length: 28 min.
Date: 1994
Cost: $19.95

Source: American Portrait Films, Inc.
P.O. Box 19266
Cleveland, OH 44119
(800) 736-4567

This tape provides a history of the development of liberty in the United States and examines the major events leading to the founding of America. The purpose is to rediscover the heritage of the nation.

The Deep Waters of Evolution
Type: 1/2-inch videocassette
Length: 28 min.
Date: 2000
Cost: $14
Source: Reasons To Believe
P.O. Box 5978
Pasadena, CA 91117
(800) 482-7836
http://www.reasons.org

Scientists such as Matti Leisola, a biochemist; Dean Kenyon, a biologist; and Siegfried Scherer, a microbiologist, raise doubts about the validity of the Darwinian theory of evolution, focusing on the limits of natural selection.

Dr. Bob Jones, Sr. (1883–1968)
Type: 1/2-inch videocassette
Length: 48 min.
Date: 2000
Cost: $14.95
Source: ShowForth Videos
Bob Jones University Press
Customer Services
Greevnille, SC 29614
(800) 845-5731

This video includes two segments: the first provides an overview of the life of Bob Jones, Sr., founder and first president of Bob Jones University; and the second is a sermon that Jones preached on Luke 23, entitled "Calvary."

Education and the Founding Fathers
Type: 1/2-inch videocassette
Length: 60 min.

Date: 1993
Cost: $20
Source: Wallbuilders
P.O. Box 397
Aledo, TX 76008
(817) 441-6044

Arguing against the "revisionists" who deny the importance of the Christian religion to education, David Barton emphasizes the educational works of Founders such as George Washington, Gouverneur Morris, and Fisher Ames, who upheld biblical teaching. Barton refers to the original textbooks and writings of the Founders to support his claim.

Election '94: We Have One Chance Left to Save America's Christian Republic

Type: 1/2-inch videocassette
Length: 60 min.
Date: 1995
Cost: $20
Source: Christian Crusade Newspaper
P.O. Box 977
Tulsa, OK 74102
(918) 665-2345

Billy James Hargis gives a rundown of the November 1994 election results, viewing them as an indication that Christians are becoming more active politically. Hargis, however, warns about future attacks on Christians by socialists and "extreme liberals."

End of the Cold War

Type: 1/2-inch videocassette
Length: 30 min.
Date: 1994
Cost: $19.95
Source: American Portrait Films
P.O. Box 19266
Cleveland, OH
(216) 531-8600

Combining elements of scripture and economics, Baptist Pastor Sherman Smith investigates the end of the Cold War and its significance for the church.

End-Times Video Collection
Type: 1/2-inch videocassette
Length: 6 hrs.
Date: Not available
Cost: $99.95
Source: Christian Book Distributors
        P.O. Box 7000
        Peabody, MA 01961-7000
        (978) 977-5060
        http://www.christianbook.com

This four-video collection of fictionalized biblical prophecy (*A Thief in the Night, A Distant Thunder, Image of the Beast,* and *The Prodigal Planet*) begins with a young woman awaking one morning to discover that her husband and millions of others have been raptured and that she now faces the coming great tribulation.

Environmental Agenda
Type: 1/2-inch videocassette and audiocassette
Length: 50 min.
Date: 1992
Cost: $20 videocassette; $6 audiocassette
Source: John Hagee Ministries
          P.O. Box 1400
          San Antonio, TX 78295-1400
          (210) 494-3900

Although initially stating that he supports action to preserve the environment, John Hagee launches into an attack on the environmental movement, which is supposedly dominated by the political left, the occult, the "New World crowd," and the New Age movement. The environmental crisis is depicted as a fabrication. God is assumed to have the environment under control without the help of the environmental movement.

The Evidence for Creation: Examining the Origin of Planet Earth
Type: 1/2-inch videocassette
Length: 60 min.
Date: 1994
Cost: $9.95
Source: Christian Book Distributors
          P.O. Box 7000
          Peabody, MA 01961-7000

(978) 977-5060
http://www.christianbook.com

Roger Oakland asserts the logic of creationism, maintaining that evidence derived from observations of the galaxy as well as rock formations on earth support the creationist theory of the origin of the earth.

The Evolution Conspiracy
Type: 1/2-inch videocassette
Length: 48 min.
Date: 1989
Cost: $19.95
Source: Creation Moments, Inc.
         P.O. Box 260
         Zimmerman, MN 55398-0260
         (800) 422-4253

This program, hosted by Roger Oakland, claims that evolution theory, far from being scientific fact, suffers from many inconsistencies. The ultimate purpose of the tape is to provide scientific facts that support biblical creation and hence to strengthen Christians' belief in a creator.

Evolution: Fact or Fiction
Type: 1/2-inch videocassette
Length: 61 min.
Date: 1994
Cost: $9.95
Source: Christian Book Distributors
         P.O. Box 7000
         Peabody, MA 01961-7000
         (978) 977-5060
         http://www.christianbook.com

Roger Oakland examines the theory of evolution, discounting it as a plausible explanation for the origin of humankind. On the basis of available evidence, Oakland concludes that evolution is subject to serious challenge.

Evolution: Science or Religion?
Type: 1/2-inch videocassette
Length: 30 min.
Date: 1995
Cost: $35

Source: Creation Moments, Inc.
P.O. Box 260
Zimmerman, MN 55398-2060
(800) 422-4253

This program appears on the first tape in the *Origins* series, along with "Lessons from a Thunderstorm." In the evolution program, Luther Sunderland deals with the definition of science, how creation and evolution can be taught in the public schools, Darwin's contributions to science, and the impact of evolution on theology.

Explaining Inerrancy
Type: 1/2-inch videocassette
Length: 5 hrs.
Date: 1989
Cost: $129
Source: Ligonier Ministries
P.O. Box 7500
Orlando, FL 32854
(800) 435-4343

This program presents an extended examination of the doctrine that the Bible is without error.

False Gods of Our Time
Type: 1/2-inch videocassette
Length: 100 min.
Date: 1989
Cost: $19.95
Source: Jeremiah Films
P.O. Box 1710
Hemet, CA 92343
(800) 828-2290

Narrated by Christian theologian Dr. Norman Geisler, this tape offers a fundamentalist view of today's "false gods": the New Age movement, the occult, evolution, humanism, and atheism.

The Feminist Movement
Type: 1/2-inch videocassette and audiocassette
Length: 50 min.
Date: 1992
Cost: $20 videocassette; $6 audiocassette
Source: John Hagee Ministries
P.O. Box 1400

San Antonio, TX 78295-1400
(210) 494-3900

Although John Hagee supports such women's issues as equal
pay and protection from sexual harassment, he attacks the so-
called feminist war on America and associates the feminist movement with pagan beliefs. Hagee focuses on the biblical notion
that women should be submissive to their husbands.

Fingerprints of Creation
Type: 1/2-inch videocassette
Length: 34 min.
Date: 1994
Cost: $19.95
Source: American Portrait Films, Inc.
P.O. Box 19266
Cleveland, OH 44119
(216) 531-8600

Dr. Robert Gantry argues that radio halos from polonium, a
naturally radioactive metallic element, are scientific proof that
the earth was formed in just a few thousand years rather than
millions of years. Hence, these halos provide support for
creationism.

Fossil Evidence of Creation
Type: 1/2-inch videocassette
Length: 27 min.
Date: Not available
Cost: $19.95
Source: American Portrait Films
P.O. Box 19266
Cleveland, OH 44119
(800) 736-4567

Arguing for a "young earth," this video presents fossil evidence
of creation, including the rapid development of coal, petrified
forests, and the discovery of unfossilized dinosaur bones, suggesting that dinosaurs became extinct more recently.

Foundations of American Freedom
Type: 1/2-inch videocassette
Length: 100 min. (2 tapes)
Date: Not available
Cost: $29.99

Source: Gateway Films
P.O. Box 540
Worcester, PA 19490-0540
(800) 523-0226
http://www.visionvideo.com

This video, which includes interviews with contemporary historians, presents an account of the values and principles said to be most important to early American leaders. Religious beliefs are said to have played a major role in the development of the nation.

Foundations of American Government
Type: 1/2-inch videocassette
Length: 60 min.
Date: 1993
Cost: $20
Source: Wallbuilders
P.O. Box 397
Aledo, TX 76008
(817) 441-6044

David Barton discusses the biblical principles that once influenced American government and points to contemporary religious right and conservative political leaders who are striving to reintroduce those principles.

Gay Rights/Special Rights
Type: 1/2-inch videocassette
Length: 45 min.
Date: 1994
Cost: $19.95
Source: Jeremiah Films
P.O. Box 1710
Hemet, CA 925456
(800) 828-2290

This tape provides a conservative Christian view of what is considered the "homosexual agenda." The observation is made that homosexuals wish to amend the 1964 Civil Rights Act to make sexual preference a right guaranteed under the Constitution.

The Genesis Quandary: Why Two Creation Accounts and Other Puzzles
Type: audiocassette

Length: 40 min.
Date: 1994
Cost: $3.50
Source: Reasons To Believe
P.O. Box 5978
Pasadena, CA 91117
(800) 482-7836
http://www.reasons.org

Dr. Hugh Ross examines the two creation stories of Genesis, explaining why the book contains two creation accounts. Among the subjects addressed are the authorship of the two Genesis accounts, the discovery of a large number of new species during a relatively short time period, fossil records, and contemporary human beings as descendants of cave dwellers.

Get Out the Vote: 20% More in '94
Type: audiocassette
Length: 25 min.
Date: 1994
Cost: Distributed free of charge to pastors
Source: Family Life Ministries
370 L'Enfant Promenade SW, Suite 801
Washington, DC 20024
(409) 246-2885

On this tape, produced for Christian pastors, Tim LaHaye presents a litany of social evils of concern to the religious right (school prayer, abortion, sex education, pornography, homosexuality, and organized crime). He calls on pastors to assist in increasing the Christian vote in the November 1994 elections in order to throw "liberal secularizers" out of government and to repeal their secularist policies.

God and Science
Type: audiocassette
Length: 120 min.
Date: 1998
Cost: $19.95
Source: Reasons To Believe
P.O. Box 5978
Pasadena, CA 91117
(800) 482-7836
http://www.reasons.org

Noted conservative columnist and talk show host William F. Buckley moderates this debate between atheist Peter Atkins, an Oxford professor, and William Lane Craig, who received a doctor of theology degree from the University of Munich. The participants consider whether Christian theism or atheistic naturalism best explains the preconditions to science and what science might have to say about the existence of God.

God's Power and Scripture's Authority
Type: 1/2-inch videocassette
Length: 49 min.
Date: 1994
Cost: $24.95
Source: Creation Moments, Inc.
P.O. Box 260
Zimmerman, MN 55398-0260
(800) 422-4253

Dr. Walter T. Brown Jr. uses examples from biology, astronomy, and earth science in an attempt to demonstrate that the earth is young and that evolution is impossible. He answers questions about the biblical flood.

God's Providence in History
Type: 1/2-inch videocassette
Length: 59 min.
Date: 1989
Cost: $24.95
Source: Bob Jones University Press
Customer Service Department
Greenville, SC 29614
(800) 845-5731

Old Testament history is examined in the context of contemporary events. The tape makes the case for the Bible's relevance to modern times.

The Gospel of Liberty
Type: 1/2-inch videocassette
Length: 37 min.
Date: 1997
Cost: $19.99
Source: Gateway Films
P.O. Box 540

Worcester, PA 19490-0540
(800) 523-0226
http://www.visionvideo.com

This video explores the possible influence that religious leaders such as George Whitefield and Samuel Davies, who were involved in the religious revival known as the Great Awakening during the early eighteenth century, had on the subsequent development of the United States.

The Guiding Hand
Type: 1/2-inch videocassette
Length: 21 min.
Date: 1994
Cost: $19.95
Source: American Portrait Films, Inc.
P.O. Box 19266
Cleveland, OH 44119
(800) 736-4567

This anti-Clinton film investigates the former Arkansas governor's outcome-based education program in that state. The tape associates President Clinton's education program with homosexuality, abortion, Eastern philosophy, socialism, and communism.

The Harder Truth
Type: 1/2-inch videocassette
Length: 95 min.
Date: 1992
Cost: $15
Source: Christian Research Institute
P.O. Box 500
San Juan Capistrano, CA 92693-0500
(800) 443-9797

This video is a graphic presentation of arguments against abortion. It is presented as a useful tool against pro-choice advocates, portraying abortion as murder. A study guide accompanies the tape.

Has the Human Body Been Designed?
Type: 1/2-inch videocassette
Length: 30 min.
Date: 1995
Cost: $35

Source: Creation Moments, Inc.
P.O. Box 260
Zimmerman, MN 55398-0260
(800) 422-4253

In this first program on the second videotape of the *Origins* series (second program: "Creation and Psychology!"), John Meyer, professor of science at Baptist Bible College, examines the complex structures of the brain and the heart from a creationist perspective.

Have You Been Left Behind?
Type: 1/2-inch videocassette
Length: 20 min.
Date: Not available
Cost: $10.95
Source: Christian Book Distributors
P.O. Box 7000
Peabody, MA
(978) 977-5060
http://www.christianbook.com

This video employs a popular tool of evangelicals, portraying those who have been "left behind" following the rapture, an event premillennialists expect based on their interpretation of the Book of Revelation. Reverend Vernon Billings delivers a message to those left behind with the objective of persuading people now to become believers in order to avoid the great tribulation.

Hell's Bells: The Dangers of Rock and Roll
Type: 1/2-inch videocassette
Length: 185 min. (2 tapes)
Date: 1990
Cost: $49.95
Source: American Portrait Films
P.O. Box 19266
Cleveland, OH 44119
(800) 736-4567

Through film clips and interviews with performers, this video explores the effects of popular music, claiming that America's youth are being seduced by the medium.

Homosexuality: Alternative or Abomination
Type: 1/2-inch videocassette and audiocassette

Length: 50 min.
Date: 1992
Cost: $20 videocassette; $6 audiocassette
Source: John Hagee Ministries
P.O. Box 1400
San Antonio, TX 78295-1400
(210) 494-3900

John Hagee supports the religious right position on homosexuality, arguing that the Bible declares it a sin against God. Much of the presentation focuses on the spread of AIDS.

How Should We Then Live?
Type: 1/2-inch videocassette
Length: 360 min.
Date: 1978
Cost: $79.95
Source: Christian Book Distributors
P.O. Box 6000
Peabody, MA 01961-6000
(978) 977-5060

This series features the conservative Christian thinker Francis Schaeffer. Each of twelve half-hour programs treats a historical era and offers biblical answers to contemporary problems. A study guide accompanies the videotapes.

In the Image of God
Type: 1/2-inch videocassette
Length: 28 min.
Date: 1998
Cost: $19.95
Source: American Portrait Films
P.O. Box 19266
Cleveland, OH 44119
(800) 736-4567

This video provides "compelling new evidence" about the creation of human beings through an act of divine will rather than evolution. It provides arguments against the evolution of human beings from ape creatures such as *Homo habilis* and Piltdown Man.

Irreducible Complexity: The Biochemical Challenge to Darwinian Theory
Type: 1/2-inch videocassette

Length: 101 min.
Date: 2000
Cost: $29.95
Source: Reasons To Believe
          P.O. Box 5978
          Pasadena, CA 91117
          (800) 482-7836
          http://www.reasons.org

Michael Behe employs examples from biochemistry to argue that irreducible complexity in biological systems refutes neo-Darwinian theory. Behe suggests other explanations for the existence of complex life, including the possibility of intelligent design.

Is Science Religious?
Type: audiocassette
Length: 60 min.
Date: 1994
Cost: $5
Source: Reasons To Believe
          P.O. Box 5978
          Pasadena, CA 91117
          (818) 335-1480
          http://www.reasons.org

Dr. Hugh Ross discusses the relationship between science and religion with Dr. Eugenie Scott, an anthropologist and head of the National Center for Science Education, an organization opposed to scientific creationism.

Israel: The Apple of God's Eye
Type: 1/2-inch videocassette and audiocassette
Length: 60 min.
Date: 1992
Cost: $20 videocassette; $6 audiocassette
Source: John Hagee Ministries
          P.O. Box 1400
          San Antonio, TX 78295-1400
          (210) 494-3900

In line with the premillennialist interest in Israel and that nation's role in the end-times drama, John Hagee claims that God will hold the United States responsible if it fails to defend Israel. Reference is made to Jewish assistance during the American Revolution to indicate that the Gentiles have been blessed through the Jewish people. Hagee uses Old Testament references to illustrate what disasters await those who persecute the Jews.

Journey toward Creation
Type: 1/2-inch videocassette
Length: 60 min.
Date: 1998
Cost: $25
Source: Reasons To Believe
          P.O. Box 5978
          Pasadena, CA 91117
          (800) 482-7836
          http://www.reasons.org

Hugh Ross, astronomer and president of Reasons To Believe, conducts a journey back in time to examine such phenomena as nebulae, black holes, and quasars. Ross does not accept the more fundamentalist belief in a seven-day creation, but concludes that God created the universe and human beings.

Keys to Good Government
Type: 1/2-inch videocassette
Length: 59 min.
Date: 1994
Cost: $20
Source: American Opinion Book Services
          P.O. Box 8040
          Appleton, WI 54913
          (414) 749-3783

David Barton examines the advice for good government given by such early Americans as William Penn, Benjamin Rush, John Adams, and George Washington. Barton concludes that morality remains the key characteristic of good government.

The Late Great Planet Earth
Type: 1/2-inch videocassette
Length: 87 min.
Date: 1987
Cost: $9.99
Source: Video Treasures
          1767 Morris Avenue
          Union, NJ 07083
          (201) 964-5604

Orson Welles narrates this video based on Hal Lindsey's bestseller by the same name. Biblical prophecy is interpreted from a premillennial perspective in predicting future disasters for the planet.

Leadership in the John Birch Society
Type: 1/2-inch videocassette
Length: 28 min.
Date: 1994
Cost: $15
Source: American Opinion Book Services
P.O. Box 8040
Appleton, WI 54913
(414) 749-3783

Members of a local chapter of the society are portrayed in action. By describing the operation of local organization in the Birch Society, this tape provides insight into the advantages of grassroots political activity that has been the focus of many religious right organizations.

Left Behind
Type: compact disc and audiocassette
Length: 5 hrs.
Date: 1995
Cost: $16.95 cassette; $24.95 CD
Source: Christian Book Distributors
P.O. Box 7000
7000 Peabody, MA 01961-7000
(978) 977-5060
http://www.christianbook.com

These audio presentations offer a rendition of Jerry Jenkins's and Tim LaHaye's first novel about the end times, based on the Book of Revelation.

Left Behind: The Movie
Type: 1/2-inch videocassette and DVD
Length: 120 min.
Date: 2000
Cost: $24.95
Source: Christian Book Distributors
P.O. Box 7000
Peabody, MA 01961-7000

(978) 977-5060
http://www.christianbook.com

This movie is a film adaptation of the Tim LaHaye and Jerry Jenkins novel about the prophesied end times. Millions of people around the world disappear in the "rapture," and those remaining on earth are left to contend with the resulting chaos and the tribulation that some Bible interpreters claim is predicted in scripture.

Left Behind: Where'd Everybody Go?
Type: 1/2-inch videocassette
Length: 100 min.
Date: 1994
Cost: $19.95
Source: This Week in Bible Prophecy
P.O. Box 1440
Niagara Falls, NY 14302-1440
(800) 776-7432

Beginning with a dramatization of the chaos that results after Christians are taken to heaven in the rapture, the remainder of the tape, supposedly "prerecorded" for those left behind, gives advice for resisting the influence of the Antichrist who will rule during the seven-year period preceding Christ's thousand-year reign on earth. Noted premillennialists such as Hal Lindsey, John Ankerberg, and Zola Levitt explain the meaning of Bible prophecy.

Massacre of Innocence
Type: 1/2-inch videocassette
Length: 85 min.
Date: 1988
Cost: $19.95
Source: American Portrait Films
P.O. Box 19266
Cleveland, OH 44119
(800) 736-4567

This video explores the sociological and medical history of abortion. The claim is made that "spiritual forces" are behind the continuation of the practice, including such rituals as child sacrifice and feminist goddess worship.

Monkey Trial
Type: 1/2-inch videocassette

Length: 50 min.
Date: 1998
Cost: $24.95
Source: Teacher's Video Company
P.O. Box AHR-4455
Scottsdale, AZ 85261
(800) 262-8837

This video is a historical account of the prosecution of John Thomas Scopes for violating a Tennessee state law prohibiting the teaching of the theory of evolution in the public schools. The video includes original film footage from the trial, which was held in Dayton, Tennessee, in 1925.

Moody!
Type: 1/2-inch videocassette
Length: 57 min.
Date: 1988
Cost: $24.95
Source: ShowForth Videos
Bob Jones University Press
Customer Services
Greenville, SC 29614
(800) 525-8398

This account of the life of nineteenth-century evangelist Dwight Lyman Moody focuses on Moody's involvement in the formation of the Moody Bible Institute, the development of the Sunday school movement, and the establishment of the Young Men's Christian Association (YMCA). Moody was influential in establishing the tradition of well-organized evangelism campaigns.

MTV Examined
Type: 1/2-inch videocassette
Length: 30 min.
Date: 1994
Cost: $19.95
Source: American Portrait Films
P.O. Box 19266
Cleveland, OH 44119
(800) 736-4567

Based on an examination of the content of the cable television station MTV, this video charges that the music station must take responsibility for increased violence, sexual activity, rebellion, and moral relativism among young people.

Nations United in the End
Type: audiocassette
Length: 60 min.
Date: 1994
Cost: $5
Source: Reasons To Believe
P.O. Box 5978
Pasadena, CA 91117
(800) 482-7836
http://www.reasons.org

Dr. Hugh Ross explains why coalitions among nations in pursuit of peace are in fact the prelude to Satan's war against Christians. Ross examines the future of Iraq, Israel, Jordan, and Lebanon on the basis of scripture.

New Age Movement
Type: 1/2-inch videocassette
Length: 30 min.
Date: 1995
Cost: $35
Source: Creation Moments, Inc.
P.O. Box 260
Zimmerman, MN 55398-0260
(800) 422-4253

Ellen Myers, cofounder of the Creation Social Science and Humanities Society, explains that evolution predates Darwin by centuries. She explores the origins of the New Age movement and argues that biological evolution has been used to authenticate "spiritual evolution." This program is the first half of the third video in the *Origins* series, which concludes with "Biblical Hermeneutics."

The Omega Code
Type: 1/2-inch videocassette
Length: 100 min.
Date: 1999
Cost: $19.95
Source: Christian Book Distributors
P.O. Box 7000

Peabody, MA 01961-7000
(978) 977-5060
http://www.christianbook.com

This film, produced by the Trinity Broadcasting Network, proved to be a commercial success at theaters, likely due to the interest of evangelical Christians. Some of the events described in the Book of Revelation are placed in dramatic form. The plot revolves around the attempt to understand a biblical code that supposedly foretells the events of the last days. The Antichrist proves to be the "European Union Chairman."

Our Military under Siege
Type: 1/2-inch videocassette
Length: 30 min.
Date: 1994
Cost: $19.95
Source: American Portrait Films, Inc.
P.O. Box 19266
Cleveland, OH 44119
(800) 736-4567

This highly critical presentation of President Clinton's policy on gays in the military provides interviews with military persons who are strongly opposed to changing the policy on homosexuals in the military. The issue is presented as a choice between national security and satisfying the demands of a special interest group.

Putting Creation to the Test
Type: 1/2-inch videocassette
Length: 6 hrs.
Date: Not available
Cost: $69.95
Source: Reasons To Believe
P.O. Box 5978
Pasadena, CA 91117
(818) 335-1480
http://www.reasons.org

Astronomer Hugh Ross, biochemist Fuz Rana, philosopher Kenneth Samples, and moderator Mark Clark examine what they consider a testable creation model. They claim that a theory of creation has been developed that satisfies scientific requirements while remaining faithful to the biblical account.

Raging Waters
Type: 1/2-inch videocassette
Length: 28 min.
Date: 1997
Cost: $19.95
Source: American Portrait Films
P.O. Box 19266
Cleveland, OH 44119
(800) 736-4567

Examination of such physical phenomena as ripple marks, marine fossils in mountain ranges, and the rapid development of coal deposits in Australia are presented as evidence for a Genesis flood. The video also refers to the legends of Australian Aborigines that describe a general flood.

The Religion of Secular Humanism
Type: 1/2-inch videocassette
Length: 40 min.
Date: 1998
Cost: $19.99
Source: Gateway Films/Vision Video
P.O. Box 540
Worcester, PA 19490-0540
(800) 523-0226
http://www.gatewayfilms.com

The video considers secular humanism to be an identifiable worldview accepted by many influential people in the United States. The claim is made that the viewpoint of secular humanism is the dominant position presented in contemporary public education.

Revelation
Type: 1/2-inch videocassette
Length: 97 min.
Date: 1999
Cost: $27.95
Source: Christian Book Distributors
P.O. Box 7000
Peabody, MA 01961-7000
(978) 977-5060
http://www.christianbook.com

This fictionalized account of the end times deals with the Antichrist coming to power and establishing a worldwide government. Government representatives are distributing virtual reality headsets that all are to wear on a "Day of Wonders." The Christian underground attempts to foil the evil plan.

Revelation Illustrated
Type: 1/2-inch videocassette
Length: 46 min.
Date: 1992
Cost: $14.95
Source: Christian Book Distributors
P.O. Box 7000
Peabody, MA 01961-7000
(978) 977-5060
http://www.christianbook.com

This retelling of the prophetic Book of Revelation includes narration from the original text, the artwork of Pat Marvenko Smith, and music by the Back Choir of Pittsburgh.

Roundtable on Genesis One
Type: 1/2-inch audiocassette
Length: 120 min.
Date: Not available
Cost: $30
Source: Reasons To Believe
P.O. Box 5978
Pasadena, CA 91117
(800) 482-7836
http://www.reasons.org

Four scholars, James Buswell, Hugh Ross, Robert Saucy, and Dallas Willard, present differing interpretations of the Genesis account of creation. Among the issues discussed are the length of a creation day, the problem of evil and suffering, and the origin of death.

Science and Genesis
Type: audiocassette
Length: 120 min.
Date: Not available
Cost: $36
Source: Reasons To Believe
P.O. Box 5978

Pasadena, CA 91117
(800) 482-7836
http://www.reasons.org

Hugh Ross, who is noted for his attempts to bring modern science and the Genesis account of creation into agreement, examines some of the crucial issues in the debate. The four separate tapes in this series are titled "Comparing Different Creation Accounts," "Creation Days," "Dinosaurs, Cavemen, and the Fossil Record," and "The Flood."

Science, Creation, and the Bible
Type: 1/2-inch videocassette
Length: 49 min.
Date: 1993
Cost: $19.95
Source: American Portrait Films
P.O. Box 19266
Cleveland, OH 44119
(800) 736-4567

Dr. Walter Brown, a former evolutionist, explains how evolutionary theory challenges the Christian faith and conflicts with science. Brown presents evidence from fossil records.

A Scientist Looks at Creation
Type: 1/2-inch videocassette
Length: 80 min.
Date: 1994
Cost: $19.95
Source: American Portrait Films
P.O. Box 19266
Cleveland, OH 44119
(800) 736-4567

This two-part program explaining creationism claims to show why many physicists, engineers, and astronomers have changed their minds on the debate between evolution and creation.

The Signature of God
Type: 1/2-inch videocassette
Length: 160 min. (2 tapes)
Date: 1997
Cost: $29.95
Source: Christian Book Distributors

P.O. Box 7000
Peabody, MA 01961-7000
(978) 977-5060
http://www.christianbook.com

Grant R. Jeffrey argues that Hebrew codes in the Bible reveal highly accurate biblical prophecies. Jeffrey claims to have developed a mathematical formula to prove that the Bible is the revealed word of God.

The Spirit of the American Revolution
Type: 1/2-inch videocassette
Length: 55 min.
Date: Not available
Cost: $20
Source: Wallbuilders
P.O. Box 397
Aledo, TX 76008
(817) 441-6044

David Barton discusses the importance of the Christian faith to the colonists during the American Revolution. Barton refers to the faith of prominent Americans at the time, such as John Adams, George Washington, Samuel Adams, and Patrick Henry, and focuses on the role they saw God playing in the course of the Revolution. God is portrayed as an unqualified supporter of the American revolutionaries.

The Story of America's Liberty
Type: 1/2-inch videocassette
Length: 65 min.
Date: 1994
Cost: $19.95
Source: American Portrait Films, Inc.
P.O. Box 19266
Cleveland, OH 44119
(800) 736-4567

This treatment of America's Christian heritage focuses on the alleged miracles that God performed in assisting the American birth.

Suffer the Children
Type: 1/2-inch videocassette
Length: 60 min.

Date: 1999
Cost: $25
Source: American Family Association
P.O. Drawer 2440
Tupelo, MS 38803
(662) 844-5036

In order to counter a prohomosexual video titled "It's Elementary: Talking about Gay Issues in School," the American Family Association produced this video, based on what the organization considers a biblically correct view of the issue.

Test of Faith
Type: 1/2-inch videocassette
Length: 55 min.
Date: 1989
Cost: $29.95
Source: Russ Doughten Films, Inc.
5907 Meredith Drive
Des Moines, IA 50322
(800) 247-3456

A physics professor, claiming that faith is an enemy of science, pressures a young college student to abandon his belief in biblical creation and to concentrate instead on scientific thinking. The tape ultimately points to the errors in the professor's position.

Tribulation Force
Type: audiocassette and compact disc
Length: 5 hrs.
Date: 1999
Cost: $16.95 cassette; $24.95 CD
Source: Christian Book Distributors
P.O. Box 7000
Peabody, MA 01961-7000
(978) 977-5060
http://www.christianbook.com

In a sequel to Jerry Jenkins's and Tim LaHaye's fictional depiction of the end times as prophesied in the Book of Revelation, this audio presentation continues the story of the last days.

The Universe: Accident or Design?
Type: 1/2-inch videocassette
Length: 60 min.

Date: Not available
Cost: $19
Source: Reasons To Believe
P.O. Box 5978
Pasadena, CA 91117
(818) 335-1480
http://www.reasons.org

Dr. David Block, director of the religious right organization Reasons To Believe South Africa, presents slides and graphs to demonstrate the wonder of the universe and the awesomeness of its creator.

Winning the Sexual Revolution
Type: 1/2-inch videocassette
Length: 35 min.
Date: Not available
Cost: $19.95
Source: American Portrait Films
P.O. Box 19266
Cleveland, OH 44119
(800) 736-4567

James Dobson, head of Focus on the Family, actor Ricardo Montalban, and movie critic Michael Medved emphasize the importance of family values and how to defend them against the humanistic influences of the public schools and the mass media.

Wolf in Sheep's Clothing: Theological Liberalism
Type: audiocassette
Length: 45 min.
Date: 1998
Cost: $4
Source: Ligonier Ministries
P.O. Box 547500
Orlando, FL 32854
(800) 435-4343

R. C. Sproul, head of Ligonier Ministries, follows in the footsteps of early twentieth-century theologian J. Gresham Machen, taking to task liberal Christian doctrine that arose in the nineteenth century challenging such fundamental Christian beliefs as the virgin birth of Jesus and Jesus' resurrection from the dead. Like Machen, Sproul contends one cannot be a liberal and a Christian at the same time.

The Wonders of God's Creation
Type: 1/2-inch videocassette
Length: 189 min. (3 tapes)
Date: 1993
Cost: $24.95
Source: Christian Book Distributors
P.O. Box 7000
Peabody, MA 01961-7000
(978) 977-5060
http://www.christianbook.com

Intended for elementary school children, the three videotapes in this series ("Planet Earth," "Animal Kingdom," and "Human Life") present the wonders of nature and attribute them to a creator. Biblical references are frequently provided during each presentation.

Audiotapes and Videotapes about the Religious Right

This section provides three types of sources on the religious right. The first analyzes the characteristics of religion and the religious right; the second deals with issues of concern to the religious right from an alternative perspective; and the third presents a critical treatment of religious right positions and activities.

Religion and the Religious Right

Apocalypse!
Type: 1/2-inch videocassette
Length: 120 min.
Date: 1999
Cost: $19.98
Source: PBS Video
1320 Braddock Place
Alexandria, VA 22314-1698
(800) 344-3337

The notion of an apocalypse, the end time of devastation for the sinful and deliverance for the faithful, has influenced human thought for over two millennia. This video explores the ways in which the meaning of the idea has changed in more recent times.

The Battle for the Bible
Type: 1/2-inch videocassette

Length: 60 min.
Date: 1992
Cost: $89.95
Source: Films for the Humanities and Sciences
P.O. Box 2053
Princeton, NJ 08543-2053
(800) 257-5126
http://www.films.com

This second video in the Bill Moyers series *God and Politics* deals with the liberal-conservative conflict within the Southern Baptist Convention. Fundamentalists have wrested control of the Convention from moderates and ultimately want to affect American politics.

The Bible in Translation: God's Word vs. Man's Words
Type: 1/2-inch videocassette
Length: 47 min.
Date: 2000
Cost: $149 purchase; $75 rental
Source: Films for the Humanities and Sciences
P.O. Box 2053
Princeton, NJ 08543-2053
(800) 257-5126
http://www.films.com

Fundamentalists, who often hold to a doctrine of biblical inerrancy, are sensitive to differing scriptural translations. In this video Elizabeth Castelli, Paige Patterson, Rabbi Burton Visotzky, and others debate such issues as the influence of the Greco-Roman world on the Bible, the use of gender-neutral language in more recent translations, the accuracy of more recent Bibles compared with the King James version (the only acceptable translation for many fundamentalists), and the use of the Bible in the pre–Civil War United States both to defend and denounce slavery.

In the Name of God
Type: 1/2-inch videocassette
Length: 50 min.
Date: 1995
Cost: $19.95
Source: ABC, Inc.
77 West 66th Street

New York, NY 10023
(800) 222-7500

Originally an ABC News special presentation narrated by Peter Jennings, this tape looks at growing churches and examines the techniques they use to attract people. Although mainline churches have been losing members, Pentecostal-oriented churches have been flourishing. Some observers voice the concern that these popular churches sacrifice basic Christian beliefs.

The Kingdom Divided
Type: 1/2-inch videocassette
Length: 90 min.
Date: 1992
Cost: $129
Source: Films for the Humanities and Sciences
P.O. Box 2053
Princeton, NJ 08543-2053
(800) 257-5126
http://www.films.com

This tape, the first in the Bill Moyers series *God and Politics*, focuses on the effect that a conflict between two different interpretations of Christianity (liberation theology and evangelicalism) is having on American foreign policy in Central America.

On Earth as It Is in Heaven
Type: 1/2-inch videocassette
Length: 60 min.
Date: 1992
Cost: $89.95
Source: Films for the Humanities and Sciences
P.O. Box 2053
Princeton, NJ 08543-2053
(800) 257-5126
http://www.films.com

Bill Moyers, in this third program in the *God and Politics* series, examines Christian Reconstructionism, a radical religious movement that advocates political activity to achieve a government that adheres to strict biblical standards. Moyers concludes that this movement may prove to be more significant than the religious right of the 1980s.

The Religious Right
Type: 1/2-inch videocassette
Length: 60 min.
Date: 1992
Cost: $89.95
Source: Films for the Humanities and Sciences
          P.O. Box 2053
          Princeton, NJ 08543-2053
          (800) 257-5126
          http://www.films.com

Bill Moyers reports on the "National Affairs Briefing" of religious right members after the 1992 Republican National Convention. Conservative leaders such as Pat Buchanan, Oliver North, Donald Wildmon, and Phyllis Schlafly state positions on homosexuality, feminism, abortion, and the media.

With God on Our Side: The Rise of the Religious Right in America
Type: 1/2-inch videocassette
Length: 6 hrs.
Date: 1996
Cost: $119.98
Source: PBS Video
          1320 Braddock Place
          Alexandria, VA 22314-1698
          (800) 344-3337

Containing archival footage and interviews, this video demonstrates how evangelical Christians became involved in mainstream politics and popular American culture.

Religious Right Issues

Abortion: The Moral Dilemma
Type: 1/2-inch videocassette
Length: 28 min.
Date: 1995
Cost: $89.95
Source: Films for the Humanities and Sciences
          P.O. Box 2053
          Princeton, NJ 08543-2053
          (800) 257-5126
          http://www.films.com

This program discusses the troubling dilemmas underlying the pro- and antiabortion positions. The Christian parents of one healthy child, having already lost two babies to a fatal inherited disease, but still wanting another child, must face the abortion option.

Battle over the Blackboard
Type: 1/2-inch videocassette
Length: 26 min.
Date: 1991
Cost: $149
Source: Films for the Humanities and Sciences
P.O. Box 2053
Princeton, NJ 08543-2053
(800) 257-5126
http://www.films.com

This program deals with the fundamentalist reaction against what is regarded as the secular humanist intrusion into the American educational system. A major topic is the book selection process for schools and public libraries.

Faith: Talking with Peggy Noonan
Type: 1/2-inch videocassette
Length: 60 min.
Date: 1995
Cost: $89.95
Source: Films for the Humanities and Sciences
P.O. Box 2053
Princeton, NJ 08543-2053
(800) 257-5126
http://www.films.com

This thoughtful presentation examines the possible effects of expelling religion from public institutions and investigates the role that faith might still play in the public realm. Father Richard John Neuhaus, Michael Lerner, and Bill Moyers are featured.

God and the Constitution
Type: 1/2-inch videocassette
Length: 60 min.
Date: 1994
Cost: $89.95
Source: Films for the Humanities and Sciences

P.O. Box 2053
Princeton, NJ 08543-2053
(800) 257-5126
http://www.films.com

Bill Moyers hosts a discussion about the legality of school prayer with Martin Marty, professor of the history of modern Christianity at the University of Chicago, and Leonard Levy, editor of *The Encyclopedia of the American Constitution*. The participants also discuss the issues of tax exemption for religious institutions and religious symbols on public property.

Liberal Protestantism in the '90s: Forrester Church
Type: 1/2-inch videocassette
Length: 30 min.
Date: 1995
Cost: $89.95
Source: Films for the Humanities and Sciences
P.O. Box 2053
Princeton, NJ 08543-2053
(800) 257-5126
http://www.films.com

Bill Moyers, program host, and Forrester Church, pastor of All Souls Unitarian Church in New York City and son of the late Senator Frank Church, discuss the state of religion in America from a liberal Protestant perspective. Church deals with the ambiguities of his ministry and what can be learned from the variety of religious positions, including the religious right.

Religion, Politics and Our Schools
Type: 1/2-inch videocassette
Length: 90 min.
Date: 1988
Cost: $69.95
Source: American Humanist Association
7 Hardwood Drive
P.O. Box 146
Amherst, NY 14226-0146
(716) 839-5080

Seven religious leaders discuss the separation of church and state and its relevance to the public schools.

With a Vengeance: The Fight for Reproductive Freedom
Type: 1/2-inch videocassette
Length: 40 min.
Date: 1990
Cost: $225 purchase; $75 rental
Source: Women Make Movies
225 Lafayette Street, Suite 212
New York, NY 10012
(212) 925-0606

This video is a reaction to the religious right's opposition to abortion, focusing on the reproductive rights of women. The struggles over abortion rights in the 1960s and 1980s are compared.

Treatments Critical of the Religious Right

Blowing the Whistle on Pat Robertson
Type: 1/2-inch videocassette
Length: 60 min.
Date: 1988
Cost: $49.95
Source: American Humanist Association
7 Hardwood Drive
P.O. Box 146
Amherst, NY 14226-0146
(716) 839-5080

The former producer of Pat Robertson's *The 700 Club* television program provides an exposé of the televangelist and presidential candidate.

Defending the Rights of Evangelism's Victims
Type: 1/2-inch videocassette and audiocassette
Length: 2 hrs.
Date: 1988
Cost: $49.95 videocassette; $9 audiocassette
Source: American Humanist Association
7 Hardwood Drive
P.O. Box 1188
Amherst, NY 14226-7188
(716) 839-5080

Richard Yao and James Luce, founders of Fundamentalists Anonymous, recount cases of religious "indoctrination" and the "deprogramming" of the "victims" of evangelism.

Facing the Fundamentalist/Vatican Challenge
Type: audiocassette
Length: 60 min.
Date: 1994
Cost: $9
Source: American Humanist Association
7 Hardwood Drive
P.O. Box 1188
Amherst, NY 14226-7188
(716) 839-5080

This tape challenges humanists to respond to the religious right's attack on fundamental freedoms. Ed Doerr argues that humanists must face the challenge of Vatican opposition to birth control, abortion, and freedom of choice.

Inherit the Wind
Type: 1/2-inch black-and-white videocassette
Length: 127 min.
Date: 1960
Cost: $19.95
Source: Movies Unlimited
6736 Castro Avenue
Philadelphia, PA 19149
(800) 523-0823

This fictionalization of the 1925 Scopes trial in Dayton, Tennessee, stars Spencer Tracy and Frederick March, who play roles corresponding respectively to Clarence Darrow and William Jennings Bryan. Fundamentalism is treated in a far from favorable light.

Quality Science Education versus Creationism
Type: 1/2-inch videocassette and audiocassette
Length: 60 min.
Date: 1988
Cost: $49.95 videocassette; $9 audiocassette
Source: American Humanist Association
7 Hardwood Drive
P.O. Box 1188
Amherst, NY 14226-7188
(716) 839-5080

Laurie Godfrey, John R. Cole, Ronnie Hastings, and Steven Schafersma, Humanist Contributions to Science Award recipients, present scientific evidence in support of evolution and sometimes humorous arguments against creationism.

Sources of Power for the Religious Right
Type: audiocassette
Length: 60 min.
Date: 1994
Cost: $9
Source: American Humanist Association
7 Hardwood Drive
P.O. Box 1188
Amherst, NY 14226-7188
(716) 839-5080

Russ Bellant investigates religious right organizations that attempt to evangelize Americans through participation in political party politics. In addition, Ed Doerr discusses separation of church and state and describes legal cases won against the religious right.

Today in America, Sex IS Politics
Type: 1/2-inch videocassette
Length: 60 min.
Date: 1988
Cost: $49.95
Source: American Humanist Association
7 Hardwood Drive
P.O. Box 146
Amherst, NY 14226-0146
(716) 839-5080

This video presents a lecture by Dr. Sol Gordon who focuses on what he considers the absurdity of sex education from the conservative perspective.

Radio and Television Programs

Conservative religious organizations broadcast a wide variety of programs that touch on political and social issues in some way. We include a selection of such programs here. Usually these programs do not appear at a uniform time nationwide but are syndicated. Readers should check local station and cable listings to determine if individual programs appear in their area.

Beverly LaHaye Today

Beverly LaHaye, president of Concerned Women for America, interviews various activists in the religious right on this daily radio program. LaHaye focuses on cultural issues such as education, the moral upbringing of children, marriage tax relief, and decency in the entertainment industry. Segments of the program can be heard via the Internet: http://www.oneplace.com/ministries/Beverly_LaHaye_Today.

Billy James Hargis Television Program

Billy James Hargis hosts this program that appears on World Harvest and National Christian Networks, Saturday and Sunday nights. It provides a forum for Hargis and his traditional conservative Christian style of political commentary. Although not as well known nationally as he was in the 1960s, Hargis still represents a politically more strident element in the religious right.

Cornerstone with John Hagee

This fundamentalist program is telecast from John Hagee's Cornerstone Church in San Antonio, Texas, and can be seen on Trinity Broadcasting Network at 8 A.M. EST on Sunday mornings. Although not as explicitly political as other broadcasts, such as Billy James Hargis's television program and Jerry Falwell's *Old Time Gospel Hour,* Hagee often offers, with passion and without apology, the religious right position on such social issues as homosexual rights, abortion, and the women's movement. He is highly critical of the Clinton administration and the "atheists in Washington." Hagee often presents evidence from scientific authorities for his positions on social issues, but the Bible is his ultimate authority.

Creation Moments

This radio program, produced by Creation Moments, Inc., is heard on 700 radio outlets in the United States and around the world. The program presents a creationist understanding of science, offering facts about nature and demonstrating their connection to a creator. Among the networks carrying Creation Moments each weekday are Moody Broadcasting System (1:40 P.M. EST) and Family Radio Network (12:30 P.M. EST). Call (800) 422-4253 for local station information.

Focus on the Family

This daily radio program hosted by Dr. James Dobson is broadcast over 1,450 stations across the country. Although not an explicitly religious program, Dobson and his guests deal with topics related to Christian family values.

Issues, Etc.

Pastor Don Matzat of the Lutheran Church Missouri Synod (LCMS) hosts this daily three-hour radio talk show, which originates from the LCMS's St. Louis, Missouri, Jubilee Network. Approximately 200 radio stations nationwide broadcast the program. The program's stated purpose is "to call the Church back to the proclamation of Law and Gospel, Sin and Grace." Matzat interviews various religious figures, many of whom are from the religious right.

John Ankerberg Show

Headquartered in Chattanooga, Tennessee, this syndicated evangelical Christian television program, hosted by John Ankerberg, presents defenses of orthodox evangelical Christianity against various cults and perceived heresies. Representatives of "heretical" groups are invited to take part in debate. The program presents conservative Christian positions on such issues as abortion and pornography.

Old-Time Gospel Hour

This program, which is seen on nearly 400 television stations and heard on 500 radio stations, features former leader of the Moral Majority Jerry Falwell. Falwell presents his fundamentalist beliefs and offers his views in opposition to abortion, homosexual rights, pornography, and crime. He often expresses strong criticism of liberals in government.

Reasons To Believe

This television program appears on Trinity Broadcasting Network and deals with evidence for the existence of God. The basic theme of the program is that science and Christianity can be allied in the fight against secularism.

The 700 Club

Produced and syndicated by the Christian Broadcasting Network and hosted by Pat Robertson, this television program follows a talk- and variety-show format and offers news analysis from a conservative Christian perspective. Viewers are invited to call for counseling and prayer.

CD-ROMs

Answers
Publisher: Reasons To Believe
Distributor: Reasons To Believe
P.O. Box 5978
Pasadena, CA 91117
(800) 482-7836
http://www.reasons.org
Price: $29.95

This CD-ROM provides information from the Handbook of Christian Apologetics and from unpublished materials gleaned from Hugh Ross, director of Reasons To Believe. Its purpose is to demonstrate the compatibility of faith and reason and the Bible and science. Among the entries are individuals who have investigated issues of faith and concluded that Christianity has the answers.

Multimedia Family Bible for Windows
Publisher: Infobases, Inc.
Distributor: Infobases, Inc.
875 South State Street, No. 3100
Orem, UT 84058
(800) 537-7823
Price: $79.95

An example of the type of biblical sources available, this Bible reference contains forty-four dramatizations of stories from the King James version of the Bible. The product also contains color maps of the Mediterranean area and the Holy Land and Bible study helps, including Hebrew and Greek definitions.

R. C. Sproul Digital Library on CD-ROM
Distributor: Ligonier Ministries
P.O. Box 547500
Orlando, FL 32854-7500
(800) 333-4233
http://www.ligonier.org
Price: $99.95

This source includes five books by Ligonier Ministries head R. C. Sproul: *Grace Unknown, The Last Days According to Jesus, The Holiness of God, Chosen by God,* and *Essential Truths of the Christian Faith.* In these books, Sproul presents his understanding of the reformed faith, the end times, and the basic beliefs of historical Christianity.

Internet Resources

About the Religious Right
http://www.pfaw.org

Claiming to be "the largest resource of religious right materials," People for the American Way presents information critical of conservative Christian political activities. The organization claims to be a watchdog, monitoring and countering information that religious right organizations submit to the mass media.

The Advocate
http://www.advocate.com

The Advocate, a national gay and lesbian newsmagazine Internet site, contains segments critical of those organizations and individuals on the religious right, such as the Christian Action Network, that oppose attempts by homosexuals to gain recognition of various rights.

American Reformation Project
http://www.americanreformation.org

This site, dedicated to reforming American politics and churches, contains commentary on such topics as abortion, crime, national defense, gun control, drug abuse, education, and election reform. Links are provided to recent news stories.

The American Religious Right
http://www.webpan.com/dsinclair/rright.html

This site, which is critical of conservative Christian political activity, provides links to many other sites related to the religious right. The site includes quotes from religious right organizations and leaders.

American Theological Library Association
http://www.atla.com

The American Theological Library Association offers for purchase a religion database that includes 366,000 journal articles, 14,500 edited works containing 192,000 articles, 357,000 book reviews, and 1,461 journal titles (600 of which are currently indexed).

Antigay Propaganda of the Religious Right
http://parent.qrd.org/www/RRR/propag.html

This site offers evaluations of the religious right position on homosexuality and includes sources on such topics as gays in the military, attacks against gays, and civil liberties.

Attacks on the Freedom to Learn Online
http://www.pfaw.org

This website newsletter, maintained by People for the American Way, reports on school censorship and what the organization considers an assault on public education by religious right groups, including attempts to introduce school prayer, the teaching of creationism in science courses, and passage of "parental rights" legislation.

Bibleinfo.com
http://www.bibleinfo.com

This site contains resources for those wishing to study the Bible. Over 340 Bible topics are available. Individuals may ask Bible questions and make prayer requests. A page gives answers to frequently asked questions.

Biblical Conservatism: Toward a Definition of a Political Philosophy
http://www.natreformassn.org/statesman/96/polphil.html

James L. Sauer discusses conservatism and Christianity, stating that "there is a sense in which all Christians, at least all consistent, orthodox and Biblical ones, are conservative."

The Bully Pulpit
http://www.geocities.com/bullypulpit_org

Reverend Jon Lands's weekly newspaper column is available on this site. Land comments on various political issues.

Center for Reclaiming America
http://reclaimamerica.org

This website, maintained by D. James Kennedy's Coral Ridge Ministries, asserts that it "provides nonpartisan, interdenominational information, training, and support to all those interested in positively affecting the culture and renewing the vision of our Founding Fathers." Topics covered include the homosexual rights movement, abortion, and the importance of morality in law.

Christian
http://www.ii.uib.no/~magnus/lists/christian.html

This site provides a "nonhostile environment" for Christians who wish to participate in an Internet discussion group.

Christian Action Fact Sheet
http://ourworld.compuserve.com:80/homepages/cafs

This site advocates profamily strategies, describing what are considered government and corporate threats to family values. Information is available on such topics as the Disney boycott, the RU-486 abortion drug, pornography, and education.

Christian Broadcasting Network
http://www.christianity.com/cbn

The Christian Broadcasting Network (CBN), founded by religious right leader Pat Robertson in 1960, offers information about the network's history, its present organization, and individuals involved in its management. CBN requests donations from those visiting the site.

Christian Reconstructionism
http://parent.qrd.org/www/RRR/recon.html

This site contains several sources on Christian reconstructionism, a postmillennial view that Christians have the obligation to establish moral government here on earth prior to Christ's return.

Christian Reconstructionism, Dominion Theology and Theonomy
http://www.religioustolerance.org/reconstr.htm

This site contains information about Christian reconstructionism, a belief that contemporary society, which is morally degenerate, must be reformed according to biblical principles.

Christianity and Liberalism
http://libertarian.faithweb.com

This site argues that libertarianism and Christianity have much in common. A bookstore and links to other sites are provided.

Christianity: Bogus Beyond Belief
http://members.aol.com/bbu84/biblicalstupidity/home.htm

This website contains highly cynical and caustic commentary on Christianity and the Bible. Included are articles on such subjects as the humanist rejection of the Bible, the impossibility of a Christian God, and atheist arguments against Christian doctrine.

Christians on the Net
http://www.christiansnet.com

The site contains over thirty-five Christian e-mail discussion lists, including those engaged in Bible study, conservative Christian discussion, and the history of evangelical Christianity.

Creation Research Society
http://www.creationresearch.org

The Creation Research Society adheres to a creationist view of the origins of the universe, which it calls "scientific special creation." The Society sells books and videotapes and publishes the *CRS Quarterly*.

Culture Watch Online
http://www.igc.org/culturewatch

A project of the Data Center in Oakland, California, Culture Watch provides information critical of organizations and leaders on the religious right. The site presents an annotated bibliography of recent publications describing religious right activities.

The Eagle Cross Alliance
http://www.eaglecross.net

The website of the Eagle Cross Alliance offers positions on political issues of special concern to the religious right, including abortion and other "profamily" topics, and supports candidates for public office. The site contains the organization's newsletter, *The Eagle and the Cross*.

Eleven Things You Can Do to Fight the Religious Right
http://www.galah.org/11things.html

The organization Gay and Lesbian Atheists and Humanists suggests methods that those sympathetic to their cause can employ to oppose the religious right.

Ethics and Religious Liberty Commission
http://www.erlc.com

Associated with the Southern Baptist Convention (SBC), this site contains information about current political and social issues. For instance, the site includes the 1997 SBC Resolution on Moral Stewardship and the Disney Company, which charges that Disney promotes "immoral ideologies such as homosexuality, infidelity, and adultery." The resolution urges Southern Baptists not to purchase Disney products.

Ex-gay "Ministries"
http://parent.qrd.org/www/RRR.exgay.html

Taking a skeptical look at the religious right's claim that homosexuals can choose to renounce the homosexual lifestyle, this site contains many sources on ex-gay organizations and evaluations of the success of such efforts.

Fight the Right Action Kit
http://parent.qrd.org

This site, from the National Gay and Lesbian Task Force, includes information on various topics, including religious right views of homosexuality and race and religious right organizations such as the Christian Coalition and Concerned Women for America. Strategies are suggested for competing with religious right organizations in the political arena.

Gospel Communications Network Online
Christian Resources
http://gospelcom.net

Gospel Communications Network, an association of organizations committed to traditional Christian beliefs, is dedicated to disseminating information about the gospel on the World Wide Web.

A Guide to the Religious Right
http://bsd.mojones.com/mother_jones/ND95/stan_guide.html

Maintained by *Mother Jones* magazine, this site contains brief descriptions of key public figures on the religious right.

How to Fight the Right Wing
http://parent.qrd.org

Stuart Norman offers advice to those concerned about the religious right's opposition to gay rights, arguing that gay rights can gain strength by being associated with other social causes such as feminism, pro-choice abortion policies, and antiracism.

Institute for the Study of Religion and Politics (ISRP)
http://www.isrp.org

Although this organization holds many of the same beliefs espoused by those on the religious right—including labeling "secular humanism" a major threat to humankind—it opposes the intrusion of religion into politics.

Interfaith Alliance
http://www.interfaithallliance.org

The Alliance dedicates itself to protecting the basic freedoms of speech, press, and religion from the restrictive tendencies of groups that wish to exercise political power. The group intends to assist in building a mainstream religious movement active in civic participation.

Internet Pro-Life Journal
http://www.ibiblio.org/bgreek/archives/greek-2

This site offers the *Internet Pro-Life Journal,* a newsletter containing recent "political, scientific, and intellectual information about the pro-life movement." The newsletter contains advice about how to begin a pro-life group.

Kingdom Identity Ministries
http://www.kingidentity.com

This site contains a doctrinal statement of Kingdom Identity Ministries, an organization contending that God has chosen a select group of people for salvation. Also included are a directory of radio broadcasts and a catalog of books, audiotapes, and videocassettes that may be purchased.

Liberty Council
http://www.lc.org

This website is maintained by the Liberty Council, which describes itself as a religious civil liberties education and legal defense organization. The site includes news accounts of issues of importance to the religious right, including advocacy of prayer in the public schools.

Mainstream Opinion
http://www.mainstreamop.org

This website attempts to demonstrate that the objectives and activities of the religious right represent a threat to the basic values that Americans hold. According to the site, conservative Christian leaders such as Jerry Falwell and Pat Robertson regard as anti-Christian those who oppose their politics.

Militias and the Religious Right
http://apocalypse.berkshire.net/~ifas/fw/9610/militias.html

Kenneth S. Stern explores possible links between the religious right and militia groups. Stern acknowledges a crucial difference between the two groups: while religious right leaders work within the electoral system, militia groups employ extralegal strategies.

Promise Keepers Online
http://promisekeepers.org

This site contains information about future conferences sponsored by the Promise Keepers, described as "a Christ-centered ministry dedicated to uniting men through vital relationships to become godly influences in their world."

Promise Keepers Watch
http://cdsresearch.org/promise_keepers_watch.htm

On this site, the Center for Democracy Studies offers information about the Promise Keepers and its founder, Bill McCartney. This male-only self-improvement organization is said to advance "the strategic political agenda of the Christian right."

The Quarterly Journal
http://www.pfo.org/qjournal.htm

Maintained by Personal Freedom Outreach, this site contains articles from back issues of *The Quarterly Journal* that offer critical analyses of Christian right evangelists and other religious personalities.

Religion in the Public Schools
http://www.adl.org/religion_ps/prayer.html

The Anti-Defamation League (ADL) presents information about the issue of prayer in schools, including religion in the curriculum, the evolution versus creationism controversy, student religious clubs, dress codes, teachers' religious expression, and teaching about religious holidays.

Religious Freedom
http://www.religious-freedom.org

This website provides information about laws that protect religious freedom as a fundamental right, and informs individuals about the right to worship as they wish. A key concern is the Religious Freedom Restoration Act, which was intended to protect free exercise of religion.

Religious Right Influence
http://www.mainstream.org/influence.htm

Maintained by the Republican Mainstream Committee, this site provides an update on the influence of the religious right in the various states. A map of the United States is included, which indicates the states in which such influence is either "dominant," "considerable," or "insignificant."

Rightguide's Conservative Directory
http://www.rightguide.com/links-alpha.htm

This site contains a large alphabetical listing of conservative organizations—including those on the religious right—and links to their websites.

Society of Humanist Philosophers
http://www.infidels.org

The Society of Humanist Philosophers presents critical commentary on various aspects of the religious right, including political candidates and the issue of evolution versus creation.

Steeling the Mind of America
http://www.steelingthemind.com

Steeling the Mind of America is an annual Bible conference organized by Compass International, Inc., a nondenominational Christian ministry. Conference speakers include Frank Peretti,

John Ankerberg, David Barton, and Alan Keyes, and topics include education, Christians and politics, and Bible prophecy.

Threats to Civil Liberties
http://www.aclu.org/about/relright.html

Maintained by the American Civil Liberties Union (ACLU), this site provides information and critical commentary on the activities of various religious right organizations in such areas as the public schools, homosexual rights, and censorship in the mass media.

Toward Tradition
http://www.towardtradition.org

Toward Tradition is an educational group of Jews and Christians dedicated to limited government, representative democracy, the free market system, a strong military, and morality in the political realm. Rabbi Daniel Lapin, the organization's president, has conducted a series of lectures that are available for purchase.

Turning Point
http://www.gnnradio.org/framedj.htm

This website presents an online version of David Jeremiah's radio program of the same name. The site states that "Turning Point stands for the supreme authority of the Word of God."

The Watch
http://thewatch.paganteahouse.com

The site contains information critical of the religious right, offers links to like-minded sites, and provides the opportunity for discussion. Also included are a list of "Christian hate, propaganda and misinformation websites."

What's Wrong with the Religious Right
http://parent.qrd.org/orgs/CITIZENS/essays/whatswrong.txt

David Bruce bases his critical evaluation of the religious right in this 1993 essay on an investigation of literature obtained from Focus on the Family as well as attendance at one of the organization's Community Impact Seminars.

Glossary

Anti-Christ   A beguiling satanic figure who supposedly will wreak havoc on the earth, particularly upon Israel and the Jews, until his ultimate destruction by Jesus. The Antichrist has been identified with everyone from the Catholic popes, Charles I, and George III to Napoleon, Hitler, and Saddam Hussein.

apocalypse   Derived from a Greek word, *apocalypse* means "to uncover or reveal the future," specifically regarding the second coming of Christ. Apocalyptic literature not only points toward the deliverance of God's people from earthly travail, but also looks beyond the end of time. For examples of such writing, see Mark 13:3–31, II Thessalonians 2:3–12, Revelation, and Daniel.

baptism of the Holy Spirit   *See* pentecostalism.

Bible code   The Bible, especially the Old Testament, allegedly contains a detailed account of past and future events presented in a secret code. Although Isaac Newton and others attempted to discover such a code, recent advocates of the idea claim that the discovery and deciphering of secret biblical messages required the invention of modern computers. In the 1980s and 1990s three Jewish scholars, Eliyahu Rips, Doron Witztum, and Yoav Rosenberg, claimed to have found evidence for the existence of a skip code involving every fifth letter, revealing such events as assassinations, wars, and natural disasters. Subsequently several other authors, including journalist Michael Drosnin, have popularized the idea. Skeptics attribute the popularity of these claims to many people's desire to believe there is a divinely established order in the universe.

born again   In John 3:3–7 Jesus tells Nicodemus that he "must be born over again" in order to "see the kingdom of God." Accordingly, in contemporary parlance, a "born-again Christian" is one who allegedly has had a personal, emotional encounter with God through Jesus.

Cane Ridge Revival   This was an enormous camp meeting near Lexington, Kentucky, in August 1801. Noted for its emotional excesses, such as the "jerks" and the "barks," this revival fueled the Second Awakening in the American West and gave momentum to such evangelicals as Methodists, Baptists, Cumberland Presbyterians, and, later, Disciples and Christians.

charismatic movement   Characterized by emotional, ecstatic forms of worship in which speaking in tongues and faith healing are encouraged, this is a twentieth-century phenomenon. Protestants and Catholics, especially since the 1960s, have been influenced by this movement.

charitable choice   This term refers to the practice of allowing faith-based organizations to bid on federal contracts for various social services, such as housing, job training, and drug and prison rehabilitation. The welfare reform legislation passed in 1996 permits this, and many religious and social conservatives applaud it, convinced that religious institutions do a better job than secular ones at providing certain services for the needy. A concern of many critics is that charitable choice, aside from the fundamental issue of church-state separation, neither proscribes faith-based organizations from proselytizing nor ensures compliance with federal laws regarding such things as gender, sexual, and racial discrimination.

chiliasm   *See* millennialism.

Christian reconstructionism   Drawing primarily upon Genesis 1:26–28 and Matthew 28:16–20, this movement, which apparently evolved from teachings at J. Gresham Machen's Westminster Theological Seminary, attempts to reconstruct society in accordance with God's law. Guided by the example of the seventeenth-century Puritans, who sought to build the Massachusetts Commonwealth on biblical principles, Christian reconstructionists want to subordinate all aspects of life to God's authority. Accordingly, they encourage Christian schooling, certain that public education has been corrupted by secular humanism; condemn the modern state, convinced it has usurped the authority of God; and embrace an optimistic eschatology, persuaded of the possibility of constructive change. In pursuit of their objectives, however, Christian reconstructionists do not advocate civil disobedience.

civil religion   Broadly, the term refers to the use of transcendent religious symbols to explain national purpose and destiny. On one hand, civil religion provides a unifying set of values for Americans of all persuasions, values that inspire the pursuit of justice and equality of treatment for all people; on the other hand, when suffused with an intense nationalism where God and country become one, civil religion easily gives support to aggression abroad and intolerance at home.

compassionate conservatism   Derived in large part from Marvin Olasky's *The Tragedy of American Compassion* (1992), compassionate conservatism nourishes both the soul and the body, in contrast to the "false compassion" of the existing welfare state that allegedly doles out material aid without imposing discipline on the poor or providing spiritual guidance. Based on the assumption that religion and government have in America's past worked closely together, compassionate conservatism today looks to faith-based institutions to administer various programs to help the needy. And for doing this, faith-based institutions would receive tax support.

creationism (scientific creationism)   First enunciated in *What Is Darwinism?* (1874) by Charles Hodge, a noted Presbyterian theologian at Princeton Theological Seminary, creationism is the belief that the Genesis account of the world's origin is historically true and accurate. Promoted today primarily by conservative Christians, creationism is an alternative explanation to Darwinian evolution for human origins. Although all creationists attribute creation to God, as described in the early chapters of Genesis, they differ among themselves on critical points. Those who tend to be biblical literalists insist that God created the various species, each of which reproduces its own kind, in a short span of time. Those who interpret Genesis allegorically are inclined to agree with conventional geologists regarding the earth's ancient origins. Although creationists are divided over geology, creationists are usually united in their opposition to Darwinian biology.

death of God theology   Based upon *The Death of God* by Gabriel Vahanian, this movement gained attention in the 1960s. Arguing that many educated Americans no longer relied on God to explain phenomena once attributed to the divine, such as natural disasters and sickness, Vahanian labored to recast Christian theology without a doctrine of God. Many conservative Christians saw this movement as just another indication of the nation's growing godlessness.

dispensational premillennialism   A theory popularized by C. I. Scofield of Dallas, Texas, in 1909. Scofield divided history into seven dispensations, or eras, each beginning with a divine covenant and ending with God's judgment. He believed humanity was nearing the end of the sixth dispensation, which would culminate in the second coming of Jesus, who then would preside over the world for a millennium.

dominion (kingdom) theology   Used by politically involved evangelicals, this term lends biblical sanction to efforts to Christianize the nation's political, economic, legal, educational, military, and communications institutions. Dominion theology undergirds much of Christian reconstructionism.

election (predestination)   The belief that certain people and groups have been foreordained to fulfill God's divine purposes. This view undergirds Israel's position as God's chosen people, as well as the New Testament belief of humanity's undeserved grace. Given the influence of such conservative Presbyterians as Charles Hodge, Benjamin Warfield, J. Gresham Machen, and Carl McIntire, this sentiment runs deep among many American fundamentalists.

eschatology   Derived from two Greek words, *eschatology* means "end" or "final." Central to eschatology, therefore, are beliefs about death, resurrection, the second coming, judgment, and the kingdom of God. In both the Old and New Testaments, eschatological writers were concerned with the ultimate triumph of God over evil.

evangelical   Derived from a Greek word meaning "good news," *evangelical* refers to those Christians who emphasize a personal relationship to Jesus ("born again"), biblical authority in matters of faith and practice, and the necessity of sharing the gospel with others (witnessing). Since the late 1940s many conservative Christians, such as Billy Graham, have preferred to be known as evangelicals rather than fundamentalists.

faith movement   Characterized by a frank equation between godliness and materialism, the faith movement looks upon religion primarily as a means to a prosperous and healthy future. This is not startling, for traces of such sentiment are evident in the seventeenth-century Puritans. And in the late nineteenth century the Baptist minister Russell Conwell made a career of one sermon, "Acres of Diamonds," which he preached approximately 6,000 times and which was essentially an exhortation to get rich. Perhaps the only thing that sets such contemporary televangelists as Oral Roberts, Robert Tilton, Kenneth Copeland, Benny Hinn, and Frederick Price apart from Conwell is the degree of blatancy. With slogans like "name it, claim it," "success-n-life," and "have a need, plant a seed," many of today's prominent evangelists assure listeners that prosperity goes hand in hand with faith. One has only to give (plant a seed) to receive (wealth).

fundamentalism   By the 1920s the terms *fundamentalist, evangelical,* and *conservative Christian* were more or less synonymous, each referring broadly to those Christians who subscribed to the five or six basic fundamentals set forth at the Niagara Bible Conference of 1895 and in *The Fundamentals: A Testimony to the Truth* (1910–1915), edited by R. A. Torrey, A. C. Dixon, and others. But the term *fundamentalism,* coined in 1920, increasingly became identified with an aggressively strident and exclusionist variety of conservative Christianity, and critics increasingly applied the term pejoratively and indiscriminately to all conservative Christians. As a result, conservative Christians such as those who founded the National Association of Evangelicals in 1942 preferred the term *evangelical* to *fundamentalist.* The difference today between a fundamentalist and an evangelical is more a matter of temperament than theology. Outside the United States, the term is often applied to staunchly conservative elements of other faiths such as Islam or Judaism.

glossolalia (speaking in tongues)   Apparently coined in the nineteenth century, *glossolalia* refers to the New Testament practice of "speaking in tongues." Acts 2:4 reports that on the day of Pentecost the Apostles "were all filled with the Holy Ghost and began to speak with other tongues as the Spirit gave them utterance." Christians have never been of one mind regarding this practice. Today, for instance, Pentecostal bodies, such as the Assemblies of God, encourage tongues, but the Baptist fundamentalist Jerry Falwell disapproves.

Gog, Magog   Various biblical passages—Daniel 11:15, Jeremiah 1:14, Ezekiel 38, and Revelation 20:8—allude to an evil ruler, Gog, from the northern land of Magog. In the Cold War aftermath of World War II many America fundamentalists identified Russia as Magog and interpreted conflicting American and Russian interests in Israel and elsewhere in the Middle East in light of biblical prophecy. Such views influenced even former President Ronald Reagan.

heterodoxy (heresy)   Departure from established beliefs and traditions. For fundamentalists, for instance, the denial of such things as the virgin birth and resurrection of Jesus would be heterodoxy.

higher criticism   This is a scientific examination of biblical texts, attempting to determine authorship, date of composition, and place of origin. Higher critics study such questions as, Did Moses write all of the Pentateuch? and Was there a second Isaiah? To many conservative Christians from the nineteenth century to the present, this kind of scrutiny undermines the veracity of the scriptures.

Identity Christianity   Based upon the belief that white Anglo-Saxons are God's chosen people and that Jews and all other nonwhites are a subspecies of humanity, Identity Christianity unites such white supremacist groups as the Ku Klux Klan and Aryan Nations.

imminency   The belief that the second coming of Christ could occur at any moment. This idea fuels much of the millennial speculation regarding the end of time.

inerrancy   A belief common among many Protestants since the latter nineteenth century that the Bible is without error in its "original autographs" with regard to history, science, and accounts of its literary origins. A remarkable similarity exists between Presbyterian inerrantists Charles Hodge and Benjamin Warfield of the 1880s and Southern Baptist inerrantists of the 1980s. For both, the Bible would be an unreliable guide on matters of salvation and humanity's relationship to God if it were known to be in error on matters of history and science. Inerrantists do concede that scribal errors have over time slipped into existing biblical texts.

lower criticism   A scientific examination of biblical texts, lower criticism seeks to ascertain the actual words of a manuscript as it was originally written by the author; or, slightly differently, to determine how accurately existing translations reflect what was said or written. This kind of study poses no serious problem for conservative Christians, for they too are concerned about the accuracy of existing biblical texts and translations. Although insisting that the Bible is inerrant in its "original autographs," conservative Christians concede that scribal errors and discrepancies have slipped into the texts over time.

mark of the beast   Quite similar to Daniel 7:2–8, Revelation 13:1–18 describes a beast, or an Antichrist that rivals Jesus in the final days and ascribes to it the number "666." The followers of the beast were to be branded on either the right hand or the forehead with the triple six.

millennialism   This refers to a thousand-year period in which the kingdom of God will prevail. Christians are usually divided over whether the second coming of Jesus will occur before (premillennialists) or after (postmillennialists) the thousand-year reign. Millennial expectations are fueled by the apocalyptic portion of the Bible, especially Revelation, and groups such as the Seventh-Day Adventists and Jehovah's Witnesses reflect the influence of millennial ideas.

modernism   Although many conservative Christians by the 1920s used the term *modernism* loosely to cover a multitude of alleged sins, scholars usually use the term more precisely to mean the adjustment of religious ideas to contemporary culture, the immanence of God in human development, and the belief that history is evolving toward the kingdom of God. As this suggests, modernism is an optimistic view, one at sharp odds with the conservative Christian emphasis upon original sin and human depravity.

natural theology   Broadly, the belief that God can be fathomed by reason alone without the need of scripture or revelation. For instance, subscribers to this view would argue that the order of nature, as well as purposeful human existence, affords rational evidence of an intelligent creator. This attempt at human self-sufficiency disturbs many Christian thinkers who believe that God is more than can be grasped by reason alone. To many Christians, the God of natural theology is little more than a projected image of humanity, a God limited by the human senses.

New Age movement   Drawing upon both Eastern and Western religious traditions, this phenomenon gained momentum in the 1980s. Its adherents subscribe to an eclectic assortment of beliefs and practices, such as reincarnation, astral projection, astrology, extraterrestrial life, astrology, immortality of the soul, miracles, angels, and yoga.

original autographs   This refers to the original biblical manuscripts that were untainted by scribal errors. Although these texts do not exist, inerrantists in the tradition of Charles Hodge, Benjamin Warfield, and J. Gresham Machen contend that the Bible cannot be proved to be in error unless the discrepancy exists in the original autographs, which, of course, are unavailable for scrutiny.

original sin   Based primarily upon the creation story and the fall of Adam and Eve from grace in the opening chapters of Genesis, this is the Christian doctrine of flawed humanity.

orthodoxy   Derived from the Greek words *orthos*, "correct," and *doxa*, "opinion," orthodoxy refers to "correct" or "right" beliefs.

pentecostalism   Drawing upon Acts 1:1–5 and 2:4–21, modern pentecostalism stresses those gifts resulting from "baptism in the Holy Spirit," such as glossolalia, prophecy, healing, and exorcism. Historically, contemporary pentecostalism emerged from the Holiners tradition within Methodism and the Asuza Street revival in Los Angeles, California, in 1906. Although its early adherents were largely poor and disinherited, Pentecostals have become increasingly middle-class. The Assemblies of God, Jimmy Swaggart's original denomination, is the largest Pentecostal body in the United States today.

postmillennialism   The belief that steadily improving world conditions will culminate in the second coming. By this interpretation, Jesus will return *after* a millennium of human progress. This optimistic viewpoint not only reinforced the reform efforts of liberal social gospel ministers in the late nineteenth and early twentieth centuries, but also undergirds the labors of contemporary Christian reconstructionists.

premillennialism   The belief that steadily deteriorating world conditions (wars and rumors of wars) will precede the second coming, at which time Jesus will establish a thousand-year reign. Thus, Jesus will return *before* the millennium. This viewpoint is generally more harmonious with a conservative, pessimistic assessment of contemporary world conditions.

pro-life (right-to-life) movement   Originating among Roman Catholics, this movement today embraces Catholics, Protestants, and others opposed to abortion. The Supreme Court's decision in *Roe v. Wade* (1973), which legalized abortion during the first two trimesters of pregnancy, gave impetus to the movement.

prophecy   Derived from a Greek word meaning "one who speaks for another," *prophecy* supposedly is an expression of divine will. Unlike apocalyptic literature, however, which forecasts the end of time, prophetic literature is focused on the present, predicting dire consequences in this life if "God's people" persist in their wicked ways. Examples of the prophetic tradition among the ancient Hebrews are Amos, Joel, Isaiah, Jeremiah, Ezekiel, and Elijah.

rapture   Refers to that moment when Christ supposedly will come to resurrect the righteous who have already died and to remove, or harvest, the righteous who are still alive. This action will leave the forces of evil in complete control of the earth for seven years, the period of the "great tribulation." In both literature and art, many contemporary Christians portray a world in chaos after the rapture.

revivalism   Refers to a reawakening or quickening of the divine spirit, an awakening sometimes accompanied by emotional fervor. Scholars usually trace the phenomenon from Solomon Stoddard, Jonathan Edwards, and George Whitefield to James McGready, Barton Stone, and Charles G. Finney. The Great Awakening (1720s–1740s) swept the eastern seaboard, while the Second Awakening (1790s–1830s) carried the gospel via emotional camp meetings across the western frontier. Methodists, Baptists, Cumberland Presbyterians, and Disciples prospered during this second wave of revivalism. Of particular interest to scholars have been the techniques of revivalism, with debate sometimes centering on whether revivals were "sent down" by God or "worked up" by more human methods.

schism   Refers to a factious division, or split, of a religious body. Although sometimes used synonymously, *schism* and *heresy* are not the same. Heresy always involves doctrinal matters, whereas schism results primarily from disputes over authority and organizational structure.

Scofield Reference Bible   Published in 1909 by Oxford University Press, this perhaps has been the most influential source of dispensational premillennial teachings for American Protestants. Annotated by Cyrus I. Scofield, a lawyer turned Congregational preacher, it was originally meant to be a portable reference for missionaries. Because Scofield's commentaries appeared on the same page as the biblical text, it was easy for readers to forget whether a particular idea came from Scofield or the Bible. By 1967, when a revision was released, at least five million copies had been sold.

secular humanism   The belief that humans, relying upon reason and acting independently of God, are sufficient unto themselves. Some intellectual spokesmen for the religious right, such as Francis Schaeffer, trace this human-centered view from the Greeks through the Renaissance to the Enlightenment. An alleged consequence of this outlook is the replacement of God-centered absolutes with moral relativism. Much like "modernism" in the 1920s, secular humanism today has become for the religious right a popular catchall for practically all social ills.

situation ethics   Coined in 1959 by Joseph Fletcher, situation ethics was a pragmatic and relativistic method for making moral judgments. It aroused the ire of many conservative Christians,

implying as it did an abandonment of absolute standards of morality.

social gospel   A movement that emerged among more liberal Protestants in the late nineteenth century and reached its peak in the optimistic years preceding World War I. Convinced that the gospel message was social as well as personal, ministers such as Washington Gladden and Walter Rauschenbusch sought to focus the attention of the churches on social ills spawned by industrialization and urbanization. Many conservative Christians objected to the social gospel, believing its social emphasis detracted from the primary responsibility to individuals.

theonomy   Coined by Cornelius Van Til of Westminster Theological Seminary, *theonomy*, derived from two Greek words, *theos* ("God") and *nomos* ("law"), is submission to God's law. As such, it is an argument for Christian reconstructionism, one steeped in Calvinistic influences. To Van Til, God's elect could grasp divine laws and live accordingly, while those who relied on human judgment, or autonomy, lived in darkness. Broadly, theonomy holds that Old Testament law differentiates between right and wrong and, therefore, should be the basis for modern society.

Index

The ABCs of Globalism: A Vigilant Christian's Glossary (Rae), 261–262

Abortion, 9, 48, 70, 104, 113–114, 139, 155, 163

Operation Rescue, 51, 113, 181

Roe v. Wade, 9, 23, 29, 45, 69, 172, 180

RU-486, 9, 10, 27, 90, 189

survey data on, 134

Abortion: A Rational Look at an Emotional Issue (video and audiocassette), 292

Abortion: The American Holocaust (video and audio cassette), 291

Abortion: The Moral Dilemma (video), 329–330

About the Religious Right (Web site), 338

Abraham, Ken, 215

The ACCC Report (periodical), 280

Ackerman, Paul D., 232, 298

The Act of Marriage: The Beauty of Sexual Love (LaHaye & LaHaye), 269

Active Faith: How Christians Are Changing the Face of American Politics (Reed), 262

Active Faith: How Christians Are Changing the Face of American Politics (audiocassette), 292

Adding Cross to Crown: The Political Significance of Christ's Passion (Noll), 259

Aderhalt, Robert 60

The Advocate (Web site), 338

After the Revolution: How the Christian Coalition Is Impacting America (Reed), 262

The Age of Consent: The Rise of Relativism and the Corruption of Popular Culture (Knight), 240

Ahlstrom, Sydney E., 196

AIDS: What you Haven't Been Told (video), 292

Albert, James A., 193

Alcorn, Randy C., 139, 250

Alexander-Moegerle, Gil, 215

All about the Second Coming (Lockyer), 278

All Rapped Up (video), 293

Allen, Leslie H., 196

Alley, Robert S., 215

Alliance Defense Fund, 157

America Conquered (Peters), 261

America: To Pray or Not To Pray (Barton), 251

American Association of Christian Schools (AACS), 158

American Atheists (AA), 187

American Center for Law and Justice (ACLJ), 19, 25, 158–159

American Civil Liberties Union (ACLU), 39

American Coalition of Unregistered Churches (ACUC), 159

The American Covenant (video), 293

An American Dream (Whitehead), 267

The American Evangelicalism: Conservative Religion and the Quandary of Modernity (Hunter), 203

American Evangelicalism: Embattled and Thriving (Smith), 212

American Evangelicals and the Mass Media (Schultze), 211

American Family Association (AFA), 160

American Family Association Journal, 280

American Freemen Association (AFA), 160

American Humanist Association (AHA), 187–188, 285

The American Leadership Tradition: Moral Vision from Washington to Clinton (Olasky), 260

American Life League (ALL), 161

American Political Theology: Historical Perspective and Theoretical Analysis (Dunn), 201

American Reformation Project (web site), 338

American Religion: The Emergence of the Post-Christian Nation (Bloom), 198

The American Religious Right (web site), 338

American Scientific Affiliation. *See* creationism

American Society for the Defense of Tradition (ASDT), 161

American Theological Library Association (web site), 338–339

Americans United for God and Country (AUGC), 161–162

Americans United for Separation of Church and State, 23, 71, 188, 193, 283

America's Christian History: The Untold Story (DeMar), 235

America's Dates with Destiny (Robertson), 263

America's God and Country: Encyclopedia of Quotations (Federer), 236–237

America's Godly Heritage (video), 293

Ammerman, Nancy Tatom, 196

Ancient Man: Created or Evolved (video), 294

And Nothing But the Truth: Real-life Stories of Americans Defending Their Faith and Protecting Their Families (Seculow & Fournier), 265

Anderson, Leith, 232

Ankerberg, John, 232–233, 316, 346

Anonymous Tip (Ferris), 254

Answers (CD-ROM), 337

The Answers Book (Ham, Snelling, & Wieland), 237

The Anti-Abortion Movement and the Rise of the Religious Right: From Polite to Fiery Protest (Blanchard), 216

Antichrist, 347

Anti-Defamation League, 53–54, 68; founding of, 188

Antievolution before World War I (Numbers), 208

Anti-evolution laws, passage of, 39, 40

The Antievolution Pamphlets of Harry Rimmer, The (Davis), 200

The Antievolution Pamphlets of William Bell Riley (Conklin), 213

The Antievolution Works of Arthur I. Brown (Numbers), 209

The Antigay Agenda: Orthodox Vision and the Christian Right (Herman), 223

Antigay Propaganda of the Religious Right (web site), 339

Anti-Saloon League, 39

Apocalypse, 347

Apocalypse! (video), 326

Apocalypse Code (Lindsey), 277, 278

Apocalypse Planet Earth (video), 294

Apocalypse Theory and the Ends of the World (Bull), 199
Apollyon: The Destroyer Is Unleashed (LaHaye & Jenkins), 276
Appleby, R. Scott, 206
Are We Living in the End Times? (LaHaye & Jenkins), 277
Armageddon, battle of, 47
Armageddon, Oil and the Middle East Crisis: What the Bible Says about the Future of the Middle East and the End of Western Civilization (Walvoord), 249
Armey, Dick, 163
Ashcroft, John, 29, 30, 55, 70, 155, 163
Assassins (Lahaye & Jenkins), 276
Associates for Biblical Research (ABR), 162
Atkins, Peter, 309
Attacks on the Freedom to Learn Online (web site), 339
Auburn Affirmation, 39, 40
The Awesome Forces of God's Creation (video), 294–295

Bahnsen, Greg L., 250
Baker, Howard H., 48
Bakker, Jim, 15, 49, 85, 109, 233, 268
Balch, David L., 196
Ball, William B., 233
Balmer, Randall, 197
Barkun, Michael, 216
Barr, Bob, 56, 60
Barr, James, 152, 197
Barton, Charles D., 251
Barton, David, 233, 294, 302, 307, 314, 323, 346
Batten, Don, 297
Battle for Our Minds: Worldviews in Collision (video and audiocassette), 295
The Battle for the Bible (video), 326–327
Battle for the Blackboard (video), 330
Bauer, Gary, 62, 64, 83, 173
  biography of, 73–75
  support of McCain, 74–75
Baumgartner, Frederick J., 197
Bawer, Bruce, 197

Bayh, Birch, 13
Bear arms, right to, 150
Beating the Unbeatable Foe: The Story of the Christian Anti-Communist Crusade (Schwarz), 271
Becker, Frank J. 43
Beckman, M. J. 151
Beginning of the End: The Assassination of Yitzhak Rabin and the Coming Antichrist (Hagee), 272–273
Behe, Michael J., 233–234, 296, 313
Bellant, Russ, 334
Benham, Flip, 10, 69, 181
Bennett, William, 16, 106
Bernall, Cassie 59
Between Jesus and the Market: The Emotions that Matter in Right-Wing America (Kintz), 224–225
Beyond Evolution: Human Nature and the Limits of Evolutionary Explanation (O'Hear), 243
The Bible and the Ballot Box: Religion and Politics in the 1988 Election (Guth & Green), 223
The Bible and the Constitution of the United States (Hall), 256
Bible Believers: Fundamentalists in the Modern World (Ammerman), 196
Bible code, 347
The Bible Code (Drosnin), 236
The Bible in Translation: God's Word vs. Man's Words (video), 327
The Bible Tells Them So: The Discourse of Protestant Fundamentalism (Boone), 198
Bibleinfo.com (web site), 339
Biblical Conservatism: Toward a Definition of a Political Philosophy (web site), 339
Biblical Hermeneutics (video), 295
Biblical inerrancy, 140–141
Biblical Solutions to Contemporary Problems: A Handbook (Walton), 267
Billings, Robert, 11, 138, 178
  biography of, 75–76
Billings, Vernon, 311

Billy Graham: A Parable of Ameri-
can Righteousness (Frady), 194
Billy Graham: The Road to
Armageddon (video), 295–
296
Billy James Hargis' 90-Minute Video
Tape Alert (video), 296
Billy James Hargis Television
Program, 335
Biological Evidence for Design, The
(video), 296
Biological Evidence of Creation
(video), 296–297
Blackstock, Terri, 269
The Blame Game: Why Society
Persecutes Christians (Stanley),
247
Blamires, Harry, 234
Blanchard, Dallas A., 216
Bleeding Hearts and Propaganda:
The Fall of Reason in the
Church (Spencer), 247
The Blessings of Liberty: Restoring
the City on the Hill (Heath),
257
Blinded by Might: Can the Religious
Right Save America? (Thomas
& Dobson), 25, 59, 266
Block, David, 325
Bloom, Harold, 198
Blowing the Whistle on Pat
Robertson (video), 332
Blue Book of the John Birch Society
(Welch), 249–250
Board of Education v. Mergens. See
Equal Access Act
Bob Jones University, 48, 64, 86,
92, 94
Bolton, Richard, 251
Bond, Julian, 8, 55
The Book of Jerry Falwell:
Fundamentalist Language and
Politics (Harding), 194
Boone, Kathleen C., 198
Bork, Robert 50
"Born again," defined, 347
Borst, W. A., 251
Boston, Robert, 193, 216–217
Boyer, Paul, 198
Boys, Don, 147, 251–252, 271
Bozell, L. Brent, 19, 53
Brasher, Brenda E., 217

Briggs, Charles A., 37
Bright, Bill, 234
Bringing in the Sheaves:
Transforming Poverty into
Productivity (Grant), 256
Brown, Arthur I., 209
Brown, Walter T., Jr., 234, 309, 322
Brownback, Sam, 163
Bruce, David, 346
Bruce, Stephen, 217, 218
Bruner, Jerome 44
Bryan and Darrow at Dayton
(Allen), 196
Bryan Bible League, 40
Bryan, William Jennings, 39, 40,
186
biography of, 78–79
Buchanan, John, 11, 14, 18
Buchanan, Pat 51, 69, 329
Buckley, William F., 16, 309
Bull, Christopher, 218
Bull, Malcolm, 199
The Bulletproof George Washington:
An Account of God's
Providential Care (Barton),
233
The Bully Pulpit (web site), 339
Bundy, Edgar C., 5
biography of, 79–70, 169
founds Church League of
America, 79
Burgess, Stanley, 199
Bush, George W., 1, 18, 26, 28–29,
60, 62, 63, 65, 67, 70, 71, 86,
105, 108, 121, 138
on compassionate
conservatism, 141
meeting with gay Republicans,
66
on RU-486, 69
signs the Texas Religious
Freedom Restoration Act, 61
speech at Bob Jones University,
64
support of vouchers, 58
on taxation, 151
Bush, Jeb, 60
Buswell, James, 321
By This Standard: The Authority of
God's Law Today (Bahnsen),
250
Byers, Marvin, 271

Campus Crusade for Christ
  International (CCCI), 162, 182
Cane Ridge Revival, 347–348
Cantor, David, 218
Caplan, Lionel, 199
Capps, Charles, 271–272
Capps, Walter H., 218
Carnahan, Mel, 29
Carpenter, Joel A., 219
Carson, D. A., 252
Carter, Jimmy, 10, 11, 13, 46, 83
  elected president, 45
  withdraws from Southern
    Baptist Convention, 69
Carter, Stephen L., 199
Castelli, Elizabeth, 327
Center for Christian
  Statesmanship (CCS), 163
Center for Reclaiming America
  (CRA), 163
  Web site, 339–340
Chalcedon Foundation, 164
Chalcedon Report, 281
Change the Hostile Climate
  (Shields), 229
*The Changing of the Guard: Biblical
  Blueprints for Political Action*
  (Grant), 255–256
Charismatic movement, 348
Charitable Choice, 55, 348
  Falwell and Robertson on, 71
  public support of 71
Cheney, Richard, 26
Chosen by God (Sproul), 337
Christian (web site), 340
Christian Action Fact Sheet (web
  site), 340
*Christian America? What
  Evangelicals Really Want*
  (Smith), 229
The Christian and Politics
  (Thoburn), 266
The Christian and the Income Tax
  (Sileven), 265
Christian Anti-Communism
  Crusade (CACC), 51, 114,
  164, 288
Christian Beacon, 281
Christian Book Distributors Catalog,
  281
Christian Broadcasting Network
  (web site), 340

Christian Century, 281
Christian Coalition, 2, 8, 16–17,
  18, 22–23, 28, 52, 54, 118,
  165–166, 174, 193
  difficulties of the mid-'90s, 20–21
  founding of, 51
  loss of tax-exempt status, 61
*The Christian Coalition: Dreams of
  Restoration, Demands for
  Recognition* (Watson), 231
Christian Coalition of America
  (CCA), 164–165
Christian Crusade, x, 6, 165–166
Christian Crusade Newspaper, 281,
  296
Christian Defense League (CDL),
  166
Christian Family Renewal (CFR),
  166
A Christian Guide to Prosperity
  (Fries & Taylor), 255
Christian Heritage Center (CHC),
  166–167
Christian Law Association (CLA),
  167
A Christian Manifesto (Schaeffer),
  246
Christian News (periodical), 282
Christian Patriot Association
  (CPA), 167–168
Christian Reconstruction
  (periodical), 282
*Christian Reconstruction: What It Is,
  What It Isn't* (North &
  DeMar), 260
Christian Reconstructionism (Web
  site), 340
Christian Reconstructionism,
  Dominion Theology, and
  Theonomy (Web site), 340
Christian Research (CR), 168
*Christian Research Book and Tape
  Catalog*, 282
Christian Research Institute, 90,
  168–169
Christian Research Journal, 282
The Christian Right and Congress
  (Moen), 226
Christian Standard, 283
Christian Voice, 12, 16, 169
  founding of, 46
  morality report cards, 46

Christian Wives: Women Behind the Evangelists Reveal Their Faith in Modern Marriage (Schaffer), 270

The Christian Worldview (periodical), 283

Christianity and Liberalism (Machen), 241

Christianity and Liberalism (web site), 340–341

Christianity and the Constitution (Eidsmoe), 254

Christianity: Bogus Beyond Belief (web site), 341

Christianity in Crisis (Hanegraaff), 237–238

Christianity Today (periodical), 283

Christians on the Net (web site), 341

Church & State (periodical), 283

Church, Forrester, 331

Church, Frank, 13

Church League of America (CLA), 169

Circuit Riders 41

City of Boerne v. Flores, 56

and Religious Freedom Restoration Act, 52

Civil religion, 348

Clark, Harold W., 209

Clark, James Freeman, 35–36

Clarkson, Frederick, 219

Clinton, Bill, 4, 63, 68, 89, 166, 174

faces impeachment, 56–57

signs Religious Freedom Restoration Act, 52

Clinton, Hillary, 56

Clinton's Circle of Power (video), 297

Cloning of the American Mind: Eradicating Morality Through Education (Eakman), 253

Close Encounters with the Religious Right: Journeys into the Twilight Zone of Religion and Politics (Boston), 216–217

Closed: 99 Ways to Stop Abortion (Scheidler), 264

Coalition for Religious Freedom (CRF), 170

Cole, John R., 333

The Collapse of Evolution (Huse), 238

Colson, Chuck, 234, 252

Columbine High School, 59–60

Columbus and Cortez: Conquerors for Christ (Eidsmoe), 254

The Coming Collision: Global Law versus U.S. Liberties (Hirsen), 257

Commager, Henry Steele, 14–15

Comparing Creation Accounts (video), 29

Compassionate conservatism, 26, 141–142, 348–349

Compassionate Conservatism: What It Is, What It Does, and How It Can Transform America (Olasky), 260–261

Conkin, Paul K., 200

Conklin, Edwin Grant, Jr., 213

Connections, 283

Conservative Protestant Politics (Bruce), 217

The Conservative Revolution: The Movement That Remade America (Edwards), 222

Contemporary Evangelical Political Involvement : An Analysis and Assessment (Smidt), 229

Continuity and Change in the Rhetoric of the Moral Majority (Snowball), 230

Contract With America, 20

Controversy in the Twenties: Fundamentalism, Modernism, and Evolution (Gatewood), 202

Conway, Flo, 152

Copeland, Kenneth, 168

Coppes, Charles H., 272

Cornerstone with John Hagee (television program), 335

The Correspondent (periodical), 284

Cotton, Ian, 200

Coughlin, Charles E., biography of, 80–81

Council for Secular Humanism (CSH), 188

Council of Bible Believing Churches in the U.S.A. (CBBC), 171, 288

Countdown to Armageddon
(McGuire), 278
Countdown to Eternity (video), 298
Craig, William Lane, 309
Cranston, Alan, 13
Creation and Evolution (Hayward),
238
Creation and Psychology! (video),
298
Creation and the Last Days (video),
298
Creation and the Supreme Court
(audiocassette), 299
*Creation and Time: A Biblical and
Scientific Perspective on the
Creation-Date Controversy*
(Ross), 245
*Creation and Time: A Report on the
Progressive Creationist Book by
Hugh Ross* (Van Bebber &
Taylor), 248
Creation Compromises (Thompson),
248
Creation Days (video), 299
Creation-Evolution Debates
(Numbers), 209
*Creation? Evolution? Resolving the
Controversy* (audiocassette),
299
*The Creation Hypothesis: Scientific
Evidence for an Intelligent
Designer* (Moreland), 242
"Creation Moments" (radio
program), 335
Creation or Evolution? (video), 300
Creation Research Society,
171–172
Web site, 341
Creationism, 3, 90–91, 143–144,
349
Edwards v. Aguillard, 49
founding of American Scientific
Affiliation, 41
founding of Creation Research
Society, 43–44, 171–172
Institute for Creation Research,
174–175
public support of, 62
*Creationism in Twentieth Century
America* (Numbers), 208–209
*Creationist Writings of Byron C.
Nelson* (Nelson), 207

*The Creationists: The Evolution of
Scientific Creationism*
(Numbers), 227
Crismier, Charles, 235
Criswell, W. A., 12
Cromartie, Michael, 219–220, 227
Crouch, Paul, 185, 272
*The Culture of Disbelief: How
America Law and Politics
Trivialize Religious Devotion*
(Carter), 199
*Culture Wars: Documents from the
Recent Controversies in the
Arts* (Bolton), 251
Culture Watch Online (web site),
341
Culver, John, 13
*A Cup of Trembling: Jerusalem and
Bible Prophecy* (Hunt), 274

Danforth, John 48
D'Antonio, Michael, 153, 220
Darby, John Nelson, 36, 41, 73
biography of, 81–82
dispensational
premillennialism, 81–82
influence of, on C. I. Scofield
and J. Frank Norris, 81
*Dark Cures: Have Doctors Lost
Their Ethics?* (DeParrie), 236
Darrow, Clarence 39, 79
Darwin, Charles, 35
Darwin on Trial (Johnson), 239
Darwinism, 3, 35, 79, 82, 143–144
Darwinism on Trial (video), 300
*Darwin's Black Box: The Biochemical
Challenge to Evolution* (Behe),
233–234
*Darwin's Leap of Faith: Exposing the
False Religion of Evolution*
(Ankerberg & Weldon),
232–233
Davies, Samuel, 310
Davis, Edward B., 200
Davis, Percival, 235
Dawn's Early Light (video), 300
Day of Deception (Hargis), 256
*Day of Deception: Separating Truth
from the Falsehoods that
Threaten Our Society* (Hagee),
273
Dayton, Donald, 200

Death of God theology, 349
The Deep Waters of Evolution
(video), 301
*Defeating Darwinism by Opening
Minds* (Johnson), 239
*Defenders of God: TheFunda-
mentalist Revolt against the
Modern Age* (Lawrence), 204
*Defenders of the Faith: Religion and
Politics form the Pilgrim
Fathers to Ronald Reagan*
(Edel), 201
*Defending the Rights of
Evangelism's Victims* (video
and audiocassette), 332
Defense of Marriage Act, 56
Delay, Tom, 119
*Deliver Us from Evil: Restoring the
Soul in a Disintegrating
Culture* (Zacharias), 250
DeMar, Gary, 138, 235, 260
Dembski, William A., 235
*The Democratization of American
Christianity* (Hatch), 202
Denhert, Eberhard, 208
Denton, Michael, 325–236
DeParrie, Paul, 236
Devos, Dick, 236
Dewey, John 40
Diamond, Sara, 153, 220–221
*Dictionary of Pentecostal and
Charismatic Movements*
(Burgess & McGee), 199
Dionne, E. J., 28
Dirksen, Everett, 43
*Disciples and Democracy: Religious
Conservatives and the Future of
American Politics* (Cromartie),
219–220
*Disciplining the Nations: The
Government upon His Shoulder*
(Woods), 268
*Disney, the Mouse Betrayed: Greed,
Corruption, and Children at
Risk* (Scheizer), 264
Dispensational premillennialism,
349
*The Dispossessed: Homelessness in
America* (Grant), 255
Dixon, A. C., 350
Dobson, Edward, 25, 59, 120, 252,
266

Dobson, James C., 24, 73, 75, 142,
158, 172, 268–269, 325
biography of, 82–83
founds Focus on the Family, 82,
173
on politics, 148
Doerr, Ed, 333, 334
Dole, Elizabeth, 62
Dole, Robert, 76
Domingo, Roger, 252–253
Dominion theology, 349
Doner, Colonel V., 253
biography of, 83–84
on politics, 148
Dowd, Maureen, 29
Dr. Bob Jones, Sr. (video), 301
Drosnin, Michael, 236, 347
Dulles, John Foster, 122
Dunn, Charles W., 201
Durham, James R., 221
Dwyer, James G., 221

E Quake (Hayford), 273
The Eagle Cross Alliance (web site),
341
Eagle Forum, 8, 171, 172
*The Eagle's Claw: Christians and the
IRS* (Richardson), 262
Eakman, B. K., 253
Early Creationist Journals
(Numbers), 209
*The Early Writings of Harold W.
Clark and Frank Lewis Marsh*
(Numbers), 209
Eckerd, Jack, 252
*The Economy to Come in Prophetic
Context* (Goetz), 272
Edel, Wilbur, 201
Education and the Founding Fathers
(video), 301–302
Edwards, Jonathan, 354
Edwards, Lee, 222
Edwards v. Aguillard, 49, 299
Eidsmoe, John, 253–254
Eighteenth Amendment, 1, 38,
186
Eisenhower, Dwight D., 1, 87,
99–100, 122
Election, concept of, 349
*Election '94: We Have One Chance
Left to Save America's Christian
Republic* (video), 302

Election of 1994, 18–19, 53
  "Revolution of '94,"19–20, 24,
  56
*Eleven Things You Can Do To Fight
  the Religious Right* (web site),
  341–342
*The Empire God Built: Inside Pat
  Robertson's Media Machine*
  (Foege), 222
En Route to Global Occupation
  (Kah), 257
*Encyclopedia of Religion in
  American Politics* (Schultz,
  West, & Maclean), 211
The End of Man (Whitehead), 250
The End of the Age (Robertson),
  279
End of the Cold War (video), 302
*End Times Events: Journey to the
  End of the Age* (Capps), 271
End-Times Video Collection (video),
  303
Engel v. Vitale. See school prayer
Environmental Agenda (video and
  audiocassette), 303
Equal Access Act, 48, 117
  upheld by Supreme Court,
  51–52, 117
Equal Rights Amendment (ERA),
  4, 7, 8, 9, 14, 85, 110, 171
Escape from Reason (Schaeffer),
  245–246
Escape the Coming Night
  (Jeremiah), 274
Eschatology, 350
*Essential Truths of the Christian
  Faith* (Sproul), 337
*Eternal Hostility: The Struggle
  Between Theocracy and
  Democracy* (Clarkson), 219
*Ethics and Religious Liberty
  Commission* (web site), 342
Evangelical, defined, ix-x, 350
Evangelicalism and Modern America
  (Marsden), 205
*Evangelicalism: The Coming
  Generation* (Hunter), 203
*Evangelicals and Foreign Policy:
  Four Perspectives* (Cromartie),
  219
*Evangelicals and Protestants
  Together: The Christian Mission*

  in the Third Millennium
  (report), 53, 54
Every Prophecy of the Bible
  (Walvoord), 280
*Evidence for Creation: Examining
  the Origin of Planet Earth*
  (video), 303–304
Evolution: A Theory in Crisis
  (Denton), 235–236
The Evolution Conspiracy (video),
  304
Evolution: Fact or Fiction (video),
  304
Evolution: Science or Religion?
  (video), 304–305
Ex-gay "Ministries" (Web site),
  342
Explaining Inerrancy (video), 305
*The Extermination of Christianity: A
  Tyranny of Consensus*
  (Schenck & Schenck), 264

*The FACE That Demonstrates the
  Farce of Evolution*
  (Hanegraaff), 238
*Facing Millennial Midnight: The
  Y2K Crisis Confronting
  America and the World*
  (Lindsey & Ford), 277
*Facing the Fundamentalist/Vatican
  Challenge* (audiocassette),
  333
*Facing the Wrath: Confronting the
  Right in Dangerous Times*
  (Diamond), 220–221
Facts & Faith, 284
Facts for Action, 284
Facts for Faith, 284
*Faith, Hype, and Clarity: Teaching
  about Religion in American
  Schools and Colleges* (Nash),
  207
Faith movement, 350
Faith of Our Founding Fathers
  (LaHaye), 258
Faith: Talking with Peggy Noonan
  (video), 330
*Fall from Grace: The Failed Crusade
  of the Christian Right*
  (D'Antonio), 220
False Gods of Our Time (video),
  305–306

False Security: Has the New Age Given Us a False Hope? (Parks), 243

Falwell: An Autobiography (Falwell), 269

Falwell, Jerry, x, 2, 4, 7, 8, 11–12, 14–15, 16, 18, 25, 27, 49, 54, 59, 65, 70, 75, 82, 95, 109, 110, 120, 142, 146, 170, 177, 191, 269, 297
  apocalyptic beliefs, 47, 98
  biography of, 84–86
  on charitable choice, 71
  founding of Moral Majority, 46, 85
  on homosexuality, 63, 144–145
  on Jews and the Antichrist, 58
  "People of Faith 2000," 28, 66, 121
  on political activism, 146

Family Research Council (FRC), 172–173

The Famous Sourcebook of Foundational Biblical Truths (Torrey), 248

Feder, Don, 222, 254

The Federal Reserve Scandal (Hargis), 257

Federer, William J., 236–237

Feinberg, Charles L., 248

Feminist Majority Foundation (FMF), 189–190

Ferris, Michael, 254

Fight the Right Action Kit (web site), 342

Final Dawn over Jerusalem: Why Israel's Future Is So Important to Christians (Hagee), 256

The Final Victory: The Year 2000 (Byers), 271

Fingerprints of Creation (video), 306

Finney, Charles G., 354

First Things, 285

Fiske, John, 36

Flynn, Tom 60

Focus on the Family, 173. *See also* Dobson, James

Focus on the Family (periodical), 285

"Focus on the Family" (radio program), 335–336

Foege, Alec, 222

For God and Country: Conservatism and American School Policy (Lugg), 226

Forbes, Steve 62

Ford, Cliff, 277–278

Foreman, Joseph L., 254–255

Fossil Evidence of Creation (video), 306

Foster, Henry 55

Foster, Marshall, 293

Foundations of American Freedom (video), 306–307

Foundations of American Government (video), 307

Fournier, Keith, 265

Foxman, Abraham 54, 68

Frady, Marshall, 194

A Fragrance of Oppression: The Church and Its Persecutors (Schlossberg), 247

Free Congress Research and Education Foundation (FCREF), 173–174

Freedom Council (FC), 174

Freedom from Religion Foundation (FRF), 190

Freedom of Conscience: A Baptist/Humanist Dialogue (Simmons), 212

Fries, Michael, 255

From Daniel to Doomsday (Hagee), 273

From Intimidation to Victory: Regaining the Christian Right to Speak (Sekulow), 264

From Sea to Shining Sea (Marshall & Manuel), 258–259

Fuller, Charles, founds Fuller Theological Seminary, 41

Fuller, Robert C., 201

Fundamentalism, 37, 41, 152, 160
  coined, 39
  defined, 350

Fundamentalism (Barr), 197

"Fundamentalism" and the Word of God (Packer), 210

Fundamentalisms Observed (Marty, Appleby), 206

The Fundamentalist Movement (Gasper), 202

The Fundamentals: A Testimony to the Truth, 38, 350. *See* fundamentalism
Fundamentals for American Christians (Walton), 249

Gabler, Mel, 45, 143
Gabler, Norma, 43, 143
  founds Educational Research Analysts, 45
The Gagging of God: Christianity Confronts Pluralism (Carson), 252
Gallagher, John, 218
Gallatin, Bill, 298
Gallup, George, 2
Gamwell, Franklin I., 202
Gantry, Robert, 306
Gasper, Louis, 202
The Gates of Hell Shall Not Prevail: The Attack on Christianity and What You Need to Know to Combat It (Kennedy), 239–240
Gatewood, Willard B., 202
Gay Rights/Special Rights (video), 307
Gays and Guns: The Case against Homosexuals in the Military (Eidsmoe), 253–254
Geisler, Norman L., 266
The Gender Agenda: Redefining Equality (O'Leary), 261
The Genesis Quandary: Why Two Creation Accounts and Other Puzzles (audiocassette), 307–308
The Genesis Question: Scientific Advances and the Accuracy of Genesis (Ross), 245
Gentry, Kenneth L., Jr., 149, 255, 272
Get Out the Vote: 20% More in '94 (audiocassette), 308
Gift, Werner, 297
Gingrich, Newt, 23, 24, 54, 56, 106, 119
  resigns as speaker, 57
  on school violence, 59–60
Gladden, Washington, 355
Global Taxes for World Government (Kincaid), 258
The Glory and the Power: The

Fundamentalist Challenge to the Modern World (Marty & Appleby), 206
Glossolalia, 351
God and Caesar: Biblical Faith and Political Action (Eidsmoe), 253
God and Science (audiocassette), 308–309
God and the Constitution (video), 330
The God Who Is There (Schaeffer), 246
Godfrey, Laurie, 333
The Godless Constitution: The Case against Religious Correctness (Kramnick & Moore), 225
Godly Women: Fundamentalism and Female Power (Brasher), 217
God's Country: A Case against Theocracy (Rapp), 228
God's Daughters: Evangelical Women and the Power of Submission (Griffith), 222
God's Law in the Modern World (Gentry), 255
The Gods of Televangelism: The Crisis of Meaning and the Appeal of Religious Television (Peck), 227
God's Power and Scripture's Authority (video), 309
God's Providence in History (video), 309
God's Warriors: The Christian Right in Twentieth-Century America (Wilcox), 231
Goetz, William, 272
Gog, Magog, 351
Goldwater, Barry, 14, 47, 100
Good-Bye America? (West), 267
Gore, Al, 1, 3, 27, 28, 29, 62, 67, 68, 70, 121
Gospel Communications Network Online Christian Resources (web site), 342
The Gospel of Liberty (video), 309–310
Gould, Ezra P., 37
Grace Unknown (Sproul), 337
Graham, Billy, 5, 14, 15, 76, 77
  biography of, 86–87
Graham, Lindsey, 19

Grant, George, 143, 147, 255–256
Grant, Robert, biography of, 88
Grant Us Courage: Travels along the Mainline of American Protestantism (Balmer), 197
Great Awakening, 354
The Great Investment: Faith, Family and Finance (Jakes), 238
Green, John C., 222, 223
Green, Joyce, 23, 61
Griffith, R. Marie, 222
A Guide to the Religious Right (web site), 342
The Guiding Hand (video), 310
Guiness, Os, 237
Guth, James L., 223

Hadden, Jeffrey K., 223
Hagee, John C., 256, 272–273, 237, 291, 303, 306, 312, 313–314
  biography of, 88–90
Hall, Verna M., 256
The Hallelujah Revolution: The Rise of the New Christians (Cotton), 200
Halloween: What's a Christian To Do? (Russo), 245
Ham, Kenneth, 237, 298
Hand, W. Brevard, 49
Hanegraaff, Hank, 237–238, 168–169
  biography of, 90–92
Hard Choices, Lost Voices: How the Abortion Conflict Has Divided America, Distorted Constitutional Rights, and Damaged the Courts (Judges), 224
The Hard Truth (video), 310
Harding, Susan Friend, 194
Hargis, Billy, James, x, 5, 6, 7, 140, 143, 165, 256–257, 302
  biography of, 92–93
  founds the Christian Crusade, 42
Harrell, David Edwin, Jr., 194
Harrington, Jim 71
Harris, Gregg, 240
Harry Potter novels, 143, 191
Hart, Frank, 273
Has the Human Body Been Designed? (video), 310–311

Hastings, Ronnie, 333
Hatch, Nathan O., 202, 208
Have You Been Left Behind? (video), 311
Hayford, Jack, 273
Hayward, Alan, 238
He Shall Have Dominion: A Postmillennial Eschatology (Gentry), 272
Heath, Charles C., 257
Hell's Bells: The Dangers of Rock and Roll (video), 311
Helms, Jesse, 8, 16, 23, 48, 107
Henry, Carl F. H., 50
Henry, Jim, 55
Here I Stand: My Struggle for a Christianity of Integrity (Spong), 212–213
Herman, Didi, 223
Hertzke, Allen, 223
Heterodoxy, 351
Higher criticism, 351
Hilleary, Van, 19
Hindson, Ed, 252
Hinn, Benny, 168
Hirsen, James L., 257
A History of Christianity in the United States and Canada (Noll), 208
Hodge, Charles, 351
Hoffecker, Pamela Hobbs, 258
Hofrenning, Daniel J. B., 224
The Holiness of God (Sproul), 337
Holloway, Linda, 3, 67
Homosexuality, 9, 63, 104, 109, 117, 144–145
Homosexuality: Alternative or Abomination (video and audiocassette), 311–312
Homosexuality and the Politics of Truth (Satinover), 264
Homosexuality, Science, and the "Plain Sense" of Scripture (Balch), 196
Honest Money: The Biblical Blueprint for Money and Banking (North), 259
How Now Shall We Live? (Colson), 234
How Should We Then Live? The Rise and Decline of Western

Thought and Culture (Schaeffer), 246
How Should We Then Live? (video), 312
How To Fight the Right Wing (Web site), 343
The Humanist (periodical), 285
Hunt, Dave, 274
Hunter, James Davison, 203
Hunter, Paul, 257
Huse, Scott M., 238
Hutchinson, William R., 203

I Was Wrong (Bakker), 268
Identity Christianity, 351
If Ministers Fall, Can They Be Restored? (LaHaye), 270
Imminency, 351
In Defense of Secular Humanism (Kurtz), 204
In God's Image after All: How Psychology Supports Biblical Creationism (Ackerman), 232
In Search of a National Morality: A Manifesto for Catholics and Evangelicals (Ball), 233
In the Beginning: Compelling Evidence for Creation and the Flood (Brown), 234
In the Image of God (video), 312
In the Name of God (video), 327–328
In the Name of the Family: Rethinking Family Values in the Postmodern Age (Stacey), 230
In the Shadow of Plenty: The Biblical Blueprint for Welfare (Grant), 255
In Washington But Not of It: The Prophetic Politics of Religious Lobbyists (Hofrenning), 224
The Indwelling: The Beast Possession (LaHaye & Jenkins), 277
Inerrancy, 351
Inherit the Earth: Biblical Blueprints for Economics (North), 260
Inherit the Wind (video), 333
Institute for Creation Research (ICR), 174–175
Institute for First Amendment Studies (IFAS), 190
Institute for the Study of Religion

and Politics (ISRP) (Web site), 343
Institute of Religion and Public Life, 285
Institutes of Biblical Law (Rushdoony), 263
"Intelligent design," 3
Intelligent Design: The Bridge Between Science and Theology (Dembski), 235
Interfaith Alliance (web site), 343
International Council of Christian Churches (ICCC), 175
Internet Pro-Life Journal (Web site), 343
Iran-Contra scandal, 52
Irreducible Complexity: The Biochemical Challenge To Darwinian Theory (video), 312–313
Is Rescuing Right? Breaking the Law to Save the Unborn (Alcorn), 150
Is Science Religious? (audiocassette), 313
Is the World Running Down? Crisis in the Christian Worldview (North), 243
Israel: The Apple of God's Eye (video and audiocassette), 313–314
"Issues, Etc." (radio program), 336
It Is Finished (Pierce), 244

Jakes, T. D., 238
James Dobson's War on America (Alexander-Moegerle), 215
Jarmin, Gary, 138, 169
biography of, 93–94
Jefferson, Thomas, 1
Jeffrey, Grant R., 274, 323
Jelen, Ted G., 224
Jenkins, Jerry B., 97, 275–277, 315, 316, 324
Jennings, Peter, 328
Jenson, Ron, 234
Jeremiah, David, 274, 346
Jerry Falwell and the Jews (Simon), 195
Jesus Doesn't Live Here Anymore (Porteous), 228

A Jewish Conservative Looks at Pagan America (Feder), 154
Jim Bakker: Miscarriage of Justice? (Albert), 193
John Ankerberg Show (television program), 336
John Birch Society, 6, 18, 100, 287
founding of, 42, 175–176
Johnson, Lyndon B., 2, 87
Johnson, Phillip E., 144, 239, 300
Jones, Bob, Sr., 4, 41
biography of, 94–95
Jones, Bob, Jr., 4, 14
Jones, Bob III, 4, 65
founds college, 140
Jordan, James B., 145
Jorstad, Erling, 224
Journal of Christian Reconstruction, 286
Journey toward Creation (video), 314
Joyner, Rick, 275
Judges, Donald P., 224

Kah, Gary, 257
Katloff, Mark A., 203
Kennedy, D. James, x, 91, 158, 163, 177, 239–240, 339
biography of, 95–96
founds Evangelism Explosion International, 95
Kennedy, John F., 1, 2
Kenyon, Dean H., 235, 301
Kerrey, Bob, 20
Keyes, Alan, 346
Keys to Good Government (video), 314
Kincaid, Cliff, 258
The Kingdom Divided (video), 328
Kingdom Identity Ministries (KIM), 176
Web site, 343
Kingdoms at War: Tactics for Victory in Nine Spiritual War Zones (Bright & Jenson), 234
Kingdoms in Conflict (Colson & Vaughn), 252
Kintz, Linda, 224–225
Kirk, Jerry, 179
Kivisto, Peter, 218
Klicka, Christopher J., 240
Klusendorf, Scott, 139

Knight, Robert H., 240
Koop, C. Everett, 13
Kramnick, Isaac, 225
Kristol, William, 28

L.A. Justice: Lessons from the Firestorm (Vernon), 266–267
LaHaye, Beverly, 269–270
biography of, 96
founds Concerned Women for America, 96, 170–171
LaHaye, Tim F., 10, 44, 113, 170, 240, 258, 269–270, 275, 308, 315, 316, 324
biography of, 97
on political activism, 146–147
on secular humanism, 150
Land, John, 339
Land, Richard, 10, 54, 55
Lapin, Daniel, 346
Largent, Steve, 19
Larson, Edward J., 225
The Last Days According to Jesus (Sproul), 337
The Last Days Handbook: A Comprehensive Guide to Understanding the Different Vies of Prophecy (Lightner), 241
The Last Temptation of Christ (film), 51
The Late Great Planet Earth (video), 314–315
The Late Great 20th Century: Prelude to Catastrophe (Lindsey & Ford), 278
The Latest American Revolution? The 1994 Elections and Their Implications for Governance (Wilcox), 214
Lawrence, Bruce B., 204
Laws, Curtis Lee 39
Leadership in the John Birch Society (video), 315
Lear, Norman, 191
Left Behind (CD and audiocassette), 315
Left Behind: A Novel of the Earth's Last Days (LaHaye & Jenkins), 275
Left Behind: The Movie (video and DVD), 315–316

Left Behind: Where'd Everybody Go? (video), 316
Legislating Morality: Is It Wise? Is It Legal? Is It Possible? (Turek & Geisler), 266
Leiberman, Joseph, 28, 67, 68, 69, 121
on moral law, 145
Leisola, Matti, 301
Lemon v. Kurtzman. See Separation of church and state
Lerner, Michael, 330
Lesage, Julia, 225
Let There Be Light (Oakland & Wooding), 243
Letters of Francis Schaeffer (Schaeffer), 270
Levitt, Zola, 316
Levy, Leonard, 331
Lewinsky, Monica, 4, 57
Lewis, Larry, 54
Liberal Protestantism in the '90s: Forrester Church (video), 331
Liberalism: Fatal Consequences (Borst), 251
Liberty Council (Web site), 343–344
Liberty Federation. *See* Moral Majority
The Lie: Evolution (Ham), 237
Lienesch, Michael, 154, 226
The Light and the Glory (Marshall & Manuel), 258
Lightner, Robert P. 241
Ligonier Ministries, 289
Lindsey, Hal, 116, 241, 277, 294, 315, 316
author, apocalyptic thrillers, 98
biography, of, 98
Lippy, Charles H., 194
Living in the Shadow of the Second Coming: American Premillennialism, 1875–1925 (Weber), 214
Lockyer, Herbert, 278
Longing for the End: A History of Millennialism in Western Civilization (Baumgartner), 197
Love and Power: The Role of Religion and morality in American Politics (Perry), 210

Lower criticism, 351–352
Lowman, Myers, 41
Luce, James, 332
Lugg, Catherine A., 226
Luksik, Peg, 258
Lutheran Renewal (periodical), 286
Lynn, Barry, 22, 23, 71, 155

MacArthur, John, 241
Machen, J. Gresham, x, 39, 73, 112, 118, 241, 325, 348
biography of, 98–99
founds Westminister Theological Seminary, 40, 99
Maclean, Iain, 211
Maddoux, Marlin, 158
Maier, Fran, 10
Mainstream Opinion (web site), 344
Make Yourself Ready: Preparing to Meet the King (Miller), 278
Manion, Clarence E., biography of, 99–100
Manuel, David, 241, 258–259
The Many Faces of Babylon: The Babylonian Influences upon Our Churches (Hunter), 257
Mark of the beast, 352
The Mark: The Beast Rules the World (LaHaye & Jenkins), 277
Marsden, George M., 205
Marsh, Frank Lewis, 209
Marshall, George C., 122
Marshall, Peter, 258–259, 242
Martin, William, 195, 205
Marty, Martin, 205, 206, 331
Massacre of Innocence (video), 316
Matrisciana, Carly, 242
McAteer, Edward A., 11, 13, 16, 47, 85, 110, 123, 184
biography of, 100–101
founds Religious Roundtable, 46, 100
McCain, John, 27, 67
attacked by religious right, 27–28, 64–65
blasts Pat Robertson and Jerry Falwell, 65
defeats Bush in New Hampshire, 64
McCarthy, Joseph, 4, 53, 102, 105
McDowell, Josh, 242

McGee, Gary, 199
McGovern, George, 13
McGready, James, 354
McGuire, Paul, 259, 278
McIlhenny, Charles, 144, 259
McIntire, Carl, 5, 6, 7, 42, 95, 112,
  114, 159–160, 175
  biography of, 101–102
  founds the American Council
  of Christian Churches, 40–41
McVey, Frank L. 39
*The Meaning of Religious Freedom:
  Modern Politics and the
  Democratic Revolution*
  (Gamwell), 202
Means, Marianne 62
*Media, Culture, and the Religious
  Right* (Kintz & Lesage), 225
Medved, Michael, 325
Meese, Edwin, 83
Menendez, Albert J., 226
Meyers, John, 311
Midnight Call Magazine, 286
Militias and the Religious Right
  (Web site), 344
Millenarianism, 271–280
Millennialism, 352
*Millennium Meltdown: The Year
  2000 Computer Crisis* (Jeffrey),
  274
*Millennium, Messiahs, and
  Mayhem: Contemporary
  Apocalyptic Movements*
  (Robbins & Palmer), 210
*Millennium Time Bomb: How To
  Prepare for and Survive the
  Coming Technological Disaster*
  (Coppes), 272
Miller, Harland W., 278
Miller, William, 35
*Mind Siege: The Battle for Truth in
  the New Millennium* (LaHaye
  & Noebel), 240
*Mine Eyes Have Seen the Glory: A
  Journey into the Evangelical
  Subculture in America*
  (Balmer), 197
*Modern American Religion, Volume
  I, 1893–1919: The Irony of It
  All* (Marty), 206
Modernism, 352
*The Modernist Impulse in American

Protestantism* (Hutchison),
  203
Moen, Matthew C., 207, 226–227
*Money Matters: Making Sense of
  Economic Issues that Affect You*
  (Sproul), 265
"Monkey affair." *See* Scopes, John
  Thomas
Monkey Trial (video), 316–317
Montalban, Ricardo, 325
Moody! (video), 317
Moody Bible Institute, founding
  of, 37, 103
Moody, Dwight L., 37, 41, 115, 317
  biography of, 102–103
Moon, Sun Myung, 88, 93, 97, 170
Moore, R. Laurence, 207, 225
Moral Majority, 2, 7, 21, 47, 75, 85,
  95, 120, 123, 124, 191
  becomes Liberty Federation, 15,
  176–177
  dissolved, 85–86
  founding of, 12–15, 46, 177
Morality report cards. *See*
  Christian Voice
Moreland, J. P., 242
Morris, Henry M. 43–44
*The Most Dangerous Man in
  America?* (Boston), 193
Moyers, Bill, 55, 327, 328, 329,
  330, 331
Mozert v. Hawkins, 50
MTV Examined (video), 317–318
*Multimedia Family Bible for
  Windows* (CD-ROM), 337
Murray, William J., 183
Myers, Ellen, 318
Myth of Separation, (Barton), 251

Nader, Ralph, 29
NAE Washington Insight
  (periodical), 286
*The Naked Public Square: Religion
  and Democracy in America*
  (Neuhaus), 207–208
*Naming the Antichrist: History of an
  American Obsession* (Fuller),
  201
Nash, Robert J., 207
National Association of
  Evangelicals, 41, 182, 286, 350
  founding of, 177–178

National Christian Action
Coalition (NCAC), 178
National Coalition Against
Censorship (NCAC), 190–191
National Coalition for the
Protection of Children and
Families (NCPCF), 178–179
National Council of Churches, 2,
5, 25, 147–148, 177
National Legal Foundation (NLF),
179
National Religious Broadcasters
(NRB), 179–180
National Right to Life Committee
(NRLC), 180–181
Nations United in the End
(audiocassette), 318
Natural theology, 352
Nelson, Byron C., 207
Nelson, Paul, 207
Neuhaus, Richard John, 207–208,
227, 285, 330
New Age movement, 352
New Age Movement (video), 318
The New American (periodical),
286
*The New Christian Right,
1981–1988: Prospects for the
Post-Reagan Era* (Jorstad), 224
The New Dare to Discipline
(Dobson), 268–269
The New Millennium (Roberston),
245
*The New Religious Right: Piety,
Patriotism, and Politics*
(Capps), 218
Niagara Bible Conferences, 36, 37,
38, 82, 350
Nicolae: The Rise of the Antichrist
(LaHaye & Jenkins), 275–276
*The 90's, Decade of the Apocalypse:
The European Common
Market–The End Has Begun*
(Terrel), 248
Nixon, Richard, 87
*No Final Conflict: The Bible without
Error in All That It Affirms*
(Schaeffer), 246
*No God But God: Breaking with the
Idols of Our Age* (Os & Seel),
237
No Longer Exiles: The Religious

New Right in American Politics
(Cromartie), 219
Noebel, David A., 164, 240, 243
Noll, Mark A., 208, 259
Norris, J. Frank 81, 82
North, Gary, 142, 147, 243,
259–260
North, Oliver, 17, 18, 23, 52–53,
329
*Not By Politics Alone: The Enduring
Influence of the Christian Right*
(Diamond), 221
Numbers, Ronald L., 207,
208–209, 213, 227

Oakland, Roger, 242, 243, 294, 304
The Oath (Peretti), 244
*Objections Sustained: Subversive
Essays on Evolution, Law and
Culture* (Johnson), 239
O'Connor, Cardinal John
association with Pope John
Paul II, 104
biography of, 103–104
O'Connor, Sandra Day, 13, 14
opposition to, by Falwell, 47
*Of Pandas and People: The Central
Question of Biological Origins*
(Davis & Kenyon), 235
Office of Faith-Based and
Community Initiatives, 70
O'Hair, Madalyn Murray, 187
O'Hear, Anthony, 243
Olasky, Marvin, x, 27, 260–261,
289, 34
adviser to George W. Bush, 105,
106
biography of, 105–107
on compassionate
conservatism, 106–107
*The Old Christian Right: The
Protestant Far Right from the
Great Depression to the Cold
War* (Ribuffo), 228
Oldfield, Duane M., 227
Old-Time Gospel Hour (radio &
television program), 336
O'Leary, Dale, 261
The Omega Code (video), 318–319
*The Omega Code: Another Has
Risen from the Dead* (Crouch),
272

On Earth As It Is in Heaven
(video), 328
*On the Boundaries of American
Evangelicalism: The Postwar
Evangelical Coalition* (Stone),
213
*On the Brink: Breaking through
Every Obstacle into the Glory of
God* (Parsley), 278
One Nation under God (Walton),
267
*Onward Christian Soldiers? The
Religious Right in American
Politics* (Wilcox), 231–232
Operation Rescue. *See* Abortion
Operation Rescue (Terry), 265
Operation Save America (OSA),
181
Opitz, Edmund A., 261
Order of the Cross Society (OCS),
181
Original autographs, 352
Original sin, 353
*Orphans in Babylon: Abortion in
America. Where Are We Now?
How Did We Get Here? Where
Should We Go?* (Domingo),
252–253
Orthodoxy, 353
Our Military under Siege (video),
319
*Outcome-Based Education: The
State's Assault on Our
Children's Values* (Luksik &
Hoffecker), 258

Packer, J. I., 210
Palmer, Susan J., 210
Parks, Jerald, 243
Parsley, Rod, 278
*Pat Robertson: A Personal,
Religious, and Political Portrait*
(Harrell), 194
*Patriots: Surviving the Coming
Collapse* (Rawles), 278–279
Patterson, Alexander, 208
Patterson, Paige, 47, 327
Patton, Francis L., 36
Pearcy, Nancy, 244
Peck, Janice, 227
Pentecost, J. Dwight, 279
Pentecostalism, 353

People for the American Way, 11,
14, 155
founding of, 191
Peretti, Frank E., 244, 345
*Perfect Enemies: The Religious
Right, the Gay Movement, and
the Politics of the 1990s* (Bull &
Gallagher), 218
Perry, Michael J., 210
Personal Freedom Outreach, 344
Peters, Peter J., 146, 261
Phillips, Howard, 11, 13, 46, 85,
100, 123
Phyllis Schlafly Report (periodical),
287
Pierce, Alfred, 244
*Piety and Politics: Evangelicals and
Fundamentalist Confront the
World* (Neuhaus &
Cromartie), 227
*Pilgrims, Puritans, and Patriots:
Our Christian Heritage* (Boys),
251–252
Pitts, F. E., 244
The Plan (Robertson & Slosser),
263
Planet Earth—2000 (Lindsey), 241
Plymouth Rock Foundation
(PRF), 181–182, 284, 287
*The Political Mobilization of
Religious Beliefs* (Jelen), 224
*Politically Incorrect: The Emerging
Faith Factor in American
Politics* (Reed), 262
Porteous, Skipp, 228
*The Post-Christian Mind: How
Should a Christian Think?*
(Blamires), 234
Postmillennialism, 353
*Postmodern Times: A Christian
Guide to Contemporary
Thought and Culture* (Veith),
249
*Prayers in the Precincts: The
Christian Right in the 1998
Elections* (Green, Rozell, &
Wilcox), 222
Premillennialism, 353
*Preserve Us a Nation: Returning to
Our Historical and Biblical
Roots* (Crismier), 235
Pressler, Paul, 47

Preus, J. A. O., 44
Price, George McCready, 209
Prolife movement, 353
Promise Keepers Online (Web site), 344
Prophecy, 353
A Prophet with Honor: The Billy Graham Story (Martin), 195
A Prophetic Vision for the 21st Century: A Spiritual Map to Help You Navigate into the Future (Joyner), 275
Prosperity and the Coming Apocalypse (Bakker), 233
Putting Creation to the Test (video), 319

Quality Science Education versus Creationism (video and audiocassette), 333–334
The Quarterly Journal (Web site), 344
Quayle, Dan, 244–245

R. C. Sproul Digital Library on CD-ROM, 337
The Race for the 21st Century (LaHaye), 240
Rae, Debra, 261–262
Rae, Scott B., 242
Ramm, Bernard, 42
Rapp, Sandy, 228
Rapture, 353
The Rapture of Politics: The Christian Right as the United States Approaches the Year 2000 (Bruce, Kivisto, & Swatos), 218
The Rapture Question Answered: Plain and Simple (Van Kampen), 279–280
Rauschenbusch, Walter, 355
Rawles, James Wesley, 278–279
Reagan, Ronald, 12, 13, 18, 24, 75, 76, 82, 97, 104, 110, 122, 169
elected president, 47
endorses school prayer, 48
Reason and Revelation (periodical), 287
Reason in the Balance: The Case Against Naturalism in Science,
Law, and Education (Johnson), 239
Reasons To Believe (RTB), 182, 283, 284
"Reasons To Believe" (television program), 336
Reconstructionism, 44, 149, 348
Redeemer Nation: The Idea of America's Millennial Role (Tuveson), 213
Redeeming America: Piety and Politics in the New Christian Right (Liensich), 226
Rediscovering American Values; The Foundations of Our Freedom for the 21st Century (Devos), 236
Reed, Ralph, 8, 18, 20–21, 27, 54, 55, 56, 57, 83, 262, 292
biography of, 107–108
founds Century Strategies, 108
heads Christian Coalition, 108
on political strategy, 148
Reforming Fundamentalism: Fuller Seminary and the New Evangelicalism (Marsden), 204
Reichley, A. James, 210
Reisman, Bill, 268
Religion and Capitalism: Allies, Not Enemies (Opitz), 261
Religion and Politics in the United States (Wald), 230
Religion and Republic: The American Circumstance (Marty), 206
The Religion and Society Report (periodical), 287
Religion and the Racist Right: The Origins of the Christian Identity Movement (Barkun), 216
Religion in American Politics (Dunn), 201
Religion in American Public Life (Reichley), 210
Religion in the Public Schools (Web site), 345
The Religion of Secular Humanism (video), 320
Religion, Politics and Our Schools (video), 331–332
The Religious Challenge to the State (Moen), 207

Religious Equality Amendment, 149
Religious Freedom (Web site), 345
Religious Freedom Coalition (RFC), 182–183
Religious Heritage of America (RHA), 183
A Religious History of the American People (Ahlstrom), 196
Religious right, contrasted to 1950s, 3, 6–7
  and African Americans, 8, 55
  and John Ashcroft, 29–30
  and George W. Bush, 26–27, 64–67
  criticism of, 14–15
  decline of Christian Coalition, 20–23
  educational concerns, 8–9, 42–43
  election results, 1980, 13, 47
  election results 1999, 18–19, 53
  family concerns, 9–10, 45
  frustration with President Carter, 10–11
  and Harry Potter novels, 143
  internal dissent, 14, 23–25
  moral concerns, 10
  organizations critical of, 187–191
  organizations supportive of, 157–186
  political awakening of, 11–13, 46–47
  responses to, 152–155
  school board election, 17
  South Carolina Republican primary, 27–29
The Religious Right (video), 329
Religious Right Influence (Web site), 345
The Religious Right: The Assault on Tolerance and Pluralism in America (Cantor), 53, 218
Religious Roundtable, 12, 16, 110
  founding of, 46, 183–184
Religious Schools v. Children's Rights (Dwyer), 221
Remnant Resolves, 263
Representing God in Washington: The Role of Religious Lobbies in te American Polity (Hertzke), 223

Rescuing the Bible from Fundamentalism: A Bishop Rethinks the Meaning of Scripture (Spong), 212
Revelation (video), 320–321
Revelation and the Rapture Unveiled! Ancient Hebrew Prophecies for the Year 2000 and Beyond (Hart), 273
Revelation Illustrated (video), 321
The Revelation of Truth: A Mosaic of God's Plan for Man (Hagee), 237
Revelation Unveiled (LaHaye), 275–277
Revivalism, 354
Revive Us Again: The Reawakening of American Fundamentalism (Carpenter), 219
"Revolution of '94." *See* Election of 1994
Ribuffo, Leo P., 228
Richards, Ann, 18
Richardson, Stephen, 262
The Right and the Righteous: The Christian Right Confronts the Republican Party (Oldfield), 227
The Right Choice: The Incredible Failure of Public Education and the Rising Hope of Home Schooling (Harris), 240
Righteous Empire: the Protestant Experience in America (Marty), 205
Rightguide's Conservative Directory (web site), 345
Right-to-life movement, 353
Riley, William Bell, 38, 186, 213
Rips, Eliyahu, 347
The Rise and Fall of the Christian Right (Bruce), 217
Risen, James, 228–229
The Road to Armageddon (Swindoll, Walvoord, & Pentecost), 279
Roads to Dominion: Right-Wing Movements and Political Power in the United States (Diamond), 220
Robb, Charles, 17, 53
Robbins, Thomas, 210
Roberts, Oral, 15, 168

Robertson, Pat, 2, 7, 9, 18, 19, 20, 25, 27, 28, 29, 44, 52–53, 54, 59, 60, 61, 62, 65, 66, 67, 74, 82, 98, 107, 119, 159, 165, 174, 179, 193–194, 245, 263, 279
  attacks McCain, 64
  biography of, 108–110
  on charitable choice, 71
  endorses political assassination, 61–62
  founds Christian Broadcasting Network (CBN), 42, 109
  founds Christian Coalition, 51
  predicts battle of Armageddon, 47
  runs for the presidency, 16–17, 50–51, 109
  supports Bush in 2000, 63
  urges end to impeachment proceedings, 57–58
Robison, James, 7, 184, 270
  biography of, 100–111
Robnett, George Washington, 169
The Rock (periodical), 287
Rockford Institute, 287
Roe v. Wade, 353
Rogers, Adrian, 50
Rood, Paul W., 40
Roosevelt, Franklin, 122
The Roots of Fundamentalism: British and American Millenarianism (Sandeen), 211
Rosenberg, Yoav, 347
Ross, Hugh, 245, 297, 299, 308, 313, 314, 318, 319, 321, 322
  biography of, 111–112
Rothenberg, Stuart, 49
Roundtable on Genesis One (audiocassette), 321
Rozell, Mark J., 222, 229
Rushdonny, Rousas John 44, 164, 263
  on reconstructionism, 149
Russell, Charles Allyn, 195
Russo, Steve, 245
Rutherford Institute, 184

Salvation for Sale: An Insider's View of Pat Robertson's Ministry (Straub), 195
The Samaritan Strategy: A New

Agenda for Christian Activism (Doner), 253
Samples, Kenneth, 319
Sandeen, Ernest Robert, 211
Santorum Rick, 18
Satinover, Jeffrey, 264
Saucy, Robert, 321
Schaeffer, Francis, x, 118, 141, 245–246, 270, 312, 354
  biography of, 112–114
Schafersma, Steven, 333
Schaffer, James, 270–271
Scheidler, Joseph M., 264
Schenck, Paul, 264
Schenck, Robert L., 264
Schism, 354
Schlafly, Phyllis 8, 171, 172, 329
Schlossberg, Herbert, 247
School vouchers, 58, 60, 62, 63, 119
School prayer, 45, 48, 55, 59, 61, 63, 66, 67, 148–149
  Abington Township School District v. Schempp, 43
  constitutional amendment on, 43
  Engel v. Vitale, 42–43
  Wallace v. Joffree, 49
School Prayer: The Court, the Congress, and the First Amendment (Alley), 215
Schultz, Jeffery D., 211
Schultze, Quentin J., 211
Schwarz, Frederick, 5, 140, 164, 271
  biography of, 114
The Schwarz Report (periodical), 288
Schweizer, Peter, 264
Science and Genesis (audiocassette), 321–322
Science, Creation, and the Bible (video), 322
A Scientist Looks at Creation (video), 322
Scofield, Cyrus, x, 38, 41, 247
  biography of, 115–116
Scofield Reference Bible, 115, 354
Scofield Study Bible (Scofield), 247
Scopes, John T., 38, 78, 79, 317
  "monkey affair," 39–40, 186
Scoreboard Alert, 288

Scorsese, Martin, 51
Scott, Craig, 59
Scott, Eugenie, 313
The Search for Christian America (Marsden), 208
Seasons under Heaven (LaHaye & Blackstock), 269
Second Coming: The New Christian Right in Virginia Politics (Rozell & Wilcox), 229
Secular Darkness: Religious Right Involvement in Texas Public Education (Durham), 221
Secular humanism, 7, 44, 49, 60, 110, 113, 150, 354
  American Humanist Association, 187–188
  Council for Secular Humanism, 189
  "The Humanist Manifesto," 40
Secularization and Fundamentalism Reconsidered (Hadden & Shupe), 223
The Seduction of Power (Dobson & Hindson), 252
Seel, John, 154, 237
Sekulow, Jay Alan, 19, 25, 159, 264, 265
  biography of, 116–117
  chief counsel, American Center for Law and Justice, 116
Selected Works of George McCready Price (Numbers), 209
Selling God: American Religion in the Marketplace of Culture (Moore), 207
Separation of church and state, 49
  Lemon v. Kurtzman, 45
  Oregon v. Smith, 52
  Sherbert v. Verner, 52
  Wisconsin v. Yoder, 52
The Servant (periodical), 288
700 Club (television program), 16, 109
Sex Education Is for the Family (LaHaye), 270
A Shattered Visage: The Real Face of Atheism (Zacharias), 250
Shattering the Darkness: The Crisis of the Cross in the Church Today (Foreman), 254–255
Sheldon, Andrea, 185

Sheldon, Louis, 18, 29, 48, 185
Shields, Carole, 154, 229
Showers in Season (LaHaye & Blackstock), 269
Shupe, Anson, 223
The Signature of God (video), 322–323
The Signature of God: Astonishing Biblical Discoveries (Jeffrey), 274
Sileven, Everett, 151, 265
Simmons, Paul D., 212
Simon, Merill, 195
The Sinai Strategy: Economics and the Ten Commandments (North), 260
Situation ethics, 354
Slater, Rosalie J., 256
Slosser, Bob, 263
Smeal, Eleanor, 189
Smidt, Corwin, 229
Smith, Christian, 212, 229
Smith, Henry Preserved, 37
Smith, Pat Marvenko, 321
Smith, Sherman, 302
Snelling, Andrew, 237
Snowball, David, 230
Social gospel, 354
Society of Humanist Philosophers (Web site), 345
Souder, Mark, 19
Soul Harvest: The World Takes Sides (LaHaye & Jenkins), 276
The Soul of Politics: Beyond "Religious Right" and "Secular Left" (Wallis), 230–231
The Soul of Science: Christian Faith and Natural Philosophy (Pearcy & Thaxton), 244
Sounding Forth the Trumpet (Marshall & Manuel), 242
Sources of Power for the Religious Right (audiocassette), 334
Spencer, James R., 247
The Spirit of the American Revolution (video), 323
Spiritual Warfare: The Politics of the Christian Right (Diamond), 220
Spong, John Shelby, 212–213
Sproul, R.C., x, 142, 145, 265, 292, 295, 325
  biography of, 117–118

Stacey, Judith, 230
Stanley, Lynn, 150, 247
Stanton, Elizabeth Cady, 230
*Stealing Jesus: How
    Fundamentalism Betrays
    Christianity* (Bawer), 197
The Stealing of America
    (Whitehead), 267
Steeling the Mind of America (web
    site), 345–346
Stockman, Steven, 18, 19
Stoddard, Solomon, 354
Stone, Barton, 354
Stone, Jon R., 213
Stone v. Graham. See Ten
    Commandments
The Story of America's Liberty
    (video), 323
Straub, Gerard Thomas, 195
Strauss, David Friedrick, 35
*Strength for the Journey: An
    Autobiography* (Falwell), 269
*Studies in Religious
    Fundamentalism* (Caplan), 199
*Subtle Serpent: New Age in the
    Classroom* (Whitemarsh &
    Reisman), 268
Suffer the Children (video), 323–324
*Summer for the Gods: The Scopes
    Trial and America's Continuing
    Debate over Science and
    Religion* (Larson), 225
Survey data
    on abortion, 134
    on belief in God, 126
    on certainty of beliefs, 136
    on born again and evangelical
        Christians, 127
    on church adherence by region,
        128
    on church adherents, 128
    on extramarital sex, 132
    on homosexuality, 133
    on ideological (liberal,
        conservative) preference, 131
    on legalization of marijuana,
        132
    on marital status, 137
    on 1996 presidential preference,
        130
    on party affiliation by religious
        preference, 130
    on pornography, 133
    on religious preference by
        region, 128
    on school prayer, 135
    on support of public spending,
        131
Swaggart, Jimmy, 15, 51, 170
Swatos, Jr., William H., 218
Swindoll, Charles R., 279

Tabletalk (periodical), 288–289
Tate, Randy, 19, 20–21, 38–39, 165
    assumes leadership of Christian
        Coalition, 56, 119
    biography of, 118–120
    supports impeachment, 57
    on violence in schools, 58–59
Taxation, 151
Taylor, C. Holland, 255
Taylor, Paul, 248
*Televangelism and American
    Culture: The Business of
    Popular Religion* (Schultze),
    211
Ten Commandments, 60, 64
    Stone v. Graham, 47
Terrel, Steve, 248
Terry, Randall A. 113, 181, 265
Test of Faith (video), 324
*Thank God, I'm Free: The James
    Robison Story* (Robison), 270
Thaxton, Charles B., 244
Theological Roots of Pentecostalism
    (Dayton), 200
Theonomy, defined, 355
Thoburn, Robert L., 266
Thomas, Cal, 9, 28, 65, 66, 67, 266
    biography of, 120–121
    co-author of *Blinded by Might*,
        120–121
    disenchantment of, with
        politics 25, 59, 121
    vice-president, Moral Majority,
        120
Thomas, Judy L., 228–229
Thompson, Bert, 248
Threats to Civil Liberties (web site),
    346
Tocqueville, Alexis de, x, xi, 2, 106
Today in America, Sex IS Politics
    (video), 334
Todd, Colleen, 270–271

Torrey, Reuben A., 140, 248, 350
Toward Tradition (web site), 346
Townsend, Luther Tracy, 208
Toy, Crawford H., 36–37
Traditional Values Coalition, 18, 29, 48, 289
　founding of, 184
Traditional Values Report (periodical), 289
The Tragedy of American Compassion (Olasky), 348
Transformation of the Christian Right (Moen), 227
A Transforming Faith: Explorations of Twentieth-Century American Evangelicalism (Watt), 213
Tribulation Force (LaHaye & Jenkins), 275
Tribulation Force (CD and audiocassette), 324
Trinity Broadcasting Network (TBN), 185
Trollinges, William Vance, 213
Truman, Harry, 1, 122
Tuffnell, Sean R., 149
Turek, Frank S., 266
Turning Point (Web site), 346
The Turning Tide: The Fall of Liberalism and the Rise of Common Sense (Robertson), 263
Tuveson, Ernest Lee, 213
Twentieth-Century Shapers of Popular Religion (Lippy), 194
2001: On the Edge of Eternity (Van Impe), 279

Under God: Religion and American Politics (Wills), 214
Understanding Fundamentalism and Evangelicalism (Marsden), 205
Understanding the Times: The Religious Worldviews of Our Day and the Search for Truth (Noebel), 243
The Universe: Accident or Design? (video), 324–325
Unsecular America, 208
An Unsettled Arena: Religion and the Bill of Rights (White & Zimmerman), 214
The U.S.A. in Bible Prophecy: Two Sermons Preached to the U.S. Congress in 1857 (Pitts), 244
U.S. Religious Interest Groups (Weber), 231
U.S. Supreme Court and the Culture of Death (Catholic bishops), 69–70

Van Bebber, Mark, 248
Van Impe, Jack, 279
Van Kampen, Robert D., 279–280
Van Til, Cornelius, 355
Vaughn, Ellen Santilli, 252
Veith, Gene Edward, Jr., 143, 249
Ventura, Jesse, 62
Vernon, Robert, 266–267
Viguerie, Richard, 11, 13
Visions of Reality: What Fundamentalist Schools Teach (Menendez), 226
Visotzky, Burton, 327
Voice of Liberty (periodical), 289
Voices of American Fundamentalism: Seven Biographical Studies (Russell), 195

Wald, Kenneth D., 153, 230
Wallace v. Jaffree. See School prayer
Wallis, Jim, 230–231
Walsh, Bob, 295
Walton, Rus, 148, 182, 249, 267
Walvoord, John F., 249, 279, 280
Ward, Marian, 67
Warfield, Benjamin, 351
The Watch (Web site), 346
Watson, Justin, 231
Watt, David, 213
Weber, Paul J., 231
Weber, Timothy P., 214
Weddington, Susan, 148
The Wedge of Truth: Splitting the Foundations of Naturalism (Johnson), 239
Weicker, Lowell, 48
Weinberg, Steven, 3
Welch, Robert, 6, 73, 139, 249–250
　biography of, 121–122
　founds John Birch Society, 42, 122, 176
Weldon, John, 232–233
West, John G., Jr., 211
West, Jonathan, 267

Weyrich, Paul, 11–12, 13, 73, 85, 100, 101, 173
  biography of, 122–123
  disenchantment of, with politics, 24–25, 123
  founding of the Moral Majority, 46, 123
  founding of National Empowerment Television, 52
What's Wrong with the Religious Right (web site), 346
When All the Gods Trembled: Darwinism, Scopes, and the American Intellectuals (Conkin), 200
When the Wicked Seize a City: A Grim Look at the Future and a Warning to the Church (McIlhenny), 259
When Time Shall Be No More: Prophecy Belief in Modern American Culture (Boyer), 198
White, Andrew Dickinson 38
White, Mel, 63, 145
White, Ronald C., 21
Whitefield, George, 310, 354
Whitehead, John W., 184, 250, 267–268
Whitemarsh, Darylann, 268
Who Are the Promise Keepers? Understanding the Christian Men's Movement (Abraham), 215
Who Will Rule the Future? A Resistance to the New World Order (McGuire), 259
Who's Afraid of the Religious Right? (Feder), 222
Why America Doesn't Work: How the Decline of the Work Ethic Is Hurting Your Family and Future—And What You Can Do (Colson & Eckerd), 252
Why the Religious Right Is Wrong about Separation of Church and State (Boston), 216
Wieland, Carl, 237
Wilcox, Clyde, 214, 222, 229, 231–232
Wildmon, Donald E., 10, 51, 158, 160, 329
  biography of, 123–124

  founds Coalition for Better Television, 46, 123–124
Wills, Gary, 214
Wilson, Pete, 57
Wilson, Woodrow, 37
Winchell, Alexander, 36
Winning the Sexual Revolution (video), 325
Winning the Values War in a Changing Culture: Thirteen Distinct Values That Mark a Follower of Jesus Christ (Anderson), 232
With a Vengeance: The Fight for Reproductive Freedom (video), 332
With God on Our Side: The Rise of the Religious Right in America (Martin), 205
With God on Our Side: The Rise of the Religious Right in America (video), 329
Without a Prayer: Religious Expression in Public Schools (Alley), 215–216
Wittgenstein, Ludwig, ix
Witztum, Doron, 347
Wofford, Harris, 18
Wolf in Sheep's Clothing: Theological Liberalism (audiocassette), 325
The Woman's Bible (Stanton), 230
Woman's Christian Temperance Union (WCTU), 185–186
The Wonders of God's Creation (video), 326
Wooding, Dan, 243
Woodrow, James 37
Woods, Dennis, 268
World (periodical), 289
World's Christian Fundamentals Association, 38, 39, 40, 79, 94
  founding of, 186
Worth Fighting For (Quayle), 244–245
Wrath of Angels: The American Abortion War (Risen & Thomas), 228–229
Wright, G. Frederick, 208

Yao, Richard, 332

Young Men's Christian
   Association (YMCA), 102
Y2K (Boys), 271
*Y2K: A Reasoned Response to Mass
   Hysteria* (Hunt), 274

Zacharias, Ravi K., 250
Zimmerman, Albright G., 214
Zimmerman, Dean R., 144
   quotation on evolution, 143–144

About the Authors

Glenn H. Utter, professor and chair of the Political Science Department at Lamar University, was educated at Binghamton University, the University of Buffalo, and the University of London. Utter specializes in modern political theory and American political thought. He coedited *American Political Scientists: A Dictionary* (1993), cowrote *Campaign and Election Reform* (1997), and most recently published *Encyclopedia of Gun Control and Gun Rights* (2000). He has written a number of articles for political science journals and other scholarly publications.

John W. Storey, educated at Lamar University, Baylor University, and the University of Kentucky, is a specialist in southern religious history. His writings have appeared in numerous scholarly publications, and two of his previous studies, *Texas Baptist Leadership and Social Christianity, 1900–1980* (1986) and *Southern Baptists of Southeast Texas, 1888–1988* (1988), won the Texas Baptist Historical Society's Church History Award. He is currently professor and chair of the History Department at Lamar University.